THE AUTHOR

Anthony Powell, one of England's most distinguished men of letters, was born in London in 1905 and educated at Eton and Balliol College, Oxford. From 1926 to 1935 he worked for the publisher Duckworth, and his first novel, *Afternoon Men*, was published in 1931. He became a full-time writer in 1936.

During the war he served with the Welch Regiment and the Intelligence Corps, rising to the rank of major, and acting as Liaison Officer with the allied forces in exile. As a recognition of these services he was awarded the orders of Leopold II (Belgium), the White Lion (Czechoslovakia), and the Oaken Crown and the Croix de Guerre (Luxembourg).

Anthony Powell is best known for his great twelve-novel sequence *A Dance to the Music of Time* (1951-75), described by Bernard Bergonzi as 'the major achievement in post-war fiction'. His other novels include *Venusberg, From a View to a Death, Agents and Patients, What's Become of Waring, O, How the Wheel Becomes It!* and *The Fisher King*. He is also the author of four volumes of autobiography: *Infants of the Spring, Messengers of Day, Faces in My Time* and *The Strangers All Are Gone*. An abridged version of this sequence has been published as *To Keep the Ball Rolling*.

Anthony Powell was made a CBE in 1956, elected Honorary Fellow of Balliol College in 1974 and was created a Companion of Honour in 1988. He married Lady Violet Pakenham in 1934, and they have two sons. He lives in Somerset.

JOHN AUBREY, aged about 30, from an engraving, tinted with water colour; and taken from an oil painting attributed to Lely.

JOHN AUBREY
AND HIS FRIENDS

Anthony Powell

Newly Revised
by the Author

THE HOGARTH PRESS
LONDON

Published in 1988 by
The Hogarth Press
30 Bedford Square, London WC1B 3RP

First published in Great Britain by William Heinemann Ltd 1948
revised edition 1963
This edition copyright © Anthony Powell 1988

British Library Cataloguing in Publication Data

Powell, Anthony, 1905-
John Aubrey and his friends. – New & rev. ed.
1. Aubrey, John   2. Antiquarians – England – Biography
I. Title
930.1'092'4   DA93.A8

ISBN 0 7012 0785 X

Printed in Great Britain by
Cox & Wyman Ltd
Reading, Berkshire

CONTENTS

ILLUSTRATIONS

TO
MALCOLM

PREFACE

A YEAR or two before the Second World War I began to consider the possibility of writing a biography of John Aubrey, whose character and work had for a long time interested me; and by September 1939 a certain amount of the necessary research—and a rough outline of the projected life—had been completed. In the course of nearly six years in the army, it was occasionally possible in spare time to read contemporary authorities, to make a few notes, or to correspond about the seventeenth century: but the greater part of the writing was done on leave or immediately after demobilization, in circumstances not always ideal for sifting historical material; so that the book never enjoyed the advantage of a long single period of concentrated attention. Like Aubrey's own work, the subject was approached *tanquam canis è Nilo*, and somewhat 'tumultuarily' put together. These things may perhaps be remembered in extenuation. Many persons have helped me at different stages of the book's progress. I record my thanks to them here. While examining Aubrey's manuscripts in the Bodleian (the authorities of which accorded permission to reproduce eight of the illustrations) officials and staff—notably Dr R. W. Hunt and Mr I. G. Philip—were of the greatest help; as were those of the Public Record Office—especially my friend Mr Noel Blakeston; of the London Library; and of the British Museum. Sir William Ll. Davies, of the National Library of Wales, confirmed that the Aubrey pedigree was in the Library's copy of the Book of Golden Grove; and Dr Henry Guppy, of the John Rylands Museum, Manchester, was good enough to supply a photograph of the portrait of Aubrey (from Canon Jackson's corrected edition of the *Wiltshire Collections*) from which the frontispiece is taken. Professor Stuart Piggott kindly lent me, during the war, a photostat-copy of sections of the *Monumenta Britannica*, which Mrs Piggott conveyed personally; and Dr Albert Hollaender sent further information in connexion with his article on Aubrey in the *Wiltshire Archaeological and Natural History*

Society's Magazine. I am also indebted to that Society's Honorary Secretary, Mr B. Howard Cunnington, and Honorary Librarian, Mr C. W. Pugh, M.B.E. Through the good offices of Mr John Johnson (formerly University Printer at Oxford), the late R. T. Gunther's 'Catalogue of Aubrey's Library' has been reproduced from the *Bodleian Quarterly Record* (VI, No. 69. 1931) by permission of Dr Gunther's surviving son, Mr A. E. Gunther, and Dr Mavis Gunther, widow of his deceased son: a most valuable addition to the book. Miss Marianne Dibden allowed me to see her notes on the Aubrey family; and Mr Ralph Waley voluntarily undertook some Wiltshire investigations on my behalf. Mr Arthur Bryant attested the fact that Pepys never mentions Aubrey. Mrs Margaret 'Espinasse (Miss Margaret Wattie), of University College, Hull, then working on her *Robert Hooke*, made helpful suggestions; as did Miss Anne Whiteman, of Lady Margaret Hall, Oxford, regarding Seth Ward, Bishop of Salisbury, upon whose biography she is engaged. Mr T. A. M. Bishop, formerly Westminster City archivist, showed me the ratebooks that identify Mary Wiseman. Mrs Katherine A. Esdaile gave information about Aubrey's sculptor friends. When the book was all but finished, I found that Mr and Mrs James Williams of Endsleigh School, Colchester, were keen adherents of Aubrey; that Mr Williams was contemplating a work with the identical title *John Aubrey and His Friends*; and that Mrs Williams had transcribed the Aubrey–Wood Letters in the course of taking a B.Litt. degree, with that subject as thesis. Mr Williams did everything in his power to assist by talking over with me various aspects of Aubrey's life and work; and Mrs Williams lent me the annotated transcript of letters (to which I owe a number of notes), providing a check of inestimable value. Mr Malcolm Muggeridge, Mr Graham Greene, and Mr John Hayward made valuable comments after seeing the manuscript: Mr John Bowle and Mr R. W. Ketton-Cremer read final proofs and supplied excellent criticisms. I am deeply grateful to all of these; and to others who have discussed Aubrey with me at different times, or corresponded with me after publication of the first edition of this book.

ANTHONY POWELL

INTRODUCTION

DR WILLIAM STRATFORD of Christ Church, chaplain to the Earl of Oxford and tutor to his son, Edward Harley, wrote to the latter on 28 June, 1711: 'I have a very proper present for your Lordship. I know your love of antiquities makes you a little superstitious. I have an elderstick, that was cut in the minute that the sun entered Taurus. Such a planetary cutting of it gives virtue to stop bleeding to which you know you are subject. If you desire to know more of the time and manner of cutting it, you must consult Aubrey's *Miscellanies*. You may meet with it without doubt amongst your father's collection of mad books.' This was how the eighteenth century remembered John Aubrey; and, although his name is now widely known, Aubrey is still sometimes thought of as a whimsical amateur of astrology, an amusing if somewhat unreliable gossip, who happened to make a reputation for himself by his accumulation of anecdotes collected in the course of an aimless and rather absurd career. The present book is intended to tell the story of Aubrey's life as fully as possible, and to show that his character and gifts were both of a most unusual order. To regard him merely as an agreeable, fairly intelligent, muddleheaded spendthrift is not only unjust, but quite inadequate in relation to his place in English literary history; in which he is, indeed, one of the most arresting figures of the seventeenth century.

The only full-length biography that has ever appeared—although he has been made from time to time the subject of short, and sometimes not very accurate, studies—was published by the Wiltshire Topographical Society in 1845. This was John Britton's *Memoir of John Aubrey, F.R.S. embracing his autobiographical sketches, a brief review of his personal and literary merits, and an account of his works; with extracts from his correspondence, anecdotes of some of his contemporaries, and the times in which he lived.* Britton was an old man at the date of the publication of this book, which, with the limited material then available, gives a creditable description of Aubrey's life and writings; but haphazard arrangement of the information, a rambling and apologetic style, the intellectual prejudices of the period, and the *Memoir*'s unwieldy *format*, combine to make this relatively rare volume somewhat uneasy reading. Aubrey's own contribution to his biography, as such, was to leave some notes 'to be interponed as a sheet of wast paper only in the binding of a book'. In these rough jottings he comments that his life 'is more remarquable in an astrologicall respect then for any advancement of learning, having from his birth (till of late yeares) been labouring under a crowd of ill directions: for his escapes of many dangers, in journeys both by land and water, 40 yeares'. This scanty *curriculum vitae* gains a little additional substance from an existing list of his 'accidents' (an astrological term meaning, merely, notable events); and he adds a tag from Thomas Carew:

> *I presse not to the choire, nor dare I . . .*
> *Thus devout penitents of old were wont*
> *Some without dore, and some beneath the font.*

J. H. Shorthouse used a number of these autobiographical notes —without feeling it necessary to mention their provenance—in his popular romance, *John Inglesant*, published in 1881. His hero, apart from these personal descriptions tacked on to him, has no resemblance to Aubrey in character or career; though his adventures take place during the same period. Aubrey's own tumbledown, but one would hesitate to say unhappy, life extends over the last three-quarters of the seventeenth century. He was born a year after the accession of Charles I; the Civil Wars broke out when he was an undergraduate at Oxford; he was in his thirties at the time of the Restoration; and he died in the latter half of the reign of William III. Behind him the years of peace stretched back to the legendary glories of the Elizabethan Age, an epoch separated only by a span from medieval times. Around him portents of scientific development and political change gave indications of a new and strangely differing world already taking shape. He found himself heir to a handsome fortune, but the estate was encumbered with debt, and his business abilities insufficient (perhaps could not easily have been sufficient) to prevent all from being lost by the time he was forty-five. The remainder of his life was spent rubbing along as best he could on the goodwill of friends and relations; writing in such time as was allowed by the onerous profession of being an habitual guest in the houses of others.

Although chiefly remembered in connexion with antiquarian research and biographical memoir, there are few persons of whom it would be more true to say that they were interested in everything. Mathematics, painting, music, natural science, horticulture, heraldry, folklore, astrology, occult phenomena were all subjects—with a hundred others—that he was ever prepared to discuss and illustrate from the experiences of himself and his friends. His intellectual equipment for satisfying this universal curiosity was lively enough, although (in the English tradition) he remained always unprofessional in whatever he touched. Somewhat confusedly, he was aware of the opportunities offered by his period. Passionately attached to the past, he was at the same time attracted by the philosophical enquiries and mechanical contrivances which preoccupied so many of his acquaintances. This divided interest makes his position an uncommon one, differentiating him, on the one hand, from a friend like Anthony Wood, in love only with antiquarian investigation; and, on the other, from such as Robert Hooke, whose life was devoted to invention and experiment. His appreciation of the contemporary scene was, however, a kind of projection of Aubrey's interest in antiquity. He contemplated the life round him as in a mirror—the glass of the Lady of Shalott— scarcely counting himself as one of the actors on the stage, caring for things most when they had become part of history. He was there to watch and to record, and the present must become the past, even though only the immediate past, before it could wholly command his attention. For him the world of action represented unreality. It was, therefore, not surprising that his business affairs, troublesome enough in themselves, were conducted with results that were financially disastrous.

Recollections of his childhood show at how early an age Aubrey began to display his feeling for history, a taste rooted in him and stimulated by living in a place abounding in memories and monuments, where solitude forced him to find recreation within himself.

Such inclinations were the outcome of the Renaissance, for the Middle Ages had taken little or no interest in archaeology, and had forgotten the topographical science of classical times. In England the study of antiquity was about a century old; but had not become in any sense fashionable or popular in the years when Aubrey grew up, especially not for those living in the country, away from the academic world. It is true that Camden (who died in 1623) was still remembered in Aubrey's part of Wiltshire for his itinerary there, a pilgrimage considered eccentric enough by the local inhabitants. Indeed, opposition to antiquarian activities persisted, sometimes in unexpected places, and Milton sneered at those 'who take pleasure to be all their lifetime raking the foundations of old abbeys and cathedrals'.

Aubrey is accordingly one of the forerunners of the Romantic Revival; though the early and vigorous flowering of historical curiosity with which he was associated suffered some antagonisms under the influence of eighteenth-century 'reason', before its triumph in a far more sentimental and indiscriminate form a few decades later. For Aubrey there was still some reality in such relics of the Middle Ages as he could find and preserve. He had a peculiar gift for conveying a sense of the past, and his stories of medieval times recall a way of life that had never been entirely forgotten. They were something more than pegs upon which to hang the tattered Gothic pageantry to which a later generation, caught in the agonising grip of the Industrial Revolution, turned for some relief and respite. The familiar accompaniments of this later romanticism—the ruins, spectres, and lonely places—attracted him, too, but as a decorative element—the counterpart of 'a jiggish phancy and gypsies and ballads'—rather than as the baleful symbols of the Soul's dark journey that they were finally to become. In spite of an inability to handle practical affairs, he had too keen a sense of what everyday life was about to allow himself to fall into the mood (not uncommon in the seventeenth century) of Thomas Bushell, with his 'long gallery, which he hung all with black, and had some death's heads and bones painted'. Aubrey lacked the egoism and self-pity required for carrying his romanticism to this more extravagant stage. His acuteness of perception where others were concerned gave an outlet to talents that—in a character only slightly different—might have spent themselves in a masque of necromancy and heraldic daydream. 'If ever I had been good for anything,' he wrote, 'it would have been a painter. I could fancy a thing so strongly and have so clear an idea of it.' It was this powerful visual imagination which dominated his writing; and which, in the last resort, laid the foundation of his place in history.

Although he produced a number of other works, by no means insignificant, Aubrey owes his position in literature to his *Lives*. The eighteenth century remembered him as the author of the *Miscellanies*, whose omens and apparitions are still remarkably entertaining. The nineteenth century knew his *Wiltshire Collections* and of his discovery of Avebury. But the *Lives*—that extraordinary jumble of biography from which later historians have plundered so much of their picturesque detail—remain his masterpiece and gave him the distinction of being England's first serious biographer. Between the *Lives*' two extremes of length—forty or more pages to Thomas Hobbes, and to Abraham Wheloc the sole phrase 'simple man'—are anecdotes and descriptions of writers, clerics, statesmen, soldiers, lawyers, scientists, astrologers, schoolmasters, rakes, ladies of the town, and obscure old friends, related in a manner truly without parallel. Indeed, to the question: 'What are the English like?' worse answers might be given than: 'Read Aubrey's *Lives* and you will see'; for there, loosely woven together, is a kind of tapestry of the good and evil; the ingenuity and the folly; the integrity and the hypocrisy; the eccentricity, the melancholy, and the greatness of the English race.

Aubrey's own career is bound up with the *Lives*, both in the sense that the story of their composition is the story of the growth and decay of his friendship with Anthony Wood; and, more generally, because a large number of the persons mentioned were so well known to him that their combined portraits show the pattern of his days, and the orientation of the undeniably brilliant society through which he moved—a society in which (it should not be forgotten) merit reaped in some respects speedier and decidedly more advantageous rewards than within the complex competitive machinery of modern life.

The years of the Civil Wars form the background of Aubrey's youth and early manhood. He himself took no part in the campaigning; but by implication the political and social atmosphere of that time is keenly conveyed. The intermittent nature of the military operations, the irreconcilable opinions of families and neighbours, the widespread individual anxieties to be on the winning side at all costs, all find a place in his pages. In spite of Royalist sympathies, he is not reluctant to praise men on the other side. He hunts with Colonel Penruddock and plans a Wiltshire county history with Judge Nicholas; and, when the violence of prevailing religious and political disagreement is taken into account, the extent to which tolerance existed (and the mildness of retaliation when the Restoration took place) is wonderful in the light of the civil strife of our own day. At the same time we are given a clear idea of the desperate worries that continued to oppress persons unconnected with public affairs in the thirty years that followed Charles II's return, when another volcanic upheaval seemed always imminent. The deterioration of the affectionate relations between Aubrey and Wood was in a great part directly attributable to this ever-present element of uneasiness; and their letters are as trenchant documents as any of the period to show how men, living in a backwater from worldly ambition, feared a return to revolutionary conditions; and were harassed by each movement of the political and doctrinal weathercocks.

Isaac D'Israeli called Aubrey 'the little Boswell' of his day. The resemblance exists—not in character, but in the self-appointed mission to record, and manner of regarding the world around. Aubrey's canvas is much more diverse than Boswell's, though a devouring curiosity and willingness to play a subordinate rôle are common to both biographers. Boswell was shrewd, ambitious, vain, capable of wit, and sometimes very silly. He was not without generosity, and had a weakness for wine and the opposite sex. Aubrey, too, considered that ' 'Tis not consistent with an harmonicall soule to be a woman-hater' (his female subjects are particularly well described), and his sacrifices to Bacchus were at least adequate—though both tastes took with him a less tormenting form. He was generous to a fault, both materially and in his impulses.

In his own affairs, as little shrewd as a man well could be; not at all vain; almost without ambition, except in the hope that his researches would not be destroyed before they reached a safe resting-place; unpractical, but not silly; above all, without envy. He was sensitive and observant, something of a poet in his imagery; with a great deal of humour, though one would hesitate to call him witty. Both writers are adept at conveying a sense of their own enjoyment or discomfiture, and in indicating the demeanour of those amongst whom they found themselves.

Of his own character, Aubrey noted 'His chiefe vertue, gratitude', thinking of himself as a failure, and taking pride in the remembrance that he felt towards his benefactors an emotion not always easy to achieve. 'Never riotous or prodigall:' he wrote, 'but (as Sir E. Leech said) sloath and carelessnesse equivalent to all other vices'. When the full extent of his work is examined it will be seen that the imputation of 'sloath and carelessnesse' is unduly severe. The writings that he managed to produce in the course of a lifetime handicapped in the early stages by business worries, and latterly by poverty and debt—'leisure is a jewel I could never be master of'—were of a quantity and quality of which there was nothing to be ashamed; not to mention the correspondence (often regarding abstruse subjects) which he carried on with innumerable acquaintances. He was painstaking and very well informed; and, just as vanity is a source of weakness that can make even the most gifted appear ridiculous, so a degree of dignity and strength is inevitably conferred upon him by his modesty.

Throughout the narrative of Aubrey's life move some pungent minor characters: his patron, Lord Thanet, pompous, facetious, and perhaps rather pathetic with his personal preoccupations and his scurvy; his servant, Robinet, adept at everything from Italian translation to working in ivory; or that prince of bores and 'narrow soul'd cuckold', Thomas Gore 'of Aldrington aliàs Alderton'. For a few seconds the powerful mind of Hobbes, the eccentricities of Edmund Wyld, the equivocations of Joan Sumner are lighted up: and then the picture fades. There is that embarrassing clash of personalities when Aubrey introduces George Ent to Anthony Wood; and the painful family rows with

Aubrey's brother William. Above all there is the friendship and
quarrel with Wood—'my deare Freinde and old correspondent
Mr Anthony Wood: who (though his spleen used to make him
chagrin and to chide me) yet we could not be asunder, and he
would always see me at my Lodgeing, with his dark Lanthorne,
which should be a Relick'—a story that is moving and a little
tragic, not less so because its course is never far from becoming
ridiculous. On the whole, the passage from Tacitus, quaintly noted
down by Aubrey, in rather shaky French, as applicable to himself,
is fitting enough: 'Cneus Lentulus, outre l'honneur du consulat et
le triumphes de Getules, avoit la gloire d'avoir vescu sans
reproche dans sa pauverté, et sans orgeuil dans son opulence où
il estoit parvenu de puis par de voyes legitimes'; while some of the
lines 'To his honoured Freinde John Aubrey Esq. in imitation of
Mr Greaves's verses etc' by 'G. E. Esq.' (no doubt George Ent),
though a testament to affection rather than poetry, should not lie
altogether forgotten:

> '—one who flyes sadnesse, hates to be severe
> But with facetious jestes unbends his eare,
> Yet one that's studious too, whose boundlesse mind
> Scarce within Learning's compasse is confind:
> But cheifly Nature loves, and farre does prye
> Into her secrets with his pierceing Eye.
> These vertues in my freindship I pursue,
> And find them all conjoynd in none but you—'

JOHN AUBREY AND HIS FRIENDS

CHAPTER ONE

Ancestry, Childhood, and Schooldays (1626–1642)

I

IN JULY or August of the year 1634—afterwards Aubrey could remember only that it was in the venison season—Thomas Hobbes came to visit friends at Malmesbury in North Wiltshire, where he had been born on that Good Friday forty-six years before, when threat of the Spanish Armada had made his mother fall in labour. The philosopher was in appearance 'then a proper man, briske, and in very good habit', his hair still black (at school he had been called *Crow*), while, a sure sign of wit, his yellowish-reddish whiskers turned up naturally. For a week or more he stayed in the neighbourhood, talking, with the touch of Wiltshire speech that never left him, of Ben Jonson, Robert Ayton,[1] and the rest of the London poets. As the son of a local parson and with a brother, a glover, still living in the town, Hobbes had a large acquaintance to renew. He went to see, amongst others, his former schoolmaster, Mr Robert Latimer, who had moved from Malmesbury (he had taught Hobbes opposite the 'Three Cups') to the village of Leigh Delamere a few miles distant, where he kept his school in the church.

Mr Latimer, an old man who wore at his girdle in the manner of an earlier generation a 'dudgeon' or wooden-handled dagger with a knife and bodkin, was a good Grecian—the best they had had in North Wiltshire since the Reformation. He was widely known for his easy way of teaching by telling the boys a Latin word when they asked to 'Goe forth', which they had to repeat to him on their return, in a short time amounting to a good number of words.

[1] Both of these had advised Hobbes on his *Thucydides*, although Ayton (said to have been the first in whose verses appears *Auld Lang Syne*) is now little known in spite of Dryden's praise and an elegant memorial in Westminster Abbey.

If a boy struck him as promising, he would take pains with his education, and he would teach 'ingeniose lads' after supper, sometimes until nine o'clock at night. Hobbes had in his day been one of the favoured pupils marked down by Mr Latimer, then only nineteen years old and new to his profession; and the young schoolmaster did his best that his scholar should do credit at Oxford to his little school, when at fourteen (at the expense of his uncle, the alderman) the boy was sent to Magdalen Hall.

On this last meeting between them (because Hobbes never came into Wiltshire again and Mr Latimer died in the November of that year), the philosopher took some notice of a small boy who had arrived at the school in the church 'not as the vulgar boys, carrying a satchel on his back' but riding 'a delicate little horse'. This was John Aubrey, then aged eight, who had hacked over from Easton Pierse, a neighbouring house belonging to his grandfather. In later years Aubrey recalled this meeting as one of the memorable incidents of his life, the origin of a deep and valuable friendship. Hobbes, the subject of his first and longest biography, was always for him *Malmsburiensis*, his Wiltshire fellow-countryman and Nestor; and—among all his wide acquaintance—*par excellence* the great man of that circle and of the age.

II

Although it seems that their connexion with Wiltshire had begun only with Aubrey's grandmother, a Danvers, the Aubreys were of some consequence in this part of the world.[1] Like the families of Baskerville and St John; Bromwich, Button, and Herbert; Vaughan, Powell, Gethin, Beavan, and many another of Welsh or Cambro-Norman descent, whose names are scattered through local Subsidy Rolls, Fines and Recoveries, or Heraldic Visitations, they had come to settle in that country from the

---

[1] The Aubreys of Chadenwich, Wilts, who had been settled in the county at least since the beginning of the sixteenth century, appear to have been unrelated. They recorded a pedigree in the Visitation of 1561 (when their coat was given as *Bendy of ermine and gules*) and sold their estate in 1640.

Marches of Wales. These grazing lands of the Border sent their
wool to the North Wiltshire clothiers to transform into broad-
cloth, so that commerce linked the two regions, and accounts for
much of the Welsh migration.

The Aubreys believed themselves to be sprung from a certain
Saunders *de Sancto Alberico* or *de Alba Ripa*—of the White Cliff—a
companion of William the Bastard, said to have been brother to
the Count of Boulogne and Earl Marshal of France. The Welsh
deputy-herald, Lewis Dwnn, and the Book of Golden Grove
trace an elaborate and circumstantial pedigree from this somewhat apocryphal forebear, whose son, Sir Richard (or Reginald)
Aubrey, fought, they say, under Bernard Newmarch at the time of
his invasion of Wales (*c.* 1093), rewarded by that feudatory with
the lordships of Abercynfrig and Slwch in Brecon. Sir Richard
Aubrey is a more convincing ancestor than Saunders of the White
Cliff, but genealogists are not always in agreement as to the
descending branches of the tree, of which the generations are too
few in number adequately to cover the first five hundred years of
the family's history; so that the Aubreys at the head of the pedigree repose in twilight. There is no reason to doubt that they
were *Advenae*,[1] as the Welsh genealogists called all strangers who
settled in the Lordship, whether of direct Norman origin accompanying or immediately following the invaders of the country, or
those who by grant, purchase, or inheritance (often through marriage with a Welsh heiress) became landowners there.

In the Cathedral Church of St John the Evangelist at Brecon is
a monument to Walter (son of Walter) and Christina Awbrey of
Abercynfrig, formerly dated 1312. Two recumbent figures lie
under a canopy on which angels swing censers. The inscription
runs: *Water le Fitz Water git ici Iesus de sa alme mercie* etc. He was

[1] G. T. Clarke in his *Limbus Patrum Morganiae et Glamorganiae* says:
'All the older, and most of the later *Advenae* were connected with the
Honour of Gloucester and followed in the train of their liege lords. They
were either the heads or the cadets of families in the shires of Gloucester,
Somerset, Devon, and Cornwall, and what little is known of them is
derived mainly from the records of those counties.' The surname
'Aubrey' occurs in early fourteenth-century Somerset records.

undoubtedly a forbear. There is no doubt that by the time of
Hopkin Aubrey, of Abercynfrig, who lived during the latter half
of the fifteenth century, the Aubreys were to all intents and purposes Welsh. Even if their root was Norman, they had been
Welsh (or, to be more precise, Welsh of the Marches, perhaps a
proper distinction) for the best part of four hundred years.

This Hopkin Aubrey, of Abercynfrig, was the grandfather of
Dr William Aubrey, LL.D., the great man of the family, who
raised them out of the obscurity in which they had lived as Welsh
squires. Dr Aubrey had been Judge-Advocate of the armies of
Queen Elizabeth at St Quentin. In those French wars William
Earl of Pembroke, a distant connexion (by descent from Welsh
ancestors 'Melin and Philip ap Elydr'),[1] was Captain-General in
1557, and, in recognition of their connexion, he may have helped
this Aubrey relation's advancement. He was in any case a good
friend to William Aubrey and gave him a silver basin and ewer.
Master in Chancery, Member of the Council in the Marches,
Regius Professor of Civil Law at Oxford, Vicar-General to the
Archbishop of Canterbury, Dr Aubrey held many illustrious
appointments. At the trial of Mary Queen of Scots he had been
one of the Commissioners, and had tried to save her from the death
penalty; but, in spite of this, Elizabeth liked him and used to call
him 'her little doctor'.

Among his kinsmen, William Aubrey numbered the mathematician, man of letters and astrologer, Dr John Dee, of a Radnorshire
family descended from the Princes of South Wales, who had likewise found favour with Queen Elizabeth, to whom he had
dedicated *The Sovereignty of the Sea*; upon which Dr Aubrey had
given advice. Elizabeth was impressed by Dee, a brilliant, eccentric figure (to whose reputation justice has only latterly been done).
Dee, presented to the Queen by Lord Pembroke, his patron
also, was much occupied with such things as the reform of the
calendar and the preservation of ancient manuscripts and monuments. It is notable that the Aubrey generation born a hundred

[1] Through a female line Dr Aubrey descended from Griffith ap Howel
Melin (the Yellow), *c.* 13th cen., of the house of Blethin ap Maenarch,
a Brecon magnate, from whom the Herberts also came (Lyfvr Baglan).

years before him should have been concerned, if only through a friend, with matters so near as these to the heart of John Aubrey himself.

Dr William Aubrey died in 1595, asking for a *goodman*, meaning, it was supposed by some, a priest, rather than Dr Goodman, the Dean of St Paul's, for whom the request was commonly accepted to be. He left, with a large fortune, Abercynfrig, the ancient seat of the Aubrey family (purchased from a cousin), where he had been able to ride for nine miles together in his own land; and the Great House at Brecon, in which his study looked over the river Usk. Also he left £2,500 per annum; but his chief clerk, one Hugh George, who was also the Doctor's executor, embezzled some of this fortune and disappeared with it to Ireland. The will entailed the property in such a manner that Dr Aubrey's great-grandson, John Aubrey, the little boy whom Hobbes had noticed at Mr Latimer's school, was eighteenth in the remainder,[1] a circumstance that was to cause him much financial and legal embarrassment when he grew up; and make him think often of Donne's lines:

> *And what doeth it availe*
> *To be twentieth man in an entaile?*

Apart from Dr William Aubrey, the Aubreys remained undistinguished—'*Heroum filii noxae*' remarked his great-grandson, 'he engrossed all the witt of the family, so that none descending from him can pretend to any'. In consideration of their father's efforts to prevent his mother's execution, James I knighted the doctor's two eldest sons and invited them to Court; but they preferred a country life, and 'modestly and perhaps prudently declined'. Their diffidence did not have its reward in the conduct of the generation that followed them, amongst whom were a number of distressing examples of extravagance and dissipation.

[1] 'He made a deed of entaile which is also mentioned in his will, whereby he entailes the Brecon estate on the issue male of his eldest son, and in defailer, to skip the 2d son (for whom he had well provided, and had married a great fortune) and to come to the third. Edward the eldest had seaven sonnes; and his eldest son, Sir William, had also seaven sonnes; and so I am heire, being the 18th man in remainder.' See J. Lloyd's *Hist. Mem. of Brecon*, p. 22 for Dr Aubrey's Inq. P.M.

One cousin, for example, refers in his will to 'what little estate God hath left me', and bequeaths something towards settling his son as an apprentice 'if he is capable', hoping that the house might be saved and 'humbly desiring on the knees of my hart' (a phrase that has something of the true Aubrey ring) that this will be performed. The son in question was even less fortunate than his father. Twice married, the validity of his first alliance was contested and successfully set aside. But the relations of his first wife, unreconciled to this (in their view) bigamous act, visited their former brother-in-law some years later and took the opportunity of smothering him when he was lying drunk in bed. The records speak also of family affrays at Brecon fair, and, although not all the clan came to violent ends, more than a few wasted their substance in quarrels, speculation, and law-suits.

The behaviour of these collateral relatives has, of course, no direct bearing on the character of John Aubrey himself, except in so much as their vagaries suggest that he may have had in him some strong hereditary strain of irresponsibility. And yet it is hard to say to what extent, if at all, the Aubreys were more riotous and prodigal than other families of the same sort. Chancery proceedings or the records of Star Chamber, for the sixteenth and first half of the seventeenth centuries, show that life, certainly in the more remote parts of the country, was as fierce and disorderly as it had been in the Middle Ages. Especially was this true of Wales and the Border, where litigants disputing the confines of an estate would lead bands of armed servants in war against their neighbours. Heiresses were abducted. Justices of the Peace practised illegal arrest. Moreover, in this secluded and mountainous region, the difficulties of maintaining law and order, for the time at least, had been increased by the comparatively recent introduction of forms of tenure and administration not yet generally understood or accepted by the people of the land.

Among the many Welshmen who made careers for themselves under the Tudors, a considerable proportion were 'Silurians'—men from the Marches, often from stock connected with the Aubreys themselves, 'for the Welshmen are all kinne'. But the cadet branch of the family to which John Aubrey belonged, either by leaving the shadow of the Black Mountains or by the generous infiltration of English blood, seems to have become gentler and less intransigent. The stormy squanderings and unhappy matrimonial adventures of their cousins were transmuted in them to a mere inability to transact business and a baneful and persistent indecision. Milder influences were at work that gave the Aubreys of North Wiltshire a more balanced approach to life than, since the time of Dr Aubrey, the founder of their fortunes, many of their name seem to have possessed in Wales.

III

Dr William Aubrey had for a time lived at Kew, and was therefore neighbour, as well as friend and kinsman, of Dr Dee, whose house was at Mortlake. In the latter's curious diary he mentions more than once a 'Mr Awbrey'. This was John Aubrey, Dr Aubrey's son (grandfather of the subject of this book), who on his father's death was left to the guardianship of John Whitgift, Archbishop of Canterbury,[1] whose Vicar-General Dr Aubrey had been. The Archbishop married his ward at the age of eighteen, or thereabouts, to Rachel, daughter of William Danvers of Tokenham in Wiltshire, thereby allying the Aubreys with an ancient and influential family, soon to increase in importance. The Danvers relationship was to be of notable assistance to this John Aubrey's grandson during the lean years.

After their marriage, John and Rachel Aubrey settled at a property now called Burlton Court, purchased for them by Dr Aubrey in 1594 at Burghill in Herefordshire; and in 1603 a child was born to them whom they named Richard. John Aubrey died at about thirty-eight years of age on 11 June, 1616. He was buried at Burghill, where there is a mural brass commemorating him. His son Richard was then about eleven years old. His

[1] The Archbishop 'kept a noble household and that with admirable order and œconomie', although 'there was not one woman in the family'. Whitgift, a strong opponent of puritanism, figured largely in the Mar-Prelate controversy. Aubrey says that John Penry, accused of writing *Martin Mar-Prelate*, 'was kin to my great grandfather'.

widow, Rachel Aubrey, married (as his fourth wife) John Whitson, alderman and benefactor of the city of Bristol.

Whitson was a self-made man, who had raised himself to be a Member of Parliament, Mayor of Bristol, Colonel of Train Bands (at his funeral their pikes had black ribbons and their drums were covered with black cloth), a rich and popular figure whose life story seems an echo of the nineteenth rather than the sixteenth century, who left large sums in charitable bequests to Bristol. He taught his stepson, Richard Aubrey, to be a good falconer, but did not at all concern himself with his education; and he also cut down the woods on the Aubrey estates, without giving Richard any satisfaction for the loss of timber. If this was allowed to happen it is not unlikely that the property was badly administered in other respects, and that Richard Aubrey was the victim of a species of ill-fortune perpetually referred to in chronicles of the past—a long minority.

When Richard Aubrey was some twenty-two years of age he married Deborah, daughter and heir of Isaac and Israel Lyte. The Lytes were another Wiltshire family, who had come in the county from Somerset, where at Lytescary the main branch of their line had lived since the end of the thirteenth century. They were said to have been brought to Wiltshire, from Somerset, by the de Yeoviltons, who had succeeded the Fitzpiers family about the year 1300 as the owners of the Easton Pierse estate. Aubrey says that there was a picture of Thomas Lyte of Lytescary hanging at Wilton (perhaps on account of his second marriage, which was to Lady Sydney),[1] so that the Aubreys' connexion with the Herberts may have brought them in touch with the Lytes.

If the distant ramifications of the paternal branch of Aubrey's family hint of strife, disintegration, and ruin, similar offshoots of the maternal side suggest, in equally general terms, some of Aubrey's own varied interests, and the firmly established civilised kind of life which he loved, but which seemed always to elude him.

[1] Widow of Sir John Sidney, brother of Sir Philip Sidney. The son of this marriage also married a Lyte, according to Aubrey.

Several of the Lyte family[1] shared his preoccupation with horticulture and heraldry, and were scholarly country gentlemen, not without some distinction, holding positions at Court and in the Law.

The eldest child of Richard Aubrey and Deborah Lyte was born on 12 March, 1626, and was christened John. The peculiarities of his character may be interpreted to some degree by considering the antagonistic elements compounded in the offspring of these strongly contrasted lineages.

IV

The day after he had seen him at Mr Latimer's school, Hobbes visited John Aubrey's relations, who lived by Kington St Michael, about half-way between Malmesbury and Chippenham, at the house known as Easton Pierse, the name of one of the two large tithings into which Kington was divided. The property belonged to Isaac Lyte, Aubrey's maternal grandfather, whose family had been tenants under lease at Kington until 1574, when they had bought the place from the poet, Thomas Sackville, Lord Buckhurst.[2] The Lytes sold the manor house and the farm to the Snells (a local family to whom they were related) for £385 in the

[1] There was, for example, Henry Lyte, of whom Aubrey writes that he translated the *Niewe herball* of Rembert Dodoens (published in 1578) into English, which he dedicated to Queen Elizabeth. 'He had a pretty good collection of plants for that age: some few whereof are yet alive 1660.' This Henry Lyte also wrote 'a little pamphlet, which I have called *The Light of Britaine* being a short summary of the old English history', which he presented to Queen Elizabeth when she went in state to St Paul's to return thanks for the defeat of the Spanish Armada. In addition to this he 'began the genealogy of King James, derived from Brute: which his eldest son Thomas Lyte, aforesaid finished and presented to King James', a work which 'Mr Camden much admired, and at the foot writt six or eight verses with his own hand'.

[2] Author of *Gorboduc*, and later 1st Earl of Dorset. He was ancestor of the better known 6th Earl of Dorset, to whom Aubrey sometimes refers, also a poet and author of *To all you ladies now at land*.

following year, keeping part of the land for themselves; and, on the brow of the hill, they built a house called Lower Easton Pierse (or Percy), though the full name—derived from the extinct family of Piers or Fitzpiers, the former owners of the land—was rarely used. It faced south-east above the brook, where later Aubrey bored clay 'as blue as ultramarine', and on the banks of which (he says), among the oaks and witch-hazel, flowered 'calver-keys, hare-parsley, wild vetch, maiden's honesty, polypodium, foxgloves, wild vine, bayle, and many vulnerary plants now by me forgot. There growes also adder's tongues, plenty.'

A book of 'prospects' of this mansion and its grounds, drawn and coloured by Aubrey himself, is still in existence. The drawings show what extensive alterations (if not entire rebuilding) must have taken place at some time during his early life; although, strangely enough, he makes no mention of this in his writings, except to refer to 'the artificers that came there', whom, as a child, he loved to watch. Some of the drawings show a rustic manor house, set among trees and seeming, more or less, to answer his description: 'the archetecture of an old English gentleman's house, especially in Wiltshire and thereabouts, was a good high strong wall, a gate-house, a great hall and parlour; and within this little green court where you come in stood on one side the barne. They then thought not the noise of the threshold ill musique.'

Other designs in the same collection illustrate something far more ornate, a Palladian villa, in place of the earlier buildings. This Italianate mansion, with its cupola and classical proportions—even allowing for some additional flourish on the part of the draughts-man—would have been a place of uncommon beauty. The garden was laid out on three different levels, each raised above the other and ascended by a flight of steps, while on the lawn of one of these was a pillar, standing half as high as the house and surmounted by a 'volant Mercury'. In the lowest of the gardens was a 'jeddeau', throwing its water to a height of thirty feet, about which were planted groups of trees that seem to be cypresses. Some have doubted whether this house was even built.

All has gone now, razed at the end of the eighteenth century and replaced by a colourless farm; but Aubrey's biographer, Britton,[1] writing as an old man in 1845, could remember this house, tumbled down, still full of ancient, forgotten oddments and pieces of rusty armour. The diarist Kilvert, whose father was vicar of Langley Burrel (where he was himself later curate), visited the place on St Bartholomew's Day, 24 August, 1871. The house he describes[2] appears to be that in which the Snell family lived in Aubrey's time, and he gives a vivid account of a decay that was no doubt of the same gradual but devastating sort which fell upon Easton Pierse. Such was the fate of the elegant houses of the seventeenth century if their owners went downhill; but if Aubrey had managed to keep his money, and his descendants had prospered, Easton Pierse might have remained as one of the architectural masterpieces of the period; for this is what the drawings suggest that Aubrey's home could have been. Even now the position in which the farm is placed and the view across the lonely fields—the

[1] John Britton (1771–1857) was an interesting figure, who had himself been born at Kington St Michael, and, from very humble beginnings, had won a place in the contemporary world of archaeology and letters.

[2] 'We put up the carriage at the Vicarage [Kington] and Edward Awdry walked up with us to Easton Pierse, by the old paths which I used to travel and which seemed so familiar to me. From the meadows above Lower Easton we caught the first glimpse of the grey gables. The old manor house has fallen into sad ruin since I used to come here to see old Mrs Buckland seven years ago. The great hall and the grand staircase both gone. All the back of the house tottering and the tall carved chimney stack trembling to its fall. From the huge oak beam which runs across and supports the vast ruined kitchen chimney, we stripped off large pieces of the bark which had never been removed and which looked as fresh as when the beam was placed there, perhaps hundreds of years ago. The house seemed empty and deserted. Heaps of stone and rubbish lay round the yards. The orchards were tangled and overgrown, the garden run wild with weeds, rank and neglected. Pink stonecrop and some straggling Virginia Stock ran over the heaps of waste and rubbish stone. There was not a sound or a sign of life or living thing about the ruinous deserted place. Nothing but silence and desolation! A shepherd lives in a part of the house which still stands but as the staircase is fallen he is obliged to go out of doors and across a rude scaffolding stage before he can reach his bedroom.'

'thin blew lanskape'—once the 'ploughed campania' of the Cots-
wolds, call up something of 'that most lovely seate' where Aubrey
was bred in 'an eremiticall solitude'.

v

There he had been born of 'longaevous, healthy kindred' at
about sunrise on 12 March—St Gregory's Day[1]—1626, in the
room where the escutcheons[2] of his grandparents' families, the
Lytes and the Brownes, were painted on the chimney, an appropriate setting for the reception of a lifelong amateur of heraldry.
In other respects, however, the omens, especially those astrological,
were inauspicious, Saturn directly opposing his ascendant. Indeed,
the child was weak and seemed so likely to die that he was christened[3] before morning prayers. Alderman Whitson was his
godfather.

This poor health continued until he was about twelve years old,
when the attacks of vomiting and ague, to which he had previously
been subject at regular periods, became rarer and, from being
fortnightly and monthly, they became quarterly and half-yearly,
at last ceasing altogether (though the issue in the 'coronall' of his
head continued to run until he was twenty-one); but much harm
had by then already been done, and 'this sicknesse nipt my strength
in the bud'. His memory was bad, too, though he always retained
graphic impressions of the surroundings and customs of childhood,
when 'the children's shoes were printed with silver figures, as the
back of horn books, with St George on horseback on red leather
and they wore yellow shoes, which I think they do still'. He learnt
his alphabet from one of these hornbooks, and his nurse used to

[1] In later life he sometimes used to sign himself as 'Gregorovius'.

[2] *Gules a chevron between three swans argent, a mullet sable for difference*
(Lyte): *azure an eagle displayed sable, legged gules, on its breast a besant or*
(Browne).

[3] 'John Awbrye, Sonne of Richard Awbrye: gent: was baptized the
xij Daye of March', 1626, Kingston St Michael Parish Register.

sing a ballad to him, of the history of England down to the time of
Charles I:

> *Yea, Rosamond, fair Rosamond,*
> *Her name was called so,*
> *To whom Dame Elinor our Queen*
> *Was known a deadly foe . . .*

Perhaps it was the nurse who by this medium intoxicated her
charge with dreams of the past, the anodyne to which he was addicted as early as he could remember, and with which throughout
his life he could never dispense.

His education and observation continued, so that: 'When about
1632 I learnt to read of John Brome the Clarke of Kington St
Michael, his old father (above eighty) who had been Clarke there
before, dayly wore a gowne like an undergraduate's at Oxford,
with the sleeves pinned behind. I doe believe that about the later
end of Queen Elizabeth's time 'twas the fashion for grave people
to wear such gownes. Mr William Shakespeare, Poet, in his monument in the Church at Stratford upon Avon his figure is thus: a
tawny sattin doublet, I think, pinked: and over that a black gown:
the sleeves of the gown do not cover the arms, but hang loose
behind.'

From his earliest years he was fascinated by the idea of knowledge of all sorts, especially of a mechanical kind: 'I was from
childhood affected with the view of things rare: which is the begining of philosophy.' He liked to watch the joiners, carpenters,
coopers, and masons at work (no doubt rebuilding Easton Pierse),
and to make plans and drawings as if he were himself an engineer: 'I was wont (I remember) much to lament with myselfe that
I lived not in a city, *e.g.* Bristoll, where I might have accesse to
watchmakers, locksmiths, etc.'

For a time he did indeed live in or near Bristol with his grandmother, Mrs Whitson, who had been bequeathed by her husband,
as a jointure, the manor of Burnet in Somerset. This was about four
miles from Stanton Drew, so that at an early age Aubrey was
familiar with the local group of prehistoric stones there, called The
Wedding, a kind of introduction to his later interest in megaliths.
In Bristol he used to hear the story, 'fresh as but of yesterday', of

how Black Will Herbert[1] (later Earl of Pembroke), then 'a mad fighting young fellow', wearing the blue coat and badge of a servant of the house of Worcester, had killed one of the sheriffs of the city, escaped through the Great Gate into the Marsh, and fled to France. After this incident the Bristol authorities had walled up the Gate and made in its place a little postern door with a turnstile.

Aubrey has left remarkably little information about either his father or his mother. They had been married just nine months before his birth, Richard Aubrey being nearly twenty-two and Deborah Lyte fifteen 'and as much from January to June'. Whether it was the long minority, the operation of Dr Aubrey's entail, the rebuilding of the house, or simply his own financial ineptitude, which ate up Richard Aubrey's fortune, there can be no doubt that for one reason or another he never managed to put his domestic and business affairs upon a satisfactory basis. Easton Pierse, it is true, was the property of the Lytes; but possibly Richard Aubrey contributed liberally to its improvement. Perhaps the trade depression of the sixteen-twenties among the Wiltshire clothiers may have affected him indirectly. It is not unlikely that he had interests in this commerce. He was a Justice of the Peace *tempore Caroli Primi*, and, in the commission of 1631, he made composition in the sum of £10 to avoid the degree of knighthood: as did also his father-in-law, Isaac Lyte, and for the same amount.

Before he went to Mr Latimer's school, Aubrey had been grounded in his accidence by Mr Hart, the curate of another neighbouring village, Yatton Keynell, who had taught his pupils

[1] Aubrey is sometimes unreliable about the early history of the Herberts; and it seems, in fact, to have been the 1st Earl of Pembroke, of the first creation of that title in the Herbert family, who was called Gwilim Ddu or Black William, rather than the 1st Earl of Pembroke of the second creation, to whom this anecdote refers, the latter being a grandson of the former by a bastard son. The incident at Bristol took place in 1527 when a great fray was made by the Welshmen on the King's Watch on Midsummer Night. On the following day, St James's Day, the Mayor was returning from a wrestling match, and one, Richard Vaughan, a mercer, was killed by William Herbert, the cause being 'a want of some respect in compliment'.

'by a faire and spreading ewe-tree in the churchyard as was common heretofore. The boyes took much delight in its shade, and it furnished them with their scoopes and nut-crackers. The clarke lop't it to make money of it to some bowyer or fletcher, and that lopping kill'd it: the dead trunk remaines there still.'

He notes that: 'At eight I was a kind of engineer; and I fell then to drawing, begining first with plaine outlines, *e.g.* in draughts of curtaines. Then at nine (crossed herein by father and schoolmaster, having nobody to instruct me; copied pictures in the parlour in a table book).' This was because: 'he cared not for play, but on play-dayes he gave himself to drawing and painting. At nine a portraiter.' Another note refers again to these pictorial activities: 'As Mr Walter Waller's picture drawn after his death; *è contra*, I have done severall by the life.' Mr Waller was the vicar of Broad Chalke, where Aubrey's cousins, the Brownes—and later the Aubreys themselves—lived. Aubrey's portrait of this divine no doubt owed something to his own inventive gifts, as the vicar died in 1629, when the painter can have been only in his fourth year. He was an observant boy, however, and remembered in 1634 the sight of Alderman Wellington of Hereford, the only person he ever saw so old-fashioned as to wear trunk-hose.

When older: 'my studies (geometrie) were on horseback and in the house of office: (my father discouraged me).' Whether these objections on the part of Richard Aubrey were founded on an innate distrust for art and letters, as such, or because occupations of this sort ran counter to plans of his own, is not explained by his son. They seem unreasonable, because, in a house where he had to provide his own amusement, there can have been little else for the boy to do; for there were no other children with whom to play, his brothers, William and Thomas, not being born until he had gone up to Oxford; and the rest of Richard and Deborah Aubrey's children died in infancy. Richard Aubrey's health seems never to have been sound and this may have made him irritable and moody. Aubrey notes, among some remedies and traditional cures, that '*For a pinne and webbe in the eye*, a pearle, or any humour that comes out of the head—my father laboured under this infirmity, and our learned men of Salisbury could doe him no good.

At last one goodwife Holly, a poore woman of Chalke, cured him in a little time. My father gave her a broade piece of gold for the receipt.'

Of his mother, he says almost less than of his father, though all his character points to a strong maternal influence. He mentions that once at Broad Chalke she saw in the sky an unusual solar effect at a time when she was 'going to see what a clock it was at an horizontal dial', and she had 'bunches of Glastonbury Thorne for a flower pott several Christmases'. On one occasion at least, as will be seen later, she persuaded him to alter his plans in a way to which he always looked back afterwards as disastrous. When her death came at seventy-five, it was an overwhelming grief to him. This is all, or nearly all, that we know about her.

At nine years old an incident took place which remained in his mind 'as if it were but yesterday'. He was in Gloucester with his father, where they had gone to see a Mr Singleton, an alderman and woollen draper, who had in his parlour over the chimney the whole description of Sir Philip Sidney's funeral, engraved and printed on papers pasted together. This marvel was at least the length of the room when extended. The paper turned upon two pins so that in action the figures mourning the Elizabethan paladin ('whose fame will never die whilest poetrie lives') moved past in slow parade; and revived in their procession the half-forgotten glories of an heroic, legendary age.

VI

There was another source which fed this 'strong and early impulse to antiquities', and a figure who, more than anyone else at Easton Pierse, dominated Aubrey's precocious imagination. This was his grandfather, Isaac Lyte, like Mr Latimer old-fashioned enough still to wear a dagger, who belonged to the remote days when parsons had been called 'Sir Richard of Stratford' or 'Sir William of Monkland', as if they had been knights; and when the shepherds

> *Did pray to God and St Oswold*
> *To bring the sheep safe from the fold,*

sometimes in their ignorance imploring the Saint under the name of 'St Twasole'.

Isaac Lyte had known some of the famous men of Elizabeth's time and before; and when (like his grandson) he had begun his Latin at the vicar's school at Yatton Keynell, Mr Camden, on one of his tours of investigation to collect material for his *Britannia*, had come to inspect the church. On that occasion the great antiquary took note of some escutcheons, particularly remarking a little painted-glass window in the chapel, which a later, and unworthy, incumbent walled-up to save himself the charge of glazing.

Aubrey's grandfather had been a friend of Sir Carew Raleigh, Sir Walter's brother, and used to say of him that he had 'a delicate cleare voice, and played singularly well on the olpharion[1] (which was the instrument in fashion in those days), to which he did sing'; and Aubrey had heard his grandmother say that when she was young 'they were wont to speak of this rebus, viz.

> *The enemie of the stomack, and the word of disgrace[2]*
> *Is the name of the gentleman with the bold face,'*

meaning Sir Walter Raleigh. Sir Walter was remembered in North Wiltshire with some misgiving, because he had persuaded Sir Charles Snell (of the family to whom the Lytes had sold the manor house at Easton Pierse) to invest in a venture that had gone amiss; and Aubrey wrote of Snell: 'My good neighbour, an honest young gentleman, but kept perpetuall sott, he engaged him to build a ship (the Angel Gabriel) for the designe for Guiana, which cost him the mannor of Yatton-Keynell, the farme at Easton Pierse, Thornhill and the church-lease of Bishop's Canning; which ship, upon Sir Walter Raleigh's attainder, was forfeited.'

Sir Charles Snell had also employed 'a graceful servant', Jack Sydenham, who used to carry Aubrey, as a child, in his arms; and years after, when Aubrey had grown up, Sydenham (who also

---

[1] Aubrey notes of this musical instrument: ''Tis as big as a lute, but flat bellyed with wire springs.'

[2] *i.e.* Raleigh, pronounced 'Raw-lie'.

sang rarely) would tell him stories of his former master, the mysterious and eccentric Thomas Bushell, Francis Bacon's ganymede, 'whose genius lay most towards naturall philosophy, and particularly towards the discovery, drayning, and improvement of the silver mines in Cardiganshire'; and (like Sir Walter Raleigh) 'had the strangest bewitching way to drawe in people (yes, discreet and wary men) into his projects that ever I heard of.'

In those distant days, says Aubrey, there had been less affectation of good manners. 'The use of "Your Humble Servant" came into England by the marriage of Queen Mary, daughter of Henry IV of France: derived from "Votre tres Humble Serviteur"; and never heard of before; but "God keep you", "God be wi' ye", "How dost doe?" with a thump on the shoulder. Till this time the Court itself was unpolished and unmannered—King James's Court was so far from being civill to woemen, that the ladies, nay the Queen herself, could hardly pass by the King's apartment without receiving some affront.'

Aubrey's grandfather could remember when smoking was still so uncommon that pipes, sometimes made of silver ('the ordinary sort made of a wallnut shell and a straw'), would be handed round the table from man to man: when the apothecaries sold sack in their shops, and the shopkeepers would reckon with counters. He was even a link with that dim, gothic age when the *tregetours*—those itinerant illusionists, who recall the stories of King Arthur's court—had exhibited the mysteries of their art:

> For oft at festes have I well heard say,
> That tregetores, within an hall large,
> Have made come in a water and a barge
> And in the Hall rowen up and doun.
> Sometimes hath seemed to come a grim lioun
> And sometimes flowers spring up as in a mede
> Sometimes a vine and grapes white and red:
> Sometimes a castel of lime and stone
> And when .him listed, voiden him anone:
> Thus seemed it to everyman's sight.

Isaac Lyte had talked with old father Davis, who had seen such things as Chaucer's lines (quoted by Aubrey) speak of done at a gentleman's hall in Gloucestershire at Christmas in the time of King Henry VIII, when shows of this kind had already become rare. His grandson was never tired of enquiring about such matters, and asking questions about the rood-loft, the ceremonies at the priory, or the manuscripts from Malmesbury that had been dispersed broadcast at the time of the Dissolution. Much of the neighbourhood had been church lands, held of Glastonbury, and there had been a nunnery at Kington, so that many of these manuscripts were still to be found, here and there, throughout the country. They were often used by glovers, that flourishing local trade, to wrap up their wares; and it was also the fashion to save the covers of books by giving them a jacket of parchment that was, more often than not, a medieval document. Music books, account books and copybooks were also bound in this material. Aubrey had noticed these covers at school, and had admired the elegance of the script and the illuminated initial letters. It grieved him that the Rector, Mr Stump (related to the famous William Stump, the great clothier who had purchased the site of the Abbey, together with some of its neighbouring lands) should use the manuscripts he possessed to stop the bung-hole of his barrel of special ale; but the Rector was so far from being persuaded to the contrary that he was accustomed to assert repeatedly that for stopping a bung-hole there was nothing in the world like an ancient parchment manuscript.

VII

In North Wiltshire there were many local customs still existing, which were soon to join these memories of the past. 'Riding at the Quintin (in French *Quintaine*) at weddings was used by the ordinary sort (but not very common) till the breaking-out of the Civill-warres. When I learned to reade I sawe one at a Wedding of one of the Farmers at Kington St Michael; it is performed at a crosse ways and it was there by the pound, and 'twas a pretty rustique sport.' He could remember at weddings seeing the bride and bridegroom kiss over the bride-cakes at the table, and the bridegroom wait at dinner. In those days the maids used to stick up in the chinks and joists of the roof 'midsummer men' made of orpins, two and two, which by inclining to or from one another told of love or aversion; or, if either withered, of death. Even the cats were different, and Aubrey could recall when 'the common English Catt was white with some blewish piednesse *sc* gallipot-blew, the race or breed of them are now almost lost'.[1] There were tales, too, of the fairies. 'When I was a boy, our country people woulde talke much of them: they swept up the Harth cleane at night: and did sett the shoes by the fire, and many times they should find a threepence in one of them. Mrs Markey (a daughter of Serjeant Hoskyns, the Poet) told me that her mother did much use that Custome, and had as much money as made her (or bought her) a little silver cup of thirtie shillings value.'

In this lonely and still unchanged countryside Aubrey spent his childhood, in a land whose atrabilious inhabitants he has well described: 'According to the severall sorts of earth in England (and so all the world over) the *indigenae* are respectively witty or dull, good or bad. . . . In North Wiltshire, and the vale of Gloucestershire (a dirty clayey country) the *Indigenae* or Aborigines speak drawlinge, they are phlegmatique, skins pale and livid, slow and dull, heavy of spirit; hereabout is but little tillage or hard labour: they only milk cows and make cheese: they feed chiefly on milk meats, which cool their brains too much and hurts their inventions. These circumstances make them melancholy, contemplative and malicious; by consequence thereof come more lawsuits out of North Wilts, at least double the number to the Southern parts. And by the same reason they are generally more apt to be fanatiques: their persons are generally plump and feggy; gallipot eies and some black; but they are generally handsom enough. It is a woodsere country, abounding much with sowre and austere plants, as sorrel &c, which make their humours sowre and fixes their spirits. In Malmesbury Hundred &c (the wett clayey parts) there have even been reputed witches. On

---

[1] Aubrey says that Archbishop Laud had been 'a great lover of Catts. He was presented with some Cypruss-catts, our Tabby-catts, which were sold at first for 5*li* a piece. This was about 1637 or 1638.' Tabbies are still called 'cyprus cats' in Norfolk.

the Downes, *sc* the Southpart where 'tis all upon tillage, and where the shepherds labour hard, their flesh is hard, their bodies strong. Being weary after hard labour they have no leisure to read or contemplate religion, but goe to bed to their rest, to rise betimes the next morning to their labour.'

Such was the picture of the landscape and the people round him which impressed itself upon the imagination of this thoughtful child.

VIII

The death of Mr Latimer in 1634, and his own sicknesses and agues, interrupted Aubrey's education for some years. In October 1634 a fever, the worst illness he had ever suffered, nearly carried him off; and he had another narrow escape in 1639, when 'my Uncle Anthony Browne's bay nag threw me dangerously the Monday after Easter. Just before it I had the impulse of the briar under which I rode, which tickled him, at the gap at the upper end of Berylane.' Meanwhile, he was under several dull and ignorant 'rest-in-house'[1] teachers; and then, when he was stronger, he was sent to board at the grammar school at Blandford St Mary's in Dorset, at that time 'the most eminent school for the education of gentlemen in the West of England'.

Aubrey gives 1638 as the year he went to Blandford; but from the masters he mentions by name as teaching there in his time, it seems possible that his arrival may have been a year or so earlier than that date. In the light of much that he says later on the subject of his own views as to what a school should be, it is clear that, in the beginning at least, Aubrey was not very happy there. 'I was exceedingly mild of spirit,' he wrote of himself, 'mightily susceptible of fascination. My idea very cleer; phansie like a mirrour, pure chrystal water which the least wind does disorder and unsmooth—so noise or etc. would.' It is a striking description of a sensitive nature. For such a boy a boarding school was, inevitably, a painful introduction to many common enough aspects of disagreeable human behaviour. However, his health improved

---

[1] The reading is doubtful as the MS. is blurred.

and he suffered less from 'the belly-ake: paine in the side'. He
made headway in his Latin and Greek, becoming the best scholar
among his contemporaries. He could not escape the effects of
his solitary upbringing. ' 'Twas a great disadvantage to me in my
childhood to be bred up in a kind of Park far from neighbours and
no child to converse with so that I did not speak till late. I was
eight years old before I knew what theft was. So I had a fine box
top which was stolen from me. My father had one to teach me in
the house and I was pent up in a room by myself melancholy. At 12
I was put to publick school at Blandford under Mr Sutton B.D.
like a bird that has gott out of his cage among the free citizens
of the aire.'

Mr Sutton, the headmaster (who had been a schoolfellow of
Bishop Lancelot Andrewes, whom he remembered as a 'great long
boy'), was 'ill-natured', says Aubrey; and 'he wrote much but
printed nothing save a little 8vo[1] against the Papists'. As the
Blandford St Mary parish register records the date of William
Sutton's burial as 23 October, 1632, it was probably his son
William Sutton, Jr., that Aubrey knew, for his arrival there as a
new boy at the age of six seems highly improbable; although the
impression that he went to Blandford before 1638 is borne out by
his mention of Mr William Gardiner, who followed Mr Sutton
as headmaster, and died in 1636.

Aubrey had a slight stammer or impediment in his speech,
which added to his difficulties, and he says that he knew nothing
of the world and the 'wickedness of boies. Often boors mocked at
me and abused me that were stronger than myself: so I was faine
to make friendship with a strong boie to protect me.[2] I was sensible of the inconvenience of my former private education to this
very day. Besides it impaired my health. Melancholy. Spleen.'
The 'envy and treachery' of schoolboys was new to him, and there
was 'at Blandford as much Roguery as at Newgate'. Discipline was
maintained with the violence considered appropriate to education,
and Aubrey says: 'I very well remember that excessive whipping

[1] Mr Sutton's book was in fact 4to (Anon.) 1629, reprinted by his son
12mo 1635.
[2] There are two initials above this comment, 'G.P.' or 'G.D.'
Possibly they are 'G.J.', see p. 192 about George Johnson.

when I was a little child did make a convulsive pain in my tender braine, which doubtless did doe me a great deal of hurt.' He and others of his acquaintance would dream when middle-aged men of 'this tyrannie at Blandford' and that they were back again at '*Hic, Haec, Hoc*'. However, all the masters were not uniformly ferocious, and 'that worthy and gentle schoolmaster Mr Gardiner of Blandford was wont to say that the calling of a schoolmaster was next to that of a Divine's but for the Bedle's office of whipping'. Others of the staff, equally out of sympathy with the tenets of their profession, did their best to make learning interesting and attractive. There was Mr Stephens,[1] only five or six years older than Aubrey himself, who was 'usher about a yeare and by whom I reap't much information'. He was 'a very good ingeniose person, who had instructed Lord Buckhurst in grammar', and encouraged Aubrey by lending him Cowper's *Dictionary*, which helped him with his Terence and his Cicero. Another usher, Mr William Browne (son of the Rector of Churchill in Dorset), who had himself been at school at Blandford under Mr Gardiner, was Aubrey's special friend, in later life often corresponding with him.

Among his fellow pupils for four years were Sir Walter Raleigh's grand-nephews, clever, proud, quarrelsome boys with tunable (but small) voices, who played their parts well on the viol. These young gentlemen informed Aubrey that their great-uncle had had an 'apparatus' for the second part of his *History of the World* 'which he, in discontent, burn't and sayd, "If I am not worthy of the World, the World is not worthy of my workes" '.

Early school at Blandford began at six in the morning, which Mr Gardiner, 'his life jaded by his scholars', seems to have enjoyed as little as anyone. 'And for my part,' says Aubrey, 'for want of perspiration, I did nothing but gape an howre or two: the teares running downe abundantly as if I had wept, which teares

---

[1] Afterwards Stephens went (among other places) to 'the great school at Dublin', and Aubrey at a later date 'desired him to tell me freely if the Irish Boyes had as good a witte as the English; because some of our severe witts have ridiculed Irish understanding. He protested to me that he could not find but they had as good witts as the English; but generally speaking he found they had better memories.'

should have been perspiration.' The picture is not an engaging one: yet Blandford was probably no worse than other schools of the period; perhaps it was better. At least it had the supreme merit of having grounded Aubrey in a good education and stimulated his intellectual interests. His own views as to how a school should be organised will be seen later, when his *Idea of the Education of a Young Gentleman* is examined.

Sandys's translation of Ovid's *Metamorphoses* fell into his hands at Blandford, and was 'a wonderful help to my phansie'. In the holidays he found a copy of Bacon's *Essays* belonging to his mother, 'which first opened my understanding to moralls (for Tullie's Offices was too crabbed for my young yeares) and the excellence of the style, or hints and transitions'. The reading of Bacon (traces of whose influence, with that of Burton's *Anatomy of Melancholy*, can be recognised in Aubrey's writing) was also encouraged by one Theophilus Wodenote,[1] who 'did me much good in opening of my understanding; advised me to read Lord Bacon's *Essayes* and an old book of proverbs (English); answered me my questions of antiquities, etc.'

In his spare time Aubrey continued to draw. '*Blandfordiae, horis vacuis*, I drew and painted Bate's . . . (*quaere nomen libri*).'[2] He also wrote blank verse, but without adroitness: and he used to visit the shop and furnaces of 'Old Harding, the only country glasse painter that ever I knew'. There were occasional contacts

---

[1] Wodenote, an Etonian and Kingsman, was brother-in-law of Mr Peyton (who had succeeded Mr Waller as Vicar of Broad Chalke), with whom he lived for two years 'being obnoxious to danger of arrests; and wrote 'in his solitude at Chalke a little manuall called *Good Thoughts in bad times*, as I take it.' The mention of Chalke, where the Aubreys, so far as it appears, were not yet living, and the 'danger of arrests' seems to place the acquaintanceship at a date later than the Blandford period; but Aubrey certainly speaks of it as 'when I was a school boy'. Wodenote was first cousin of Nicholas Ferrar of Little Gidding, brother or cousin of the 'Mr Woodnot' who, according to Izaak Walton, attended George Herbert on his deathbed. *Good Thoughts in Bad Times* was the title of a work by Thomas Fuller published in 1645.

[2] Clark suggests *The Mysteries of Nature and Art viz. . . . drawing, colouring*, by J[ohn] B[ate], a quarto published in 1645.

with the outside world, and sage remarks like that of Mr Basket, 'a reverend divine, who was wont to beg us play-dayes, would always be uncovered before the schoolboys, and sayd that "'twas the Lord Burleigh's custome, for (saith he) *here is my Lord Chancellor, My Lord Treasurer, my Lord Chief Justice, &c. predestinated"'*. There were also such local traditions to be remembered as that of the country people of Blandford, who used to say that Cardinal Morton (of 'Morton's fork' fame) was a shoemaker's son of Bere in Dorset.[1]

Another chance encounter made an impression on Aubrey. At the bowling green at Blandford was a German gentleman, who had been driven from his estates and his country by the wars that raged there. In exile, this distressed foreigner was forced to maintain himself by surveying the land; and he was accustomed to remark: 'Before the wars I had as good an estate as any of you.' When he thought over these words, the necessity for everyone to know some means of earning a living struck Aubrey; because no man was safe from such misfortunes.

These were the odds and ends that made up the memories of his schooldays, while political unrest had already begun to cast a dark shadow across the English scene, which, in Clarendon's nostalgic retrospect 'had enjoyed for so many years the most uninterrupted prosperity, in a full and plentiful peace, that any nation could be blessed with; and as there was no apprehension of trouble from within, so it was secured from without by·a stronger fleet at sea than the nation had ever been acquainted with, which drew reverence from all neighbouring princes'. Such easy and unwarlike days were already numbered, and—like the exiled German on the bowling green—many were soon to lose their estates, and be forced, like him, to seek refuge over the sea, earning their bread by such resourcefulness as they might find in themselves.

[1] Aubrey, later, noted that the Cardinal's coat of arms was *quarterly gules and ermine in the first quarter a goat's head erased*, somewhat resembling the three goats' heads of the Shoemakers' arms.

CHAPTER TWO

Oxford, the Middle Temple, and Avebury (1642–1650)

I

ON 3 MAY, 1642, when hope of compromise between the King and Parliament was in reality at an end, Aubrey was entered as a gentleman-commoner at Trinity College, Oxford; and, writing his name according to college custom in the buttery book, paid the required caution money of £3. He was then in his seventeenth year.

Trinity was the college of Mr Browne, the friendly usher at Blandford, and may have been chosen for that reason. Its President was still the eccentric Dr Kettle, close on eighty years of age and a person of 'terrible gigantique aspect' in gown, surplice, and hood. For over forty years he had held his post, and although not in the front rank of scholars, added some ability and good sense to his fits of odd behaviour and outspoken speech. He was a strong Church of England man. When Laud had sent him a gift of venison he had refused it, and asked the servant who brought the offering if the Archbishop of Canterbury intended to put any scholars or fellows into Trinity as he had done at All Souls. Although a great believer in keeping down the *juvenilis impetus*, the President, Aubrey says, was generous to 'diligent boys that he ghessed had but a slender exhibition from their friends, and would many times put money in at their windows'. He had also observed that the houses in Oxford which provided the smallest beer had the most drunkards. Accordingly, he had arranged that Trinity should have the best brew in the University.

The undergraduates laughed at Dr Kettle and mocked him; but they were afraid of him for his great gift of scolding in Latin. He had a habit of rebuking them by name in sermons, and calling them *Tarrarags*, *Blindcinques*, *Scobberlotchers*, and using even cruder and more explicit invective when displeased. Even the dons felt

44

the edge of his tongue, for Aubrey says that in one of his sermons the Doctor 'told 'em that they should keepe their bodies chast and holy: "but," said he, "you fellowes of the college here eate good commons and drinke good double-beer and breede seede, and that will gett-out." ' 'He dragged with one foot a little,' says Aubrey, 'by which he gave warning (like a rattlesnake) of his coming. Will Egerton (Major-General Egerton's younger brother), a good wit and mimick, would goe so like him, that sometime he would make the whole chapell rise up, imagining that he had been entring in. . . . He sang a shrill high treble; but there was one (J. Hoskyns) who had a higher, and would play the wag with the Doctor to make him straine his voice up to his.'

Kettle is a characteristic figure in the general picture of seventeenth-century university life, which, in spite of bright high-lights marked by contemporary anecdote, is not always brought easily into focus. Not long since, undergraduates had come into residence at ten (and even eight) years old; and although by Aubrey's time the average age was fifteen to seventeen, with a sprinkling of young men of nineteen or twenty, the atmosphere of the Oxford of his day remained that of a loosely disciplined school.

The great majority were preparing themselves for the Church, and a few for the Bar. The universities had scarcely become at this date a recognised stage in a gentleman's education; although they had already changed considerably from an earlier conception of them as monastic centres for 'poor scholars'. There were a few rich young men among a large number from families of comparatively modest means. The latter had come to acquire an academic training with which to make a livelihood. This was the picture, moving gradually to the familiar one of nineteenth-century Oxford, with a general level of comparatively well-to-do undergraduates, who had been sent there to be 'finished' rather than trained. This last conception, too, began to change rapidly as grants and scholarships increased in number and different social conditions arose; so that, on the one hand, Aubrey's Oxford seems to have altered hardly at all in three hundred years, and, on the other, he seems to speak of an institution curiously remote from the university of the twentieth century.

There was, as ever, a tendency for older people to suspect 'de-
bauchery' among the young men. Some even questioned the moral
soundness of the Fellows. The latter, traditionally immune from
self-criticism, were disposed to add their own voices to the volume
of complaint regarding the undergraduates, over whom they tried
to maintain an uneasy discipline by fines, the docking of food, and
in some cases by blows, treating the junior members of the university sometimes as tiresome children, sometimes as scholars and
men of the world. Of a former way of life traces still remained.
'I remember,' says Aubrey, 'at Oxford (before the Civill Warres)
the custome was that some day of the Whitsune-Holidayes the
Master Cooke (for that yeare) with the rest of his Brethrene were
marched in silk doublets on Horseback, and rode (I thinke) to
Bartholemews or Bullington-green, [to] fetch in the Flye:[1] the said
master-cooke treated his bretheren before they rode out. (At Exeter
Coll. 1642) I sawe them drinke their mornings draughts: and on
Michaelmas day they rode thither again to convey the Fly away.
Methinks this old Custome lookes as if it were derived from that
mentioned in Pliny.'

II

His first residence at Oxford was short, though he had time to
make some friends and to develop for Oxford life an appetite
which never left him. He 'lookt through Logique and some
Ethiques' and various incidents of his life as a freshman always
remained in his mind: such as Robert Sanderson, Bishop
of Lincoln, being, on account of his bad memory, 'out in the
Lord's Prayer' when he gave his first lecture; or the story told by
the nephew of another bishop—Dr George Webb, Bishop of
Limerick—of how the body of his uncle had been dug up by the
Irish when they captured the town.

In London events were taking an ominous shape. War had become inevitable, and, within a year, Oxford was to change from a

[1] 'The Fly' means a familiar demon (in this case presumably the
spirit of cookery), from the notion that devils were accustomed to
assume the form of flies.

peaceful university town to a metropolis crowded with officers
and courtiers, ambassadors and dragoons, grass-widows, bawds,
and parasites of all kinds. To persuade the undergraduates
to attend lectures or to take their studies with reasonable seriousness in this commotion became for the University authorities an
increasingly difficult problem. The scholars and 'privileged men'
began to train in New College gardens, watched by the ten-year-
old Anthony Wood. There were road-blocks by Magdalen, and
trenches from Wadham to St John's. The well where St Edmund,
when Archbishop of Canterbury, had sometimes conversed with an
angel ('like Numa Pompilius with the nymph Egeria', remarks
Aubrey) was stopped up when the town became a garrison.
Exercises took place with two squadrons of musketeers, one of
pikes, and one of halberts. These, 'after they had byn reasonably
instructed in the wordes of commaund and in their postures',
were (wrote Anthony Wood) 'put into battell arraye and skyr-
mished together in a very decent manner'.

Through this throng moved also many notorieties of one kind or
another. Although he speaks with regret of such military activity,
and the inconvenience brought in its train, the opportunities for
meeting new people must have compensated Aubrey, always
trying to draw the chill of his childhood's loneliness from his
bones, for much of the discomfort and insecurity.

Later in the summer 'Bellona thundred', and the first brush of
hostilities took place near Banbury, between detachments under
the Earl of Northampton and Lord Brooke, Parliament's philosopher general. Already signs were appearing in Oxford of what
might be expected from the warring factions. When Aubrey was
attending one of Dr Kettle's rhetoric lectures in hall, the President
having left the room for a minute, a foot-soldier came in. Jack
Dowch (later a clergyman, whose name suggests the prototype of
the loutish undergraduate of all time) pointed to the Doctor's
hour-glass. The soldier took the hint, and broke it. This was a
portent of the spirit that was abroad.

There were also distractions of another sort. 'Our grove was the
Daphne for the ladies and their gallants to walke in, and many
times my lady Isabella Thynne (she lay at Balliol College) would

make her entrey with a theorbo or lute played before her. I have
heard her play on it in the grove myselfe, which she did rarely:
for which Mr Edmund Waller hath in his Poems for ever made
her famous . . . She was most beautiful, most humble,
charitable, etc. but she could not subdue one thing. I remember
one time this lady and fine Mistress Fenshawe, her great and
intimate friend who lay at our college (she was wont, and my
lady Thynne, to come to our Chapell, mornings, halfe dressed,
like angells) would have a frolick to make a visitt to the President.
The old Doctor quickly perceived that they came to abuse him;
he addresses his discourse to Mistress Fenshawe, saying "Madam,
your husband and father I bred up here, and I knew your grandfather; I know you to be a gentlewoman, I will not say you are a
whore; but gett you gonne for a very woman." The dissoluteness
of the times grieved the good old Doctor, his dayes were shortened,
and he dyed.'

Aubrey's father, nervous, and with reason, about the disturbing
events of the day, sent for his son to return home; and, on 9
August, 1642, Aubrey with great grief obeyed this summons,
carrying back with him to the country Thomas Browne's *Religio
Medici* (hot from the press, for it was published in that year),
'which first opened my understanding'. He went probably to
Broad Chalke, a village about seven miles from Salisbury, where
his great-uncles, the Brownes, lived. Here Richard Aubrey had
rented from Lord Pembroke (who owned much of the land thereabout) the manor farm, said to have been given nine hundred
years before by King Edgar to the nuns of Wilton.

III

The Aubreys had Royalist sympathies, and when the King's
army marched into the west, one of their many cousins, Major
Morgan of Wells,[1] fell sick of a malignant fever, and was brought
dangerously ill to the house at Broad Chalke. He was lodged

[1] The Aubreys had claim to quarter Morgan arms, though the
exact relationship with this family is not apparent. Elsewhere he refers
to 'Major John Morgan of Wells' as possessing a folio 'which speaks of

secretly in a garret, and 'there came a sparrow to the chamber window, which pecked the lead of a certain panel only, and only one side of the lead of the lozenge, and made one small hole in it. He continued this pecking and biting the lead during the whole of his sickness (which was not less than a month). When the Major went away, the sparrow desisted, and came thither no more.'

In September 1642 the Parliamentarian forces occupied Oxford, and, 'the Lord Viscount Say and Seale came (by order of the Parliament) to visit the colleges, to see what of the new Popery they could discover in the chapells'. At Trinity, says Aubrey, 'on the backside of the skreen, had been two altars (of painting well enough for those times, and the colours were admirably fresh and lively). That on the right as you enter the chapell was dedicated to St Katherine, and that on the left was the taking of our Saviour off the Crosse. My Lord Say saw that this was done of old time, and Dr Kettle told his Lordship, "Truly, My Lord, we regard them no more than a dirty dish-clout"; so they remained untoucht till Harriss time, and then were covered over with green. The windowes of the chapell were good Gothique painting, in every columne a figure: *e.g.* St Cuthbert, St Leonard, St Oswald.'

Meanwhile, the soldiers of Parliament, 'very untractable and undocile in their postures', began to quarrel among themselves. The Blue-coated regiments fought the Russet-coated regiments, and Lord Saye, finding them unwilling to be pacified, sent some to prison and told the rest he cared not for their help, and bade them begone. The men objected that they had had no pay, so that Lord Saye, exhausted with their brawling, took coach and retired to his house at Broughton. However, the Commissioners had not opportunity at that moment to interfere further in the university, because Edgehill was fought in October 1642. The King

the Knights' fees at Glaston'. Another cousin, William Morgan of Wells, had been 'chamber-fellow' to Sir Edmund Berry Godfrey, murdered in 1678 at the time of the 'Popish Plot'. It is possible that Aubrey may have confused the Christian names of the Morgans, as he speaks of William Morgan as captain or major. Colonel John Morgan of Wells, D.L. for Somerset, was buried at Corsham, aged 73, 1684.

marched into Oxford, which, as Clarendon wrote, 'was the only
city of England that he could say was entirely to his devotion;
where he was received by the university (to whom the integrity
and fidelity of that place is to be imputed) with that joy and ac-
clamation as Apollo should be by the Muses'.

In due course Aubrey persuaded his father to allow him to
return to Trinity. On the journey there signs of war showed themselves. 'I remember in February 1643 as I rode to Oxford neer the
Barrow on Cutchinlow-hill were certain soldiers belonging to the
King's Garrison in Abington, perhaps a dozen or more, that kept
watch and guarded themselves in a great pitt, thereby, so that if an
enemie came, there was nothing to be shott at but their heads.' He
found the Court at Oxford, and the town crowded with soldiers
and camp-followers.

Aubrey used to go down to Christ Church to see the King at
supper. One night there, he heard Charles say 'that as he was
hawking in Scotland, he rode into the quarry, and found the covey
of partridges falling upon the hawk', adding, 'And I will swear
upon the Book 'tis true'. Aubrey repeated the words to his tutor.
'That covey was London', sagely remarked the don.

In this same year there was a sale of the poet William Cartwright's library (' 'tis not to be forgott that king Charles 1st dropt
a teare at the newes of his death') and Aubrey bought Dr Featly's
Handmayd to Devotion and many other books. His first recorded
piece of practical antiquarianism also took place at this period, in
connexion with the ruins of Osney, the twelfth-century priory
near Oxford founded by the Norman baron Robert d'Oyly.[1]
Aubrey, realising that the ruins were in danger of destruction,
caused several drawings to be made of them, employing a hedge-
priest called Hesketh, a pupil of William Dobson, the King's
Serjeant-Painter. Dobson was himself in Oxford, working at

[1] His wife noticed in that neighbourhood the noise of 'chattering
pies', explained by her confessor as the complaint of souls in purgatory.
Her husband accordingly caused a religious house to be built there.
Lands of Osney were held by ancestors of Aubrey's patron Lord
Abingdon. The artist was possibly Roger Jerome Hesketh, Benedictine,
1639, but see Surtees Soc. for an earlier painter, Thomas Hesketh
(inform. Margaret Toynbee).

conversation pieces and portraits of courtiers and officers, and at least one of the drawings is considered to have been executed by his hand. Another of the drawings was handed over to William Dugdale (then Rouge Dragon Pursuivant, and engaged in delivering royal warrants, demanding the submission of garrisons in arms against the King), for his great work *Monasticon Anglicanum*. Aubrey's fears for the ruins proved to be justified, because the remains of the priory were pulled down soon after the drawings were made, and the very foundations of this ancient place uprooted and destroyed.

In April there was smallpox about in the town (Anthony Wood's mother sent him with his brother Christopher, and a horse and a man, into the country out of harm's way). Aubrey caught the disease. While he was recovering, he used to gossip with Mr Saul, an old servant of Sir Robert Poyntz (knight of the Bath and last of an ancient line), and Mr Saul was no doubt his informant on the subject of Sir Robert's grandfather having built Newark 'to keep his whores in': and how Sir Walter Raleigh, 'in a stand at Sir Robert Poyntz' park at Acton tooke a pipe of tobacco, which made the ladies quitt it till he had donne'. William Radford, an undergraduate then in his third year at Trinity, was also accustomed to visit Aubrey while he was ill at this time, and they would spend several hours together in the room where Aubrey lay, in which there was a coloured glass window of St Gregory, appropriate to his birthday; and presumably put there at his own expense, though he does not say so. These visits were very welcome, 'or I think melancholy would have spoyled a scurvey antiquary'. Radford's name crops up more than once in Aubrey's reminiscences of Oxford. He was 'an honest, sequestered fellow', a Wykehamist, who eventually became a schoolmaster, and remained Aubrey's friend until his death in 1673.

On one occasion at least Radford had fallen foul of Dr Kettle, who, says Aubrey, 'was irreconcilable to long hair: called them hairy scalpes, and as for periwigges (which were then very rarely worn) he believed them to be the scalpes of men cutt off after they were hanged, and so tanned and dressed for use. When he observed the scolars hair longer than ordinary (especially if they were

scolars of the house) he would bring a paire of cizers in his muffe
(which he commonly wore) and woe be to them that sate on the
outside of the table. I remember he cut Mr Radford's haire with
the knife that chipps the bread on the buttery hatch.'

After this excursion as an amateur barber, the President, as if to
emphasise his disregard for the feelings of those who might have
hoped later with the same knife to cut some bread to eat, sang a
snatch from 'an old play of Henry VIII's time'[1]:

> *And was not Grim the collier finely trimmed?*
> *Tonedi, Tonedi.*

He then turned to John Lydall, another of Aubrey's close friends.
' "Mr Lydall," sayd he, "how doe you decline *tondeo*? *Tondeo,
tondes, tonedi?*" '

Radford was a friend of Thomas Mariet, later to share chambers
with Aubrey in the Middle Temple, and he knew Edward Wood
(Anthony Wood's brother), who served with the King's army
when garrisoned at Oxford. These three, Radford, Mariet, and
Ned Wood (at some moment after Aubrey's first year), having
never seen London, decided by way of a 'frolique' to walk there
from Oxford. Passing through Windsor, they called on one of the
Fellows of Eton, 'the ever-memorable John Hales', famous in his
own day, but now almost forgotten except for his remark 'that
there was no subject of which any Poet ever writ, but he would
produce it much better treated of in Shakespeare'. The three
undergraduates persuaded Hales (who was uncle of John Sloper, a
later vicar of Broad Chalke) to entertain them on the grounds that
they were Oxford scholars; and 'he treated them, well and putt
into Mr Wood's hands ten shillings'. The incident conveys the
medieval flavour that academic life in some respects retained; and
it is a good example of a kind of adventure considered very wag-
gish at the period of Aubrey's Oxford days.

---

[1] This is what Aubrey calls it; but the quotation is from Richard
Edwards' play *Damon and Pithias*, probably acted before the Queen in
1564 (but not licensed until 1567) and not from *Gammer Gurton's
Needle*, as Aubrey says.

IV

When he recovered from smallpox in June 1643, Aubrey returned again to the country, where he lived 'a sad life' for three years. His father's health was bad. Among other complaints, he suffered from some form of cataract or other ocular disorder, and the family's legal entanglements were already beginning to become more than a little troublesome. Richard Aubrey was out of sympathy with his son—'for in those dayes fathers were not acquainted with their children'—but this did not prevent him from being often in a state of exaggerated paternal anxiety on his behalf. Mrs Aubrey clearly fussed too; and much of their son's chronic inability to grapple with the problems of everyday life was no doubt in part accountable to his parents' determination to continue to treat him as a child.

This exile in the country he describes as 'almost a consumption'. There were scarcely any good books; and the only conversation was that of servants, rustics, and the soldiers quartered in the neighbourhood. Among the latter were Sir Thomas Ashton's regiment, one of the troopers of which was brother to John Birkenhead, author of *Mercurius Aulicus*, that piece of embryonic journalism that appeared at Oxford after Edgehill. This, however, was small consolation for the dullness; and there could be only a limited number of local reminiscences to be gathered, rare as those of old goodwife Dew (who had had three bastards and died in 1649 at the age of 103), who could remember how King Edward VI was in this country and 'he lost his courtiers, or his courtiers him, a hunting, and found him again in Falston-lane'. '*Odi prophanum vulgus et arceo*', Aubrey noted of these dismal years, when he existed only on his memories of Oxford and the friends he had made there.

However, although no longer, 'walking and singing under Merton College Gate', could he mark how 'the note would be returned with a loud hum from the Gothic, irregular vaulting', there were the encounters and anecdotes of his two Oxford interludes upon which to reflect. There was, for example, that curious figure (and, it might be added, typically English minor literary celebrity) John Taylor, 'the water-poet', who had visited the University in 1643.

Then about sixty-three, Taylor, says Aubrey, was 'of middle stature, had a good quicke looke, a black velvet, a plush-gippe and silver shoulder belt; was made much of by the scholars and was often with Josias Howe at Trinity College'.

Taylor had had an adventurous career since he had been 'mired' in his Latin accidence at Gloucester Grammar School. Instead of growing up into a scholar, he had been pressed for the navy, seen the siege of Cadiz, and travelled as far afield as Prague. In an effort to sail down the Thames in a boat constructed of brown paper, he had narrowly escaped drowning. After any such exploit he was accustomed to publish a pamphlet, his collected works having appeared in 1630. He had plied for hire as a Thames waterman, and at the time of this Oxford reception (for he had visited the University on other occasions) he kept a public-house in Long Acre, where the sign was his own head—and said to be a good likeness. His verse was by no means without talent, and his conversation incomparable 'for three or four mornings' draughts'; but, as the hours passed and the glasses filled and refilled again, his audience had to brace themselves to hearing all over again the burden of his words, in the besetting repetition common to so many good and convivial talkers.

Josias Howe was one of the Fellows of Trinity. He was a great admirer of the water-poet and held that he could choose out six verses from Taylor's works 'as good as you will find in any other'. Howe, about thirty years old when Aubrey came up to Oxford, was the son of the rector of Grendon-Underwood in Buckinghamshire; and later, when Aubrey wrote of Shakespeare, he noted: 'The humour of[1] . . . the constable in *Midsomernight's Dreame* he happened to take at Grendon in Bucks—I think it was Midsomer night that he happened to lye there—which is the roade from London to Stratford, and there was living that constable about

[1] Aubrey could not remember the name of 'the constable', so that we are left in uncertainty as to whether he intended Dogberry in *Much Ado about Nothing* (as Britton assumes), Elbow in *Measure for Measure*, Dull in *Love's Labour's Lost*; or whether he was, indeed, thinking of one of the characters in *A Midsummer Night's Dream*, in which no constable is found.

1642, when I first came to Oxon; Mr Josias Howe is of that parish and knew him.'

Another of the Trinity Fellows was George Bathurst, 'who had a henne to hatch egges in his chamber, which they daily opened to discern the progress and way of generation', on the occasions when Dr Harvey, expounder of the theory of the blood's circulation, came to visit him. Aubrey could remember these meetings, and he had also seen Harvey after Edgehill fight, where the Doctor had been present as physician to the king, the Prince of Wales and Duke of York being put under his charge during the battle. Aubrey was 'then too young to be acquainted with so great a doctor'; but later he came to know him (and, indeed, to be treated by him), learning from Harvey that Francis Bacon's 'delicate, lively hazel eie' was 'like the eie of a viper'.

George Bathurst was the father of Ralph Bathurst, another of Aubrey's friends, though 'the currish fellows would not suffer their pupils' to read his books. The younger Bathurst subsequently became President of Trinity and Vice-Chancellor of the University. He was intimate with many of Aubrey's later friends— Petty, Thomas Willis, Seth Ward, and many of the circle who formed the elements of the Royal Society. Anthony Wood wrote: 'A man of good parts, and able to do good things; but he has a wife that scornes that he should be in print—a scornful woman, scornes that he was deane of Wells.' Bathurst gave Aubrey the incorrect information that Ben Jonson came from Warwickshire; and, with Anthony Ettrick, William Hawes, and John Lydall, he was one of the Trinity men named in the draft of a will made by Aubrey ten years later.

Among others of the older generation upon whom Aubrey could ponder was Dr Hannibal Potter, who became President of Trinity when Dr Kettle died in 1643, notable insomuch that he 'whipt his scholar with his sword by his side when he came to take leave of him to goe to the Innes of Court'. His brother, Francis Potter, a less menacing figure, was one of Aubrey's great friends, and 'a rare inventor of machines'. He had devised a graduated compass, and, like Harvey, held theories on such scientific subjects as the transfusion of the blood, an idea that had come into his head while reflecting on the story of Æson and Medea. He had also devoted himself to the Number of the Beast, on which thesis he took his degree as a Bachelor of Divinity (in the form *An Papa sit Anti-Christus*); and he published an *Interpretation of the Number 666*, which was translated into French, High Dutch, Low Dutch, and Latin. Pepys at a later date found the book 'mighty ingenious'. This mystery, too, had been revealed to the author unexpectedly one night, as he went upstairs to his brother the President's room. More will be said of Potter when Aubrey's personal friends are considered together.

Such were the memories of the university that Aubrey took back with him to Wiltshire. Disturbed and short as his contact with Oxford had been, it was enough to convince him of the direction in which lay his intellectual interests. The impact on his sensibility of this residence is shown best by fragments in the *Lives*, and elsewhere in his writings, that refer to friends he made there, and personalities who struck his imagination at this formative stage of his life. His account of these figures is often disconnected, but it hints at a profundity of experience that could be obtained at Oxford during those years, among much that was at the same time pedantic, wearisome, and brutal.

V

In September 1645 his former schoolmaster, William Browne, wrote news of the Civil Wars, and said that he had appropriated Aubrey's gown and converted it into a 'Divine's gowne' for himself, because it was lying musty for want of use. He suggested that Aubrey should come to Oxford to take his degree, but said that, if his father prevented this, he advised him to try and come to London, 'but I doubt your Mother and your Grandfather will stoppe all good motions'. London, said Browne, would be as cheap as Oxford, and Aubrey would be better placed as regards 'a bad but prospering and good but declining cause'. The country certainly had little to recommend it for those with Royalist politics. On 8 January, 1646, the Parliamentarian committee constituted to raise money from the neighbourhood of Broad Chalke, and sitting

at Falstone House near Wilton, noted in their day-book:
'Richard Aubrey of Broadchalke, gent., has already paid £7 in
North Wilts towards his five-and-twentieth part there. Now
he pays us at Falstone £33 in sixty fat sheep and £60 in money
accepted for his fine here and in Herefordshire.'

These demands were an additional burden on the family's
resources. Aubrey himself was in Herefordshire at this time, perhaps overseeing the negotiations in connexion with the necessary
compounding for the estate there, because he saw the Puritan and
Parliamentarian committee-man, Edward Broughton, 'neer 80,
the handsomest shaped man that ever my eies beheld', famous as
the father of the beautiful woman of the town, Elizabeth Broughton, who (like the other courtesan of good birth, Venetia Stanley)
had been kept by Richard Sackville, 5th Earl of Dorset. She had
become such a byword that Aubrey had seen a ballad that went
like a litany.

> From the watch at twelve a clock
> And from Bess Broughton's button'd smock,
> Libera nos, Domine.

It seems also to have been on this visit to Herefordshire that the
old parson, Richard Hill of Stretton, recalled that Ben Jonson,
when employed as a bricklayer, had worked on the garden wall
of Lincoln's Inn, next to Chancery Lane; and it had been on
this spot that a bencher, hearing him repeat some verses from
Homer, was so struck with his intelligence that he sent the poet to
Cambridge.

At last, with much effort, Aubrey persuaded his father to allow
him to go to London, and was admitted a student of the Middle
Temple on 6 April, 1646. Oxford surrendered in the following
June, and many Royalists came to London, among them a number
of acquaintances Aubrey had made at an earlier date among the
cavalier entourage. So far as intellectual life was concerned, he
still felt himself suffering in that respect from the deprivations of
country life. At first he did not find that the companionship
brought by life in London was the society of which he had dreamed,
and now sought. 'I loved not debauches,' he wrote, 'but their

martial conversation was not fitt for the Muses', meaning that, in spite of the change, his life was still dull rather than dissipated. However, in November 1646, to his great delight, he was able to return for a time to Trinity; and 'was made much of by the Fellows, had their learned conversation, lookt on books, musique'.

In this way for the next two years he divided his time, agreeably enough, between Oxford and the Inns of Court. Owing to his father's illness and business worries, he never succeeded in settling down to much work at the law. It is unlikely that he would in any circumstances have exerted himself greatly in that direction. The common ways of life always took him by surprise. 'At the Innes of Court they do not learn the Rules of Justice *ab origine*: but insted, Chicanerie and Trickum Legis: the art of wrangling and ill aquation, overreaching, and opression. . . . I remembered a grave barrister of the Middle Temple and a good student: he had a great memorie and would have quoted any case in the Reports: but had you put the case to him, altering but the very name, he was at a loss and a stand: could goe no further just like a Grayhound when the Hare is masked through the Hedge. He could not hunt it out.'

However, he looked back afterwards on this period as on the whole the happiest time of his life, 'when ingeniose youths as rosebuds, imbibe the morning dew', the days of his youth growing perhaps more idyllic in retrospect, as business cares increased. It was now, when he was drinking, gossiping, and occupied with fresh people and new ideas, that he began to accumulate the mass of impressions and anecdotes which was to be his contribution to history. This was how the barristers talked among themselves: 'I remember about 1646 (or 1647) that Mr John Maynard (now Sir John and serjeant), came into the Middle Temple Hall, from Westminster-Hall, weary with business, and hungry, when we had newly dined. He sate down by Mr Bennet Hoskyns[1] (the only son of Serjeant Hoskyns, the Poet), since baronet and some others; who having made an end of the commons, fell into various discourse, and what was the meaning of the text (Rom. 5. 7.): "For a just man one would dare to die; but for a good man one would

---

[1] Father of Aubrey's friend, John Hoskyns.

willingly die." They asked Mr Maynard what was the difference between a just man and a good man. He was begining to eate, and cryd: "*Hob!* You have eaten your dinner, and now have leisure to discourse; I have not!" He had eate but a Bitt or two when he replied: "I'le tell you the difference presently: *Serjeant Rolle is a just man and Matthew Hale is a good man*"; and so fell to make an end of his dinner. And there could not be a better *interpretation* of the text. For Serjeant Rolle[1] was just, but by nature penurious; and his wife made him worse: Matthew Hale was not only just, but wonderfully charitable and open handed, and did not sound a trumpet neither, as the Hypocrites doe.'

It was at the Middle Temple, too, in this year that Aubrey heard an octogenarian Norfolk lawyer called Dunstable affirm that Sir Edward Coke, the great Lord Chief Justice, was born to but three hundred pounds of land, while others there said it was but forty pounds a year; and one night, at about this time, he remembered that Sir John Denham lost two hundred pounds gambling at the New-Cut.

VI

On Christmas Eve, 1648, Richard Aubrey's state of health became so grave that his son was once more summoned from Oxford 'to looke after his country businesse and solicite a law-suite'. He returned to Wiltshire for a while, where a chance episode took place, the recording of which, even if he had taken no further interest in such matters, would alone have given Aubrey a place in the annals of English archaeology. This was his discovery of Avebury. When the erratic surmises of his own and subsequent

[1] 'When I was a Student of the Middle Temple from 1646 to 1656', wrote Aubrey, 'I many times went to the King's Bench Court: and I very well doe remember (although Judge Rolle was of the Parliament faction yet) he would never obey Comitee Lawe: and when Councill [would many] times allege that the Plaintiff or Defendant was a Cavaleer: he would be peevish at it and say what is this to the Cause; what is this to the matter, how does this concern the merit of the Cause before us? All that knew him in that Station will say, that he never warp't in his administration of Justice.'

generations are taken into account, the impression made on him
by this chance find shows that at the age of twenty-two he had an
uncommonly sound instinct for what was of major antiquarian
interest. 'Salisbury-plaines and Stonehenge I had knowne from
eight years old: but I never sawe the country round Marlborough
till Christmas 1648, being then invited to Lord Francis Seymour's, by the Honourable Mr Charles Seymour, with whom I
had the honour to be intimately acquainted, and whose friendship
I ought to mention with profound respect to his memorie. There
was my honoured friend and neighbour Colonel John Penruddock
of Compton Chamberlayne and that good old Gentleman Mr
Stephen Bowman, steward to the Lord Marquess of Hertford: we
went together: and Mr W. Levet, &c. The morrow after twelf-
day Mr Charles Seymour and Sir William Button of Tokeham,
baronet, met with their pack of hounds at the Greywethers.
These Downes look as if they were sowen with great Stones, very
thick, and in a dusky evening they look like a flock of Sheep: from
whence they take their name: one might fancy it to have been the
scene where the Giants fought with great stones against the Gods.
'Twas here that our game began and the chase led us (at length)
through the village of Aubury,[1] into the closes there: where I was
wonderfully surprised at the sight of those vast stones, of which I
had never heard before, as also the mighty bank and graffe[2] about
it. I observed in the enclosure some segments of rude circles made
with these stones, whence I concluded they had been in the old
time complete. I left my Company a while, entertaining myself
with a more delightful indagation: and then (steered by the cry of
the Hounds) I overtook the company and went with them to
Kynnet, where was a good Hunting dinner provided. Our Repast

---

[1] Speaking of the spelling of Avebury, Aubrey wrote elsewhere:
'But in the legier-book of Malmesbury Abbey it is written *Aubury*; and
so it is in the records of the Tower. But here, methinkes, I see some
Reader smile to himself, thinkinge how I have strained the Place to be of
my own Name: not heeding that there is a letter's difference, which
quite alters the signification of the words.' The oldest spelling seems, in
fact, to have been some form of *Avebury*.

[2] Ditch.

was cheerful, which being ended, we remounted and beat over the Downes with our Greyhounds. In the afternoon's diversion I happened to see Wensditch,[1] and an old camp, and two or three sepulchres. The evening put a period to our sport, and we returned to the Castle and Marleborough, where we were nobly entertained; *juvat haec meminisse*. I thinke I am now the only surviving Gentleman of that company.'

The company themselves are, indeed, of no little interest; and, on examination, it seems not impossible that this notable gathering of Royalists had met to discuss matters more vital than the hunt, or the prehistoric monuments of that neighbourhood.

'Lord Francis Seymour', or, more accurately, Francis Seymour, 1st Lord Seymour of Trowbridge (so created 19 February, 1641), was the younger brother of William Seymour, Marquess of Hertford (so created 3 June, 1640), and later 2nd Duke of Somerset. Lord Hertford had been exiled for going through a form of marriage with Lady Arabella Stuart in 1610; but, later, on his return to England, he had been appointed governor to the Prince of Wales. In 1616 he had married Lady Frances Devereux, daughter of Elizabeth's favourite, Essex. At the time of the meet at the Greywethers, Hertford had already taken an energetic part in the Civil Wars: at the defence of Sherborne Castle in 1642, and in 1643 at Lansdowne.

Aubrey's friend 'the Honourable Mr Charles Seymour' (whom he sometimes calls 'Lord Charles Seymour') had been born in 1621, and was included by Aubrey in his list of special friends, who are discussed in a later chapter. Colonel John Penruddock was son of Sir John Penruddock, of Compton Chamberlayne, High Sheriff of Wiltshire. About six years older than Aubrey, and like him educated at Blandford, he had gone up to Queen's College, Oxford, and become a student of Gray's Inn. At the time of the meet two of his brothers had been killed, not long since, fighting for the King; and his own tragic death was not far off.[2] Stephen

[1] Wansdyke.

[2] In March 1655, Colonel Penruddock led the rising, which was a prelude to the rule of the Major-Generals, and which Cromwell, to strengthen his own hand, may have allowed to take form. Penruddock

Bowman was another energetic Royalist, and he may have been the 'Mr Bowman' who preserved the notes of Serjeant Glynne's death sentence on Penruddock, referred to as 'my cosen Bowman' by Mrs Penruddock, who wrote so memorable a last letter to her husband before his execution. Like Aubrey's father, Stephen Bowman[1] had been one of those mentioned in the Falstone day-book of the Parliamentarian committee. Sir William Button,[2]

and his companions in arms occupied Salisbury, seized Judge Rolle (the 'just man' of Mr Maynard of the Middle Temple) and Judge Nicholas (a Wiltshire magnate, to appear later as an antiquarian acquaintance of Aubrey), both of these judges being then on circuit. Penruddock proclaimed Charles II; but he was surprised and taken prisoner some days after this exploit, when he had moved on with his forces to Blandford and the West. He was tried before Serjeant Glynne, and, in spite of his plea that he had committed no legal high treason, and had surrendered only on articles promising security for life and estate, he was beheaded at Exeter, on 16 March, 1655.

[1] In the Falstone day-book, dated 1645: '26 May, Stephen Bowman, of West Harnham, gent., hath made his composition with us and paid presently in two horses, the one delivered to Captain William Ludlow, the other to Captain D'Oyley, valued at £10 and promises £10 more at Michaelmas. He formerly paid £50 to Colonel Edmund Ludlow, as appeareth by ticket. All which we accept as full composition. 29 September, received £10 for his twenty-fifth part. He was an active man of Lord Hertford's rendezvous at Dogdean, encouraging the people to join the Marquis and Prince Maurice.' No doubt Stephen Bowman was a relative of 'Mr Seymer Bowman' (if he is not, indeed, the same person) referred to in the *Miscellanies* (*Marvels*) by Aubrey as having seen a woman cured of the King's Evil in her eye by being touched by Charles I, then a prisoner in Carisbrooke Castle. This 'Mr Bowman', who was M.P. for Old Sarum in 1660, is also mentioned (with Mr Gauntlet, maker of the famous Wiltshire pipes) as having told Aubrey that: 'In the reigne of King James I, as the boyes were at play in Amesbury street, it thundered and lightened. One of the boys wore a little dagger by his side, which melted in the scabbard, and the scabbard was not hurt. This dagger, Edwarde, Earle of Hertford, kept among his rarities. I have forgotten if the boy was killed.'

[2] Sir William Button's home, West Tokenham Court, had been looted to the extent of some £700 or £800 in June 1643 by the forces of Sir Edward Hungerford, who was in command of the Parliamentarian troops in Wiltshire; a depredation that was repeated in the same month

baronet, who died in 1654, had a son of the same name, who succeeded him and died in 1659. It was, presumably, the father who attended the Greywethers meet. Like the rest of the field Button was a strong Royalist, and had suffered at the hands of the Parliament's soldiers. 'Mr W. Levet' was William Levett,[1] of Savernake in Wiltshire and Mazefield in Sussex, who had been Page of the Bedchamber (or Page of the Backstairs) to King Charles I, and also 'one of the Prince's Highness's Guard'. He had been involved in the King's attempt to escape to Holland at Christmas, 1646, and had conveyed £800 to the Dutch captain who undertook the passage, the scheme being eventually abandoned.

In this company Aubrey was in the centre of local Cavalier intrigue: and, since he frequented similar circles in London (as will be seen later), it is surprising that he always avoided the net cast by Cromwell's ubiquitous spies. That some specific plot was being hatched at the time of the meet is, of course, purely problematical; but the names of the gentlemen collected together to follow the hounds were those of men calculated to cause some apprehension to Wiltshire Roundheads.

But to return to Aubrey's discovery of Avebury—when the extraordinary archaeological interest of the remains is considered in relation to the years of neglect that preceded and succeeded

in 1644, when some £500 worth of his belongings were plundered. Button was also fined £2380 in 1646 for 'delinquency'. He had been a member of Sir Arthur Hopton's embassy through France and Spain, and he was noted for his charitable works. The Button (or de Bitton) family had been settled in Wiltshire since the thirteenth century, and, like the Aubreys, were said to be Welsh *Advenae*.

[1] Later, Levett became Solicitor-General, and wrote defending the view that the King, and not Dr John Gauden, had written *Eikon Basilike*, stating that when he had attended Charles I at Carisbrooke, he had often observed him at work on the manuscript. His Wiltshire estate, when he was forced to compound, was estimated at only £20. Anthony Wood noted in his diary in March 1692: 'William Levet, author of a letter to show that Dr John Gauden did not write *Eikon Basilike*, died in his house near Marlborough in Wilts.' In the list of Wiltshire gentry given in the *Brittania* in 1673, Seymour Bowman, 'of New Sarum', and William Levett, 'of Swindon', both appear.

Aubrey, the significance which he at once attached to this fortui-
tous discovery is a remarkable example of his early developed and
acute judgment in such matters. He often visited Avebury on
subsequent occasions, and his theory (generally held until comparatively recent years) was that the stones had been placed there
by the Druids. It is now known that the people responsible for the
erection of this huge group of megaliths, the laying out of the extensive grass avenues across the downs, lived between three and four
thousand years ago—as long before the Druids as Aubrey lived
after them; and in all probability the place was a ritual centre to
which pilgrims of the Bronze Age travelled, often from distant
parts of Europe. It would, however, be unreasonable to expect
Aubrey to have guessed this, as such conclusions are based on a
mass of general information on the subject not available in the
seventeenth century. Aubrey's theories showed a better appreciation
of the possibilities than, for example, those of Inigo Jones, who
held that the stones were of Roman origin; while eighteenth-
century antiquarians, equally wide of the mark, allowed their
minds to dwell on Serpent Temples and other such mythological
figments of the imagination.

The hand of man was, as usual, not idle in attempts to remove
all trace of these relics of a former age, Parson Brunsdon, of
Monkton, being Aubrey's informant on this melancholy subject. 'I have *verbum sacerdotum* for it, that these mighty stones, as
hard as marble, may be broken in what part of them you please,
without any great trouble: *sc.* make a fire on that line of stone,
where you would have it crack; and after the stone is well heated,
draw a line with cold water and immediately give a knock with a
smith's sledge, and it will break like Collets at the Glass-house.'

VII

William Browne continued to send letters about the progress of
the Civil Wars, often in Latin and, as befitted his profession,
signed '*Guil. Fuscus.*' He was a scholar of the old-fashioned kind,
who used to dispute fiercely. 'I thinke it was an epidemick evill of
that time,' says Aubrey, 'which I thinke now is growne out of

fashion, as unmannerly and boyish.' In 1647 Aubrey had gone to visit Parson Stumpe to see if any of the parchment manuscripts remained, but the vicar's sons were 'gunners and soldiers' and had disposed of them, though he showed several old deeds 'granted by the Lord Abbot with their seales annex'd'. In 1648 he went over to Wootton-Basset, and Mr Jacob, eighty-year old tenant of Lady Inglefield, told of the tradition that King Richard III had been born there. In 1649 Aubrey met Emanuel Decretz,[1] Serjeant-Painter to Charles I (Dobson had died in 1646), who told him that the *catafalco* at James I's funeral had been designed by Inigo Jones. At a countryman's house in Herefordshire he picked up a copy of *De duplici methodo libri duo*, by Sir Everard Digby, who had been executed at the time of the Gunpowder Plot; and in the following year he encountered Father William Harcourt, also destined to be hanged, drawn, and quartered at Tyburn in 1679, on which occasion a butcher-boy snatched out of the fire a piece of the unfortunate priest's kidney. 'The wonder is, 'tis now absolutely petrified. I have seen it', wrote Aubrey, at a later date.

Another correspondent was John Lydall, his Trinity contemporary, who came to stay with the Aubreys, and whose neatly written letters about books and Oxford friends (he sometimes mentions Dowch, who had caused the soldier to break Dr Kettle's hour-glass) are full of gratitude for his friend's generosity, sometimes to a point almost of obsequiousness. With the development of his antiquarian and scientific interests, Aubrey had begun to combine a lasting curiosity on the subject of occult matters; and he was trying to collect information about the 'just devil of Woodstock' —that is to say, the origin of the mysterious noises that had disturbed the Parliamentarian Commissioners in that village.[2] On 11 March, 1650, Lydall wrote: 'Concerning that which happened at Woodstock, I was told by Mr Hawes (who now lives with Sir

[1] Aubrey thus describes him, perhaps confusing Emanuel with his brother John, who succeeded Dobson.

[2] These were the incidents that gave Scott some of the background for his novel *Woodstock: or the Cavalier. A Tale of the year 1651*, in which book the Royalists, to impede the sequestration, pretend that they are ghosts.

William Fleetwood in the park) that the committee which sat in
the Mannour were pelted out of their chambers by stones thrown
in at the windows; (but from what hands the stones came they
could not see); that their candles were continually put out, as fast
as they lighted them; and that one with his sword drawn to defend
a candle, was with his own scabbard in the mean time well cud-
gelled: and others were forced to remove, some of them to Sir
William Fleetwood's house, and the rest to some other places. But
concerning the cutting of the ôak, in particular, I have nothing.'

Lydall's letter raises the question of Aubrey's credulity, a
label rarely omitted by any writer who mentions him, and a trait
which was a source of such regret to his biographer, John Britton.
Like most of his contemporaries, Aubrey believed in witches,
supernatural occurrences, and astrology. To dismiss as mere rubbish the first two of these, in the light of anthropological enquiry
and the examination of poltergeist phenomena, for example, is no
longer so enlightened as might once have been supposed; while the
conception that the circumstances attendant on a birth may have
far-reaching effects on the life of an individual should be thought
of in relation to the stage of development attained by seventeenth-
century science and the growing movement to co-ordinate
information of all kinds. Aubrey habitually records a local belief
(notably in the *Remains of Gentilism*) as if it were an established
fact. This does not always mean that he accepts it as such. Indeed,
the words are often half-humorously written, like a remark made
in passing conversation, a characteristic that his writings always
retain. The method is all part of his presentation of life as a picture
crowded with odd figures, occupying themselves in unexpected
and sometimes inexplicable pursuits. He wrote down what appeared to him the truth, but it is often the truth of poetry rather
than the truth of science. To demand otherwise is to ask that he
should have been some man other than John Aubrey; and as he
himself remarked: 'I know that some will nauseate these old
Fables: but I doe profess to regard them as the most considerable
pieces of Antiquity I collect.'

CHAPTER THREE

London and Broad Chalke (1649–1659)

I

IN 1649 THE KING was beheaded. The act shocked the country, and Europe, in a sense bringing an end to an epoch; but the existence of individuals like Aubrey, who had played little or no personal part in the Civil Wars, was scarcely at all changed; for political disorder and arbitrary government had already become part of their lives for a number of years. He mentions that at about this time (which was when his mother fell from her horse and broke an arm) he was suitor to Mistress Jane Codrington; but he gives no details about this lady, probably a member of one of the several families of Codrington living on the borders of Wiltshire and Gloucestershire.

A year or more later, in April 1651, on returning to London, a deeper attachment was formed, when 'I sawe that incomparable good conditioned gentlewoman Mrs M. Wiseman, with whom at first sight I was in love—*haeret lateri*'.[1] This Mary Wiseman is named again in the rough draft of his will (of which more will be said later), in which she is described as 'of Westminster', and was bequeathed Aubrey's best diamond ring.

The address 'of Westminster' provides the first clue to Mary Wiseman's identity, for the Westminster rate-books for the parish of St Margaret's show that a 'Mr John Wiseman' lived in the Great Sanctuary (sometimes called the Broad Sanctuary) between 1648 and 1655. After that date his name disappears. On 31 January, 1656, the nuncupative will of 'John Wiseman, late of the City of Westminster, Esqr.' was proved by Rebecca Wiseman, his wife and executrix. This will had been declared in the presence of

[1] ——*letalis arundo.* Verg., *Aenid*, IV. 73. Aubrey put his pen through the phrase after writing it, perhaps thinking Dido an unsuitable comparison.

Sir Roger Higgs, Knight, John Young, Esquire, and Robert Jones, Gentleman, at a time when John Wiseman, 'on or about 28th November, 1655', was 'sick of the sickness whereof he died'. This documentary record mentions bequests to 'my sonne' and 'every-one of my daughters', but does not set forth the children indivi-dually by name. A further search reveals the burial of 'Thomas, son of John and Rebecca Wiseman' in the parish register of St Martin-in-the-Fields in 1635; but the records of the baptisms of the Wiseman children have not come to light.

The marriage licences at the Faculty Office, however, supply some additional information towards the identification. This entry occurs for 1661:

'Jan. 3rd, John Saintloe of St Dunstan-in-the-East, London, bachelor, 30 & Mary Wiseman, spinster, 20, daughter of Rebecca Wiseman of St Clement Danes, widow, who consents; at St Martin Outwich, London.'

There can be little doubt that this licence refers to the girl who had enchanted Aubrey; more especially when it turns out that the Saintloes (sometimes 'Saintlowe' or 'St Loe') were a Wiltshire family, a branch of whom, often mentioned by Aubrey, lived at Broad Chalke.[1] The family of this John Saintloe (who obtained a Faculty Office Licence) recorded a pedigree in the Heralds' Visitations of London in 1664. He was a merchant, and his father and grandfather had also been named John Saintloe. The former had been of St Dunstan-in-the-East, 'citizen & Fishmonger & merchant', and he had married Mary Andrewes, niece of Bishop Lancelot Andrewes. John Saintloe, the father, had acted as executor to the Bishop when he died. John Saintloe, the grand-father, of Knighton at Broad Chalke, had married Elizabeth, daughter of Sir Lawrence Hyde and aunt of Edward Hyde, 1st Earl of Clarendon.

---

[1] 'Edward Saintlowe of Knighton, Esq., was buried in the Church of Broad Chalke, May the 6th, 1578, as appeares by the Register Booke. The snow did then lie so thick on the ground that the bearers carried his body over the gate in Knighton field, and the company went over the hedges, and they digged a way to the church porch: I knew some ancient people of the parish that did remember it'.

In this pedigree Mary Wiseman's father is noted as 'Groom of the Privy Chamber to King Charles I'. If we now turn to the Visitations of Essex, among the large families of Wiseman of Felsted and elsewhere (said to have come to that county 'from the North'), John Wiseman 'of the privie chamber' appears in 1634. His father was 'of the Society of Goldsmiths', and most of his near relations seem to have done relatively well for themselves in the world.

Until the date of her birth can be ascertained, it cannot be said with any certainty whether Mary Wiseman was indeed only eleven years old when marked down by Aubrey as 'an incomparable good-conditioned gentlewoman'. Many girls (for example, John Evelyn's wife), married at fifteen, were engaged when mere children; but Aubrey's not infrequent mistakes regarding the chronology of his early life, combined with the fact that marriage licence affirmations were intended primarily to show that the parties were 'of age' (and are often unreliable on the point of actual years stated) must both be taken into account. The registers of St Martin Outwich (which was under the patronage of the Merchant Taylors Company and was demolished by fire in 1873) go back only so far as 1670, so that no record exists there of the Wiseman-Saintloe marriage.

Yet another licence in the Faculty Office, by its hint at Mary Wiseman's early death, may provide a footnote to what little we know of the story. It must be emphasised, however, that there is nothing to suggest that the same John Saintloe was one of the parties, except that the name and age make the identification applicable, together with the Wiseman[1] family's connexions with

[1] A marriage licence, dated 12 June, 1663, was taken out by 'Andrew Paschall' and 'Rebecca Wiseman', possibly Aubrey's friend, Andrew Paschall, rector of Chedsey in Somerset, and a sister of Mary Wiseman's. However, this is pure guesswork, as both Paschalls and Wisemans were numerous in Heraldic Visitations of Essex. There is a small but not uninteresting point to be considered regarding the Wisemans. Among the witnesses of the nuncupative will of Mary Wiseman's father, John Wiseman of Westminster, was 'John Young. Esq.' Is it not possible that this was the 'Jack Young (afterwards knighted)' stated by Aubrey to be responsible for the famous inscription

Essex, where John and Mary Saintloe may have settled after their marriage:

'1667 April 3 John Saintloe of Woodford, Co Essex, widower, 36, & Margaret Porter of the Precinct of the Cathedral Church of the Holy Trinity in the City of Norwich, sister of William Porter.'

II

Apart from his love affairs, Aubrey remembered 1651 as the year in which the new rulers of England began to make their power felt. On 22 August at Tower Hill he saw the beheading, following a sentence for high treason, of the puritan minister Christopher Love, who had fallen foul of the Independents and become involved in the intrigues of the Scotch Presbyterians. In the course of 'Love's Plot' its author had corresponded with Charles II and Queen Henrietta Maria. Love, says Aubrey, was 'the only person that ever I saw decollated. It was after dinner and as cleare a sky as ever I sawe. Shortly after his suffring the skye began to thicken and at last was envellopt in blacke dismall Cloud, and all that night and till next noon such Thunder,

in Westminster Abbey O RARE BEN IONSON? In the passage which refers to this memorial, Aubrey writes, a few lines lower, that Ben Jonson received £50 a year to use his influence with King James I to keep 'Sir W. Wiseman of Essex' from being pricked for sheriff. Presumably this refers to Sir William Wiseman of Canfield Hall, Essex, baronet (a connexion of the Wisemans of Westminster), who served as sheriff for his county in 1639—sure enough, the year after Ben Jonson died. This concatenation of the names Wiseman, Young, and Ben Jonson in this Westminster setting may be coincidence; but it seems worth recording. It must be added that a 'Mr John Young' was buried in the Abbey on 5 May, 1699, whose will was proved as 'John Young, of St Margaret's, Westminster, gent.' and names no relations but speaks of his 'school at Westminster'. 'Jack Young' turns up in Aubrey's Lives as a friend of Suckling and Davenant, making an assignation with 'a very pretty young girle' and being locked into his room as a madman as a practical joke on the part of his friends. Little seems to be known of this Jack or John Young, but see Notes and Queries, CXCII, 442, 1947, Whitmore, for Sir John Young and his family, which makes the Ben Jonson connexion unlikely.

lightning, and Tempest as if the Machine of the world had been dissolving.'

Although political matters obtruded themselves to some extent throughout this period, more congenial subjects, such as Flying Chariots and Submarine Navigation, occupied the letters that passed between Aubrey and Francis Potter, who spent some time staying with the Aubreys in the country. Like so many of his correspondents, Potter speaks gratefully of Aubrey's generosity; but his brother, Hannibal Potter (now exiled from the Presidency of Trinity by the Parliamentarian Chancellor of the University, Philip, 4th Earl of Pembroke), writes some time later complaining that Aubrey was too fond of encouraging Francis in his wild schemes, and worse still, 'recommends him to his face', a habit unfavourable to brotherly relations, as Francis had 'a wonderful conceight of himself'.

There were also plans to be considered for visiting Italy. Aubrey had by now met William Harvey, whom he had admired so much from far off as an undergraduate. Harvey (physician and friend of 'my cosen Montague'[1]) gave him advice in 1651 about this projected tour; telling him what should be seen, what company kept, and what books read—in this last respect recommending Aristotle, Cicero, Avicenna, 'and did call the neoteriques shitt-breeches'. Aubrey was also in touch with that eccentric, impecunious figure of Polish origin, Samuel Hartlib,[2] on the subject of going abroad. On 8 March, 1652, Hartlib wrote that he would 'improve any opportunity that shall offer itselfe for some Travellers next month into Italy'. The letter also refers to the 'large and particular' account of Francis Potter, promised by Aubrey, who even at the age of twenty-five seems to have been turning his attention to biography, and shared Hartlib's interest in educational reform.

However, Aubrey's mother, to her son's great disappointment, dissuaded him from leaving England. This was no doubt largely on account of his father's state of health, because Richard Aubrey, affected by some bronchial disorder, was already sinking. The family doctor, Samuel Bave, wrote a statement in Latin, expressing

[1] Sister of John Aubrey of Llantrithyd, later baronet.

[2] For Hartlib's acquaintance with Aubrey, see *Notes and Queries*, CXCV, 2, 1950, Turnbull.

the gravity of his case. He died at Broad Chalke on 21 October,
1652, his son receiving what he took to be an occult indication
of his father's imminent demise. 'Three or four days before my
father died, as I was in my bed about nine o'clock in the morning,
perfectly awake, I did hear three distinct knocks on the bed's
head, as if it had been with a ruler or ferula.'

Richard Aubrey was buried on 26 October, 1652, in the south-
east corner of the chancel at Kington St Michael, under the
window where, as a boy, his son could remember the picture of 'the
Ladie Cicelie Bodenham in her cope and robes,' lady prioress of
the nunnery at Kington, later promoted to Wilton, of which she
was abbess until the Dissolution. The will was proved in the
following April. With small bequests to charity and to servants,
Richard Aubrey left his eldest son the farm at Broad Chalke and
the manor of Burlton in Herefordshire, with other less important
properties in Brecon and Monmouth. There was £500 for each
of the younger sons, William and Thomas, to be paid by Aubrey
to his brothers. According to Aubrey there was also £1800 worth
of debts. Easton Pierse would, naturally, remain occupied by the
Lyte grandparents.

'I doe hope to live so long to erect a little inscription in white
marble to the Memory of my father: about an ell high or better',
wrote Aubrey. 'Alexander Brome has an elegy on him in his
Poemes which he made at the request of his next neighbour and
friend Mr Isaac Lyte, Alderman of London, my Kinsman.' The
projected inscription was in Latin, and speaks of Richard Aubrey[1]
as 'vir pacificus et fidelis amicus'.

[1] The following record is entered, probably in Aubrey's own hand,
at the end of the First Parish Register Book at Broad Chalke: 'Richard
Awbrey of Broad Chalke, Esq. died at Chalke 21 of October and buried
Kington St Michael, the 26 of the same month anno 1652. Kington is
near Chippenham in N. Wilts.' Alexander Brome (said to have been
learning Latin grammar at the age of four and a quarter) is remembered
for 'I have been in love, and in drink, and in debt, This many and many
a year', his drinking songs, and ballads ridiculing the Roundheads. His
brother was Henry Brome, a London bookseller. The Clerk of Kington
St Michael (who had taught Aubrey to read) was called John Brome (see
p. 31).

III

The death of his father was a milestone in Aubrey's career. From that moment he was plunged into financial difficulties from which he never managed to extricate himself; while for the next fifteen years lawsuits beset him like a nightmare. Now he lived chiefly at Broad Chalke; and, riding about the country there, spent much of his time in reflection:

' 'Twas about these purlieus that the Muses were wont to appear to Sir Philip Sydney, and where he wrote down their dictates in his table book, though on horseback.[1] For those nimble fugitives, except they be presently registered, fly away and perhaps can never be caught again. But they were never so kind as to appeare to me, though I am the usufructuary. It seems they reserve their grace only for the proprietors, to whom they have continued a constant kindness for a succession of generations of the no less ingeniose than honourable family of the Herberts. These were the places where our Kings and Queens used to divert themselves in the hunting season. Cranbourn Chase which reaches from Harnham Bridge at Salisbury near to Blandford, was belonging to Roger Mortimer, Earle of March: his seate was at his castle at Cranbourne. If these oakes here were vocal as Dodona's some of the old dotards (old stagge-headed oakes, so called) could give us an account of the amours and secret whispers between the Great Earle and the faire Queen Isabell.'

In these enchanting vales the shepherds were still accustomed to wear the traditional Arcadian attire, 'a long white cloak with a very deep cape, which comes halfway down their backs, made of the locks of the sheep. There was a sheep-crooke (*Vide* Virgil's *Eclogues* and Theocritus), a sling, a scrip, their tar-box, a pipe or flute, and their dog. But since 1671, they are grown so luxurious

---

[1] 'My great-uncle Mr Thomas Browne, remembered him; and sayd that he was often wont, as he was hunting in our pleasant plaines, to take his table book out of his pocket, and write down his notions as they came into his head, when he was writing his *Arcadia* (which was never finished by him).'

as to neglect their ancient warm and useful fashion, and goe *à la mode*.'[1]

Among the 'romancy plaines and boscages' of Wiltshire, Aubrey, now twenty-seven years old, began to consider what he had done in life. '*Quid digni feci hîc process. viam?*' he wrote, adding, 'Truly nothing; only umbrages, *sc.* Osney abbey ruines, etc., antiquities.' He came to the conclusion that he was a kind of whetstone, against which others sharpened their wits. There was, however, the distraction of occasional visits to London, where Francis Potter wrote to him in December 1652, directing his letter to 'the signe of the Rainebowe,[2] a stationer's shop in Fleetstreet by Temple'. Wilton, a centre of life and gossip, was not far away from Broad Chalke, and, as a neighbour and distant connexion of the Pembrokes (in spite of dislike of some individual members of the family and disapproval of their Roundhead politics), he was invited often there, where he had known the names of the subjects of the portraits in the galleries since the age of eight. It was at Wilton in the same year that he found Sir John Denham, poet and wit, whose considerable contemporary reputation has not stood up to the test of time. Denham, 'being in some straits', was staying with Lord Pembroke, having recently returned from conveying the Dukes of York and Gloucester to safety in France. Aubrey's Trinity friend, Josias Howe (at this period evicted from his fellowship by the Parliamentarians), had known Denham at Oxford, 'where he was the dreamingest young fellow'. Howe told Aubrey that he had

---

[1] Shepherds had a special fascination for Aubrey, and he noted later, when writing of Surrey: 'The Shepherds of these Downs use a half horn, *scil.* slitt *secundum longitudinem*, naild'd to the end of a long staff (about the length of our Western Sheep Crooks) with which they can hurl a stone a great distance, and so keep their sheep within bounds, or from straggling into the corn. Such I have seen in some old hangings (*viz.* the King's designed by Rafael de Urbino) and before the first edition of Sir Philip Sydney's *Arcadia*: but never saw the thing before I passed over these pleasant Downs.'

[2] The shop of Daniel Pakeman, who published Judge Rumsey's 'little 8vo book' *Organon Salutis*, which described his whalebone instrument for clearing the throat (see p. 81); a poem of Vaughan's refers to this.

'never expected such things from him as he has left the world. When he was there he would game extremely: when he had played away all his money he would play away his father's wrought rich gold cappes.' Some of the pleasure of Denham's companionship was in his stories of the famous Sylvanus Scory, who had known Elizabeth's court at the time when the King of France was the great Queen's suitor. Christopher Wase ('Kit Wase', an Eton scholar who had gone on to both King's, Cambridge, and Queen's, Oxford, and who was to become a lifelong friend) was also at Wilton, as tutor to William, Lord Herbert[1] of Cardiff; and Aubrey used to follow the hounds with pupil and tutor, between their Latin lessons.

He was in touch with John Lydall about companions for the projected tour abroad, and the latter wrote to him, on 5 April, 1653, saying that Ralph Bathurst was 'not minded to travel', neither was Thomas Willis able to accompany Aubrey. Lydall excuses himself on the grounds of his own 'crazy and sickly constitution of body' and also on account of the expense of the journey. But the Grand Tour was fated never to take place, and Aubrey wrote: 'I made my will and settled my estate on trustees, intending to have seen the antiquities of Rome and Italy, for [some] years, and then to have returned and married, but *Diis aliter visum est superis*, my mother to my inexpressible grief and ruine, hindred this designe, which was my ruine.' The terms in which Aubrey speaks of his mother's opposition are unusually strong. Clearly he felt that now was some turning-point in his life; in what way, remains unexplained.

The surviving draft will (already mentioned in connexion with Aubrey's Trinity friends and with Mary Wiseman) is probably the one referred to above, because Ralph Bathurst became 'Dr' in 1654. Bequests to Jesus College were presumably on account of the family's Welsh associations, and the fact that Dr William Aubrey had been of that house. Later, Hawes and Bathurst each came to be President of Trinity, and Lydall (who died in 1657) became a Fellow of Trinity. It was 'Will Hawes' who told Aubrey that Dr

[1] Grandson of Philip, 5th Earl of Pembroke, with whom, according to Aubrey, 'the glory of English hunting breathed its last.'

Hannibal Potter's election to the presidency of Trinity had been illegal, and that, if Lord Falkland had not been killed at Newbury, Dr William Chillingworth, the great controversialist, would have had the place. John Davenant was a son of Dr Edward Davenant, the mathematician. Dr Davenant, Prebend of the Church of Sarum, was a good friend to Aubrey later, when he was in trouble, and his daughter Anne, 'a notable Algebrist', married Anthony Ettrick, a Trinity friend, now a barrister, who shared Aubrey's antiquarian and occult interests.

The terms of the draft are as follows:

'To my loving grandfather, Mr Isaac Lyte, 50*li*, and to my grandmother, 50*li*. A decent inscription of white marble for my father, and the like for myselfe: the Epitaphe to be made by Mr A. Ettrick.

Item, to Anthony Ettrick of Berford, in the county of Dorset, Esq., I bequeathe ten pounds to buy a piece of plate, my saphire ring, Sir Walter Raleigh's history, and Philip Comineus.

Item, my will is that my executors buy for Trinity Colledge in Oxon a colledge pott of the value of ten pounds, with my arms thereon inscribed; and ten pounds which I shall desire my honoured friends Mr Ralph Bathurst of Trinity Colledge and Mr John Lydall to lay out upon mathematicall and philosophicall books.

Item, I give to the library of Jesus Colledge in Oxon my Greek Chrystomus, Bede's 2 tomes, and all the rest of my bookes that are fitt for a library, as Mr Anthony Ettrick or Mr Lydall shall think fitt, excepting those bookes that were my father's which I bequeathe to my heire.

Item, I bequeathe to John Davenant of the Middle Temple, esq., a ring of the value of 50*s*. with a stone in it.

Item, to Mr. William Hawes of Trinity Colledge aforesaid a ring of the like value.

Item, to Mr John Lydall of Trinity Colledge aforesaid a ring of the like value.

Item, to Mr Ralf Bathurst of Trinity Colledge a ring of the like value.

Item, to Mris Mary Wiseman of Westminster, my best diamond ring and . . .'

He seems to have been unable to decide on the additional bequest to Mary Wiseman, for the rest is blank.

In December 1653, in the court at the house of Sir John Snell (of the Kington St Michael family, whom the graceful Jack Sydenham had served), 'we saw our shadows on the fogg as on a wall by the light of the lanternes, sc. about 30 or 40 foot distance or more'. This was the kind of spectacle that always interested Aubrey, and in 1654, when staying with his cousin, John Aubrey of Llantrithyd, he 'began to enter into pocket bookes philosophical and antiquarian remarques', and also the notes on natural phenomena (and, indeed, on almost every conceivable subject) which were to form the basis of some of his later writings. On this visit to Glamorgan, he saw across the Bristol Channel 'the mountaines of Devonshire all white with snow'. Back in Wiltshire he acquired a purge from Dr William Harvey (Aubrey kept the prescription), and recalled how Harvey was accustomed to ride, 'his man following on foote, as the fashion then was, which was very decent, now quite discontinued'. In 1654 the Doctor described a contrivance he had seen at Carshalton or Beddington in Surrey, 'a pretty Machine to cleanse a House of Office sc. by a small streame no bigger than a man's finger, which hung upon its centre of gravity, so that when it was full (perhaps it held a gallon) a considerable quantity of water fell downe with some force and washed away the Filth.'

It was at about this period, too, that Aubrey met 'the ever memorable' John Hales, of whom he had already heard much from Hales's nephew, Mr Sloper, the vicar of Broad Chalke; and, also, from Tom Mariet, William Radford, and Ned Wood, after their famous walk to London. Hales, like Howe from Trinity, had been ejected from his Eton fellowship by the forces in power; and Aubrey says that 'The Ladie Salter (neer Eaton) was very kind to him after the sequestration: he was very welcome to her ladyship and spent much of his time there. At Eaton he lodged (after the sequestration) at the house next the Christopher (inne), where I sawe him, a pretty little man, sanguine, of a cheerful countenance, very gentle, and courteous: I was received by him with much humanity: he was in a kind of violet-coloured gown and was reading Thomas à Kempis: it was within a year before he deceased, 1656. He loved Canarie: but moderately, to refresh his spirits.' Afterwards, Aubrey found that the information given him by Mr Sloper as to Lady Salter (who was sister to Brian Duppa, Bishop of Salisbury) was a mistake. Hales had come to her house, but ' 'twas to teach her sonne, who was such a blockhead he could not read well'.

In June 1655 Aubrey had a fall at Epsom, and broke one of his ribs 'and was afraid it might cause an apostumation'.

IV

Inigo Jones's book on Stonehenge, the first to be wholly devoted to the subject, appeared in 1655, a work written by the direction of King James I and entitled *The Most Notable Antiquity of Great Britain, vulgarly called Stone-heng, on Salisbury Plain, Restored by Inigo Jones, Architect-Generall to the late King*. The author had died in 1651, and the book was issued by his son-in-law, John Webb, who, in fact, seems to have composed most of the volume from Jones's rough notes, in which the theory was propounded that the stones had been set up by the Romans as a temple of the Tuscan order of architecture, dedicated to the god Cœlus, father of Saturn. Aubrey read this study 'with great delight', and says:

'There is a great deal of learning in it, but, having compared his scheme with the Monument itself, I found that he had not dealt fairly, but had made a Lesbian's rule, which is conformed to the stone; that is, he framed the monument to his own Hypothesis, which is much differing from the thing itself: and this gave me an edge to make more researches, and further opportunity was that my honoured and faithfull friend, Colonell James Long, of Draycot, since Baronet, was wont to spend a week or two every Autumne at Aubury [Avebury] in Hawking, where several times I have had the happiness to accompany him. Our Sport was very good and in a Romantic country: sc. the Prospects noble and vast, the downe stock't with numerous Flocks of Sheep, the Turfe rich and fragrant with Thyme and Burnet,—

Fessus ubi incubuit baculo, saxoque resedit
Pastor arundineo carmine mulcet oves;[1]

nor are the Nut-brown Shepherdesses without their graces. But the flight of the Falcons was but a parenthesis to the Colonell's facetious discourse, who was *Tam Marti quam Mercurio* and the Muses did accompany him with Hawkes and Spanniels.'

In order to support his theory that the stones were from 'the Quarries at and about Aibury' and that they had been set up somewhat later than the time of Agricola (A.D. 79), Inigo Jones had altered in his plan the position of many of the megaliths; and he had added others, the illustrations to his book being, as Aubrey remarks, most inaccurate. The 'Lesbian's rule' was a mason's rule made of lead, which could be bent to suit the curves of a moulding, so called from the style of the buildings on the island of Lesbos, where the stones were said to be laid, not so as to form an even front, but each stone alternatively projected and retired. So far as Avebury was concerned, this misrepresentation was not accepted by Aubrey, who had no bias as to any particular pattern that the remains might or might not take. He produced his own plan of what he called 'an ill-shaped monument' in the form that he found it; thereby setting an example of archaeological integrity from which later investigators in the same field sometimes fell sadly short.

v

Aubrey's thirtieth year may be said to mark the beginning of his career as a writer, as he began his first serious literary work, the *Natural History of Wiltshire*, in 1656. One of his portraits also belongs to this period and there is a note, dated 1671, on the title page of the manuscript of his *Monumenta Britannica*:

'My Lord Charles Seymour had my picture, *aetat* 30, which his lady now hath. *Quaere* Sir John Erneley for it.' This may possibly have been the minature by Samuel Cooper, stolen from the Ashmolean in 1691, after it had, perhaps, been returned to Aubrey by

[1] Noted by Aubrey as Ovid, *Trist.* lib. IV. See illustration facing page 80 for his picture of himself hawking with Long.

Seymour's widow, Lady Ernle. It seems, however, more probable that the picture was the portrait attributed to Lely, which shows Aubrey leaning against a column with his hand on the head of a young negro. If the style of dress and hair is compared with that of Dobson's canvas of Colonel John Penruddock,[1] the resemblance between the two pictures may be remarked. The latter, unless posthumous, must have been painted before 1655, the year of its subject's death.

Mary Wiseman is mentioned again in Aubrey's 'accidents' for the year 1656, which is recorded as 'a strange year to me, and of contradictions;—sc. love M.W. and lawsuites'. These 'amours with Madame Wiseman' continued—to what extent of intimacy we do not know—as did also 'the chargeable and taedious' litigation on the subject of the entail, a matter of six hundred pounds a year, mostly in Brecon, but a little in Monmouthshire. In his efforts to clear up this question Aubrey had to go to Chaldon, in Surrey, and search the parish register for the record of the burial[2] of his great-grandmother, Wilgiford Williams, the relict of Dr William Aubrey, who had married a Mr Browne of Willey in that parish. On 30 March, in the same year, Aubrey had been one of the parties to an indenture disposing of the advowson of Yatton Keynell (which he held with William Stumpe, George Ivy, and his grandfather, Isaac Lyte) to William Duckett, Esq., of Hartham: a slight, but significant, indication of the direction in which his affairs were moving.

[1] The Penruddock portrait is reproduced in the *Wilts Arch. Mag.*, vol. 16. It is, of course, not impossible that Aubrey's portrait was also by Dobson or one of his pupils. Its whereabouts is not known; but there is an engraving from it, inscribed: 'John Aubrey, Esqr. F.R.S.' together with the Aubrey coat of arms. In the John Rylands Library at Manchester is Canon Jackson's copy of this reproduction, described in Dr Albert Hollaender's article in the *Wilts Arch. Mag.*, vol. 49, as a watercolour, stated to be about 1790 in date. This picture bears the further inscription: 'From the original painting by Sir P. Lely in the possession of Edmund Lodge, Esqr., Lancaster Herald.' Lodge published *Portraits of Illustrious Personages in Great Britain*, 1821 and 1834.

[2] John Browne, and his son, John, sold the manor, 1613, to Richard Betenson (called Beteston by Aubrey), see Manning and Bray's *Surrey*, which says Aubrey was mistaken in thinking Dr Aubrey formerly owned it.

These lawsuits on the Welsh border were not without their amusing side, on account of the persons he met while attending them, and the anecdotes that were told. Dr William Watts, a Canon of Hereford, recounted the story of what had happened when Dr Daniel Price, the Dean, 'a mighty pontificial prowd man', had insisted, contrary to custom, on riding a mare in a church procession, when a nearby stallion had broken loose; and Judge Haggit of Bristol, perhaps rather improperly, 'told us that a Client's wife of his hath no manner of signall either of man or woman'. 'Old John Tussell, my attorney' probably belongs to this period, too, who said that Sir Edward Coke, when Lord Chief Justice, had 'gott a hundred thousand pounds in one yeare'. Walter Rumsey, one of Aubrey's counsel in these cases, speaking of the increase in litigation, pointed out that there were twenty-four attornies even in the small county of Brecon. Rumsey was later a judge on the South Wales circuit.

'He was an ingeniose man,' says Aubrey, 'and had a philosophicall head; he was most curious for grafting, inoculating, and planting, and ponds. If he had any old dead plumbe-tree, or apple tree, he let them stand, and planted vines at the bottom, and let them climbe up, and they would beare very well. . . . He had a kindnesse for me and invited me to his house and told me a great many fine things, both naturall and antiquarian. He was very facetious and a good musician, played on the organ and the lute. He could compose. He was much troubled with the flegme one winter at the court of Ludlow (where he was one of the councellours), sitting by the fire spitting and spawling, he took a fine tender sprig, and tied a rag at the end, and conceited he might put it down his throate, and fetch up the flegme, and he did so. Afterwards he made an instrument of whalebone. I have often seen him use it. I could never make it go downe my throat, but for those that can 'tis a most incomparable engine. If troubled with the wind it cures you *immediatly*. . . . I had a young fellow (Marc Collins) that was my servant that used it incomparably, more easily than the Judge; he made of them. In Wilts, among my things, are some of his making still.'

It was also in 1656 that Aubrey, back in London, went with his friends, John Hoskyns (grandson of the famous wit of that name) and Stafford Tyndale, to see William Lee's invention[1] for the weaving of stockings by an engine of his contrivance, shown by a weaver in Pear-Pool Lane. The Tyndales were Wiltshire neighbours, and Stafford Tyndale was apparently the son of Thomas Tyndale, regarded by Aubrey as a typical gentleman of the old school. They lived at the Priory, near Easton Pierse; and in the same year old Mistress Tyndale, who had known Dean Overall's lovely wife ('so tender-hearted that (truly) she could scarce denie any one'), repeated a song about this lady to Aubrey, which went somewhat like:

> The deane of St Paule's did search for his wife,
>   And where d'ee thinke he found her?
> Even upon Sir John Selbye's bed,
>   As flat as any Flounder.

Aubrey had seen a picture of this famous beauty, painted by Hoskins (uncle of his friend, Samuel Cooper, the miniaturist), and there was a ballad about her in a book belonging to Ralph Sheldon, another friend of whom more will be said later. In July 1656 Dr William Harvey died. Aubrey was present at the funeral at Hemsted in Essex, and helped to carry the body into the vault.

Among the 'accidents' for December in the same year occurs the ill-omened note: 'Veneris Morbus'[2]—yet another indication that the malign influence of the Paphian goddess was at work in his life. One may speculate as to whether this misfortune has some connexion with the lasting regret he felt for his mother's insistance in preventing him from leaving England. Did Aubrey feel that, by getting away from the country for a time, he might have avoided some otherwise inevitable and disastrous relationship which wrecked his health and his career? The gravity of this

---

[1] Lee, a poor curate, 'observing how much paines his wife took in knitting a payre of stockings, he bought a stocking and a halfe, which he designed in his loome, which (though some of the appendent instruments of the engine be altered) keepes the same to this day'. Cromwell had passed an Act making the transportation of this invention a felony.

[2] Venus is denoted in the manuscript by her planetary sign.

infection may have been inconsiderable, and should not be exaggerated. Dr Samuel Bave and Dr Bidgood discussed the matter together in Latin letters. It was an additional ill to bear, unless (somewhat improbable in that day) the cure was rapid.

There was a new blow in November 1657, when 'domina Katherina Ryves, with whome I was to marry' fell sick and died. He notes only the decease of this lady, adding that her portion was more than £2000 and that her husband was to be the guardian of her brother's estate, worth £1000 a year. Her identity is provided by a will, dated 2 November, 1657, and proved in 1660. In this document Katherine Ryves describes herself as 'of the Close, Sarum, Wilts., daughter of George Ryves, Esq.', and gives directions that she should be buried 'by my father and mother at Blandford Forum'. The £2000, spoken of by Aubrey, was left to her brother, together with special instructions that, before distributing her several bequests to the poor, he should make himself well informed as to where real want lay. £350 was left 'to my deare ffriende Mr John Awbrey' and a mourning ring to 'Mrs Awbrey, his Mother'. Similar rings were bequeathed to Katherine Ryves's four aunts: Mary and Margaret Miller, and Anne and Joan Sadler.

From the information given in the will as to her parentage, it appears that Katherine Ryves belonged to an old and distinguished Dorset family, several of whom had become (like Aubrey) members of the Middle Temple, among them possibly her father, George Ryves: although the connexion with Blandford would be sufficient to account for friendship with the Aubreys. It should be noted that it was Katherine Ryves herself who is described as 'of the Close' and not (as the printed list of wills states) George Ryves. Her father presumably lived in or near Blandford, since he was buried there. For his daughter's residence at Salisbury the following explanation can be offered.

Among the aunts mentioned above, in Katherine Ryves's will, were Anne and Joan Sadler. Now it so happens that Aubrey speaks of visiting 'about 1656' a Mrs Sadler at 'the great House in the close in Salisbury', where the 'pitched causeway' in the court, lying untended during the times of Civil War, was so overgrown with weeds that it seemed to have disappeared. 'The Great House' was Sherborne House (or Sherborne Place) on the west side of the Close, often called The King's House, after the visit paid there by James I, where the Sadler family (a branch of that of Wootton-Basset in North Wiltshire) had lived since the end of the sixteenth century. Thomas Sadler, sometime Registrar of the Bishopric, had commanded a troop of horse in the King's service. His widow Mary (daughter of William Urwin of Stanton St Bernard) died on 23 September, 1659. In her will she bequeathed her real and personal property, including the house in the Close, to her cousin Mary Miller, and to her kinsman John Sadler the elder, of Gotacre, a Chancery suit being required to adjust the differences of the two latter. Mary Miller was, of course, another of the aunts mentioned in Katherine Ryves's will, and, as will be seen later, became an old friend of Aubrey's. No doubt the Great House with its pitched causeway was where Katherine was living with her aunt, or aunts, when Aubrey was paying his addresses to her.

The generous legacy to Aubrey suggests that the engagement may have been something more than a prelude to a formally arranged marriage, although he himself mentions no emotion beyond his regret at the loss of the money. Elsewhere he says that he believed that 'in matters of generation we ought to consult more with our sense and instinct, than our reason and prudence, fashion of the country, and interest. We see what contemptible products are of the prudent politiques, weake, fooles, ricketty children, scandals to nature and their country. The heralds are fooles—*tota errant via*. A blessing goes with marriage for love on a strong impulse.'

However, in spite of the disapproval he expresses here for alliances contracted with a view to impaling a famous coat, or linking a pedigree with an ancient line, the fear that a young man might so easily make a detrimental match is one that recurs in Aubrey's letters, and in his essay on education. This fear is, indeed, almost an obsession, no doubt inculcated by his parents from his earliest years. At times, too, he writes that this man or that[1] was 'too

---

[1] *e.g.* Descartes, and Thomas Bushell (who did, in fact, marry) in the *Lives*.

wise to encumber himself with a wife'—perhaps rather bitterly, since he certainly came near enough himself to matrimony on a number of occasions. It is possible that, with Mary Wiseman so recently in his mind, and with the consciousness of the load of debt that weighted him down, the Ryves fortune may have been the foremost consideration in the marriage. Twenty-three years later he was still on the best of terms with Katherine Ryves's aunt, Mary Miller.

VI

Meanwhile, he toyed with his 'memoires of naturall remarques' and watched the covers of his books[1] in the closet at Broad Chalke stain—until 'in feaverish autumns' he could not tell the colour of the leather—with a 'hoare mouldiness', from the damp mists of the downs. In this idyllic retreat, undisturbed by the tribe of duns and attorneys, for a while at least he could work and muse. 'By my Parlour window' grew 'a Bon-Chrestien Peare tree against the wall' of curious shape: in the garden beyond 'a Warden-peare neer to a Ewe-tree, that is to say within a yard or lesse, the peare-tree reclines from the ewe tree, as by an antipathy, and lookes as if it were shorne that way'. Sometimes he tested the monosyllabic echo in the kitchen-garden 'sullen and mute till you advance [some] paces on the easie ascent, at which place one's mouth is opposite to the middle of the height of the house at right angles'; sometimes he fished in the stream which he had stocked with crayfish. These had not lived, because the water was too cold for them; but the trout there were two feet long.

The walls of the church 'and of the buttery at the farme there doe shoot out besides nitre, a beautiful red, lighter than scarlet: an oriental horseflesh colour'. The village was also so fortunate as to possess 'one of the tunablest ring of bells in Wiltshire which hang advantageously, the river running near the churchyard, which meliorates the sound'; though 'when Horses come from North Wiltshire (or other parts) to Broad Chalke, when they

[1] For the contents of Aubrey's library, see Appendix B.

come to drinke of the water there they will sniff and snort, it is so cold and acrimonious, so much impregnated with nitre'. If Aubrey and his friend, Sir George Penruddock (whose family had been tenants of Broad Chalke farm before it had been leased to the Aubreys), had not arranged in 1659 for themselves to be appointed churchwardens, 'the fair church had fallen, from the niggardliness of churchwardens of mean condition'. A beam in the belfry and the sixth bell, which they added to the existing five, commemorate their period of office.

The living of Broad Chalke was in the gift of King's College, Cambridge, and the incumbents who occupied the vicarage in Aubrey's day—Walter Waller, Robert Peyton, and John Sloper, all of whom he mentions from time to time in his writings—were accordingly scholars of Eton and King's.

Walter Waller, 'a very learned man', who had come to Chalke in 1622, had taught his kinsman, Edmund Waller, the poet, at Cambridge. In 1627 he had married Elizabeth, daughter of John Saintloe and sister of the John Saintloe who became the husband of the incomparable Mary Wiseman. Waller died in 1629, and, as will be remembered, Aubrey at the age of three or thereabouts made a posthumous portrait of him. His curate had been Launcelot Morehouse, who had written against Francis Potter's book 666, *the Number of the Beast*; and who, when speaking with Aubrey of the 'Ho-ho-ho of Robin Goodfellow', did 'averre to me, *super verbum sacerdotis*, that he did once heare such a loud laugh on the other side of a hedge, and was sure that no Human voice could afford such a laugh'.

Walter Waller was followed by Robert Peyton, a younger brother of Sir John Peyton, baronet, of Isleham, Cambridge, and a gentleman who 'had travelled into Italy, studied the law, and was a Justice of the Peace, but afterwards took Holy Orders'. He could remember 'when the play called *Ignoramus* (made by one Ruggle of Clare Hall) was acted with great applause before King James, they dressed Sir Ignoramus like Chief Justice Coke and cutt his beard like him and feyned his voice', a drollery which was thought to have had the unforeseen result of setting the lawyers against the clergy, 'and shortly upon this Mr Selden wrote of Tythes *non jure divino*'. Robert Peyton, it will also be recalled, was brother-in-law of Theophilus Wodenote, who had recommended Bacon's *Essays* to Aubrey when a boy, encouraged him to talk about anti-quities, and gossiped of such matters as the Earl of Radnor's grandfather having been a furze-cutter in Cornwall. Peyton's large and widely connected family were related to those of Danvers and Bertie, both of which clans played a great part in Aubrey's life.

This vicar had died in 1644, and was succeeded at Chalke by John Sloper, whose mother was sister to the 'ever-memorable' John Hales. Sloper, when a boy at Eton, had seen Benjamin Oughtred, then a very old man, the 'Butler' (or, more accurately, the Registrar) of the College, and father of William Oughtred, the famous mathematician. Aubrey was godfather to Mr Sloper's son John (who was baptised 7 February, 1649); and he noted of Abigail Sloper, the vicar's daughter: 'Pride; Lechery; ungrateful to her father; married . . . runne distracted . . . recovered.' John Sloper himself died in 1691.

VII

'A little before the death of Oliver, Protector, a whale came into the river Thames, and was taken at Greenwich', wrote Aubrey. ' 'Tis said Oliver was troubled at it.' On the afternoon of 3 September, 1658, the day following the great hurricane—'Oliver's storm'—Cromwell had died of 'a bastard tertian ague'. He was not buried until 23 November.

From Broad Chalke in 'March 1659' (probably 1660, *N.S.*) Aubrey attended 'a Meeting of gentlemen at the Devizes for choosing of Knights for the Shire', when 'it was wish'd by some that this Country wherein are many observable Antiquities, were surveyed in imitation of Mr Dugdale's *Illustration* of Warwick-shire: but it being too great a taske for one man, Mr William Yorke, (Counsellor at Lawe and a great lover of this kind of learn-ing) advised to have the labour divided. He himself would under-take the Middle division. I would undertake the North. T. Gore, Esq., Jeffrey Daniel, Esq., and Sir John Erneley would be assistants.

Judge Nicholas was the greatest Antiquary as to Evidences that this Country hath had in the memory of man: and had taken notes in his *Adversaria* of all the auncient Deedes that came to his hands. Mr Yorke had taken some memorandums too.' Aubrey adds a note: 'Who had these *Adversaria*? Ask Capt Chaloner and Mr Hulbert of Cosham his son-in-law for 'em.'

William Yorke was of Basset's Down and a member of the Middle Temple. He was married to Elizabeth, daughter of William Bower, of West Lavington, and widow of Henry Danvers,[1] of Baynton. He was a Member of Parliament in 1654 and 1661, and one of the trustees of Philip, Earl of Pembroke. In the Falstone day-book is noted: 'William Yorke, of West Lavington, gent., His goods and estate were for a short time under restraint on suspicion of delinquency, but enfranchised in April, 1649.'

Thomas Gore, of Alderton, was an amateur herald and genealogist, a great crony of Aubrey's, who often writes '*Quaere* T.G. *de hoc*' when uncertain on some tricky point of local history or heraldic lore. Later, as will be seen, they quarrelled; and Aubrey took to referring to his old acquaintance as 'the cuckold of Alderton'[2] and to complaining of his tiresome fads. Gore must, indeed, have been a pedant and bore of no common order. He came of a Wiltshire family of considerable antiquity and the name of his ancestral parish, Aldrington, had been corrupted in the course of time to Alderton. For this reason he would always—even when giving a receipt for a small sum—write 'Aldrington', usually identifying it as 'Aldrington *aliàs* Alderton'. The great event of his life was when he was pricked for High Sheriff of Wiltshire in 1680–81. He has left an elaborate account of this ceremony, from his setting out from his own door at 'Aldrington *aliàs* Alderton', of his ride to Salisbury Assizes, of all that was done there, and of the journey home. During his shrievalty he managed to become involved in some political squabble, and published his defence, which was called *Loyalty displayed and Falsehood unmasked in a letter*

---

[1] Great-grandson of Silvester Danvers (b. 1518). See chart II.

[2] The designation may have had reference to the Gore arms: *Or, three bulls' heads caboshed sable*. An effigy of Gore's brother, d. age 6, survives in Alderton Church. A Thomas Gore of Alderton was presented for a base born child. 1683.

to a friend, 1681. His will, too, is a document remarkable for its length, its extraordinary jumble of items, and its finical precision. Gore was, in short, a figure who steps straight from one of the comedies of the past (Mr Justice Shallow embodies his type for all time), obsessed with his own importance, always true to form in his eccentricity and irascibility, and—inevitably—the supposed victim of matrimonial deception.

Jeffrey Daniel was of St Margaret's, Marlborough, where members of the Daniel family were stewards to the Earls of Pembroke. Sir John Erneley (or Ernle) of Whetham, near Calne, was many years later (in 1672) to marry the widow of Aubrey's friend Charles Seymour; and to become Chancellor of the Exchequer in the first year of James II.

Robert Nicholas,[1] of Roundway (or Rynd-way), a house near Devizes, where the Nicholas family had lived since 1300, was a Baron of the Exchequer and a local figure of some mark. His daughter, Anne, was married to Thomas Hulbert, of Corsham, to whom Aubrey refers in his note about the *Adversaria*, together with Captain Robert Chaloner. Captain Chaloner (son of John Chaloner, of Lloran in Denbigh) appears to have leased Roundway in 1657 from Robert Nicholas (one of whose brothers had married Chaloner's sister Joan). Chaloner was Bluemantle Pursuivant in 1660, and Lancaster Herald from 1667 to 1675, when he died. In Aubrey's life he seems to have played some disagreeable part; and more will be said of him.

This meeting to elect the Knights of the Shire conveys clearly

[1] Judge Nicholas was of the Long Parliament and had been prosecuting counsel at Laud's trial, when he had spoken violently against the archbishop. He had also been appointed one of the assistant judges to try King Charles I; but he seems to have been shrewd enough somehow to have avoided attending the proceedings on this occasion. Anthony Wood said of him: 'In his pleadings some sense, but was extream, virulent, and had foul language at his command.' A few years before this meeting he had come near to being hanged during Penruddock's rising, when, with Judge Rolle, he had been seized at Salisbury and ordered to proclaim the King. As a prominent supporter of the Commonwealth Government, it was proposed at the Restoration to exempt him from indemnity; but a warrant for his pardon was issued and he settled at Seend in Wiltshire.

the mixed political opinions and party adherences of Aubrey's country neighbours, the presence of Judge Nicholas, and no doubt others, considerably modifying the predominantly Cavalier flavour. The mingling also suggests March 1660, rather than 1659—Cromwell dead some eighteen months—when 'the system of extemporary government which had been held together only by force, naturally fell into fragments when the force was taken away'. It does credit to the serene outlook of these gentlemen of Wiltshire that, at a moment when the political confusion that had descended upon the country was of a kind to have excused some apprehension, they should have found this antiquarian project an important item on the agenda. However, in spite of their excellent intentions, 'this good design vanished *in fumo Tabaci* and was never thought of since', says Aubrey, who alone stuck to his undertaking, and began his second work on the county—*An Essay towards the Description of the Northern Division of Wiltshire*. For the next eleven years much of his time in the country was spent in examining churches, transcribing memorial inscriptions, and picking up any chance scraps of information which might be supplied by the tradition of the houses he visited. All this promiscuous research went towards forming his *Wiltshire Collections*.

VIII

In February 1659 his grandfather, Isaac Lyte, had died; and Aubrey nearly broke his own neck in Ely 'Minster', presumably engaged there in executing one of those feats of precarious balancing demanded of those who engage in archaeological enquiry. The following day his horse tumbled 'over and over', but without serious mishap to the rider. In April he went with Edmond Hobbes, brother of Thomas Hobbes, into the room where the philosopher had been born, a visit he recorded in case posterity might have supposed that Edmond Hobbes's own house in Malmesbury had been the scene of this event. In July his friend Stafford Tyndale wrote from Alençon trying to persuade Aubrey to make a further effort to come abroad: 'Allow yourself but two hundred pounds a year and in the company I'le bring you acquainted with, you may live and travel like a Prince. But if you think to performe any thing alone, your expenses will doubly increase, besides the hazards you'l expose your self to. I speake this by a Spirit of Prophecy, foreknowing that you will have a rambling fitt before you dye, and passe this occasion, you will never meet soe good againe, while you live; whether you consider the conjuncture of affaires at this present; or the cheapnesse of travelling, when you will be obliged to not more than the care of your owne person, and a little laquay, or none if you please, because our servants shall supply that place.'

All this time Aubrey was keeping the terms of the legal year in London, and moving about among the wide circle of *virtuosi*, where the arts, philosophy, science, and politics found some common ground. Except that Cromwell ruled 'with kingly and more than kingly power', the upheaval of the Civil Wars had left much untouched. When the Protector, dining at Hampton Court in 1657 or 1658, told Lord Arundel of Wardour and Lord Fitzwilliam that he had been in all the counties of England and that Devon husbandry was the best, Aubrey overheard the remark, and, vesting it with the authority that the chance words of princes bear, noted this opinion in his chapter on the agriculture of Wiltshire.

Some of Aubrey's London friends, like those in Wiltshire, used to run a risk of being caught in dangerous political enterprises. Nicholas Tufton[1] (later Earl of Thanet, and a patron when misfortunes overtook Aubrey) was imprisoned in the Tower on two occasions for nearly a year on suspicion of having plotted against Cromwell. Another friend, Tom Mariet, whom Aubrey had known at Trinity (where he had made a name for

---

[1] Nicholas Tufton, 3rd Earl of Thanet: b. 1631: styled Lord Tufton, 1632–1664; lived in France during some of the period of the civil wars, but imprisoned in the Tower, Dec. 1655–Sept. 1656, and Sept. 1657–June 1658; succeeded to the peerage, May 1664. By the death of his cousin, Lady Alathea Hungerford, 1678, he became, in right of his maternal grandmother, Lord Clifford; mar. April 1665 Elizabeth, d. of Richard Boyle, Earl of Burlington. d.s.p. 1679 aged 48.

himself by his 'sharpe Repartie' to the Parliamentarian Visitation
—that he would submit~to their authority 'with all my heart if
you'll submit to the King'), was engaged in Royalist intrigue.
Mariet, who was 'of Whitchurch, in Warwickshire, Esq.',
shared rooms with Aubrey in the Middle Temple. This was about
the year 1654 (and no doubt earlier), because Aubrey speaks of
Colonel (or rather Major-General) Massey[1] being a party to the
discussions. Massey and Mariet were 'in London privately',
corresponding with the King, 'who wrote them letters with his
own hand which I have seen'. Mariet was also 'tampering' with
General Monk to see if his attitude could be sounded regarding
the possibility of the King's return; 'and they could not find any
inclination or propensity in G[eorge] M[onk] for this purpose
scil. to be instrumentall to bring in the king. Every night late, I
had account of all their transactions abed,' wrote Aubrey, 'which
like a sott as I was, I did not while fresh in my memory, committ
to writing, as neither had T[homas M[ariet]: but I remember in
the maine, that they were satisfied he had no more intended or
designed the king's restauration, when he came into England or
first came to London, then his horse did.'

IX

Since the death of Charles I, any eccentricities in forms of government had seemed possible, and in spite of Royalist sympathies,
Aubrey was enough a child of the age to share contemporary taste
for experiment in political theory. This showed itself in his membership of the Rota Club, founded by James Harrington, a friend
whose 'genius lay chiefly towards politiques and democraticall
government'.[2] Harrington (who had been in the service of the

---

[1] Afterwards Sir Edward Massey, who had deserted the King for
Parliament in 1642; but, as a Presbyterian unacceptable to the officers of
the New Model, had to escape to Holland in 1648, taking service with
Charles II. He was distrusted by the Royalists, but engaged in much
plotting, being in England in 1654 and 1656, and also soon after Oliver
Cromwell's death.

[2] In a lively and sometimes moving account of Harrington's life,
Aubrey writes: 'He was by order of the Parliament made one of his

Elector Palatine and was a close friend of Andrew Marvell) was the author of *The Commonwealth of Oceana*, a political romance, published in 1656, which, in the manner of the period, depicts the author's conception of an ideal Government. At the head of the state was to be a prince or Archon (antitype of Cromwell), elected like all the other magistrates by the people, who are controlled by a moderate aristocracy on the Venetian model, estates being limited to £3000 a year. An elaborate system of rotation and balloting was to secure the equilibrium of all interests; and it was after this aspect (developed in other writings by him) of Harrington's constitution that the club was named. The *Oceana* was also intended to provide a criticism of the political theories of Hobbes.

These conceptions were not in themselves specially interesting or original, though Harrington was not without a grasp of the limitations of government in its relation to social life, and of the unavoidable nature of the contemporary struggle for power. The idea of a political debating society was, on the other hand, something entirely new; and Harrington's circle may be compared with the political clubs that sprang up at the time of the French Revolution. The meetings took place at the Turk's Head in New Palace Yard, 'at one Miles's where was made purposely a large ovall table, with a passage in the middle for Miles to deliver his Coffee. About it sat his disciples and the virtuosi. The discourses in this kind were the most ingeniose, and smart, that ever I heard, or expect to heare, and bandied with great eagernesse: the arguments in the Parliament howse were but flatt to it. . . . Here we had (very formally) a ballotting-box, and balloted how things should be varied, by way of tentamens. The room was every evening full as it could be cramm'd. I cannot now recount the whole number:—

Majestie's bedchamber at Holmeby, &c. The King loved his company; only he would not endure to hear of a Commonwealth: and Mr Harington passionately loved his Majestie. Mr Harington and the King often disputed about government. He was on the scaffold with the king when he was beheaded; and I have at these meetings oftentimes heard him speake of King Charles I with the greatest zeale and passion imaginable, and that his death gave him so great a griefe that he contracted a disease by it; that never anything did goe so near him.'

Mr Cyriack Skinner, an ingeniose young gentleman, scholar to
John Milton was chaire-man.' The rest of the company included:
Harrington's great friend Henry Nevile; Maximilian Petty, 'a very
able man in these matters, and who had more than once turn'd the
councill-board of Oliver Cromwell, his kinsman'; Edward Bagshaw; Pepys (whose shrewd and practical instincts were too strong
for such political romanticism to attract him for long); and many
others in Aubrey's circle. Thomas Mariet and John Hoskyns
occur in this list, but later he struck out their names, perhaps
because he did not feel sure enough about their presence at the
Rota. Aubrey himself—with the Earl of Tyrconnel, John Birkenhead (author of *Mercurius Aulicus*), and 'several officers'—was only
an 'auditor'.

Although greatly enjoyable, the meetings (which lasted from
November 1659 to February 1660) were not always peaceable:
'We many times adjourned to the Rhenish-wine howse. One time
Mr Stafford and his gang came in, in drink, from the taverne, and
affronted the Junto (Mr Stafford tore the orders and minutes).
The soldiers offered to kick them downe stayres, but Mr Har-
rington's moderation and persuasion hindred it.'

To Aubrey, detached, easy-going, and, it must be admitted,
fundamentally uninterested in the practical problems of government, there seemed much to be said for the King, much to be said
for the views of theorists like Harrington; but little or nothing
to recommend the men who were then in power; and, as he
remarked:

'The doctrine was very taking, and the more because, as to
human foresight, there was no possibility of the king's returne.
But the greatest part of the Parliament-men perfectly hated this
design of rotation by ballotting; for they were cursed tyrants, and
in love with their power, and 'twas death to them, except 8 or 10,
to admitt of this way, for H. Nevill proposed it in the Howse, and
made it out to them, that except they embraced that modell of
government they would be ruined—*sed quos perdere vult Jupiter etc. hos
&c.* Pride of senators for life is insufferable; and they were able to
grind anyone they owed ill will to powder; they were hated by the
armie and their countrey they represented, and their name and

memorie stinkes—'twas worse than tyranny. Now this modell
upon rotation was:—that the third part of the senate should rote
out by ballot every third yeare, so that every ninth yeare the Howse
would be wholly altered; no magistrate to continue above three
yeares, and all to be chosen by ballot, than which manner of
choice, nothing can be invented more faire and impartial.'

However, the time was near when General Monk was to make
'all these airie modells' vanish: and then ''twas not fitt, nay
treason, to have done such; but I well remember that he [Harring-
ton] several times (at the breaking up) sayd, "Well, the king will
come in. Let him come in, and call a Parliament of the greatest
Cavaliers in England, so they be men of estates, and let them sett
but seven years, and they will all turn Common-wealthe's men"'
—a prophecy which was to prove not far wide of the mark.

Events were taking shape in England. At Oxford in 1658 the
Mayor, with his civic officials and the troopers guarding them,
when they tried to proclaim Richard Cromwell 'Protector', were
pelted with turnips and carrots; and at a later stage Aubrey noted
that an anonymous commentator wrote these words on the door of
the House of Commons:

> *Till it be understood*
> *What is under Monke's hood*
>   *The citizens putt in their hornes.*
> *Untill the ten days are out*
> *The Speaker haz the gowt,*
>   *And the Rump, they sitt upon thornes.*

As for Monk, he came out on horseback one February evening in
1660, and the mob, says Aubrey, 'were so violent that he was
almost afryd of himself, and so, to satisfie them (as they use to doe
to importunate children) *Pray be quiet, yee shall have a free Parliament.* This about seven, or rather eight as I remember at night.
Immediately a loud holla and shout was given, and the bells in the
city ringing, and the whole citie looked as if it had been in a flame
by the bonfires, which were prodigiously great and frequent and
ran like a traine over the citie, and I saw some balcones that began
to be kindled. They made little gibbetts, and roasted rumps of

mutton: nay, I sawe some very good rumps of beefe. Healths to the king, Charles II, were drunke in the streets by the bonfires, even on their knees; and this humor ran by the next night to Salisbury, where there was the like joy; so to Chalke, where they made a great bonfire on the top of the hill; from hence to Bland-ford and Shaftesbury, and so to the Lands-end: and perhaps it was so over all England.'

CHAPTER FOUR

The Royal Society; and Joan Sumner (1660–1669)

I

ON HIS birthday, 29 May, 1660, King Charles II, after the bleak years in the wilderness, again entered London. The 'lowd musick' played him in, says Aubrey, to the accompaniment of one of the brisk works of William Yokeney, the Wiltshire lutenist and composer of songs; encouraging, but still a reminder that to the question of royal popularity there might yet be two sides:

> What if the King should come to the City
>   Would he be then received I trow,
> Would the Parliament treat him with rigor or pity?
> · Some doe think yea, but most doe think no, &c.

For the time being at any rate there was, however, little doubt upon this point, the people on the whole showing themselves delighted that 'they were freed from the chaines of darknesse and confusion which the presbyterians and phanaticks had brought upon them'; and, as Anthony Wood added to this entry in his diary, 'some of them seeing what mischief they had done tack'd about to participate of the universal joy, and at length clos'd with the royal partie'. Celebrations continued, and Aubrey recalled that at Malmesbury 'were so many and so great vollies of shot, by the inhabitants of the Hundred, that the noise so shook the pillars of the Tower, that one pillar and the two parts above fell down that night'.

Poor Harrington was arrested, committed to the Tower, and then sent with sad results to Portsea Castle, a confinement described by Aubrey:

'His durance in these prisons (he being a gentleman of a high spirit and hot head) was the procatractique cause of his deliration

or madnesse; which was not outrageous, for he would discourse
rationally enough and be very facetious company but he grew to
have a phancy that his persperation turned to flies, and sometimes
to bees—*ad cetera sobrius*; and he had a timber *versatile* built in
Mr Hart's garden (opposite to St James's parke) to try the experiment. He would turn it to the sun and sit towards it; then he had
his foxtayles there to chase away and massacre all the flies and
bees that were to be found there, and then shutt his chassees.
Now this experiment was only to be tried in warm weather, and
some flies would lie so close in the cranies and the cloath (with
which it was hung) that they would not presently show themselves.
A quarter of an hower after perhaps, a fly or two, or more, might
be drawen out of the lurking holes by the warmth; and then he
would 'crye out, "Doe not you see it apparently that these come
from me?" 'Twas the strangest sort of madnes that ever I found
in any one: talke of anything else, his discourse would be very
ingeniose and pleasant.'

For others—and often not the most worthy—there were rewards; while much fluttering took place within formerly Cromwellian dovecotes in a belated effort to prove that the inmates had
in reality never had anything but the King's true interests at heart.
Batten (Pepys's superior in the Navy Office) was knighted, who
not long since had, from the sea, bombarded Henrietta Maria, so
that the Queen had been forced to leave her bed and take refuge
under a bank in the open fields. On the other hand, another and
older acquaintance of Pepys's, Aubrey's friend Captain Silas Taylor, the antiquary (who used to play and sing his part at the
musical meetings at Oxford attended by Anthony Wood), had to
fly the country; although, when all-powerful Parliamentarian
sequestrator in Hereford, he had earned the regard of the King's
party by his civility and restraint. From his exile at Dunkirk he
wrote Aubrey letters about gavelkind, sending him a copy of his
book on this subject. Aubrey's cousin, John Aubrey, of Llantrithyd, whose estates had been sequestrated during the interregnum,
was created baronet: and Josias Howe, that 'very great cavalier and
loyalist, and a most ingenious man', was restored to his fellowship
at Trinity, whence he had been driven by intruding commissioners.

In short, the processes that follow a great political upheaval took their accustomed and erratic course.

II

When he considered that the Restoration was a matter of certainty, Aubrey had written to Hobbes in Derbyshire strongly advising him to come to London, to be there before the King's arrival. Aubrey's plan was that a meeting should take place between Charles II and the philosopher at the studio of Samuel Cooper, for whom both Hobbes and Aubrey himself had recently sat; and had also drawn another friend, William Petty, at Aubrey's instigation.

'Knowing his majestie was a great lover of good painting,' says Aubrey , 'I must needs presume he could not but suddenly see Mr Cowper's curious pieces, of whose fame he had so much heard abroad and seen some of his worke, and likewise that he would sitt to him for his picture, at which place and time he would have the best convenience of renewing his majestie's graces to him.' Hobbes took Aubrey's advice; and 'it happened, about two or three days after his majestie's happy returne, that, as he was passing in his coach through the Strand, Mr Hobbes was standing at Little Salisbury-house gate (where his lord then lived). The king espied him, putt off his hat very kindly to him, and asked him how he did. About a weeke after he had orall conference with his majesty at Mr S. Cowper's, where, as he sate for his picture, he was diverted by Mr Hobbes's pleasant discourse. Here his majestie's favours were reintegrated to him, and order was given that he should have free accesse to his majestie, who has always much delighted in his wit and repartees.'

Aubrey calls Cooper[1] 'the prince of limners of this last age' and

---

[1] It was at Samuel Cooper's in 1669 that Dr Hugh Cressy told Aubrey that he had been the first to bring the works of Socinus to England; and that Lucius Cary, Viscount Falkland, reading them, had become the first English Socinian. Aubrey adds that Falkland had been painted by 'Jacob de Valke, who taught me to paint', indicating that his practical interest in painting had survived boyhood. This was probably

says that Hobbes's portrait was 'as like art could afford, and one of the best pieces he ever did'; adding that Charles II purchased this picture, and kept it in his closet at Whitehall. Aubrey was as familiar as Pepys with the world of painters' studios, and among the artists whom he frequented was Cooper's brother, Alexander Cooper, 'limner to Christina, Queen of Sweden, who was familiarly acquainted with Des Cartes'. He had stories to tell, much appreciated by Aubrey, about the great French philosopher and mathematician; though Samuel Cooper had remarked to Aubrey that 'Frenchmen are all ingeniose, few excellent; they (generally) want patience to goe through knotty studies'.

Another artist friend was Wenceslas Hollar, a Bohemian born at Prague, who had left his country on account of the wars there, earning his living in England by drawing, 'so that what he did for his delight and recreation only when a boy, proved to be his livelyhood when a man'. Hollar (whose father was a Knight of the Empire 'which is by letters patent under the imperial seale (as our baronets, I have seen it') had gone to the Low Countries on the outbreak of the Civil Wars, where he had stayed until 1649, and 'I remember he told me that when he first came to England (which was a serene time of peace) that the people, both poore and rich, did looke cheerfully, but at his returne, he found the countenance of the people all changed, melancholy, spightfull, as if bewitched. . . . He was a very friendly good-natured man as could be but shiftless as to the world, and dyed not rich'—a career and character that Aubrey was in a position to appreciate.

David Loggan,[1] a Dantziger, was also of this circle, and Aubrey had plans to borrow the portrait of Hobbes, bought by the King, in order to have it engraved by Loggan. Close contact still existed between art and science, painting and sculpture not yet remote from decoration and handicraft. Loggan recommended to Aubrey

Gerard Valck, a Dutch engraver employed by Loggan. Such pictures of Aubrey's as exist show an attractive sense of colour, but unfortunately the reddish-brown, yellow, and green tints which they usually contain become blurred and dull in reproduction.

[1] Aubrey's portrait by Loggan, now lost, was drawn for the *Natural History of Wiltshire* in 1686. (See p. 310 n 1.)

the manciple of one of the Oxford colleges, Edwards, who 'doth cut in Wood very well'; and Edward Marshall, Master Mason to the Crown (who had made Michael Drayton's monument in Westminster Abbey), is often cited by Aubrey as an authority on memorials and inscriptions. Another sculptor he knew was William Marshall; and he speaks with admiration of the statuary of the eccentric John Bushnell, and of his rival, Caius Gabriel Cibber ('Mr Sibbart', father of Colley Cibber), both acquaintances.

Bric-à-brac, also, could always claim Aubrey's attention. 'About the begining of March, 1660, I bought accidentally a Turkey-stone ring (it was not of the fine Hew rock but a greenish). It was then wholly serene. Towards the latter end of the month it began to be nubulated: and it continued to change the shape of its clouded face. This ring became very famous and I parted with it to the Honble. Roger Boyle.'

III

In July 1660 Aubrey (perhaps trying to forget the impending marriage of Mary Wiseman) visited Ireland with his friend Anthony Ettrick, an antiquary full of whims, member of the Middle Temple, who seems to have been something of an authority on Irish gossip. Another friend, William Petty (who had been of the Rota, where he had plagued Harrington with his troublesome statistics), may have provided some Irish introductions. Petty had already made—and lost—a fortune in Ireland, where the estates granted to him by the Commonwealth Government in payment for his famous 'Down Survey' had perforce to be returned to their former owners at the Restoration. Now he was in London, repairing his affairs with notable success, and moving about with his customary activity throughout intellectual circles and in the neighbourhood of the Court.

Aubrey stayed in Ireland for a month, spending some of his time drawing 'landskips on horseback symbolically' and observing the peculiarities of the Wild Irish, 'whom you will see sometimes on holidays, a whole parish running like madmen from hedge to hedge wren-hunting.' He also saw there a Testament 'in Saxon Character' in which the Magi were described as Druids. His return

journey across the pernicious waters of St George's Channel nearly
ended in disaster, as there was grave danger of shipwreck off
Holyhead. Later he wrote his impressions of that unhappy island
to Hobbes: 'From North Wales I went into Ireland, where I saw
the manner of living of the natives, scorning industry and luxury,
contenting themselves only with things necessary. That kingdom
is in a very great distemper, and hath need of your advice to settle
it; the animosities between the English and the Irish are very
great, and will 'ere long, I am confident, break into war.' Aubrey
goes on to thank Hobbes for the trouble he had taken in sitting
for his portrait—referring apparently to the picture executed by
John Baptist Caspars,[1] which Aubrey lent to Hollar to be engraved. In a letter on this subject Hollar prudently advised: 'If
you had occasion to aske for me of the people of the house, then
you must say the Frenchman Limner, for they know not my name
perfectly.' This portrait was subsequently presented by Aubrey to
the Royal Society.

Aubrey's friend John Hoskyns was travelling abroad at this
period, and he wrote several letters from Venice, where he stayed
at the time 'when the Duke marries the sea'. In one of these, dated
July 1661, Hoskyns says that he has nothing to report of the
famous Venetian courtesans but 'that their beauty is only fatness
and what is an easy product of it, impudence', adding: 'Pray get
me some of Mr Hobbs his future bookes before the Hangman burns
them.'

On 21 August, 1661, Stafford Tyndale wrote: 'The Algebraick
Questions are resolved and I have them for Mr Davenant or yourself. I saw your Mistress the other day in the street, soe that I can
tell you she is well, though I spake not to her. She simpar'd as if
you had been treating of the Portion in Yorkshire; and I must tell
you (to her advantage) that I esteeme her prettier then she was in
Spring Garden, or at Cooper's. . . . I have been urgent with Mr
Gaspar, but Mr Hobs his picture is not yet donne; I am angry and
troubled at it, yet no thing will prevaile he is so busy about his new

[1] Caspars (sometimes 'Jasper' or 'Gaspar') was a painter much employed by General Lambert. After the Restoration he became assistant to
Lely, and later to Kneller.

house, and some worke abroade . . . some vessels are gone already
to Portugall, and others are ready to transport Sir Richard Fanshawe, that all things are matured; and if you intend that journey,
you must hasten. But you have time sufficient and to spare, to prepare for Messrs Caspar and Faithorne the first of which (I beleeve)
will hardly see the Low Countries this yeare; and the other not till
Michaelmas be past, will think of Paris. Mr Anderton, long before
you wrote to me your first letter, had sold the pieces you speake of,
and sayes that you made no bargain with him at all; 'tis true you
fancied a couple of Landskips, but not imagining that you would
come to the price, he put them off to the next comer.'

It appears from this that Aubrey had had some idea of accompanying Sir Richard Fanshawe's embassy to Portugal, a mission to
carry Charles II's portrait to his bride, Catherine of Braganza.
Aubrey's association with painters is again indicated, and his rather
apologetic thanks to Hobbes for sitting for the Caspars portrait
are explained by the delays that had taken place. William
Faithorne,[1] planning to visit the Low Countries, was the elder
painter of this name, who drew Aubrey's portrait a few years later.
Faithorne had been involved in the Civil Wars and had now
established himself as an engraver and print-seller near Temple Bar,
where he carried on a considerable trade in Italian, Dutch, and
English prints. Henry Anderton painted historical subjects and
portraits, and was patronised by the King. We do not know the
identity of the lady referred to as Aubrey's mistress. 'Cooper's'
was no doubt Samuel Cooper's, the painter, and Tyndale's expressed preference for her appearance may have been in the flesh
rather than in a picture of her hanging in the studio. He returns to
her in a letter of 7 May, 1662, in which he writes to Aubrey: 'Wee
are not able to live here without your company, doe what we can
to preserve our selves. For your Queen has been very ill; her mother
is so at present with a Tertian; and our good friend Mr Hoskins is
sadly vexed with a violent and almost continued feaver.'

One morning in this same year Aubrey called on Hobbes,

[1] Faithorne was imprisoned for a time by the Roundheads. Later
he was released on condition that he left the country; and for a period he
lived in France. He had been allowed to return in 1650.

whose 'Greek *Xenophon* lay open on the board: sayd he, "had you come but a little sooner you had found a Greeke here that came to see me, who understands the old Greeke: I spake to him to read here in this booke, and he sang it: which put me in mind of what Mr Charles Cavendish had told me."' Hobbes had thought of Cavendish, says Aubrey, because he had travelled 'into Greece, all over; and that would not serve his turne but he would goe to Babylon, and then his governour would not adventure to goe any further with him: but to see Babylon he was to march in the Turks' armie. This account I had many years since, *scilicet* 1642, from my cosen Edmund Lyte, who was then gentleman usher to his mother the countess dowager [of Devonshire].' Cavendish had said that the Greeks sang their language which reminded Aubrey of the Herefordshire speech, and of how 'our old vicar of Kington St Michael, Mr Hynd, did sing his sermons rather than read them'.

IV

On 15 July, 1662, the Royal Society received its first charter. The group dated back to 1645, or even earlier, though that it was identical with 'the Invisible College'[1] is thought improbable. It was an institution that played a great part in Aubrey's life and of which he was proud to write himself a member. He had been concerned before its existence as a corporate body with that particular name: perhaps as far back as 1651, when scientific meetings had been held in William Petty's rooms, and elsewhere, in Oxford; where Petty had at one time 'kept a body that he brought by water from Reding a good while to read on, some way preserv'd or pickled'. '*The first begining of the Royal Society*,' wrote Aubrey, '(when they putt discourse in paper and brought it to use) was in the chamber of William Ball, Esqr., the eldest son of Sir Peter Ball of Devon, in the Middle Temple. They had meetings at tavernes before, but 'twas here when it formally and in good ernest sett up. In Dr Spratt's History [of the Royal Society] you may see when the patent was granted.'

He returns to the subject in his life of John Wilkins, Bishop of Chester. 'He was the principall reviver of experimentall philosophy

[1] See Syfret, *Notes & Records of the Royal Society*, Vol. 5, No. 2.

(*secundum mentum domini Baconi*) at Oxford where he had weekley an experimental philosophicall clubb, which began 1649, and was the *incunabula* of the Royal Society. When he came to London, they mett at the Bull-head taverne in Cheapside (*e.g.* 1658, 1659, and after) till it grew too big for a clubb, and so they came to Gresham College parlour.' By December 1660 the number of members of this Society was fifty-five, and the weekly subscription one shilling.

His own nomination as a Fellow, on 20 May, 1663, gave Aubrey outward and visible status as a 'professed virtuoso', and was a mark of recognition of which he was appreciative, in spite of the criticism and denigration to which the Society had from some quarters to submit. These attacks were by no means negligible. Roger North says that this distinguished assemblage was, at its inception, 'made very free with by the ridiculers of the town'. Samuel Butler composed verses making fun of it, and even a number of years later Evelyn could note in his diary: 'Then follow'd Dr South, the University's orator, in an elegant speech, which was very long: and not without some malicious and indecent reflections on the Royal Society, as underminers of the University, which was very foolish and untrue, as well as unseasonable.' Dr South, as will be seen in connexion with Anthony Wood, many years later, was fond of making tart remarks, to his cost. However, Charles II gave the newly founded body every encouragement, attended its meetings, and granted the Society a coat of arms. The membership was soon increased to some two hundred and fifty, a large number considering the total of literate persons existing at that time. Men of widely different character, attainment, and aim were included. Sir Kenelm Digby, William Petty, and John Evelyn were on the council, while Dryden, Wren, and Hooke were nominated at the same time as Aubrey.

Pepys was, of course, a member, and it is a little surprising that he never mentions Aubrey in his diary: though to one of his methodical and acquisitive character, Aubrey's happy-go-lucky nature and looming bankruptcy may have suggested a cautious approach, even in the early days. In Aubrey's writings, Pepys appears only twice, in an account of Merton Abbey, where Aubrey says: 'the Bells of St Mary Overy did come from this Abbey: for so Mr Pepys and the Parishioners do say'; and, in a second place, when Aubrey is discussing the origin of the Broad Arrow as a Royal Mark (which Aubrey thought to have been brought in by the Normans with cross-bows): 'Mr Secretary Pepys, Secretary of the Navy, tells me that all his Majestie's timber trees for the Navy are marked with this Marke: and all ships, boates, &c, vessels that are impressed for his Majestie's service are marked with this marke.' A colleague of Pepys in the Navy Office, William, 2nd Viscount Brouncker, was the first President of the Royal Society, considered by the diarist 'a rotten-hearted false man', and one of whom to beware. Others, as will be seen, took the same view of Brouncker, who was, however, an accomplished mathematician.

'I remember one St Andrewe's day,' says Aubrey, '(which is the day of the generall meeting of the Royal Society for annuall elections), I sayd "methought 'twas not so well that we should pitch upon the Patron of Scotland's day, we should rather have taken St George or St Isidore" (a philosopher canonised). "No," said Sir William Petty, "I would rather have it on St Thomas day, for he would not beleeve till he had seen and putt his fingers in the holes", according to the motto [of the Society] *Nullius in verba.*' Aubrey had more in common with the general work of the Society than might be thought, even if his interests were, on the whole, in the past rather than the future, and the present most appealed to him in so far as the characters and behaviour of contemporaries were concerned. The atmosphere of enquiry and learning, often of a distinctly unprofessional sort, engendered by the meetings, was one in which he felt himself at home; and it was through his membership that, in 1663, he came in contact with Charles II.

The King, 'discoursing one morning with my Lord Brounker and Dr Charleton concerning Stonheng, they told his Majestie what they heard me say concerning Aubury [Avebury] *sc.* that it did as much excell Stoneheng as a Cathedrall does a Parish Church. His Majestie admired that none of our Chorographers had taken notice of it: and commanded Dr Charleton to bring me to him the next morning.' Dr Walter Charleton was Physician-in-Ordinary to Charles II. He was 'a learned, unhappy man', author of a book (applauded by Dugdale and eulogised in some lines by Dryden) which appeared in 1663—intended as a counterblast to Inigo Jones's theory that the stones were of Roman origin—*Chorea Gigantum; or the most famous Antiquity of Great Britain, vulgarly called Stonehenge, standing on Salisbury-Plain, restored to the Danes*.[1] Charleton (as will be seen later) held a low opinion of Lord Brouncker, with whom the discussion was taking place. Aubrey goes on to describe his subsequent visit to the King: 'I brought with me a draught of it donne by memorie only: but well enough resembling it, with which his Majestie was well pleased: gave me his hand to kiss and commanded me to wait on him at Marleborough when he went to Bath with the Queen (which was about a fortnight after,) which I did: and the next day when the court were on their journey his Majestie left the Queen and diverted to Aubury, where I showed him that stupendous Antiquity, with the view thereof he and his Royal Highness the Duke of Yorke were very well pleased. His Majestie then commanded me to give an account of the old Camps and Barrows on the Plaines.

'As his Majestie departed from Aubury to overtake the Queen he cast his eie on Silbury-hill about a mile off: which he had the curiosity to see, and walkt up to the top of it, with the Duke of Yorke: Dr Charlton and I attending them. They went to Lacock to dinner: and that evening to Bathe; all the Gentrie and Commonaltie of those parts waiting on them, with great acclamations of joy &c.'

At Silbury the Duke of York was struck with a number of small snails on the turf of the hill-side; and commanded Aubrey

---

[1] This book suggests that the 'plain stones laid overthwart upon the Tops of the Columns' were for a 'convenient and firm footing for such [Danish] persons of honourable condition, who were principally to give their votes at the election of the King'. Aubrey notes in his transcript against this theory: ' 'Tis a monstrous height for the grandees to stand: they had need to be very sober, and have good Heads: not vertiginous. They should stand as the Wiltshire phrase is, upon Kit's brand iron.' Charleton's book was answered by Webb, Inigo Jones's son-in-law, in 1665.

to pick up some of these. Accordingly, Aubrey collected about a
dozen or more, and the next day, when the Duke 'was abed with
his Dutches at Bath', he told her of these snails, and sent Dr
Charleton to find Aubrey, so that she might see them. This was
perhaps with a view to some culinary preparation, as Aubrey
brings up the subject again in his *Surrey Collections*. 'As I rode
over Albury Down, I was wonderfully surpriz'd with those prodigious snails there, as big as two or three of ours. Mr Elias Ashmole
(Windsor Herald) told me, they were brought from Italy by the
old Countess of Arundel; who did dress them and eat them.'

Following Charles II's instructions, Aubrey surveyed Avebury
in the September of that year, 'with a plain-table and afterwards
tooke a Review of Stoneheng'. He duly presented the result of
this work to the King, who commanded him to print it. Aubrey's
excuse for not obeying this instruction was that, before offering
the public his treatise, he ought to see with his own eyes the similar antiquities in Wales; which he never 'had the opportunity to
do'. Besides which: 'There have been several Books writt by
learned men concerning Stoneheng, much differing from one
another, some affirming one thing, some another. Now I come in
the Rear of all by comparative Arguments to give a clear evidence
that these monuments were Pagan Temples; which was not made
out before: and have also (with humble submission to better
judgments) offered a *probability* that they were Temples of the
Druids . . . this Inquiry, I must confess, is gropeing in the Dark:
but although I have not brought it into a cleer light yet I can
affirm that I have brought it from utter darkness, to a thin Mist,
and have gonne further in this Essay than anyone before me.'

The papers that describe these antiquities formed the opening
chapter of Aubrey's *Monumenta Britannica*, a work which only recently achieved publication; nor did Aubrey see his way to for-
warding the King's energetic suggestion that human bones should
be sought by digging at the bases of the megaliths.[1] The stones of

[1] In 1666 Lawrence Washington, who owned the farm of West
Amesbury, which included Stonehenge, told Aubrey that 'in one of the
seaven Barrowes was lately digged up Coales and pieces of Goates hornes
and Stagges hornes'.

Avebury were also noted by Pepys, when he passed this way on the road to Marlborough some years later. Perhaps he was looking out for them as a result of conversations he had heard at Court.

V

Meanwhile there were always business worries—*opus et usus*—the borrowing of money, and perpetual riding up and down the country, where he was fortunate to have 'wonderfull credit'. In February 1662 his grandmother, Israel Lyte, died. The estates in Herefordshire were sold. Burlton went to a Wiltshire friend, Dr Thomas Willis[1] ('darke red haire (like a red pig): stammered much'), who belonged to the circle of scientists and physicians with whom Aubrey mixed in London. Dr Willis (who did some close negotiating regarding the deal) had discovered the medicinal properties in the water at the Oxfordshire village of Adstrop, and Anthony Wood calls him 'the most famous physician of his time'. On one of these returns to Herefordshire to clear up his business there, Aubrey had seen in 1660 that 'Pittiful poor old Weaver, Clarke of the Parish' of Canon-Peon, who as a handsome young man had first seduced Bess Broughton (later famous, when 'her price was very much—a second Thais'), who came of an ancient family in that neighbourhood.

The property at Stratford[2] was bought by Herbert Croft, Bishop of Hereford. The bishop was not above some haggling over this transaction, and wrote: 'I have made diligent enquiry into the estat by a neer and knowing dweller, and really I am afraid that together with the copyhold the uttermost is a hundred *per annum*: scarce any improvement to be made by the greatest industry; and whereas you talke of much wood, I am assured scarce enough for the necessary uses and fences; which are generally very

[1] Willis was brother-in-law of the redoubtable Dr John Fell, Dean of Christ Church, having married the latter's sister; and ancestor of the eighteenth-century antiquary Browne Willis, who subsequently inherited Burlton. *Cf.* 'Willisian Burleton' in Philip's poem *Cider*.

[2] This was, perhaps, Stretford, a small parish on the outskirts of Leominster.

badde and will cost much money to enclose them well. This I conceive to be the true state of the busines, and then all this considered and further that there is so much of it arable and so little meadow and pasture . . . eighteen years purchase will be in this country the full Valew: and this I shall give, paying you the total together if you please; I forgot one great inconvenience, you have only power for court Baron, the Leet another hath, which often proves vexatious to the tenants. I pray let me have your final answer that I may dispose of my matters accordingly.'

It was perhaps, on his return journey from Hereford, probably arranged so that he could visit his mother, who seems to have spent some of her widowhood in Somerset, that 'Anno 1663, June in my journey from Bristoll to Welles, walking down Dunderhill on foot, presently after a fine shower of Raine, I sawe a little thin mist arise out of the Ditch on the right-hand by the Highway's side; but coming neere to the place I could not discerne it. I had the curiosity to see whereabouts it was; and going back a little way, discerned it, and took notice of some mark by it. When I came to it my nose was affected by a smell that I remembered: but it came not immediatly into my mind *viz* the Smell of the canales that come from the Bathes at Bath to the Houses of Office which presently after came to my remembrance. By this time my Groome was come with the Horses, who though of ordinary understanding had his senses quick. I asked him if he smelt anything, who after a sniff or two, answered, the smell of the Bath. This place is about two parts of three of Dundery-hill. I have a conceit the water lies not very deep. The Owner of the Land might turne it to good Profit.'

Apparently there were other anxieties as well as those of business, for John Hoskyns (perhaps referring to the lady who simpered) wrote in January 1663: 'Some of your intimate acquaintances here have lately told me how extremely Amorous you are by nature and I am much inclined to credit that opinion when I take notice that the suddennesse of your departure from us, and the ill-pretended ground of the melancholy when you wrote last to mee, could not proceed from anything but the violent passion, the first a hopefull, the last an unsuccessful amour. Alas! and is

Shee froward, let her goe; You can doe well enough without 'hem.'

Whether or not Hoskyns's surmise was justified, we do not know. In the meantime Aubrey continued to enjoy and record his sober friendship with Hobbes. 'In 1664 I sayd to him "Me thinkes 'tis pitty that you that have such a clear reason and working head did never take into consideration the learning of the lawes '; and I endeavoured to perswade him to it. But he answered that he was not like enough to have life enough left to goe through with such a long and difficult taske. I then presented him the Lord Chancellor Bacon's *Elements of the Lawe* (a thin quarto) in order thereunto and to draw him on: which he was pleased to accept and perused: and the next time I came to him he shewed me therein two cleare paralogismes in the 2nd page (*one* I well remember was in page 2), which I am heartily sorry are now out of my remembrance.' According to Aubrey, this conversation resulted in Hobbes setting to work on his *De Legibus*, a treatise of which more will be said.

In the same year Aubrey managed to travel abroad at last, and there was an excursion to France. He landed at Calais on 11 June, 1664, and journeyed on to Paris, where Hobbes directed a letter to him as: 'Monsieur Aubray, Gentilhomme Anglois, Ches Monsieur de Houlle dans le Cloistre de St Julien le pouvre au Riche d'or; devant la Fontaine de St Severine pres du Chattelet.' Hobbes wrote approving the plan of seeing 'the Loyer and the country of Brittany and that about Geneva'. The philosopher remarked: 'I see you mean to husband all your time to the best advantage. I have nothing to add but my wishes for your safety and the continuance of your health, which is not to be despaired of in one that can temper himself from his excesses, and especially in fruit, as you can.' It is not known whether Aubrey in fact ventured as far afield as was his project. He went to Tours, and in August to Orleans, a centre (as Evelyn had rather smugly noted some years earlier) for those travellers who had a mind to indulge in the coarser pleasures. Few, indeed, who had not the taste, and the constitution, for deep potations cared to prolong their stay there; and it is therefore not surprising to learn that in this city Aubrey 'had a terrible fit of the

spleen and piles', against which ills an avoidance of fruit had
evidently proved an inadequate precaution. He also saw in the
hospital of Orleans a young man whose left cheek had been
gnawed by a werewolf, 'for, sayd he, had it been a wolfe he would
have killed me out right and eaten me up'. When, on 13 October,
he returned to England, *via* Dieppe, he brought with him a *laissez-
passer* (on which document he is described as 'Jean Aubré') for *'un
tableau de tapisserie a bordure doree Estant dans une Caisse'*, upon which
article it was recorded that the appropriate dues had been paid.

'At my returne to London from France,' says Aubrey, 'I went
to St Paul's Church to Prayers and to heare an Antheme: a French
youth that waited on me then, told me that the singing men and
boies had taken cold: they sang *enrouément*: he spake it ignorantly',
and Aubrey goes on to explain that: 'the French have much better,
stronger, and clearer voyces than the English: one may heare the
French singing from the French Church in Threadnedle Street as
far, or very near as far as the upper end of the street at St Martin-
Outwich-Church.'

This French boy, from the way Aubrey speaks of him and from
the letter that follows, was probably not 'Robert Wiseman', a
servant to whom Aubrey often refers, and of whom a word should
be said. In October 1664 George Ent (a friend of Aubrey's to
whom we shall return) wrote from Paris: 'I have enquired after
Robert and it seems his Master has taken another Servant I believe
much worse than himselfe, and the poor rogue is at present quite
destitute of a Service. I have not seen him since, but I doe intend,
next Wednesday come seven-night, and in the mean time to bring
him over to Mr Hughes: if your mind be altered since, I desire
that you would be pleased to write to mee that I may save you that
expence.' Ent adds an apology that Aubrey had previously been put
in the position of engaging a boy who had proved unsatisfactory.

These were probably the beginnings of 'my ingeniose faithfull
servant Robert Wiseman', over whose surname Aubrey often writes
the word 'Prudhome' and whom he sometimes calls 'Robinet'.
'Wiseman' was no doubt a convenient anglicisation of the French,
which also reminded Aubrey of 'that incomparable gentlewoman'
who had also borne that name. This certainly seems to be the

explanation, and there is a note 'R.W.'s daughter' beside Aubrey's comment that children of the French born in England 'doe naturally pronounce "a" fully'. Robert Wiseman's name is also noted beside another entry, referring to the Vale of the White Horse, which, wrote Aubrey, 'has the handsomest people of any part of England: and they are good-conditioned people: and there and Oxfordshire have a commendation at London for good faithfull servants'—servants presumably in the manner of Robert Wiseman. Wiseman could translate French and Italian books for Aubrey, and he became godfather to one of Hobbes's relations.

VI

In the following year, 1665, Hobbes spoke of Malmesbury, and told Aubrey 'that he was willing to do some good to the towne where he was borne: that his majestie loved him well, and if I could find out something in our country that was in his gift, he did believe that he could beg it of his majestie, and seeing he was bred a scholar, he thought it most proper to endow a free school there: which is wanting now . . . after enquiry I found out a piece of land in Bradon-forest (of about 25*li* per annum value) that was in his majestie's gift, which he had designed to have obtained from his majestie for a salary for a schoolmaster: but the queen's priests smelling out the designe and being his enemies, hindred this public and charitable intention.'

On another occasion, at about this period, Aubrey remembered going into the Strand with Hobbes, 'when a poor and infirme old man craved his almes. He beholding him with eies of pity and compassion, putt his hand in his pocket, and gave him 6*d*. Sayd a divine (*scil*. Dr Joseph Mayne) that stood by—"Would you have donne this, if it had not been Christ's command?" "Yea", sayd he, "Why?" quoth the other. "Because," sayd he, "I was in paine to consider the miserable condition of the old man: and now my almes, giving him some relief, doth also ease me." '

It must also have been in 1665 (though he notes the date as 1662) that Aubrey saw John Wilmot, 2nd Earl of Rochester, incarcerated in the Tower for abducting Elizabeth Mallet, an episode described by Pepys.[1] Aubrey mildly comments on Rochester that 'his youthly spirit and opulent fortune did sometimes make him doe extravagant actions. He was wont to say that when he came to Brentford the devil entered into him and never left him till he came into the country again to Adderbury and Woodstock.'

VII

Faithorne's portrait was executed in 1666, when Aubrey was forty years old. As a work of art this picture, intended as a frontispiece to the *Monumenta Britannica*, is an unpretentious piece, and makes Aubrey look younger than his age. The medium, a head and shoulders drawn in indian ink, the face lightly stippled in colour, need be thought none the worse of for being intended to record no more than would a photograph. Indeed, the impression conveyed of the subject is, perhaps, in accuracy much the same as that which the formality of a photographic sitting might also have presented, had such a means of taking a likeness been then available. There is the apprehensive glance, the hint of self-consciousness in the expression which recall the aspect so commonly found at a later date in albums of ceremonious photography. This is, naturally, a more lively picture than the engraved reproduction of the oil-painting attributed to Lely. The features depicted in the two portraits are sufficiently alike to make the authenticity of the subject of the earlier one tolerably certain. The ten years that passed between the two sittings seem on the whole to have improved Aubrey's appearance.

The Faithorne drawing shows a man (he was 'of middle stature') dressed apparently with more than usual elegance, whose face is so different from other seventeenth-century faces that it is tempting

---

[1] 'My Lord Rochester's running away on Friday night last with Mrs Mallet, the great beauty and fortune of the North, who had supped at Whitehall with Mrs Stewart, and was going home to her lodging with her grandfather, my Lord Haly [Hawley], by coach: and was at Charing Cross seized on by both horse and foot men, and forcibly taken from him, and put into a coach with six horses, and two women provided to receive her, and carried away.'

to suppose that the likeness is a good one. His nineteenth-century biographer, Britton, thought the features 'manly, bold, expressive, and intelligent'; but (sharing Dr Kettle's prejudice against false hair) considered that 'the monstrous and barbarous wig, however, not only disfigures the human countenance, but, like a bad and disgusting frame to a beautiful picture, was calculated to deteriorate and degrade the gem it enshrined'. The large sleepy eyes, the look of hesitation, and the lines of irony at the corners of the mouth give an air of sensibility (and suggest at the same time a lack of assurance) that has little in common with the lineaments of the soldiers, scholars, scientists, wits, and divines—saintly, dissipated, arrogant, or sceptical—who occupy the canvases of Vandyck and Dobson, Lely and Kneller. Here is the face of a man who has half explained to himself the follies of the world: who has failed; and yet achieved something—while so many of these men of action and affairs have sunk into oblivion, with the causes for which they lived and died, by some vitality less unreal than theirs, he has remained alive.

To draw from this portrait any deep conclusions about Aubrey's character would be somewhat fanciful, but the appearance it attributes to its subject well bears out the traits that emerge from his writings; the easy-going laziness, and inquisitive interest in people, blending so unaccountably an unworldliness with a deep appreciation of the world's ways, the powers of self-expression always trying to develop, yet somehow always handicapped from the start by an inherent incapacity.

VIII

Faithorne's portrait is much how he would have looked when, in the autumn of 1665, he became involved in what was perhaps the worst fiasco of his career, combining as it did, in the maximum degree, his endemic vexations at law and in love. The beginning of the mischief he notes as: 'November 1; I made my first addresse (in an ill howre) to Joane Sumner.'

The identity of Joan Sumner was for a long time unknown; and Dr Rawlinson, in his memoir published in 1719, went so far as to state that Aubrey had actually married this lady. The records of the Wiltshire Marriage Licences show that some evidence, in fact, existed which might have encouraged this erroneous conclusion. There is, however, unfortunately no reason to suppose that the misinformation has any such excusable basis as might be provided by a superficial search among these documents. Chancery proceedings and wills have provided new material, in addition to that found among the licences, scanty enough, but giving the outline of an episode which is interesting for the light it throws on the social life of the period; for the typical manner in which Aubrey is seen getting into a mess with a dangerous woman; and, not least, for the general implications of the story as an illustration of human relationships and behaviour.

The Sumners were a family living in the neighbourhood of Kington St Michael, sometimes three miles away at Sutton Benger, and sometimes at Seend, which is about twelve miles distant. Like the more eminent Childs or Methuens and many of the prosperous people in that part of Wiltshire, they were clothiers; and, although social position in the latter half of the seventeenth century is not always easy to define (as, for example, the ramifications of the Pepys family show), the available information strongly suggests that they were a family on the rising grade, moving from the middle class of merchants into that of squires and gentlemen. The prejudice against 'trade', as such, was a later development, and at this period younger sons from many great and ancient families became not only merchants but apprentices to skinners, maltsters, and such like. At the same time to be unquestionably 'a person of quality' was, naturally, a desirable thing, and metamorphosis with the help of a judicious marriage had for a long time been relatively common. It is possible that the Sumners were already looked upon as a more or less established 'county family'; but it is much more likely that Joan Sumner's union with Aubrey would be considered to have brought her advancement in the social scale.

Aubrey himself certainly held no very high opinion of the stock from which she came—the local clothiers, of whom he wrote: 'Our cloathiers combine against the Wool-masters, and keep their spinners but just alive: they steal hedges, spoil coppices, and are trained up as nurseries of sedition and rebellion.' This view is supported by records of the period. Aubrey also recounts a tradition, unsubstantiated by recent research,[1] of how the clothiers came to be at Seend and thereabouts. 'Mr Francis Lodwyck told me that mention is made in some of our histories that King Henry VII was in exile some time, and lived at the Duke of Burgundy's Court. The staple for our Wool was then at Calais, and 'twas manufactured by the Walloons. When he came to the Crown he sent for a number of them to come into England, to sett up the cloathing trade there, and Mr Lodwyck says the History says that they were settled in Wiltshire and that there are still severall of their descendants with Dutch and French names. I remember one Mr Goupy,[2] and I had to do with a merchant of his name at Tours. I remember I heard them say that heretofore this was a great place for cloathing, *sc.* about ninety and more years since. I have now forgot the reason for their removing hence to Tunbridge. The good houses were built by the Cloathiers. I know not any small country village that has so many well built houses.' Elsewhere, Aubrey says that these hypothetical Flemings had moved away, traditionally on account of a plague; but adds that he himself considered that there might have been another reason for their departure, which he attributed to the iron ore in the Seend water, unsuitable for the 'fulling' and washing of cloth.

This discovery about the quality of the water had been made by him when 'wayting then upon Joane Sumner' at her brother's house, where Aubrey was staying (accompanied by his servant, Robert Wiseman) for the Seend Revel, one of those bacchanalian rural festivals which enlivened the countryside, and which he satirised when he tried his hand later at writing a play. In the Sumners' house, the 'chalybiate waters in the well of the courtyard

[1] See *Wiltshire Woollen Industry*, by G. D. Ramsay, but for some suggested names of Flemish origin see *Wilts N. & Q.*, III, p. 380.

[2] This name, contracted to Guppy, appears at Seend and at Melksham according to Canon Jackson, who comments that the arms of the family were half English, half French: *Or, on a chevron between three roses slipped, three fleurs de lys.*

were more impregnated than any waters yet heard of in England. I sent some bottles to the Royal Society in June, 1667, which was tried with galles before a great assembly there. It turns so black that you may write legibly with it, and did there, after so long a carriage, turne as deepe as a deepe claret. The physitians were wonderfully surprized at it, and spake to me to recommend it to the doctors of the Bathe (from whence it is but about ten miles away) for that in some cases 'tis best to begin with such waters and end with the Bathe, and in some *vice versa*. I wrote severall times, but to no purpose, for at last I found that, though they were satisfied at the excellencies of the waters and what the London doctors said was true, they did not care to have the company goe from the Bathe. So I inserted it last yeare in Mr Lilly's Almanack, and towards the latter end of the summer there came so much company that the village could not contain them, and they are now preparing for building of houses against the summer. John Sumner sayth (whose well is best) that it will be worth to him 200*li* per annum.'[1]

This 'John Sumner, gent.', son of Edmund Sumner, clothier, of Sutton Benger (who had died about 1651), was brother of Joan Sumner, and owned one of the 'good houses' that Aubrey speaks of on Seend Green. The house still stands there, with its stone escutcheon above the door, bearing the arms to which the Sumners pretended.[2] This coat, like plenty of others, was unauthorised by the College of Arms, and at least one member of the family, Thomas Sumner (whose residence is recorded as bearing the ominous name of 'Passion's Mill' and who was possibly Joan's uncle), disclaimed his right to coat armour together with his usurpation of 'the name and title of gentleman' at the Visitation of 1623, when he was inscribed in the Heralds' list headed '*ignobiles omnes*'.

The family seem also to have had puritan tendencies, because Aubrey says that there had been a great deal of painted glass in Seend church, until it was 'beaten down by one William Sumner,

---

[1] Aubrey himself had some idea of profiting from this discovery, and he noted that: 'It would be a prudent way of laying out money, to build a handsome convenient House of entertainment for the Waterdrinkers at Seende and to make a fine Bowling green there.'

[2] *Vert, a fess dancetté ermine.*

of the parish, about the yeare 1648'. The clothiers, as a class, found no inconsistency in combining revolutionary sentiments with oppression of their weavers, and Seend seems to have been something of a centre of political disaffection. Judge Nicholas[1] had settled there after the Restoration. In April 1663 he had attended a vestry meeting and noted the appointment of John Sumner as one of the 'Surveyors of the Highway'. Of Joan herself, Aubrey says no more than to record his lasting regret that he ever became entangled with her. As in the case of Katherine Ryves, there is nothing to indicate a sentimental attachment. On the other hand, there exist a few trifling sidelights on Joan's character which suggest that she may have been a masterful woman of a kind that might well have exercised some sort of a hold over a man of Aubrey's temperament. He quotes, for example, her views on the subject of a local tragedy which seem to imply on her part a considerable firmness of purpose. 'A wench being great with child drowned herself in the river Avon, wher having layn twenty-four houres, she was taken up and brought into the church at Sutton Benger, and layd upon the board, where the coroner did his office. Mistress Joan Sumner hath often assured me that the sayd wench did sweate a cold sweate when she lay dead: and that she severall times did wipe off the sweat from her body, and it would quickly return again: and she would have had her opened, because she did believe that the child was alive within her and might be saved.' The discussion in itself and Joan's recommendation suggest at least an absence of squeamishness on her part with regard to such subjects. She had told Aubrey of a recipe (said to be used by thieves) to hinder dogs from barking—'Boares fatt and cummin seeds mixed in a horne'.

Another matter is of some significance. On 10 July, 1665—scarcely four months before Aubrey's 'first addresse'—a licence was

---

[1] Nicholas will be remembered as having attended the Devizes meeting of 1659, when Wiltshire antiquarian projects had been discussed. A warrant against him was applied for in 1664 on the grounds that he 'in a bragging and boasting way did glory that he was the man that drew up the charge against his late Majesty; and being reproved thereof said if it were to do again he would do the same, etc.'

taken out at Salisbury in which the parties to be married were:
'Samuel Gayford, of Bulkington, aged 27, yeoman' and 'Joan
Sumner, of Sutton Benger, aged 29, spinster'. Nine months later
another licence was taken out at the same place, but this time it
was Aubrey who was to be the bridegroom: who,[1] for his part,
recorded 1666 as a bad year. 'This yeare all my businesses and
affaires ran kim kam. Nothing took effect, as if I had been under
an ill tongue. Treacheries and enmities in abundance against me.'
There was worse in store, and the next mention of Joan Sumner is:
'Arrested in Chancery Lane at Mrs Sumner's suite.'

Legal proceedings now fell thick and fast: '1668 Feb. 24 a.m.
about 8 or 9, triall with her at Sarum. Victory and 600*li* dam-
mage, though devilish opposition against me.' And again: '1668:
July 6 was arrested by Peter Gale's malicious contrivance, the day
before I went to Winton for my second triall, but it did not retain
me above two howres; but did not then goe to the triall.' Finally:
'1669: March 5 was my triall at Winton from 8 to 9, the judge
being exceedingly made against me, by my Lady Hungerford. But
4 of the Venue[2] appearing, and with much adoe, gott the moiety
of the Sarum verdict, *viz.* 300*li*.'

A search among the legal cases of the period has thrown a little
light upon this unpleasant affair. By no means all its details are
clear, but some indication of the events leading up to the dispute
may be gathered from the papers that have been found. The two
earliest documents (neither of which are quoted in full) appear
to belong to the period November 1667, the first being *The Bill
of Complaint of John Aubrey and his Mother Deborah against Joan Sumner*,
in which the negotiations of the two former to borrow £100 from
the latter are recited; and an account is given of how 'having thereby gott some acquaintance and Intymacy with her the said Joane
and perceaving that she had a good fortune and estate which was

[1] 'John Awbrey of Easton Pierse in Kington St Michael, gent., and
Mris Joane Sumner, of Sutton Benger, sp., Bdmen: William Browne, of
Sarum, tailor, and Joseph Gwynne, of Easton Pierse, yeoman. Not
attested, but one bondsman signs: Jos. G. makes his mark only. Aprile
11, 1666.'

[2] Used in the legal sense of place of trial of an action.

at her owne dispose and the said Joane manyfestinge much kindnesse and friendship', Aubrey became a suitor, and marriage was agreed upon. However, there remained not witnesses to this 'but such as are since dead or gonne into remote parts'; while Joan 'doth now most unconsoyonably refuse to marry with and take your Orator to be her husband'. To this, Joan Sumner's 'Answeare' stated that she did not know why Aubrey should suppose that she should marry him, since his estate was 'all or for the most part' in mortgage, and he had said 'that hee thought this defendant would come to my Lady Hungerfords her Almeshowse and used other opprobrious Speeches with strange manner of usage', so that she had laid aside all thought of marriage 'conceiving that in all possibility if once the marriage should take effect his usage and carriage to this defendant would be far worse and more Extravagant'. She 'utterly refused' to marry him and 'conceives that no promise or ingagement that she has made with him can oblige her thereunto'.

Further proceedings before the Lord Keeper, Sir Orlando Bridgeman, took place on 8 February, 1669, at which Joan Sumner of Sutton Benger, spinster, complains that Edward Adye, of Seagry, gent.,[1] in or about 1664 became indebted to her for sums amounting to £50, for which he entered into the obligation of a penalty sum of £150, to be paid on a certain day, since past, as was shown by bonds that could be produced. Further, 'John Awbrey, late of Chalke, Esq., in or about 1666 became an ernest suitor in the way of marriage' to her. In the treaty of marriage that followed her acceptance of him as a husband, Aubrey had proposed to settle on Joan, for her jointure, all his lands at Easton Pierse 'discharged from all manner of incumbrances'. In spite of this undertaking, Joan Sumner alleged that the lands in question were already mortgaged for a 'great and considerable sum' to one '— Scroope, Esq., late of Castle Coombe, Wilts'. This was John Scrope, of Castle Combe, who was married to Anna, sister of Aubrey's friend Thomas

---

[1] In the *Natural History of Wiltshire* Aubrey remarks: 'Ganders are vivacious animals. Farmer Ady of Segary had a Gander that was fifty years old, what the soldiers killed. He and his Gander were both of the same age.' Perhaps 'Farmer Ady' was one with 'Edward Adye, Gent.'

Gore, 'of Aldrington *aliàs* Alderton', the amateur herald, who
had also attended the Devizes meeting. Aubrey mentions Scrope
several times in his writings, and says that his hair, 'like that of
Thomas Randolph, the poet', was 'of a very light flaxen, almost
white'.

The documents go on to recite how Aubrey, not having enough
money of his own to redeem these lands of Easton Pierse, 'prevailed' on Joan Sumner (according to her own account) to give him
the bonds mentioned above (relating to her transactions with
Adye), with which he, Aubrey, might recover the sums with interest, and use this money towards discharging the mortgage. But
'if the marriage did not take effect' the whole 'benefit' of the obligation should remain on her.

Joan Sumner's case was that the treaty of marriage had not 'taken
effect' and the bonds should accordingly have been delivered up to
her. She accused Aubrey and Adye of conspiring between them to
defraud her; and, not only of refusing to repay the money lent,
but also of failing to return the bonds 'in specie'. Adye, she complained, sometimes pretended that he had paid the sums and that
the bonds were long since cancelled; while Aubrey pretended that
she, Joan Sumner, was to have no benefit from them.

Aubrey's answer (18 February 1669) to this accusation was that
he had heard that Adye had entered into a bond with Joan Sumner;
and that when, in 1666, he himself was a suitor for her hand, he
had offered to settle on her, with other lands, the farm at Easton
Pierse. He admitted that at that time part of the land was under
mortgage to Mr Scrope for the payment of £500; but he denied
that he had 'endeavoured to prevail' on Joan Sumner to lend him
the money to redeem this mortgage. He added that he had had no
money from her except as set forth below.

'Being invited by some of the complainant's friends to become
a suitor to Joane in the way of Marriage did accordingly do the
same and on coming to her house she did very kindly receive him
and entertained him very affectionately several months together.'
It was then arranged that she should have £2000 as her marriage
portion, while Easton Pierse was to be settled on her (and her
heirs males begotten of her by Aubrey) for life. The farm was to be

surveyed, etc., by her brother and others. The settlement was sealed and Aubrey expressed a hope that the marriage should be solemnised immediately after sealing.

Joan Sumner agreed that £500 should be paid in the first place to Mr Scrope; but some of this money she wished to come from the amount that was owed by Adye. That was the whole story; and he, Aubrey, was waiting for the marriage, 'which he was always ready to have performed and still is ready to consummate the same if the Complainant shall so think fit'. He denied that Joan Sumner had given him the bonds named. She gave him bonds of money due to be paid to Mr Scrope.

Edward Adye's answer, given 29 April, 1669, was that, having need of money, he had borrowed from Joan Sumner the amounts named. He had, however, paid them back with interest 'long since'. He had heard the story of Aubrey's engagement to marry Joan. A further stage of the case was that, on 7 February, 1670, there was an Order in Chancery that an injunction be issued to stop the proceedings at law of John Aubrey against Joan Sumner until he had answered the plea put in by her. It should be added that in November 1668 Joan Sumner brought another action, similar in certain respects to her suits against Aubrey and Adye (except that no question of marriage was involved) against one Richard Lester (or Lessiter) of Wiltshire, husbandman, who utterly denied her allegation that she had lent him money.

To conclude the career of Joan Sumner herself, we find that, on 21 March, 1671, she was party to yet another marriage licence taken out at Salisbury, this time made out in the names of 'Robert Pope, of Wedmore, Somerset, gent., aged 40' and Joan Sumner of Sutton Benger, whose age is also given as 40—in all probability a slip of the pen rather than the revelation of another deceit. In March of the same year these two were married. Nine months later, in the following December, Joan, wife of Robert Pope, of Blackford, Wedmore, Somerset, died—no doubt in childbirth. In her will, dated 22 October, 1671, and proved April 1672, she expressed a wish that she should be buried in the chancel of the church at Sutton Benger. She left an exceptionally large number of petty bequests to relations and friends, symptomatic, perhaps, of her restless hope, even after death, to impose her personality on others.

In a letter dated 5 December, 1668, Aubrey wrote to Anthony Wood of some sinister part played in this affair by Robert Chaloner, mentioned earlier as the lessee of Roundway from his relations the Nicholas family, and the possible possessor of Judge Nicholas's *Adversaria*. Wood was at this period trying to obtain a post in the Heralds' College, and Aubrey says: 'There is not yet any vacancy: but he [William Dugdale] supposes one that I know that is not fitt for the place will be contented for money to resigne. He is Lancaster Herald: and one that the Office (and I thinke every body) hates, or ought to doe, if they knew him as well as I doe: for he hath been the *boutefeu*[1] to set me and my dame at Variance.'

To this Wood replied on 8 December, 1668: 'I am glad that I have such a friend as you to stir in my business. I would by no means have put you to this trouble, could I have reposed confidence in any other: The person that you mentioned in your letter that is now Lancaster Herald, his name is Chaloner, whose character I have heard from one of our neighbours that liveth at the Devizes. I know also that he hath been an Officer in the Army, a bustling man for the world, of great acquaintance with the gentry, and one that understandeth his trade well. I know that if a resignation be desired of him he will not stick to ask enough.'

What part Chaloner played in poisoning the relationship between Aubrey and Joan Sumner we do not know; but it is hard to see how the marriage could have turned out even a moderate success, unless Joan's character was in reality something very different from the aspect of her that emerges from the chancery proceedings. Aubrey, with his usual good-natured and reckless disregard for the future, after three years of litigation still stated that he was prepared to marry her; although it should be remembered that this

---

[1] *i.e.* firebrand:

      'But we, who only do infuse
        The rage in them like *boute-feus* . . .'—*Hudibras*.

Aubrey was obviously very familiar with this poem, and quotes from it more than once in his writings.

premise may well have been merely an integral and necessary part of his formal defence.

To grasp the rights and wrongs of the innumerable cases of this sort, usually involving comparatively small sums of money and deals in land, which fill the Bill Books of the Grand Sessions of the provincial circuits, is not easy, even when such cases are uncomplicated by the matrimonial considerations of this one. On the face of it the interest to be paid by Adye seems 'hard and unconscionable' enough; but parallels could easily be found for it among the unending suits of the smaller landowners, perpetually at law to recover money lent on the security of land. Even allowing for the chaotic state of Aubrey's personal affairs, and the muddling and dilatoriness with which he may have handled matters relative to the settlement, there remains on Joan Sumner's part a suspicious appearance of shuffling with the bonds, as if deliberately trying to bring off a more or less dishonest stroke. There may even have been a conspiracy on the part of some concerned to use Joan as a tool to bring final ruin to Aubrey in order to obtain his property for themselves. To have remained, in spite of her dowry, single until the age of twenty-nine or thirty in the seventeenth century suggests that some unusual impediment must have stood consistently in the way of her marriage; while the fact that she was prepared to break her engagement with Gayford to accept Aubrey's ostensibly better offer implies that her heart was not much involved in either case, especially in view of her subsequent treatment of Aubrey. There had, it appears, been others with whom a similar game had been played, for in a letter to Wood (dated 7 April, 1673), speaking of one, Dr Jolliff, Aubrey wrote: 'He found out something in Anatomy, which Mrs Sumner's business haz made me forgett: which unlucky woman amongst severall others besides yours J.A., undid the Doctor's eldest brother, who lives in the howse with her 3 yeares as I did one and 2 months: and he contracted to her and then she left him in the lurch.' It is tempting to suppose that in the end Aubrey felt some relief at having escaped Joan and her clothier relations.

Of the minor characters in the drama, the name of 'Peter Gale, yeoman' occurs among the Salisbury Marriage Licences; and again in the will (dated 21 October, 1670) of John Sumner, who had bought lands of a Peter Gale in Longley; while 'Peter Gale of Avon, yeoman' had been party to an indenture referring to the Chippenham neighbourhood in 1656. These records probably concern the author of the 'malicious contrivance' who caused Aubrey's arrest in 1668; although it must be remembered that Gale was a common name in Wiltshire, some of the Gale family being indeed (through the Lytes) distant relatives of Aubrey's. Samuèl Gayford, who had been engaged to Joan Sumner a few months before Aubrey took out his bond, appears again among the Salisbury Marriage Licences in 1671 as 'Samuel Gaysford of Kee-vil', the other contracting party being on this occasion 'Susanna Barton, of Westbury Leight, spinster'. The Lady Hungerford[1] who at Winchester used her influence with the judge against Aubrey is not with certainty identifiable, as there were at that time several women alive who bore that name and title.

When the case with Joan Sumner was over, Aubrey sold his remaining property. From this time forward his efforts to marry or settle down, or indeed to live the kind of life to which he had been born, were at an end. From now on he became an indigent wanderer, without responsibilities to maintain or appearances to keep up; and, in his own words, he never knew true happiness until he had reached this state of 'happy delitescency'.

---

[1] Frances, daughter of Aubrey's old friend Charles Seymour (2nd Lord Seymour of Trowbridge), married Sir George Hungerford of Cadenham in 1665. More probably the traducer was Margaret, widow of the Parliamentarian general in Wiltshire, Sir Edward Hungerford (1596–1648), of Farley Castle and of Corsham, and daughter of William Halliday, Lord Mayor of London. About 1670 she owned Stanton St Quintin manor, near Malmesbury. Another possible candidate is Jane Culme, second wife of Sir Edward Hungerford (1632–1711), famous for his extravagance and an acquaintance of Aubrey's. The episcopal archives in the Consistory Court at Salisbury show that Aubrey brought a case for breach of promise against Joan Sumner about 6 Feb. 1666/67, which dragged on until the spring of 1669/70. Unfortunately the documents have not come to light. (inform. Anne Whiteman.)

CHAPTER FIVE

Anthony Wood; and the Absconding (1667–1677)

I

IN THE midst of this disagreeable episode with Joan Sumner, Aubrey formed a new friendship, which was to become a major element in his life; and led, ultimately, to his undertaking his most important work and the one for which he is generally remembered—the Σχεδιάσματα as he called them, 'pieces written on the spur of the moment'—better known as the *Brief Lives*. This came about as the result of his meeting with Anthony Wood, in August 1667, an encounter at Oxford (which he himself sometimes mistakenly dates as 1665) of Aubrey's own seeking, because, rather surprisingly, he had not yet come across Wood in the course of their common interest in antiquities, in spite of Aubrey having known Ned Wood, Anthony's elder brother, at Trinity.

Anthony Wood (or 'à Wood' as he preferred to call himself, a pretentious and, at best, precarious archaism) is a figure whose many unattractive characteristics make a just account of his activities somewhat difficult to compile. He was an uneasy, bad-tempered man, whose family lived at Oxford in the house called Postmasters' Hall, that stands opposite Merton College. His father supplemented a fairly comfortable income by letting rooms and hiring out a tennis court in the garden. Wood himself occupied two garrets at the top of the house, in one of which he had built a chimney, making a hermit's cell, where he could copy out inscriptions collected from churches visited on country walks, and study books and papers that might be of use to him in his projected *History of Oxfordshire*, planned on the model of Dugdale's *Warwickshire*. He was six years or so younger than Aubrey, and had matriculated as a postmaster at Merton; but, although this status amounted to holding a scholarship at that college, his academic life had been undistinguished, and he had, indeed, taken five years to obtain a degree. Even so he might have been a Fellow if the dons could have brought themselves to support his obnoxious humours; but High Table at Merton felt otherwise on this matter. Wood settled down to his resentment and his manuscripts, having successfully foiled repeated efforts of his family to make him take up some trade or profession. He himself could hardly analyse his own attraction to the arts and to antiquity, and his aversion for the world of everyday affairs and humdrum relationships. In an effort to express these feelings, he wrote of himself:

'Heraldry, musick and painting did so much crowd upon him that he could not avoid them: and could never give a reason why he should delight in those studies more than in others, so prevalent was nature, mix'd with a generosity of mind and a hatred to all that was servile, sneaking, or advantageous for lucre sake.'

There were others, naturally enough, who took a less flattering view of Wood's character than that held by himself, but in its essential stuff this subjective outline gives a true enough picture of his attitude to people and things. In addition to his antiquarian work he kept a diary (from which the above passage is quoted), a remarkable document, containing a detailed account of his everyday life, packed with information on the subject of the ways and personalities of contemporary Oxford, including, notwithstanding his contempt for lucre, his monthly expenditure, a matter in which he was keenly interested. He has a violent, uncouth manner of writing, and, indeed, can often hardly express his meaning adequately if he has to tell a longish story or deal with ideas of a complicated sort. To this weakness as a littérateur, he adds the besetting frailty of the diarist, that is to say 'touching-up' passages at a date later than that of the original entry. Yet, with all its shortcomings, this journal has about it something that is unusual and powerful; and to read it is to understand why there were those, like Aubrey, who could suffer Wood gladly, for all his selfishness, malice, stinginess, and bad temper.

'In Dr Charlett's study', says Thomas Hearne (writing in 1705), 'is Ant. à Wood's Head taken in Plaister de Paris, which shews him to have been a melancholly thoughtfull Man.' The drawing (now hanging in the Bodleian) of this bust, representing

Wood's appearance as it was about ten years later than his meeting with Aubrey—like Faithorne's portrait of the latter—makes its subject look younger than might be expected. The lank hair hangs untidily round the sharply formed bones of the face and over the arched eyebrows. The lips part with the suggestion of a sneer, perhaps a little self-consciously. The man's character is written with an uncompromising clarity across the peevish, feminine, but not entirely unattractive countenance. Wood's liveliness, his intelligence, and his egoism all reappear in this portrait with almost as little restraint as they show themselves in the confused pages of the diary.

In spite of being at odds with almost everyone with whom he came in contact, he had obtained access to the University archives, a privilege that implied at least a measure of official recognition of researches. In short Wood was making a name for him in circles where such enquiries counted for something. The record of his first encounter with Aubrey is one of the instances when he 'wrote-up' his diary a quarter of a century after the event; and the episode gives an indication of the notoriety that Wood had already won. There seems no reason to suppose that the diarist's first impression was much at variance with the account he gives, but there is certainly some cause to doubt the accuracy of the pretended assessment of Aubrey's value as a collaborator, an estimate which can, in fact, be shown to have been very different. The clumsy sentences betray the deliberate spite of the wording. The passage in question to some extent anticipates the chronological narrative of Aubrey's life, but it is here reproduced *in extenso*, because if quoted piecemeal it looses some of its force as an exposition of Wood's nature:

'Aug. 31, [1667] John Aubrey of Easton-Piers in the parish of Kington St Michael in Wiltshire was in Oxford with Edward Forest, a Bookseller living against Alls. Coll. to buy books. He then saw lying on the stall *Notitia Academiae Oxoniensis*,[1] and asking who the author of that book was, he [Edward Forest] answer'd the report was that one Mr Anth. Wood of Merton College was the

---

[1] *Academiae Oxoniensis Notitia* was published in Oxford in 1665, and again in London in 1675. The author was the antiquarian William Fulman, who had also collected material for a life of the 'ever-memorable' John Hales, of Eton.

author, but was not. Whereupon Mr Aubrey, a pretender to Antiquities, having been contemporary to A. Wood's elder brother in Trin. Coll. and well acquainted with him, he thought he might as well be acquainted with A. W. himself. Whereupon repairing to his lodgings and telling him who he was, he got his acquaintance, talk't to him about his studies, and offered him what assistance he could make, in order to the completion of the work that he was in hand with. Mr Aubrey was then in a sparkish garb, came to town with his man and two horses, spent high, and flung out A. W. in all his recknings. But his estate of 700 *li* per annum being afterwards sold and he reserving nothing of it to himself, liv'd afterwards in a very sorry condition, and at length made shift to rub out by hanging on Edm. Wyld, Esq., living in Blomesbury near London, on James Earle of Abendon [Abingdon] whose first wife was related to him, and on Sir John Aubrey his kinsman, living sometimes in Glamorganshire and sometimes at Borstall near Brill in Bucks. He was a shiftless person, roving and magotieheaded, and sometimes little better than crazed. And being exceedingly credulous would stuff his many letters sent to A. W. with folliries and misinformations, which sometimes would guide him into the paths of errour.'

The slang phrase[1] 'flung out A. W. in all his recknings' means that Wood accuses Aubrey of getting the better of him, or cheating him, in all money matters: probably with reference to small borrowings on Aubrey's part, sometimes recorded in Wood's personal accounts. These two men were so different in so many ways that their twenty-five years of working together in comparative harmony is certainly to be wondered at, in spite of the interests they shared: for, although Aubrey was on easy terms with all kinds of persons, he mentions more than once his dislike of 'surliness and inurbanitie', defects which were so integral a part of Wood's disposition, to say no worse.

Nonetheless, each had a side to his character which, although manifesting itself in precisely opposite ways, gave them a possession in common. This was their unworldliness, a quality whose

[1] OED (1933) gives 1749 as earliest recorded use in this sense.

various forms can bind into some sort of affinity widely divergent types of men. Aubrey might move familiarly through the more or less bohemian world of intellect and fashion, which found a place on the outskirts of the Court, in the eyes of the prudent wasting his substance, and appearing only a more literate version of many another well-to-do spendthrift. Wood, in his Oxford obscurity, might be parsimonious, quarrelsome, and back-biting, one of those uninviting pedants who at any period form a scarcely avoidable ingredient of academic life. At bottom neither of them was interested in material things—in what Hobbes called 'a perpetual contention for Honour, Riches, and Authority' that goads on relentlessly the greater part of mankind. Their pleasures and their rewards were found in those shadowy and enchanted regions of the imagination where so much of their time was spent; and for both of them the past was as real—perhaps more real—than the present or the future.

There can be no doubt that Wood's initial reception of Aubrey was far removed from the patronising acceptance of him as a necessary evil, which the amended entry in the journal was intended to imply. As a lonely, unpopular recluse, haunted not seldom by his father's thoughtlessness in having omitted, at the Visitation of 1634, to enter the Wood pedigree in the Heralds' Book, not less, by the undistinguished circumstances in which his family lived and squabbled around him, Wood, even if he remained unflattered by an approach on the part of a fellow antiquary of unassailable social position (however unsound financially), must have been glad to receive the offer of practical assistance. Aubrey was in touch with people of all kinds, whose influence might be of great use and difficult to procure by someone of Wood's comportment; and a painstaking hermit could not afford to ignore the substantial advantages in such directions that might be offered by his new acquaintance.

The meetings continued. Among the regular monthly accounts kept in Wood's *Journal* occurs the item, for 31 August, 1667: 'Spent with Mr John Awbrey of Wilts at Mother Web's and the Mermaid Tavern, 3s. 8d.'; while, on 28 January, 1668, Wood, with the brother he called 'Monsieur' and others, was at a party

with Aubrey at the Crown Tavern, when at the end of the evening
Wood paid 6d. to 'Robert Prudhome' for lighting him home.
Impending disaster made it impossible for Aubrey to retain Prudhome (or Wiseman, as he was usually called) in his service, and
through Wood tried to arrange for 'Robinet' to be employed by
Ralph Bathhurst, the President of Trinity. On 19 May, 1668,
Aubrey wrote to Wood: 'I hope they [the Bathursts] like my servant Robinet'; and again, on 19 July, 1668: 'When you see an
opportunity to drop as by chance some words concerning my beloved servant Robinet, whom I wish extremely well: and it is the
height of his desire to serve Mr President which may be a happy
step to which he aimes at and to his farther preferment. Missing
the Doctor I would not write to him about it for that he might
thinke it too imposing. I could prefer him to the Earl of Worcester or Pembroke but Oxford is the place he loves and where he
would make a better livelyhood. I humbly leave the request of his
and mine to your Prudence. When I heare from you pray let me
know what you think on't.' On 17 February, 1669, he wrote: 'I am
much engaged to Dr Bathurst for his love to Robinet. I am sorry
(as it happens) he was not in England', Wiseman having (as will
be seen) taken service with Lord Northumberland, who was
travelling on the continent.[1]

On 8 January, 1667, he wrote a letter to Wood that shows how,
outwardly at least, the latter had tried to make himself agreeable
at their early meetings. After regretting that 'It is my Fate to be
plagued with a suite in Lawe', Aubrey goes on to say: 'I must
never forget your kindnesse to me when I was at Oxon. I must
assure you that I esteem myselfe very happy in your acquaintance
. . . as often as I may serve you pray let me heare from you, for I
am to my power as zealous for you as any one in this Nation.'
Wood replied to this: 'I wish I had acquaintance with more of
your public spirit, who might satisfie me of such matters, . . .

[1] On 6 September, 1672, Aubrey wrote to Wood from Lord
Thanet's seat, Hothfield: 'If Robinet's marriage doth not go on, I could
recommend him to my Lord's service here, XX per annum wages, and all
his cast cloathes, hatts, stockings, &c.' On 3 July, 1684, he wrote thanking Wood 'for his resentment of poore Robinet's condition'.

hoping for your company about a month hence.' On 5 December (there is no year, but the letter seems to belong to this period) Aubrey sent Wood a note, asking him to dine with his affluent friend Edmund Wyld at his house 'in the Great Square' in Bloomsbury, where it stood next to the Blackman's Head on the south side. Here Wyld (who was unmarried) lived with his mistress, Jane Smyth.

II

The historical survey of the city of Oxford upon which Wood had been engaged since 1661 was intended to include the university, the colleges, the monasteries, and the parish churches. The work was not on the whole original, but consisted primarily in an effort to arrange the Oxford collections of Brian Twyne, first keeper of the university archives, who had died in 1644, leaving some sixty manuscript volumes, packed with archaeological matter,[1] but unmethodically noted down. Wood had decided to divide the material he proposed to use into three sections. These were to be: first, the city and ecclesiastical antiquities: secondly, the annals of the university, with accounts of buildings, professorships, etc.; and, lastly, the antiquities of the colleges. The treaties on the city remained in manuscript until Wood's death; but through the influence of the Dean of Christ Church, Dr Fell, the treatise on the university was accepted by the University Press in October 1669. It is possible that the Dean had been persuaded to take an interest in Wood's labours by Aubrey's friend, Ralph Bathurst, President of Trinity. The terms were good, though the 'pedantical and pedagogical' Fell, as Wood called him, made certain reservations and amendments, also suggesting that short biographies of the literary and ecclesiastical celebrities who had been in residence at Oxford should be included. Wood agreed to undertake this additional task; and a development of this proposal led some years later to the compilation of the *Athenae Oxonienses*,

[1] Among these papers were two treatises written in 1592 by Aubrey's distant cousin, Henry Lyte of Lytescary—*Records of the true origin of the Noble Britons that sprang of the remains of the Trojans taken out of oblivion's treasure* and *The mystical Oxen of Oxenford*.

an 'exact history of all the writers and bishops that have had their
education in . . . Oxford' since 1500.

A correspondence now began between Aubrey and Wood that
was to last for twenty-five years, of which the most important
part consisted in Aubrey's contribution to these biographies. In
the early stages of their partnership Aubrey's help to Wood must
mainly have taken the form of lending manuscripts and documents,
of which he had been a collector for some time past. No doubt he
also offered suggestions as to the general scheme of the work,
that Wood was verifying between 1667 and 1670 by long visits
to London, where additional authorities could be consulted. It
was not, however, until the biographical side of the enterprise
took on a paramount importance that Aubrey, by his wide acquaintanceship with all sorts and conditions, and by his gift for
hitting off character or appearance in a phrase, infused a vitality
into the *Athenae* which Wood, unaided, could never have brought
to that impressive, but sometimes rather uninspired, chronicle
of names. These contributions by Aubrey were the *Lives*, to
which he owes his fame, composed between the time of Dr Fell's
instructions to Wood and the year 1680. Certainly there was a
strong element of chance in the manner that they came to be
written. At the same time it should not be forgotten that as early
as 1652 Aubrey had promised Hartlib 'a large and particular
account' of Francis Potter, and in 1667 pledged Hobbes that he
would write the philosopher's life, indications that the idea of
biographical work had always been present in his mind as a suitable medium for talents which seemed often in danger of frustra-
tion from lack of appropriate employment.

III

The passage with Joan Sumner, coincident with these early years
of friendship with Wood, had added the final and insupportable
burden to the tottering edifice of Aubrey's financial stability. Still,
he hurried backwards and forwards, ringing the changes between
Wiltshire, London, and Oxford. In April 1668, after his recent
victory over Joan Sumner at Salisbury assizes, he had attended the

funeral of Sir William Davenant, some of whose 'very young' children by his second wife were present. The coffin was of walnut, declared by Sir John Denham to be the finest coffin he had ever seen; though, to Aubrey's regret, surmounted by no laurel. With some lack of inspiration the words *O Rare Sir William Davenant* were inscribed on the grave in Westminster Abbey; and Dryden took the place as Poet Laureate of 'that sweet swan of Isis'. In this year the Clerk of St Mary Overy's, a very old man, who had been tailor to the dramatist John Fletcher, told Aubrey that Fletcher had been invited to stay in East Anglia at the time of the plague in 1625, and, having remained in London only long enough to have a suit made, had caught the malady and died. Meanwhile, Aubrey had news that Hobbes was very ill; and the philosopher, too, nearly died on this occasion, while he lay at Bristol House in Queen Street.

In 1669 Aubrey stayed with Anthony Henley[1] at one of the Henleys' houses, the Grange, Northington, near Alresford, in Hampshire, where he decided to write down some of his ideas on the subject of improvements to be made in English education, an essay that took him fifteen years to complete. He also spent some time at Easton Pierse, when, knowing that the property could not remain his much longer, he made drawings of the house and grounds (including one of the 'dog Fortune at 2 chaines distance') to remind him of 'the place where I was born, my mother's inheritance which cruel fate enforced me to part with'. These pictures survive in the album called *Designatio de Easton Piers*. On 7 August, 1669, he wrote to Wood: 'Dear Friend: I returne my heartiest respect and thanks to you for your great kindnesses to me at Oxon: which I must never forgett and without complement I never was more happy in any one's company in my life . . . I should be the happiest man to see you in Wilts: about ten dayes hence I shall know when I may be certayne to be found. I have now but one horse left fitt to be rid, els I would send one for you.'

---

[1] Anthony Henley married Mary Bertie, whose second husband was her cousin, Henry Bertie, son of Aubrey's kinsman and patron James Bertie, Earl of Abingdon. He also owned Bramshill House.

He wrote again to Wood on 2 October, 1669, desiring him: 'to speake to your neighboure the carrier's wife concerning the cloake that I left at London in the warehouse. She sent me a cloake but it is not mine: and it is shorter a great deale.' On 21 October his former schoolmaster, William Browne (who had become Vicar of Farnham in Surrey), died at the age of fifty-two of smallpox, infected while burying a corpse.

In February 1670 Robert Wiseman wrote from Rome:

'Sir, These is to aquinte you that his Lordship[1] is arrived at this famous Sity the 6 of January, which I can give good thankes, and you, Sir, that I came into this good Italy in which I am in hopes to Rise, I being now neerer to my Lord then I was when I came out of England. I had dun Mr Seymour's bisness from London to this place in French and Italian, and hie veriwell content of mee. The Great Duke interteindds his host[2] most nobley at Pisa being his winter quarters and warmer then Florence, for it is the coldest place that ever I felt in my life, though one of the finest. There the Great Duke have the finest palais that I have Sine. It seems as well furnist and the most Rishest thing in the world. [In] it we could not see the jewels, the Great Duke having the key stooll and will trust nobody with it. Here we expect the pope to be made on [?any] daye and for the want of a pope wee shall not have any Carnivall. I wish you was one of the Carnivall, the which it would be better then going to lawe with Mris Joane, but I hope your bisnes goes better then it went when I came away. My lordd intends to stay here two months and then go to Naples and Loreto and to Venice but I believe the loss of his sonn will make him goo sooner home than he would have dun, which I shall be sorry for because I would learn Italian well.—Sir, pray do me the favour to present my faithfull service to your good family and assure yourselfe that I praye God to prosper you and will stand as I am, Your faithfull and obedient servant, Rob. Wiseman.
Sir excuse me if I have nott writt sendse conveniency. We are lodged at the palazo del Moretto dans le strado del Corso.'

[1] Aubrey notes: 'The Earl of Northumberland.' This was Joceline Percy, 11th Earl of Northumberland. His only son, Henry, died on 18 December, 1669, and he himself died in the following May, when all his honours became extinct.

[2] Doubtful reading: 'host' would here mean 'guest'.

EASTON PIERSE BEFORE ITS REBUILDING, from a watercolour by Aubrey, painted in 1669.
He has marked the right-hand first-floor window as the room of his birth.

The same house after its rebuilding, Southern Elevation from a watercolour by Aubrey,
painted in 1669: note the 'volant Mercury' and 'Jeddeau'.

SIR JAMES LONG AND AUBREY HAWKING. Watercolour by Aubrey. The scene is Salisbury Plain or thereabouts. Sir James Long is presumably the figure with the telescope, as Cromwell had permitted him to wear a sword, which he also carries.

Aubrey passed on the gist of Robinet's letter to Wood, when he wrote to him on Easter Tuesday (5 April), 1670, saying: 'Honest Mr Anthony! I sent you a letter from London the last Terme by the Coachman; I never heard from you since and therefore suspect that he being then drunke, lost it. The contents of it was to give you notice that if you have occasion of search and transcription of any Records at Rome, I can have it donne for you. I am very well acquainted with the Provinciall of the Jesuits (who will send to their Generall at Rome) who hath promised me it shall be donne, if you send your Quere's or proposalls . . . I am now taking my leave of the beloved place where I first drew breathe. I have now lately ended my lawsuit with Mrs Sumner.'

IV

In 1671, as we have seen, the crash came, and Easton Pierse had to go from him. Aubrey describes himself as having at the same time to part with the farm at Broad Chalke; but he stayed there, on and off, for many years after this.[1] At some time previous to 1664 he had mortgaged the Easton Pierse estate to Thomas Gore ('of Aldrington *aliàs* Alderton') and his brother, Charles Gore, as trustees of their sister, Anna, afterwards wife of John Scrope of Castle Combe, the last of whom had been a party to Joan Sumner's business transactions. On the afternoon of 25 March, 1671, 'that most lovely seate' passed out of his possession, disposed of (through one Jonathan Rogers, presumably a solicitor) to Mr Robert Sherwin, Aubrey noting the exact time of the final stage of the deal for astrological documentation; and adding, with his incurable vagueness, that he lost '500 *li* + 200 *li* + goods + timber'.

He was overcome with a longing for monastic life, perhaps accentuated by illusions as to the peace and security he might find there to pursue his antiquarian researches: for his pleasures were never wholly of a monastic sort. 'I wished monasterys had not

[1] In 1686 Aubrey mentions again that 'Chalke must be sold', at the time of the death of his mother; but he and his brother William seem to have used the place at least as late as 1690, though no doubt the property was heavily encumbered.

been putt downe, that the reformers would have been more moderate as to that point. Nay, the Turkes have monasteries. Why should our reformers be so severe? Convenience of religious houses—Sir Christopher Wren—fitt there should be receptacles and provision for contemplative men: if of 500, but one or two. 'Tis compensated. What a pleasure it would have been to have travelled from monastery to monastery. The reformers in the Lutheran countries were more prudent than to destroy them (*e.g.* Holsatia, etc.); only altered the religion.'

He often returns (especially in the *Surrey Collections*) to his regret for the days of monastic houses and a way of life that had ceased with their dissolution. 'Absconded as a banished man,' he wrote of the straits he was now in, 'I was in as much affliction as a mortall could be'. However, in spite of these misfortunes, he found there was still much to compensate him for the loss of material wealth, so much so, indeed, that he even came to consider that he had 'never quiett, nor anything of happinesse till divested of all, 1670, 1671; at what time providence raysed me (unexpectedly) good friends—the right honourable Nicholas, earl of Thanet, with whom I was delitescent at Hothfield in Kent neer a year . . . Sir Christopher Wren; Mr Ogilby: then Edmund Wyld, esq., *Regius Societatis Socius*, of Glasely Hall, Salop (*sed in margine*), tooke me in his armes with whom I most commonly take my diet and sweet *otiums.*' This period of his life not only proved an exception to 'the strange fate that I have laboured under never in my life to enjoy one entire month or six weeks *otium* for contemplation', but also turned out to be a season when his health improved. Before these days his digestion had been weak. 'Stomach so tender that I could not drink claret without sugar, nor white wine but would disgorge': but now he could add 'not well ordered till 1670'. This last development was certainly a matter for congratulation.

Tribulations even added a stimulus to his work, and 'notwithstanding these ambarasments I did *pian piano* (as they occur'd) take notice of antiquity' and having sold all and disappointed as aforesayd of moneys I received, I had so strong an impulse to (in good part) finish my description of Wilts, two volumes in folio, that I could not be quiet till I haddonne it, and that with danger enough,

tanquam canis è Nilo, for feare of the crocodiles, *i.e.* catchpolls—
And indeed all I have donne and that little that I have studied
have been just after that fashion, so that had I not lived long my
want of leisure would have afforded me but a slender harvest.'

There was an account of Avebury to be put in order, and he was
at work on this at the same time, adding to the manuscript further
matter of general antiquarian interest, and calling the whole *Monumenta Britannica*, though at one time the title was to be *Monumenta
Druidum*. But, in spite of a philosophical attitude of mind, the obstructive circumstances remained in all their grimness. There was
danger of arrest most of the time, especially in 1671: but the
catchpolls—the crocodiles of the Nile—were somehow eluded.
Influential friends now had to be cultivated. Dr Walter Charleton, the King's Physician, sent a discouraging letter (on 4 February,
1671) regarding the possibility of obtaining Lord Brouncker's
good offices in his capacity as President of the Royal Society.
Brouncker had recently cast Charleton's nativity, notwithstanding the latter's view that astrology's 'very fundamentals seem
to be precarious and fraudulent'. The two of them, it will be remembered, had been responsible for Aubrey's presentation to
Charles II in connexion with Avebury. Some of the letter deals
with the horoscope, but Charleton goes on to advise that, 'if you
come once to that degree of infelicity to want his [Brouncker's]
assistance or depend upon his sincerity', an oblique approach
would be necessary. 'If you would make him your patron and
raiser, you have no other way to do it but by bribing his mer-
cenary —, who by that means alone became his, after she had
passed through almost as many hands as the R. S. hath members,
and many more than she has teeth in her gumms of Nature's
setting. Nor do I thinke it possible for him to oblige any but a
Miss . . .'

Aubrey himself was much involved in astrological enquiries at
this period; when Coley's horoscope was cast. That astrologer's
skill in horary questions eventually led to employment by William Lilly, when the latter's sight had grown dim and his hand
had begun to lose some of its skill in mystifying his clients.
Aubrey held a high opinion of Coley (with whom he sometimes

stayed), and, in a letter to Wood, dated 14 June, 1671, he wrote of him: 'He is a man of admirable parts, and as good a natured man as can be, and more and more to be expected from him every day. And comes by his learning meerly by the strong impulse of his Genius. He understands Latin and French: yet never learned out his grammar, his father was a joyner, one against the Theatre.' Events had by this time taken sufficiently expressive shape for even the most obtuse astrologer to present in general terms a reasonably accurate picture of Aubrey's circumstances: and Coley did not ignore these outward portents when he stated that 'the nativity is a most remarkable opposition, and 'tis much pity the starres were not more favourable to the native.' He goes on to show how the heavenly bodies 'threaten ruin to land and estate: give superlative vexations in matters relating to marriage, and wondrous contests in law-suits—of all of which vexations I suppose the native hath had a greater portion than was ever desired', adding that Aubrey would be in great danger between the ages of forty and fifty. The horoscope is in the *Collection of Genitures* made by Aubrey, intended to be part of the information about distinguished men to be supplied to Wood; to whom, on 27 October, 1671, he wrote a long letter from Broad Chalke about his affairs and plans.

'My worthy Freind,

  I returned hither this day three weekes, and am very much to blame, I have not answered your two kind letters sooner. . . . I am mightily pleased to heare it confirmed so certainly that I am beyond sea: at Salisbury 'tis for certain that I am in Italy, let it be at Bononia: these things I have given out for my own security: but 'tis perhaps prophetically true. After so many tossings and troubles in the world, where could a man better withdraw himself than into such a learned Society as that of IHS (study they must: but what they have a mind to: musick, Heraldry, Chymistry, etc.). I am well acquainted with 'em and always reserved that designe as the *ultimum refugium*. To goe to reconcile the differences of the two churches I leave to them that have nothing els to doe, and know not how to spend their paines better. . . . Now amongst others that I correspond with is Father Thimilby (brother to Sir Thomas Thim: of Yorkshire) who is now Rector of a pretty little Coll: of Novices in a

pleasant place (Watton) 6 miles from Dunkirke, who hath invited me
over to him above this 12 moneth and staye as long as I will, *i.e.* sojourne:
and after 40 what better life could a man take. Is it not better than when
one comes to be old to be scorned by his brother's cooke mayd, which I
known to be donne to a wise old gent at London, (Mr delauné) who
though worth at that time 60,000*li* was slighted by the cooke mayd.
Prithee, Mr Wood, tell Dr Bathurst and his godly Lady that you have
received a letter from Bononia and that I am in a Heaven upon Earth.
Tell 'em fryar John remembers him to them. . . . I would willingly before I leave England, finish my perambulation of Wilts which is more
than half donne. In a fortnight or three weeks I could doe the Country
part. The Records will keep cold. I thinke I must leave the finishing to
you and Mr Browne; or rather to you when you are at leisure. About
March or Aprill I hope to finish as aforesayd. Pray remember me to Mr
Browne. If he writes or sees Mr Gore let him not tell him that he sawe
me, for he is a fidling peevish fellow and something related to my adve.-
sarys . . . I am writing a comedy for Thomas Shadwell, which I have
now almost finished since I came home, *et quorum pars magna fui*. And I
shall fitt him with another, *The Country Revell*, both humours untouch't,
but of this, mum! for 'tis very satyricall against some of my mischievous
enemies which I in my tumbling up and down have collected. Now if I
would be rich, I could be a prince. I could goe into Maryland, (between
Virginia and New England) which is one of the finest *countrys of the
world* (same climate with France). I can have all the favours of my lord
Baltemore[1] I could wish—His brother is his Lieutenant there; and a
very good-natured gentleman.—Plenty of all things; There is ground
2000 miles westwards. I could be able I believe to carry a colony of
rogues: another of ingeniose Artificers; and I doubt not one might make
shift to have five or six ingeniose companions, which is enough. Now
wither of these I shall chose *dabitur illâ horâ*, but of both these I adjure
you by the friendship you beare me to be secret.'

This letter shows that Aubrey's thoughts of entering a monastic
house had some practical foundation. Father Thimelby, a Jesuit
(who worked under the assumed name of Richard Ashby) had
taught philosophy and theology at Liège, and, during the Commonwealth, had been sent to forward his Order's activities in

[1] Cecil Calvert, 2nd Lord Baltimore (who died in 1675), had been
a contemporary at Trinity with Aubrey's friend Francis Potter.

England. He was at this time rector of the house for novices at Watten, near St Omer, and, in 1672, he was appointed rector of St Omer College, the seminary to which Titus Oates obtained admission in 1677. Thomas Gore, it will be remembered, had been connected with the sale of Easton Pierse after the Joan Sumner affair. Aubrey came to dislike him more and more as years went by, and most of his letters to Wood have some uncomplimentary reference to the 'C. of A.' or 'Cuckold of Alderton'. Mr Browne was an antiquarian parson,[1] to whom Aubrey usually sends friendly messages; though, in a later letter, he wrote of Gore: 'If he should not assist me, he were an ill-natured cuck—, for he hath made me as much his slave as Sir Browne', the latter having apparently made more than reasonable demands on Aubrey's energy and good nature in the pursuit of his genealogical interests. The 'old gent' was Gideon Delaune, apothecary to Anne of Denmark.

Unhappily, the autobiographical comedy has disappeared, perhaps destroyed, perhaps bound together with other manuscripts and forgotten on the shelves of the library of some country house. *The Country Revel* remains, a rough draft dispersed throughout one of the volumes of Aubrey's miscellaneous papers, written at odd moments when any idea suitable to the play, and its dialogue, came into his head. Like the lost comedy, the piece is full of references to persons he knew, the names of their living prototypes being noted beside or above those of many of the characters. The loss of the earlier dramatic work is much to be regretted, because, although Aubrey did not possess the methodical industry necessary to a playwright, he had a promising talent for expressing himself in this form, as in most of his other literary experiments. The autobiographical side of the comedy would have added something to the facts known about his life; while the story of Joan Sumner, and the game she played, might have been passed down to posterity in an entertaining and appropriate manner. The idea

[1] On 9 October, 1671, Gore had written to Aubrey: 'I obtain'd the acquaintance of young Mr Richard Browne, and was with him at his Father's house at Myntie, where he expressed againe and againe his obligations to yourselfe.'

of emigrating recurred almost until the end of his life, though it is impossible to feel that Aubrey's temperament would have suited him to pioneering work in a new country.

Wood wrote, on 10 November, 1671: 'I am very glad that you have satisfied me on many things, and cease not to send into divers parts for further information of other men: I speake in my conscience (for I have told other men of it already) that I have had and shall have more from you as to these things then all people besides whatsoever. What I have had hitherto besides, hath been for the most part mine own industry and purse. There be three things that I strive to follow, these are: 1. To be above the desire of riches. 2. above the feare of death. 3. to be my own judge, and not to be led away by what is put into my head by sundry persons. Pray consider these things and obtain them, and Ile warrant you a true philosopher.' He also mentions an Italian book that Aubrey had sent the previous Whitsuntide for Robert Wiseman to translate.

It was, of course, all very well for Wood to recommend philosophy to Aubrey (whose natural equipment in that sphere was considerably superior to any possessed by Wood himself), but sending 'into divers parts for further information from other men' was sometimes a tedious undertaking, when combined with a chronic need to circumvent creditors. There is an undated note, written about this time, in which Aubrey asks: 'When you write to me pray remember to endorse your letter to *Mr Thomas Awbrey* at Broad Chalke to be left at the Lambe in Katherine Street, Sarum. This to avoid being discovered.'

On 28 November, 1671, Aubrey wrote to Wood: 'I have a great desire to see my honest brother Tom well settled, marryed to a good discreet wife with about 800*li* or 1000*li* which his estate (Chalke farme 250*li* per annum) does very well deserve. I wish you could find [such] another as your sister-in-law or neice if she were big enough. My great-grandmother was of Oxfordshire: and I like the people mighty well. About Chalke are no wives nearer then Salisbury, prowd and all gamesters, and unknowing or unfit for a country gent., turne and in North Wilts they will be drunken. Is it not an odd thing to send to a monk and an antiquary about such a question, but how can I tell what may happen. Some of your acquaintances may hint. I intend to be in London about Xmas. I have not enjoyed myself so much these 20 yeares as here.'

On 20 December, 1671, he wrote again to Wood from the Blackamore's Head in Stanhope Street: 'I have a desire to see you once or twice more and cannot have a more clowdy opportunity for an invisible ghost then now. I shall spend all the next month in Somersetshire. Direct your letter then to William Dorvell near the market place in Wells.' This was probably a visit to his mother, for Mrs Aubrey (though she was sometimes at Chalke) seems to have lived at Bridgwater: and was occasionally at Bristol. This appears from Aubrey's correspondence with Andrew Paschall,[1] rector of Chedsey in Somerset.

V

In January 1672 he talked with old Goodwife Faldo, aged eighty or more, who had known Dr Dee. She could remember her mother tending the thaumaturge in his last illness, which happened soon after he had entertained the Polish Ambassador at his house at Mortlake. On the 13th of the same month, Nicholas Tufton, Earl of Thanet (mentioned earlier as having been imprisoned by Cromwell in the Tower) wrote thanking Aubrey for the trouble he had taken in connexion with the 'lanthorne to travaile with', adding: 'For measuring of my Land, I am resolved not to doe it untill I finde by my writeings each particular field specified by name, how bounded, and where situated, which will take up some time afore 'tis done, of which I thought it not amiss to give you this accompt. If the sorting of my writeings and collecting of the heads of them in writeing, as Green has done, be suitable to your inclination, you shall not loase your time in taking this trouble: your answeare hereunto you may be pleased to send by the Cantebury Post, in case this finds you not out time enough to send it this weeke by the carryer, and if you acquaint me that you incline for Hothfield on those termes, you will be pleased to come down by water at the same time that one John

[1] See p. 69 n.

Warner does who is to serve me, when you will find horses at Gravesend to bring you both hither.'

Lord Thanet's suggestion was acceptable, offering as it did a refuge for the moment. Its tone (and that of Thanet's subsequent letters) is not very engaging; though it may be that the invitation was entirely charitable and the talk about employment was meant to give Aubrey a comparatively dignified *raison d'être* at Hothfield. It seems, however, more likely that Thanet had a number of tedious odd jobs to be done, and thought that Aubrey might be a useful man to do them. On 1 April, 1672, Aubrey wrote to Wood from Broad Chalke: 'On Satturday next (or fryday) I shall be, God willing, at Harewood with Mr Hoskyns in Herefordshire, where I shall stay about a moneth.'

The efforts of Aubrey's two brothers were enlisted by him to lend a hand in his antiquarian researches, and in May 1672 he wrote to Wood that 'my brother Tom searcht the register at Wilton from the begining and talk'd with old men' in an unsuccessful effort to ascertain further details of the dramatist Philip Massinger,[1] who had been one of the retinue of the Pembrokes. In the same month Samuel Cooper, 'his majestie's alluminer and my honour'd friend', died. Cooper had painted a second portrait of Hobbes, which he had promised to give Aubrey for the Bodleian. The picture had remained in the painter's keeping 'for something of the garment that was not quite finished', and Aubrey, lying low at Lord Thanet's at the time of the artist's death, could not claim it from the hands of the widow.[2]

He continued to stay from time to time at Hothfield, and still tried to find some regular means of earning a living. On 12 August, 1672, he wrote to Wood: 'I had gonne sooner into Kent, but Dr Wren, my deare Freinde, without my knowledge contrived an employment for me, which he referred to me to consider of, and so I shall till Michaelmas Terme. 'Tis this—Mr Ogilby is writing the history of all England: the map is mending already.

[1] 'This day I searched the register of St Saviour's, Southwark, by the playhouse then there, *vulgo* St Mary's Overy's: and find Philip Massinger buried March 18, 1639.' Aubrey to Wood: 31 January, 1674.

[2] She was sister to the mother of Alexander Pope.

Now the Doctor told me that if that were àll, it would be no very great matter. He was pleased to tell him that he would not meet with a fitter man for that turne then J.A. Now it's true that it suits well enough with my Genius; but he is a cunning Scott, and I must deale warily with him, with the advice of my friends. It will be in February next before I begin, and then between that and November followeing I must curry all over England and Wales . . . The King will give me protection and letters to make any inquisition, or etc. . . . my being in towne is too much knowne, but tell them that I am suddenly goeing towards France, which is true for I am going to the seacoast of Kent, perhaps I may make a step to Calais (but tother side). I shall write to this purpose to my stiffe starcht friend T.G., Cuckold & Esq.'

On 23 September, 167... Thanet wrote again to Aubrey: 'By this Groome I have sent a horse and your Portmantue, and I hope your returne hither on him will be not faster than when we went hence to Folkestone, the horse being at grasse, and since myne, neaver used to hard rideing. Some two days since, the Groome being sent with my Coachman upon some business of mine, very fairely that day went to an Alehouse and there stayed most part of the day, for which fault I enjoyne him this pennance, being to have him retourne upon his faire feet without a Launce from Coldham hither, without soe-mutch as allowing a Jugge of beer by the way. Of this keep him in ignorance till you are on horseback, else disgusted with the penance, and by way of revenge, he may neglect it lookeing to the horse as he ought, and being ready to come out, then open the commission and show him.'

No doubt it would have been in better taste for Thanet to have administered the discipline of his household through some agency other than that of his guests, especially when the latter were suffering financial embarrassments, which were certainly a matter of common knowledge; while for Aubrey, unusually benevolent to servants (often to the extent of being imposed upon) such instructions could have been nothing but disagreeable. They give, however, a good idea of the minor afflictions with which he was now surrounded.

VI

Hobbes had recovered from his severe illness of some years before, and, on 3 February, 1673, Aubrey wrote to Wood: 'The old gent. is strangely vigorous for his understanding still: and every morning walks abroad to meditate. He haz written a treatise concerning Lawe, which 8 or 9 years since I much importuned him to doe, and, in order to it, gave him the Lord Chancellor Bacon's *Maximes of the Lawe*. Now every one will doe him the Right to acknowledge he is rare for definitions and the Lawyers building on old fashioned maximes, (some right, some wrong) must need fall into severall paralogismes. Upon this consideration I was earnest with him to consider these things. To which he was unwilling, telling me he doubted he should not have dayes enough left to doe it. He drives on, in this, the King's Prerogative high. Judge Hales, who is no great courtier, had read it and much mislike it, and is his enemy. Judge Vaughan has read it and much commends it.'[1]

On 23 February, 1673 Aubrey wrote to Wood again, this time on a more intimate matter: 'Now let me take you to Scrutiny: Are you turned Roman Catholic or no? You know what I am, no Enemie to them, unless Irish Bigotts. That you are so was reported at the Vice-Chancellor's table (Dr Bathurst) and that by the Deane himselfe: but perhaps that arrow was drawn out of your godly cosen's[2] quiver. Well, I say a little superstition is a good ingredient in Government. What public spiritts are now left, nay almost I could ask what common honesty. Amongst the Clergy, Humility and Charity very rare: except you come to an Honest poor old Bachelor parson. σοὶ μὲν ἐγώ, σὶ δ'ἐμοί.[3] So now I must unbosome myselfe and desire your friendly advice and counsell, (which I have done before now) which course of life to take. I have

[1] Sir John Vaughan was Chief Justice of the Common Pleas and Sir Matthew Hale (Mr Maynard's 'good man'—see p. 59) Chief Justice of the King's Bench. Vaughan was a great personal friend of Hobbes. Vaughan and Hale had been John Selden's executors.

[2] Mary Wood, wife of Wood's brother, Robert, with whom he was on the worst of terms.

[3] *Iliad*, Bk. IV. 63.

severall good Freinds who are great men that aske me and chide me saying have you found out any good place yet; but finde it, and your Businesse shall be donne. So I have laid Queres in the Custome-howse, Tower, &c. But I am stormed anew. I am at my Witts end. They would have me turne parson and keepe an honest Curat, and I shall have a parsonage of 200 *li* per annum. What doe you thinke of this: is it honourable or prudent? Lord, how shall I looke in a Cassock! The new Newes is that we shall have warres with France. I doubt how strongly the Church of England stands. If it changes then what shall I doe. But thus much they tell me and tell me truly, that I love not businesse and rising earling[1] is death to me. In this case I shall take no paines, enjoy my friends at London or Oxon, or &c and have a gentile Competency. Pray advice me by the next post what to doe, for I am so importuned that I could scarce sleep last night.

'Pray burne or blott out some arcana of A.W. and J.A. in this letter'.[2]

In March 1673 there was one of Sir Thomas Browne's indecipherable letters from Norwich (Aubrey had complained earlier of their illegibility) giving some biographical notes about himself, and making enquiries about the progress of Aubrey's *Templa Druidum*. On 7 April, 1673, while still staying with Lord Thanet, Aubrey wrote to Wood: 'One Mr Goresuch of Woodstock dined with us at Romney Marsh, who told me that at the old Gothique-built howse of Sir Jeffrey Chaucer, that there is a picture, which goes with the howse from one to another—which see. . . . I have 3 other draughts *i.e.* draughts of the severall views of Ousney abbey besides that I gave to the monasticon in my trunke at Kington by Easton-Piers but dare not trust my brother with the key, for my bookes would be like butter-flies, and fly about all the countrye. . . . I doe long to have that narrow soul'd cuckold's Nativity, which I hope Sir Browne will not forget.' The last sentence refers to his many efforts to possess himself of Thomas Gore's horoscope, which, after ceaseless enquiries, he was finally successful in obtain-

---

[1] Slip for 'rising early'.
[2] This sentence is written on the back of the letter.

ing. On 14 April, he wrote again: 'I have a great mind to make myself once more happy in your so good, so ingeniose, innocent and friendly conversation: and whether ever I may a second time, God Knows. The starres frown untowardly on this Nation and had I not been unluckily persuaded by my brother William to loose 500*li* of which I shall never see a farthing, I could (*excepto quid non simul esset*) have been by my Lord's favour in the happiest condition I was in my life, as I shall tell you if you mind me of it, too long now to relate, and which might not be unacceptable to you at Paris: and perhaps I may yet at the long run make shift to compas it.'

If Aubrey found himself so contented at Hothfield, it is perhaps over-exacting to criticise Thanet's demeanour to him. Certainly Hothfield provided a convenient *pied-à-terre*. Aubrey inspected the parish church there, and endeavoured to establish a theory that Christian places of worship were formerly built so that their eastern elevation should be directly opposite the point on the horizon where, on the day appropriate to their patron saint, the sun rose. After making observations on the day of the vernal equinox, he found to his satisfaction the position of St Margaret's, Hothfield, to 'answer to the sun-rising on St Margaret's Day, 20th July.'

In May 1673 John Ogilby, in his capacity as 'Royal Cosmographer and Geographic Printer', granted Aubrey the promised licence[1] to survey the county of Surrey. At this time over seventy,

---

[1] The licence, which is reproduced at the beginning of the *Surrey Collections*, states that: 'By virtue of his Majesty's Warrant under his Sign Manual, dated 24 August, A.D. 1671, authorizing me to proceed in the actual survey of His Majesty's Kingdom of England and Dominion of Wales, I have constituted, ordain'd and made John Aubrey, Esq., my lawful Deputy for the county of Surrey and parts adjacent; willing and requiring all Justices of the Peace, Mayors, Bailiffs, Sheriffs, Parsons, Vicars, Church Wardens, High Constables, Constables, Headborows, and all other his Majesty's officers, Ministers and Subjects, whatsoever to be aiding and assisting my said Deputy or his Agents in the said actual Survey: and upon his reasonable request to admit him free Acess to all public Registers or other Books, whereby the Geographical and Historical description of his Majesty's said Kingdom of England and Dominion of Wales may be anyways promoted or ascertained.'

Ogilby had had an eventful career as dancing-master, soldier, and author. His wife, according to Aubrey, was one of the Fox family, of Netherhampton near Wilton, her father being a member of Lord Pembroke's entourage; and this connexion with Wiltshire may have accounted in some measure for Ogilby's decision to appoint Aubrey his deputy in Surrey. 'I entered upon the perambulation of the county of Surrey July 1, 1673,' wrote Aubrey, 'and left off about the middle of September following.' The period of time devoted to this survey (in fact Aubrey seems to have continued his researches until October) does not seem excessive in relation to the amount of ground that had to be covered but, while he was engaged in copying monumental inscriptions (of which by far the greater part of the volume consists) Aubrey must have worked hard. The book was given the double title of *A Perambulation of the County of Surrey* and *The Natural History and Antiquities of the County of Surrey*. He used Lord Thanet's house as his headquarters while he travelled about in the neighbouring county.

Before he embarked on the survey, while he 'lay at Mistress Neve's', Aubrey had a narrow escape from being run through by a drunkard on St John's Night, 'at Mr Burges' chamber in the Middle Temple', in the street opposite Gray's Inn Gate, 'a gentleman whom I never saw before, but (*Deo Gratia*) one of his companions hindred his thrust.'[1] This was just before he set out, because he had written to Wood on 17 June, 1673: 'I shall not begin my journey till this day or tomorrow sennight, for the horse will not come up till next saturday, and my brother (I thanke him) has lamed my horse just as I have occasion for him: and a good handsome horse to doe me credit, so that I shall be forced to ride my brother's, a little nagge. I have got a pretty youth to wayte on me that can write and reade and loves ingeniose things and will be adroit for my service. I long as it were with a woman's longing to

[1] Between 1650 and 1669 Aubrey also experienced 'danger of being killed by William, Earl of Pembroke, then Lord Herbert, at the election of Sir William Salkeld for New Sarum'. Salkeld does not occur in parliamentary records as an M.P., though a 'Sir William Salkeld of Rock' is mentioned by Le Neve as having a daughter who married 'a notorious counterfeiter of hands and very poor'. Salkeld, deriving from the Cumberland family, lived at Fifehide Nevile (Hutchins's *Dorset*).

see Oxford and you and the Bishop of Botley,[1] to whom I pray my respects and also Mr Newman.'

On 4 July, 1673, he was for three hours with his friend Sir Robert Moray, before the latter's death. Moray, who had had scientific and antiquarian interests, had once promised Aubrey an account of prehistoric remains in Scotland. Aubrey wrote of him afterwards: 'The Highlanders (like the Swedes) can make their own cloathes: and I have heard Sir Robert say that he could doe it. . . . He was my most honoured and obligeing friend, and I was more obliged to him then to all the courtiers besides. I had a great losse in his death, for, had he lived, he would have got some employment or other for me before this time. He had the King's eare as much as any one, and was indefatigable in his undertakings . . . His lodging when he died was the leaded pavillion in the garden of Whitehal—Had but one shilling in his pocket *i.e. in all*. The King buryed him. He lies by Sir William Davenant in Westminster Abbey.'

He found his expedition to survey very enjoyable, and, on 10 August, 1673, he wrote to Wood: 'Deare Anthony! I have had the pleasantest Pilgrimage that ever any man has had I thinke since the Reformation and find many strangers very civill to me much more than I did in Wilts.' However, the perambulation ended rather disastrously, because (as he wrote to Wood on 11 October) while he was staying at Esher, Aubrey's horse broke out of its ground, or was stolen, and he had to return on foot to London, though 'were it not for some critical coxcombes I would as soon doe this work pedestrian as equestrian'. On top of this loss, Ogilby now informed Aubrey that he was going to make no more use of him, as he would get 'what scraps he can out of bookes or by hear say'. Aubrey's horse was recovered, but there was 8s. in expenses to pay on the return of the animal. Ogilby refused to contribute to this sum, and, showing that Aubrey's earlier suspicion of his shiftiness was justified, left his deputy four or five pounds out of pocket on the cost of the survey, notwithstanding

[1] A nickname, probably of Anthony Hodges, Rector of Wytham in Berkshire. He was a great wag. John Newman was another member of Wood's circle.

the seven pounds he had had for the task in the first place. As Aubrey remarked: 'God deliver me from such men.'

A detailed questionnaire had been printed and sent round by Ogilby to persons likely to help him with antiquarian information. There is a copy of this paper attached to the manuscript of the *Surrey Collections*, and on it Aubrey has written the note: 'These queries were considered at several meetings by Christopher Wren, LL.D., John Hoskyns, Esq., RSS, Mr R. Hook, RSS, Mr Jo. Ogilby, Mr John Aubrey, Mr Gregory King. The last of these, Gregory King,[1] was a young genealogist, engraver, and statistician who etched some of the plates for the new edition of Camden's *Britannia* which was then contemplated, and eventually appeared in 1695. He had helped Ogilby in the survey of Essex, and raised money for him by a lottery of books, action more congenial to the cosmographer than Aubrey's unremunerative methods. A few years after this King was appointed Rouge Dragon Pursuivant.

Meanwhile, the third volume of Dugdale's *Monasticon* was published, in 1673, containing Hesketh's picture of Osney, engraved by Hollar, headed with a shield charged with the Aubrey arms, and bearing an inscription referring to the circumstances in which Aubrey, years before as an undergraduate, had been instrumental in contributing this illustration. In copies of the *Monasticon* the Osney plate is for some reason rare.

In this October, Aubrey's old Trinity friend, William Radford, died at Richmond, where he had kept his school, and where, only a few days before his decease, Aubrey had been with him, when they had discussed that 'honest sequestered' Wykehamist's great adventure—the time when he and Tom Mariet and Ned Wood had walked to London and seen on the way the famous Hales. Radford left a widow, a lady, says Aubrey, who 'haz a solar face (yet the sun in her horoscope could not be *in ascendente*), and thrives well, and haz a good sound judgment'.

---

[1] King laid out the streets of Soho, and Soho Square was formerly called King's Square. It has been suggested that Greek Street, formerly Grig Street, was so called after King's christian name.

VII

Aubrey continued to search for a niche into which he could creep, where he could earn enough to keep him alive, and at the same time retain opportunities to pursue his antiquarian and other interests. On returning to London after the completion of the Surrey survey, he saw much of his friend, Robert Hooke, the scientist and inventor, as appears from the latter's *Journal*, in which there are a number of entries such as: 'Lent Aubery 20 sh: he promised to repay it'; or notes of books—a *Euclid* or a *Scaliger*—bought by Hooke from Aubrey in his extremities. In March 1674 Hooke recorded: 'Mr Aubrey arrested for 200 *li*', an episode that Aubrey himself describes, when the serjeant who apprehended him was one, Gardiner, 'a lusty, faire-haired solar fellow, prowd, insolent, *et omnia id genus*'. However, Hooke was able to write in his diary four days later: 'Mr Aubery cleerd, &c.'

While under arrest, Aubrey wrote on 31 March, 1674, to Wood: 'In short I thank you for your advice concerning the Cassock, and it will be better for me to accept of 50 *li* or 60 *li* per annum which will serve my turne . . . I would knowe when Robinet comes to sett in the Exchange. I can recommend him to Ivory-turners, cane-makers where I now ly, very honest fellows and good workmen and where curious Tortoseshell knives are made and Telescopes. I would have him goe once or twice a year to Paris. Now you must know that the London Booksellers are Jewes and blockheads, and the *Virtuosi* want a Factor to buy new bookes and maps at Paris, which either are not to be gott (or if sent for) 5 times the Rate there. This would bring him in favour with all the R.S. and they would reward him well for his Factorage besides.'

On Easter Eve Aubrey's friend, Major John Graunt, died, author of *Observations on the Bills of Mortality* and other statistical studies, in working on which Graunt had been in close touch with Sir William Petty. He was a member of the Royal Society, and 'had gonne through all the offices of the city so far as common councill man', says Aubrey, but became a Roman Catholic and laid down all public employment. 'A great number of ingeniose persons attended him to his grave' in St Dunstan's in Fleet Street, and Aubrey saw Petty there, weeping.

On 9 April, 1674, Aubrey returned to discussing with Wood the possibility of emigration: 'I am like to be spirited away to Jamaica by my Lord Vaughan,[1] who is newly made Governor there, and mighty earnest to have me goe with him and will looke out some employment worthy a Gent for me. Fough! the Cassock stinkes: it would be ridiculous. I can send into England every month or six weekes.'

The sentiments expressed are characteristic of Aubrey in his manner of being, at times, so much at variance with the ways of his age. In the seventeenth century it would not be surprising to find an instance of objection to taking orders arising from some irreconcilable minutiae of theological conviction; or, alternatively, one might expect the cynical acceptance of an incumbency as a respectable means of earning a livelihood without undue exertion. 'Religious topics he seldom appears to have adverted to', remarks Britton; and Aubrey certainly had an infinite toleration for the religious opinions of others. A view of the ministry as a 'ridiculous' profession for him must, in his day, have been at least a little unusual; though there seems to be little or nothing in his writings to support Richard Garnett's view (expressed in the article on Aubrey in the *Dictionary of National Biography*) that he 'seems, nevertheless, to have inclined to the philosophy of his friend Hobbes'—if this phrase is intended to convey that Aubrey shared Hobbes's agnosticism.

Wood had something better to do than to worry about Aubrey's personal problems, because his *Historia et Antiquitates Universitatis Oxoniensis* was on the point of publication, and the part Dr Fell played in the production of this work was proving very troublesome to him. The Dean of Christ Church, says Aubrey, had 'perused every sheet before 'twas sent to the presse: and maugre the author and to his sore displeasure did expunge and inserted what he pleased. Among other authors, he made divers alterations in Mr

[1] John Vaughan, later 3rd Earl of Carbery, appointed Governor of Jamaica, 1674. Pepys called him: 'one of the lewdest fellows of the age, worse than Sir Charles Sedley'.

JOHN AUBREY F.R.S. aged 40: from a drawing in ink, lightly tinted with watercolour, made by William Faithorne in 1666.

Antonius à Wood.
Oxon. Antiquarius.
A. D. 1677.

ANTHONY WOOD, aged about 45, drawing in wash from a bust.

Wood's copie in the account he gives of Mr T. Hobbes of Malmes-bury's life . . . also in the lives of other very learned men to their disparagement.' On 23 April, 1674, Aubrey wrote to Wood on this subject:

'I received your kind letter with Dr Fell's Insertions concerning my countreyman Mr Thomas Hobbes, and sent you an answer to it, and of my delivering it to him (who remembers him very kindly to you), and that he would desire you *to write a letter of com-plaint to him of it, and he will vindicate himself in print against the Doctor, at the end of a booke he is now printing, viz. the Translation of Homer's Odysses.* I have not since heard from you, so that whether you received my letter I am doubtful. I showed it to Sir Christo-pher Wren and Dr Twisse (who remembers him to you) *cum multis aliis Virtuosis*; who all (*uno ore*) cry out of the Injustice used against you, and say againe (amongst others Mr Dugdale and Mr Ashmole) that you have no way so good to cleare yourselfe, as to print a Sheet here in London of the Doctor's Foystings, to be bound up with your Booke. Dr Twisse is sufficiently nettled (as he haz reason) and is glad to hear of such a Revenger.'

Dr Twisse was a friend of Aubrey's, and 'minister of the new church neer Tothil street, Westminster'. He (or perhaps it was only his father) was a man of 'melancholique and hypocondriaque tem-perament', a condition not improved by Dr Fell's irritating activities regarding the notice of his father, Dr William Twisse, in the *Historia et Antiquitates*. On 16 May, 1674, Aubrey wrote to Wood:

'I doe thinke it will be my fate to goe to America this Summer'; and, on 26th of the same month: 'Pray remember my Complaint about Robinet lending my rare Italian booke to Sir — Crooke.[1] For God's sake be earnest with him to gett it againe, and let him not sell *me* for a booke. I might doe him a greater courtasie then that comes to. If he abuses me, he is as ungrateful a wretch as ever served a Master.'

---

[1] 'I have left an Italian booke at Mr Stedman's for Robinet to translate', wrote Aubrey to Wood, Whitsun, 1671. In nearly every subsequent letter he wrote to Wood during this period, Aubrey refers to his desire to have this book (which was about 'carving, and foulding linnen and fencing') returned to him.

In July 1674, Wood's book appeared, in two great folios, with an engraved title and numerous headpieces: in the body of Volume II, an appreciation of Aubrey's help, fulsome enough to preclude any later claim on Wood's part to dissatisfaction at this stage of their relationship. Aubrey was pleased, though he had been anxious to figure in the preface as 'of Easton Pierse' to 'contra-distinguish him from other John Aubreys' (of whom there were, indeed, several in existence); and, on 28 July, he wrote: 'like a wild olive or polypodium my name will live upon your never-dyeing structure . . . severall of my friends dehort me from Jamaica; for why should I at this time of day, and being of a Monastic humour, make myselfe a slave and roast my selfe for Wealth? *Apage Satana.*'[1] However, if he could for the time bear with Aubrey, there were others by whom Wood felt himself deeply provoked on the subject of the book, Dr Fell being naturally the worst offender in this respect. Fell's interference with the form of the notice given to Hobbes resulted in a sharp controversy between the philosopher and the Dean, during the course of which the aggressive Doctor told Hobbes 'that he was an old man, had one foote in the grave, that he should mind his latter end, and not trouble the world any more with his papers'. This was not the language that the author of *Leviathan* was likely to take lying down; and the King himself became involved, most unwillingly, in this unseemly scuffle between the sages.

'Your Booke is generally well received,' wrote Aubrey on 15 September, 1674, 'but would have been better, had not the Dean imbittered it, so much and so often with his gall and spleen: but the Odium lyes on him, which (had not Mr Hobbes' Epistles lett the worlde knowe the Deane's intermedling) would have layn at your dore.' To his emendations and interpolations in the text, Fell had added his insistence that Wood's book should appear in Latin, making this a condition of his support. Wood, with a sound instinct for discarding an obsolete literary fashion, wished the work to be issued in English. Aubrey had written to Wood on this subject as early as 17 February, 1669: 'I thought good to advertize

---

[1] *i.e.* 'Get thee behind me, Satan.'

you that I can so bring it about that if you have a mind to have records at Rome searcht, it shall be done for you: for when I was at Paris I was acquainted with some of the Jesuits[1] who will undertake it: but one of them this day told me that he does not approve of the Universitye's design in printing first in Latin, for if it is first in English it will bring it into far more fame and sell the better.' However, Fell's habitual intractability resulted in this piece of academic obscurantism being observed; and in Latin the *Historia et Antiquitates Universitatis Oxoniensis* was finally published.

In October that year Aubrey visited for the last time his old Trinity friend, Francis Potter (who died in 1678): 'I had not seen him in three years before and his lippitude then was come even to blindnesse, which did much grieve me to behold. He had let his beard be uncutt, which was wont to be but little. I asked him why he did not get some kinswoman or kinsman of his to live with him, and looke to him now in his great age? He answer'd me that he had tried that way; and found it not so well: for they did begrudge what he spent that 'twas too much and went from them, whereas his servants (strangers) were kind to him and tooke care of him.'

On 30 November, 1674, there was a letter from Lord Thanet: 'Your last of the 7th of this Instant I receiv'd, and it being sent by the Cantebury Post, I had not made an answer to it, since this is the 10th time at least, that I desired you never to send any Letters by that way, since every Thursday about seven o'clocke the Carrier (John Godfrey) his Porter may be found at the May Pole in the Strand, and by no meanes neaver any letters does miscarry and most doe by the Cantebury: Butt since 'tis Dr Tonge's[2] concerne, I shall for the time returne an answer.

[1] Aubrey uses the sign H̶.

[2] This was Dr Ezreel Tonge, Titus Oates' foolish, rather than criminal, accomplice in the 'Popish Plot'. Oates had in 1673 been instituted vicar of Bobbing in Kent, Bobbing Place being a seat of the Tufton family. A number of Thanet's relations are buried in the church. Tonge also held livings in Kent, but does not appear to have met Oates (who was translated to Hastings in 1674) until 1676. Tonge was a friend of Aubrey, who was chiefly interested in his educational experiments.

'I am much obliged to the Doctor for concerning himself with my health; I have taken so maney Slapps of Sundry Persons as well Phisitians, as others, that I'le incline to the oppion that Apollo onely can absolutely cure mee, to whose Deity I would performe a Pilgrimage as far as the Bermudes, were I not in Diana's grove, which sweet Island certainly was that the Poet thus justly speakes on. *Hic ver perpetuum atque alienis mensibus aestas.* I have read amongst the Ancients that Bacchus was in Some Place adored for the God of health, as well as Apollo, or Esculapos; of his blessings I doubt not to participate in a few yeares, from the Bermudes and I thinke it cannot bee denyed that Naturall wine well concocted in a warme Southerne Countrey is a drinke very much conducing to man's health, and perticulerly in the Rhumatick unhealthfull countrey, where the pretious Liquor is so basely abused. . . . I want some ingeniose Person, that would goe over to the Bermudes to bound my land, give me an accompt of the soyle and many other particulars too long here to insert; and when hee hath done that hee may retourne, if he pleases on the 1st opportunity. If you can recommend any such to mee you would doe a great kindnesse to your affectionate servant, Thanet.'

This was, presumably, intended to be a suggestion that Aubrey might undertake the duties described. Thanet's family had been connected with the Bermudas since 1629, when Sir William Tufton had been appointed governor (being executed on a charge of high treason by his successor two years later), and, in spite of his glowing account of the islands, there may have been circumstances that made Thanet circumspect about making Aubrey a direct offer: a request from Aubrey's side putting the peer on safer ground if (as might easily have happened) Aubrey's genius had not proved to be adapted to the plantations.

VIII

In 1674 Aubrey's friend, George Ent, went to live in Oxford, and in August Aubrey gave him an introduction to Wood, a meeting that proved far from successful. Ent, whose family had come from the Low Countries, was the son of Sir George Ent,

friend and correspondent of Hobbes and Harvey, with the latter
of whom he had travelled in Italy. The younger Ent was a member
of the Middle Temple. His early experience of the ill-humours of
schoolmasters had perhaps soured his view of all academical persons, since Aubrey says that he had been at school under Dr Triplett,[1] who had kicked him down a flight of stairs for inciting
another boy to ask for a share in the pedagogue's pot of honey. Sir
George Ent considered this treatment unduly severe, and removed
his son to William Radford's school at Richmond, where the headmaster's memories of having his hair cut with a carving knife may
have tempered the discipline with more discretion. Be that as it
may, his pupil never seems to have acquired the art of asking
judiciously, and on a number of occasions it was necessary for
Aubrey to make apologies for Ent to Wood, to whom he wrote on
26 August, 1674: 'he is a very honest gentleman and his rhodomontades you will easily pardon'. But Wood did not easily pardon
Ent's rhodomontades. The *casus belli* narrowed itself down to the
question whether or not Ent should be allowed to borrow Aubrey's
Life of Hobbes, still incomplete but now in a coherent form. Aubrey
vacillated between a good-natured desire to gratify his friend's
curiosity and a prudent fear that, if the biography were committed
to his hands, Ent would gossip about its contents wherever he
went. On 24 October, 1674, he wrote to Wood: 'If I can I will
write today to Mr Ent. I desire he should peruse Mr Hobbes life:
but if he has a copie of it, it will fly about like lightning, and Mr
Hobbes who is something apt to be cholerique upon just cause
as this is, will be very angry and I shall loose his Friendship. . . .
The Cuckold of Alderton might have been pleased to name me
too,[2] not that I value his Testimony but he has perused my
MSS, and has done his business and now a fart for me.'

---

[1] Triplett had been brought up in a violent tradition, having himself suffered under Dr Gill of St Paul's School, who was said to spare
neither age nor sex in his delight in birching, a catholicity of taste cele-
brated in a ballad (quoted by Aubrey) of Dr Triplett's own composition.

[2] Gore had in that year brought out an enlarged edition of his
*Catalogus plerorumque omnium authorum qui de re heraldica Latine, Gallice,
Hispanice, Germanice, Anglice, scripserunt.*

On 12 January, 1675, Aubrey wrote again to Wood on the subject of Ent: 'Mr G. Ent is a very honest Gent. but you must pardon his passions sometimes. Mr Ent was so angry with me and so importunate for Mr Hobbes life that I could not deny it him: but if he should let it flye about he would infinitely disoblige me and the D[ean] of Ch[rist Church]'s faction would be nibling at it. I am obliged to him for his old Acquaintance and told him I would write to you to let me have it.'

Wood was not the man to let matters go as easily as that; and if (as was likely enough) there was a possibility of Fell and his clique making trouble about the *Life of Hobbes*, even before it appeared, there was some cause firmly to resist showing the manuscript to one who, on Aubrey's own admission, was likely to chatter about the contents. On 25 February, 1675, Aubrey wrote once more: 'I thinke to satisfye Mr Ent's longing you must showe him the life. . . . All men cry out against the Deane's spoyling your Booke. . . . In your next edition if you only mention my name in the Preface as you intended (and which the Dean I am confident scracht out) I shall be glad of the honour. I mean only shortly mentioned.'

On 28 February, 1675, Wood voiced his complaints: 'You have always told me, since Mr Ent came from London, that you are sorry that he and I have not better contexture of humours— that you doubt not but we now agree—and the such like. Now give me leave to tell you, that since he came from London last, a little before Xmas, (at which time you communicated my letter to him, which you should not have done) he hath not taken notice of me nor spoke to me. The first time that I sawe him after his returne from London, I welcom'd him home and we ate dinner togeather. I dranke to him, not taking notice of what had passed; but he I say truth not returned to me the like civility, and therefore shows himself to be no good natured man. What? Do you think that after he has vented his simplicity towards me, I shall sneak to him—No I will not. I have done enough already. Besides had he any good nature in him, he would not be quarrelsome in his liquor, but being so I have done with him, and rather glad than sorrowful for his displeasure. . . . Now you know my mind. I would not have you make it worse than this. Upon your often urging me these matters in every letter you have sent since Xmas, I now send you the truth, which reason I would have you take notice off, and thinke not that I tell you these things upon my owne will onlie.'

On 6 March, 1675, Ent sent Aubrey an account of how matters looked from his side: 'In the meantime the animall A. Wood does study to disoblige and affront me. Sir, I told you in my last letter I would see him hanged before I would ask him for Mr Hobbes's life and now I'll see him hang'd and damned before I'll do't. Why should he be courted to deliver the goods? You ought to command him to it: God and nature designed that fellow rather for a bricklayer than a historian.'

On 9 March, still trying to keep the peace, Aubrey wrote to Wood: 'I am exceedingly sorry for Mr Ent's strangeness to you: but 'tis confest his *friends* must bear with him. I did not show him your letter: but, expostulating with him, and he being cholerique, &c I read only the paragraph where he *"introduced into your company two boy-batchelors and upbrayded you with dotage"*.'

Ent kept up the bombardment, writing to Aubrey on 8 April, 1675, that he could not 'too much blame your A. Wood here, one not only very peremtory in his abuses, but, as farre as I can perceive, does ostentate and pride himself in them. I thinke he is not at present in Towne, but when he returns you would do well to command those things out of his hands, and I will then take care that they should be dispos'd of according to your commands.' On 20 April, 1675, Ent wrote again, adding at the end of his letter: 'I have sent you a shilling to drinke my health, and Mr Wiseman has sent you an Ivory Tobacco-Stopper.'

On Shrove Tuesday (9 May), 1675, Aubrey wrote to Wood: 'I am sorry G. Ent and you have no better contexture of humours. I find him to be no great lover of Antiq: but pardon him. My kind respects to Mr Browne and the merry happy gang and to Mr Wiseman when you see him. . . . I would have G.E. and you and all quarrells over a glass of Sack.' On this note dissensions seem to have died away, Wood and Ent avoiding the other's company. Aubrey tried again on 18 May: 'I *yet* wish there could be a right understanding between you'; but it was no good. Dislike was mutual and absolute.

IX

On 19 April, 1675, Lord Thanet had written to Aubrey: 'I perceive that Mr Wild has a mind to buy some land in New York which place you suppose to be a fine Countrey. You are the first that ever I heard terme that part a delicious Countrey. Corne, indeed, I heare will growe there, and in the summer they may have fatt Beef and Mutton; but in the winter, which is very long and tedious, they are like the Norwegians that live upon Salt-Meates, and Fish, and have such vast Snowes that they are forced to digg their wayes out of their houses, else they would be stifled. If he will buy land in America, lett it be in the Bermudes, where health abounds and safety is had, two cheife things which a wise man, as he, should looke after, and so much with my humble service pray let him knowe.

'Your lodging like an enchanted castle, being never to be found out, I shall in the future direct my Letters to Mr Hooke's chamber in Gressam Colledge, as you desire. . . . Your last from London dated the 24 of this instant was brought to me hither the day following by our owne Carryer. That you sent it by the right way was not surely intended, but happened either by miracle or chance.

'I am glad you have so good an opportunity to make your addresses to that excellent lady the younger Countess Dowager of Pembrooke,[1] who if your starres be favourable, may through the interests of the Dutches of Portsmouth, procure you some good employment if not neglected by a wonted trapishness incident in You. The freedome I take in mentioning that You will, I hope, easily forgive, since I doe it not by way of check, but by a friendly advertisement to beware of it; . . . If you have the same occasions of protection against your merciless creditors as you had some while

---

[1] This was Catherine, widow of Philip, 5th Earl of Pembroke, and daughter of Sir William Villiers, bart. Her son, Philip, 7th Earl of Pembroke, married on 20 May, 1675, Henrietta de Kéroualle, youngest sister of the Duchess of Portsmouth, the King's mistress.

since, I may now serve you in it, both with *salvo honore et conscientia*, provided you will be a little ruled.'

It was, of course, Aubrey's friend, Edmund Wyld, who had been thinking of buying land in New York. This rich eccentric, the owner of several estates, who lived with his mistress, Jane Smyth, in a large house in Bloomsbury, will be spoken of later in the chapter that deals with Aubrey's intimate friends. Wyld had been a Member of Parliament in Cromwell's day, and he may have thought it wise to provide himself with a property in the New World, since the times were so uncertain. The offer of protection was acceptable enough to Aubrey, and, on 3 May, 1675, Thanet wrote again:

'J. Aubrey. With this you will receive a Protection according to your desire, which when useless returne. I send it to you under this provisoe, that you are now my Sollicitor to looke after my businesse in London; and for your Sallary that is agreed on. My mother hath lent me Thanet house garden, where I intend to fit up two or three chambers for my use when I come to London privately, and intend to stay not long there, one of which as my meniall servant you may make use of when fitted up, and when it is you shall have notice.

'Sift my cosen Charles Howard as much as you can, concerning his intended voyage to the Bermudes, of which give me the speediest account possible: as likewise in what part of the world the new Caesarea lies: and whether it be a place newly discovered or that it is or hath been formerly planted. I conceave before Mr Wild goes thither, to whome I sent my humble service, you will have time enough to give me notice of it. I know he is soe civill and good natur'd a Gent, that if he buys a good pennyworth in purchases there, he will assist his humble servant in doing the like. His good Company and edifying conversation would be a great motive to make me buy a purchase there, to be his neighbour. But as to Billing and his Braine-sick crew, I must owne not to be over covetous of such Acquaintance and Neighbours. I shall not forget to acquaint Mr Wild when I send to Provence to get enough of the Acornes of the red Oake for my Freinds and Selfe, of which he may command what proportion he pleases.

'I would have you in future to take more time in writing your letters, for the last was so ill writ that I had a great deal of trouble to read some part of it.

Thanet.'

On the following day, he wrote to Aubrey once more, this time saying:

'Sir, I am not soe ignorant as not to knowe that the Stile of myne of the third Instant is much unbefitting to writ in to a Gentleman of Your Birth. The reason why I make my Selfe such a prowd ill bread Fellowe in it, is the better to disguise the business you lately enjoyned me to doe for you: and on the same score my Letters in the future shall be, by your permission, as little civill, then in case any should be questioned on the account you knowe of, in producing such, writ in soe imperious a manner, will induce all to believe that the business, although very unbefitting your belonging to me, is no otherwise than reall. Although this small service can hardly be inrolled under the notion of a Curtesy, yet I assure you 'tis the first protection I ever gave, although I have been in this nature sollicited by many. Were there anything of moment that I could serve you in, you might freely command him who is in great reallity, Your most affectionate and humble servant, Thanet.'

The general purport of Lord Thanet's two letters must be considered in the light of a peer's right—abolished some score of years later—to grant as part of his parliamentary privilege a 'Protection' to any of his 'menial' (i.e. whole-time, paid) servants to shield him from arrest upon civil process—usually arrest for debt: all such Protection being registered by the Clerk of the Parliaments. The 'prowd ill bread' letter was merely the formal document to be produced by Aubrey if necessary, since the records show that there were perpetual complaints regarding the abuse of this privilege. The enquiries in the middle part of the letter relapse into the normal style of Thanet's correspondence. It is permissible to wonder whether the letter was not at least in a small degree intended to remind Aubrey of his dependent position at the same time as it provided him with an asylum from his creditors. The facetious, self-satisfied tone of the peer's letters do not convey an attractive impression of the writer, though there can be no doubt that his patronage of Aubrey was a good-natured act. The cousin to whom he refers in the earlier letter was probably Charles Howard, F.R.S., of Deepdene, Dorking, son of Lord Arundel.

Perhaps it is unjust to suggest that Thanet's behaviour was self-important, for he makes no change in his manner of writing to Aubrey, who sent him news of his cousin, Charles Howard, and suggested a meeting with Sir James Long, at this time staying in Provence. Howard was thinking of buying land in the Bermudas, and, on 7 June, 1675, Thanet wrote to Aubrey:

'Minos (the Secretary of the Bermudan Company) may be a fitting person to inform Mr Howard of such owners. He is a scraping shurding Fellow, and will hardly answer a question unless daubed in the hand; Therefore my cousen's best way will be in treating with him, to let him know that in case he goes through with a purchase by his procurement, he will then gratifie him for his paines taken in that concerne.'

Thanet goes on to speak of the scurvy from which he suffered, a disease he seems to have despaired of curing. A year later, on 22 May, 1676, he wrote making arrangements to see someone Aubrey had recommended for his 'Bermudian Steward', closing with the words: 'Since this letter is to be left for you, I have paid the carriage of it here, not to trouble your Freindes to do it at Gresham Colledge; therefore be pleased to let me knowe, if the Porter askes anything of him for it, that I may know him againe for an errant Shirke, and hee shall be treated accordingly.'

x

In 1675, Aubrey submitted his *Natural History of Wiltshire* to the Royal Society, when 'it gave them two or three days entertainment which they were pleased to like'. He had, perhaps, hoped that they might testify their appreciation by printing the manuscript. From June to October he stayed with the Longs at Draycot. On 27 November, 1675, he wrote to Wood: 'as you were saying, if I could be Principall of Gloucester hall[1] that were a fine way of ending my dayes in peace and ingeniose innocency. I would undertake to make it an ingeniose Nest and would decoy thither several honest and ingeniose persons of either University and some from beyond Sea.' In the same year, John Evelyn, whose residence in the county concerned added weight to his opinion of the book, was shown the *Surrey Collections*, and wrote on 8 February, 1676:

[1] Gloucester Hall, Oxford, was in very low water at this period.

'Sir, with incredible Satisfaction have I perus'd your *Natural History of Surrey*, &c; and greatly admire both your Industry in undertaking so profitable a Work, and your Judgment in the several Observations which you have made. It is so useful a Piece and so obliging, that I cannot sufficiently applaud it. Something I would contribute to it if it were possible; but your *Spicilegium* is so accurate, that you have left nothing almost for those who come after you.' Evelyn goes on to give some account of his family's house, Wotton, and the 'Sugar-Loaf mountains' to the south-west of that seat, which, 'with the Boscage upon them and little Torrents between, make such a Solitude, as I have never seen any Place more horridly agreeable and Romantick'.

It was in 1675, too, that Aubrey met Dr Robert Plot, 'who had then his *Naturall Historie of Oxfordshire*[1] upon the loome, which I seeing he did performe so excellently well, desired him to undertake Wiltshire, and I would give him all my papers: as I did also my papers of Surrey as to the naturall things, and offered him my further assistance. But he was then invited into Staffordshire to illustrate that countie.'

Plot, who in February 1676 wrote to Aubrey enclosing 'the remarques of the gravediggers of Woking concerning the roots springing from dead bodies', had been born in 1640. He was an Oxford scholar of Magdalen Hall, and later of University College, where he had been responsible for the erection of the statue of King Alfred. His Oxfordshire and Staffordshire collections take much the same form as Aubrey's Wiltshire papers, the scientific theories being equally reckless, while Aubrey's mastery of the apt phrase is lacking. Plot was pushing, and he had, perhaps, more application; but he was as credulous as Aubrey in the latter's most uncritical moods, and there is no reason to suppose that he would have made of the Wiltshire material better use than did Aubrey himself. His quick wits and ambition, together with a capacity for thrusting himself forward, seem to have impressed Plot's contemporaries in disproportion to his real ability. He liked good living, and his successor as keeper of the Ashmolean, the young Welshman, Edward Lhwyd, described him as 'a man of as bad morals as ever took a doctor's degree', adding to this devastating superlative: 'I wish

---

[1] Aubrey annotated his copy of Plot's *Oxfordshire* (Ash, 1722), notably about Thomas Bushell and Francis Potter (see R. Elsley's letter in *Times Lit. Supp.*, 5 Oct. 1951).

his wife a good bargain of him, and myself that I may never meet with his like again.'

In an undated letter (or postscript), written apparently about this period, or perhaps a short time later, Aubrey wrote to Wood: 'If you die; or, one knowes not some time or other as the World runs madding, your papers may be sifted & examined. Therefore *ex abundante cautelâ*, I would entreat you to burne (or blott out) a passage[1] in a letter of mine about 1674 or 5, wherein I expressed friendship for the Ch. of R. God bless us from another Rebellion. 'Twas when I was invited to take a Benefice.' There were, indeed, new suggestions that he should enter the Church. Charles Snell, another astrologer friend, had written to him (beginning 'Dear Gossip') on 21 August, 1676: 'If the haesitation in your speech doth hinder, gett a parsonage of 4 or 500 *li* per annum, and give a curate 100 *li per annum* to officiate for you.'[2] The phrase seems to imply that Aubrey's stammer was more serious than his own references to it might suggest; but, however inconvenient this impediment may have been, the practical advice in the matter of a curate could no doubt have been followed, at least in the early days of his indigence, if Aubrey had had any such inclination.

On 29 August, 1676 (on the day upon which Henry St George, the Somerset herald, had shown him the documents at the College of Arms regarding Dr William Aubrey's funeral), Aubrey wrote again to Wood about the question of taking Orders: 'I am stormed by my chiefest friends afresh, *viz* Baron Bertie, Sir William Petty, Sir John Hoskyns, bishop of Sarum, etc., to turne ecclesiastique; "but the king of France grows stronger and stronger, and what if the Roman religion should come-in againe?" "Why then!" say they "cannot you turne too?" You, I say, know well that I am no puritan, nor an enimy to the old Gentleman on the other side of the Alpes. Truly, if I had a good parsonage of 2 or 300 *li* per annum,

[1] See p. 147.
[2] 'Charles Snell, Esq., of Alderholt, Fordingbridge', Hampshire, belonged to the Snell family, who were neighbours of the Aubreys at Kington St Michael. In one of his letters he writes from Salisbury and speaks of 'my cosen Gore's nativity'.

(as you told me) it would be a shrewed temptation . . . the next week I shall goe into Essex with my good friend Mr Wyld but shall in a weeke quickly return again, and perhaps may goe with him to Worcestershire.'

Certainly Aubrey was in an awkward position. One post, if he had succeeded in securing it, would have made Pepys his colleague, as appears from a slip (no doubt the fragment of a letter) pasted on one of the Aubrey manuscripts: 'Mr Secretary Wren's indefinite kindnesse is valuable if our lord P. know it, and Mr Collins, but *cave*. They might between them determine somewhat certaine. There are peacable places among souldiers; and now the navy office thrives, and a man can nowhere so well hide himselfe in an office as there, 'cause 'tis out of the way. I cannot get Quillettus here, but would you could find Gallus Veridicus, which you must enquire for privately. I never saw it, but Mr Oldenburg may possibly have heard of it. The want of the Royal Society is the greatest defect of our parts: possibly you have some one that for money will informe mee as you doe for love. If you find any such fix him for J.†'

'Our Lord P.' means Lord Brouncker, President of the Royal Society, and 'Mr Collins' was John Collins, F.R.S., a friend of Aubrey's and a mathematician. The German, Henry Oldenburg, mentioned towards the end of the letter, was the Society's first secretary, holding the post jointly with Dr John Wilkins, who had married Oliver Cromwell's sister. Oldenburg had lived in England for many years, sometimes employed by his native state of Bremen as a diplomatic agent, but mostly devoting his energies to scientific study and letters. In Cromwell's time objection had been raised to his appointment on the grounds that he had taken the King's part during the Civil Wars; and also because he was alleged to have a 'peculiar temper which prevented him from agreeing well with others'. This latter characteristic was in some evidence during his great quarrel with Aubrey's friend, Robert Hooke, whose own temper was not of the best, and who considered that Oldenburg had not done justice to his invention of the hair-spring for pocket-watches. The last sentence, written on the slip of paper by Aubrey, means, of course, that he misses most of all the meetings of the

Royal Society, and would willingly pay for a regular account of these.

In the lists that he composed, called *Faber Fortunae*,[1] in which he wrote down various methods by which he might make some money, Aubrey noted: '1676: from Sir William Petty—Jamaica 500 *li* gives 100 per annum: take a chymist with me, for brandy, suger, etc., and goe halfe with him.' It was probably to this trying period of his life that Aubrey referred when he wrote of Dr Edward Davenant (who had taught him algebra and Sir Christopher Wren had described as 'the best mathematician in the world' thirty or more years before): 'he was my singular good friend and to whom I have been more beholden than any one else besides: for I borrowed five hundred pounds of him for a yeare and a halfe, and I could not fasten any interest on him.' Davenant, as has been mentioned earlier, was father-in-law of Aubrey's friend, Anthony Ettrick, who supplied some of Aubrey's information about the Doctor. Both Dorset antiquaries, Ettrick was now Recorder of Poole, and later committed Monmouth after Sedgemoor. His difficulties in these years did not prevent Aubrey from carrying on correspondence with Hobbes (who had left London in 1675, to spend the rest of his days in Derbyshire, at Chatsworth or Hardwick with his patron), John Ray the naturalist, and many others who shared his interests. There seem also to have been other consolations during this melancholy period, as Hooke recorded in his *Journal*, on 13 August, 1676, that Aubrey told him 'of his living and of bouncing Pru'. When in London he lodged for the most part with Hooke at Gresham College, where the Royal Society had rooms: or at the Tobacco Roll and Sugar Loaf, 'at the upper end of Maydenhead-lane opposite the gap in Great Russell Street in St. Giles', a convenient *pied-à-terre* for Thanet House, which, latterly, stood in Great Russell Street, the owner having disposed of his mansion (built by Inigo Jones) in Aldersgate Street to Lord Shaftesbury, to whom the unfashionable position was convenient for demagogic purposes.

[1] *Faber est quisquis Fortunae suae* was one of the mottoes in a room at South Wraxall House, a seat of the Long family, and the phrase had probably struck Aubrey on a visit there. Comenius called a work *Faber Fortunae*, 1637.

Aubrey noted that: 'About 1676 or 5, as I was walking through Newgate Street, I saw Dame Venetia's bust standing at a stall at the Golden Crosse, a brasier's shop. I perfectly remembered it, but the fire had gott off the guilding: but taking notice of it to one that was with me, I could never see it afterwards exposed to the street. They melted it downe. Now these curiosities would be quite forgotten, did not such idle fellows as me putt them downe!'[1] In September 1676 John Ogilby, the Royal Cosmographer, died. During the whole of this period Aubrey spent a great deal of his time with Robert Hooke, Edmund Wyld and his mistress, Jane Smyth, with other friends, at coffee houses and taverns such as Garaway's, Jonathan's, Tooth's, Man's or Mr. Farre's, at the Rainbow in Fleet Street; meetings regularly recorded in Hooke's *Journal*.

[1] This was the memorial of the famous courtesan Venetia Stanley, who before her connexion (like Bess Broughton's) with Lord Dorset, had been, according to Aubrey, 'a miss to Sir Edmund Wyld', father of Aubrey's friend of the same name. Later she had married Sir Kenelm Digby, who, says Aubrey, was accustomed to express the opinion that 'a wise man and lusty, could make an honest woman out of a brothell-house', and who seems to have cherished no regrets regarding this matrimonial experiment. On her death in 1633, Digby set up this copper-gilt bust of his wife, recognized by Aubrey, who could remember that the monument had formerly stood 'on an altar of black marble' in one of the City churches. He recorded a little drawing of the bust in the manuscript.

CHAPTER SIX

The Lives (1677–1692)

I

IN 1677 ELIAS ASHMOLE, 'the greatest virtuoso and curioso that ever was known or read of in England before his time', as Wood called him, decided to present the University of Oxford with the collection of rarities, brought together by the Trade-scants of Lambeth. This gift was on condition that a suitable building was found for the exhibits, and 'notwithstanding that he had been courted by others to bestow them elsewhere, and that others had offered great sums for them.' Although 'Tradescant's Ark' had been bequeathed to him, Ashmole had been obliged to obtain possession of the rarities by means not over fastidious: which had in fact involved, more or less directly, the suicide of Tradescant's widow. He had, however, made numerous additions of his own to the extraordinary accumulation of objects constituting the collection, and the University accepted his offer; which resulted in the erection of the museum since known as the Ashmolean, an institution which was to play an important part in Aubrey's life.

On 31 July, 1677, Aubrey noted: 'I sold my bokes to Mr Little-bery[1]; scilicet, when my impostume in my head did break': adding 'about 50 annos impostume in capite'. On 9 September Hook recorded in his diary: 'Aubery will stand for Secretary' [of the Royal Society] and, a month later, that he 'desired Mr Aubery to spread the Designe of choosing new president to Mr Ent, Dr Millington, &c.' It was also in October, on the 24th, that Hooke 'tickld Aubery' at Jonathan's coffee-house.

In the following year he was in Oxford again, and, on 21 May, 1678, Thomas Pigott (a Fellow of Wadham and Chaplain to Lord

---

[1] A bookseller.

Ossory), with whom Aubrey often corresponded especially on the subject of 'the Universal Language', wrote: 'I never met with any persons more deserving and obligeing than Mr Aubery and his Lady . . . their company was so pleasing and advantageous that I could not part with them whilst they stayed at Oxford, not till I had seen them in the stage coach at Abington, where I left them with a great deal of regret.' The identity of the lady remains veiled. On 17 August, 1678, Aubrey wrote to Wood, condoling with him on his increasing deafness and adding: 'I am sorry that Mr Browne showed himselfe such a Clowne to you. For the Cuckold of Aldrington, 'twas no great matter.'

II

In September 1678 Titus Oates made his depositions before Sir Edmond Berry Godfrey, and consternation at the rumours of the 'Popish Plot' began to spread throughout the country. Aubrey chose this not very propitious moment to stay with his Roman Catholic friend, Ralph Sheldon, at Weston Park, a house by Long Compton in Warwickshire.

Sheldon, who (according to Hearne) was called *Great Sheldon*, and who was of an 'antient, gentile and wealthy family' of Beoley, in Worcestershire, had been put in the way of meeting Wood by Aubrey, as friends having a common interest in heraldry and antiquities. In a letter dated 1 February, 1671, Aubrey had spoken of having been 'long acquainted' with Sheldon, who hoped (continued the letter) that Wood might come and stay with him that summer; and in the same year Sheldon himself had sought out Wood at Oxford, an attention, as usual, somewhat ungraciously recorded in the diary. As was his habit, Wood also took the opportunity at a later date to comment unfavourably on the inconvenience caused to him by the relationship—in this case owing to the circumstance of his new acquaintance's religion. 'Now Mr Sheldon being a zealous Papist and A.W. afterwards often in his company, must be esteem'd a Papist also, as he was by many sniveling saints, who make it a most horrible thing to be seen in the company of any of them.'

Most of his contemporaries certainly believed that Wood was a

Roman Catholic by conviction; and it is clear from his letters that Aubrey himself was at times in doubt as to whether or not his friend had been received secretly into the Roman Church. Although his friendship with Sheldon may have seemed to confirm this suspicion in the eyes of many, there were a number of other circumstances (not least the biographies in the *Athenae*) which made the supposition reasonable enough. However, Wood himself always denied any such imputation, and no doubt he extracted from Sheldon as much as he could for the injury done to his credit by this papistical association. Sheldon and his wealth were useful in many ways, and Wood undertook the cataloguing of the library at Weston, in return for which he was to receive financial assistance towards the production of the *Athenae*. Accordingly, Wood fell into the way of descending on Weston for months at a time, a habit of which the Sheldon family became most heartily sick. At length the host could endure these visitations no longer and would abscond for a week or two to London, returning only when he had reliable intelligence that his relentless guest had withdrawn himself: behaviour that was in consequence grimly recorded, as showing sad want of manners, by his persecutor in the diary.

Among his collections, Sheldon possessed a 'ballad book', often referred to by Aubrey as giving scraps of unusual historical information, such as the query to Wood (on 8 September, 1680), 'Pray search that booke, and see if you can find the ballad, or verses, on the coronation of King James—

> *And at the erse of them marched the Scottish peeres*
> *With lowzie shirts, and mangie wrists, went pricking up their eares.'*

This unfriendly piece of contemporary observation was to have been made use of in the life of James I, a biography contemplated by Aubrey, which, for reasons that will be seen later, has not survived. There were many other pieces in the book, like the verses on Dean Overall's wife or those on 'the five woemen barbers, that lived in Drewry Lane', which chronicled droll incidents of the past and sometimes gave useful indications of the sentiment of the time. Sheldon was able to supply biographical information, too, on the subject of many of the Roman Catholic writers to be included in the *Athenae*; and both Aubrey and Wood knew how to make use of the opportunities provided by an intelligent and well-to-do friend who possesses an excellent library.[1]

In 1678 Wood had gone to stay at Weston on 5 August. Aubrey seems to have followed later in the month, or perhaps in September. The frenzy of rumours about the 'Plot' were now reaching their height, and, on 12 October, Sheldon's house was searched for arms. Aubrey left on 15 October, Wood noting in his diary: 'lent to Mr John Aubrey at his going from Weston 3*s*. 6*d*.—he saith hee'l pay my brother at Staple Inn when he comes next to London.' Wood 'tarried there' until 28 November, but a week before he left a warrant[2] was issued for Sheldon's arrest; and his host was imprisoned for a time in Warwick gaol, from which place he wrote cheerful letters to Wood, saying that he read much, and was concerned only by a rumour that Dr Plot had laid information in particular against him. On his return to Oxford, Wood suffered a great amount of unpleasantness as a result of this episode. He was questioned as to his religious beliefs by the authorities of the University, and, as an outward sign of his conformity, he took the Oath of Supremacy and Allegiance before the Vice-Chancellor. Although such political disturbances always upset him, Aubrey, in his obscurity, had no official vexations; and, on 19 October, he watched with Hooke the eclipse of the moon. On 10 April, 1679, he wrote to Wood: 'I often dream of Weston'. In May of the same year Ralph Sheldon was free and again in London, when on the 27th he wrote to Wood: 'Yesterday came to mee honest Mr John Awbrey, whose head is so full that it will not give his tongue leave to utter one word after another. I assure you he is (to my apperance) as mad as anyone almost in the university of Bedlam.'

---

[1] Mr Arthur Bryant has pointed out that Sheldon's butler was called Will Waynman; and, although there is no supporting evidence to prove that he was, indeed, identical with Pepys's servant of that name, the possibility seems to be strong enough to be worth recording.

[2] Aubrey's friend, Thomas Mariet, now High Sheriff of Warwickshire, brought the warrant to Weston.

III

On 11 April, 1679, Lord Thanet had sent a letter to Aubrey saying:

'With such devout persons as you are to morrow I conceave will be an idle day; Therefore I should be glad of your company to morrow at my Lodgings, as early as you cann, I having a little Business with you and then afterwards we will eate a dish of meate together, at which I will give you a bottle of most excellent Portugall Wine, which is all at present necessary to be said by Your affectionate servant,   Thanet.'

Eight months later, on 24 November, 1679, in the forty-ninth year of his age, died Nicholas Tufton, 3rd Earl of Thanet, 'Baron Tufton and Baron Clifford, of Westmoreland and Vipont, Lord of the honor of Skipton in Craven, High Sheriff by inheritance of the County of Westmoreland, who by his early and generous education in arts and arms,' (says his memorial inscription in Rainham church) 'improved by much travel and experience, did greatly advance his natural endowments; being a person singularly eminent for his loyalty to the prince, king Charles the Second, in the time of whose banishment he suffered three years and a half imprisonment in the tower of London; and no less renowned for his love to his country, and also for valour and magnanimity, for justice, temperance, courtesy, conjugal affection and constant friendship, highly exemplary.' Although he does not seem to have remained in the Tower more than about half the time mentioned, some of this warm appreciation of Thanet's qualities may have been not entirely unmerited, making allowances for the convention of the commemoratory slab. To Aubrey he was always 'my honoured Lord', and, whatever his fads and sententious periods, his house was a refuge in time of stress and he was a patron whom it was ill to lose. Robinet's death took place in the same year, and Thomas Pigott wrote from Oxford on 29 April: 'Poore Mr Wiseman dy'd here some time agoe and I helped to carry him to the grave.'

Meanwhile, foreign affairs were taking on a threatening appearance. On 5 June, 1679, Aubrey wrote to Wood: 'Yesterday on the

old Exchange 'twas reported that in the Catholic Countreys there
is a Sodalitie of Devoto's that goe up and downe begging for
money to carry on the Warre in England for establishing their
Religion, and that they have gotten about two millions. They
weare crosses and a crowne of Thornes on their head. 'Tis said also
that the King of France will sett-up a Patriarch . . . the next
weeke I will put on a Roman resolution, and goe to Pancrace
church. The trueth is that I and Mr E[dmund] W[yld] doe grow a
little lethargiq.' On 26 June he wrote again, much worried about
some piece of secret information that he had passed on to Tom
Mariet, through whom his words had reached Wood. This indiscretion was the result of 'my head being fuller of good wine than
prudence'. It had been written from the Royal Society's rooms,
where there were always 'Parliament men and courtiers, persons of
great intelligence' and rumours would fly about: '. . . as concerning
the Q[ueen] there is strong evidence against her.[1] Severall of our
members have copies of the Depositions which will certainly cutt
her if she stayes. They say that she will goe to the Waters at Bour-
bon, and so into her own countrey. The Judges were sent to consult yesterday or the day before and some sayd that they adjudged
it not fitt for her to goe. This day I sawe my honoured Friend Mr
Sheldon, who told me he would write shortly to you, and that he
goes out of the Towne shortly. I would more willingly incurre any
one's displeasure than his, he is so worthy and honest a gent., and
though no mortal loves solitude, contemplation, and an innocent
life &c more than I, yet the tricks that are discoursed at the
Clubbes are not agreeable to that old pious Thomas à Kempis-
way. . . . Have you seen my Lady's reply to Sir Thomas' booke.
I wish I had it. . . . My faire Lady Theodos[ia] Ivy is my most
intimate Shee-friend. Her husband (Sir Thomas)[2] and she did

---

[1] In the course of the Popish Plot scare, the Queen was accused of
attempting to poison the King.

[2] Sir Thomas Ivy (of a neighbouring family living at West
Kington) was husband of Theodosia Stepkin. In Sir John Bramston's
autobiography (Camden Society) he is stated to have been 'knighted after
the King's returne, but merited whipping rather'. He was the author of a
rare pamphlet, published in 1654, called *Alimony Arrained*, which,

afterwards cohabite, and she had a daughter by him, dyed 8 aetat 7 years since. She is married to one Mr Brian a Roman Catholic but haz no child living. Sir Thomas died about 5 years since.'

On 18 August, 1679, Hobbes wrote to Aubrey from Chatsworth where he had retired some four years earlier under the protection of Lord Devonshire: 'I thank you for your letter of Aug 2d, and pray you present my humble thanks to Sir George Ent that he accepteth of my judgment upon his booke. I feare it is rather his good nature than my merit. I am sorry for the news you write of his son.

'I have been told that my booke of the Civill Warr is come abroad, and I am sorry for it, especially because I could not get his majestye to licence it, not because it is ill printed or has a foolish title set to it, for I believe that any ingenious man may understand the wickednesse of that time, notwithstanding the errors of the presse.

'The treatise *De Legibus* at the end of it, is imperfect. I desire Mr Horne to pardon me that I consent not to his motion, nor shall Mr Crooke himself get my consent to print it.

'I pray you present my humble service to Mr Butler.

'The priveledge of stationers is (in my opinion) a very great hindrance to the advancement of humane learning.'

Sir George Ent's book which Hobbes had received was *Of the Use of Respiration*, and George Ent, the son, at this time lay on his deathbed. Hobbes's own book to which he refers was *Behemoth*: *History of the Cause of the Civil Wars of England*, which had been finished about 1668, but suppressed by the desire of the King. This work had recently been pirated and did not appear with authority until 1681. Aubrey notes: 'It was J[ohn] A[ubrey] that did putt Mr Hobbes upon writing his treatise *De Legibus*, which is bound up with his *Rhetorique* that one cannot find it but by chance; no mention of it in the first title.' Mr Horne and Mr Crooke were booksellers, the former of whom had offered to publish an

according to Aubrey, contained 'as much baudry and beastlinesse . . . as can be imagined' regarding his married life. The vagaries of the Ivys' matrimonial affairs seem to have supplied some of the material used by Aubrey in his comedy *The Country Revel*.

unauthorised edition of *De Legibus*; while Mr Butler was, of course, the author of *Hudibras*. George Ent died in September. Aubrey attended the funeral, having spent some days with his friend before the end, and discussed with him portents that Ent supposed himself to have received regarding his imminent decease.

Hobbes himself died on 4 December, 1679, in his ninety-first year, having moved the month before from Chatsworth to Hardwick in a feather-bed laid in a coach. James Wheldon, Lord Devonshire's baker, who wrote 'a delicate hand', had looked after the philosopher and acted as his amanuensis. Now he was his executor, and wrote to Aubrey, giving an account of the death and funeral, enclosing a copy of Hobbes's will, his epitaph on himself, and a list of books. Aubrey set about the production of his *Life of Mr Thomas Hobbes of Malmesburie* in its final form. Wood, apprehensive as usual, noted in his diary: 'Shrove Tuesday February, 1680. I sent to Mr Aubrey to have a care what he does if he hath a hand in it—that he write faire things or else somebody will be upon his back.'

In his preface to this work, Aubrey wrote: '*Lectori*—'Tis religion to perform the will of the dead; which I here discharge with my promise (1667) to my old friend Mr T. H. in publishing the life and performing the last office to my old friend Mr Thomas Hobbes, whom I have had the honour to know [from] my childhood, being his countreyman and borne in Malmesbury hundred and taught my grammar by his schoolmaster.' However, instead of publishing this biography, Aubrey lent the manuscript to Dr Richard Blackbourne, of Trinity College, Cambridge, whom he described as 'a general scholar, prodigious memorie, sound judgment', who was also interested in his schemes to popularise the chalybeate springs at Seend. He wrote to Blackbourne in about February 1680: 'Pray advise me whether 'twould not shew handsomest to begin with a description of Malmesbury, and then place Mr H. pedigre? But, with all, should not "Thomas Hobbes was borne at Malmesbury, Apr . . . 1588" be the initiall and, as it were, textuall, line? Shall I in the first place putt Mr H. life donne by himselfe? (If so, whether in Latin, or English, or both?) Or else, shall I intersperse it with these animadversions? I could

begin with a pleasant description of Malmesbury, &c., (all new
and untoucht) 14 leaves in 8vo, which his verses will lead to, and
which Anthony Wood seemes to desire. Pray be my Aristarchus,
and correct and marke what you thinke fitt. First draughts ought
to be rude as those of paynters, for he that in his first essay will be
curious in refining will certainly be unhappy in inventing. . . I
will speake to Fleetwood Shepherd[1] to engage the earl of Dorset
to write in the old gentleman's praise. Should mine be in Latin
or English? (and by whome the Latin, if so?) Is my English style
well enough?'

Aubrey had at first intended his contribution to Hobbes's
biography to be a sort of commentary to the short metrical autobiography written by the Philosopher himself; and published in
1680. Indeed, the first title of Aubrey's work was *Supplementum
Vitae Thomae Hobbes*, but Wood objected: 'What need you say
Supplimentum?—*sic* pray say the life of Thomas Hobbs.' Dryden
and Judge Vaughan approved the *Life*, but were insistent that such
details as Hobbes having been a page should be omitted; and
Aubrey commented: 'I never yet knew a Witt (unless he were a
piece of an Antiquary) write a proper Epitaph, but leave the
reader ignorant, what countryman, etc. Only tickles his Eares
with Elogies.' However, in 1681, Blackbourne, and not Aubrey,
produced the *Life* in Latin, as *Vitae Hobbianae Auctarium*, also re-
printing the memoirs previously published. He left out the names
of Lord Falkland and Sir William Petty, on the grounds that they
were 'ignote to foreigners', while he presented both works as
having been written by Hobbes himself. It was, on the whole, an
unsatisfactory collaboration, and Aubrey wrote to Wood: 'Dr
Blackbourne is a young man of prodigious parts, but ungovern-
able: he does not use me well in losing my papers: both yours and
some printed ones that I have lent him: but I will endeavour to

---

[1] Fleetwood Shepherd is mentioned by Aubrey elsewhere as help-
ing to break all the lamps in 'the garden at Whitehall', together with
Lord Rochester and Lord Buckhurst (later Earl of Dorset), all of whom
were coming in from their revels about the year 1674. Some time in the
1670's Shepherd discovered young Matthew Prior, serving at his
uncle's tavern, the Rummers, in Westminster, and became his patron.

returne as many of them as I can'; and, elsewhere: 'I suffer the grasse to cutt under my feet; for Dr Blackbourne will have all the Glory.'

IV

The political situation remained disturbed, and, on 17 January, 1680, Aubrey wrote to Wood: 'Dr Oates is implacably angry (I heard yesterday by an intimate acquaintance of his a Chaplain of the Duke of Yorke) with the Bishop of Oxon for his slighting of him at Oxon, and speakes reproachfully of him and sayes of him what I will not enlarge on in writing.' On 27 March he wrote again: 'George Ent was wont to say "a pox take Parties"; I say so of Plotters. Doe not I well remember the folly of the Cavaliers in their severall sensless plottes against a formed Army? Did they not still more irretiate themselves, and make their condition worse? Even as, even so. Now another plott is started, though to be more of moment then any yet projected.'

Work on the *Lives* continued, though, since he had lost his money, Aubrey was handicapped not only by his own convivial and unenergetic tastes, but also by the need for taking into account the caprices of those in whose houses he stayed; such consideration having become no longer a matter merely of good manners so much as an indispensable foundation for a livelihood. Consequently his manuscript often shows signs of composition during periods of convalescence from the effects of late hours and more wine than was judicious for one who had for many years been inconvenienced by a weak digestion. His method of work was to inscribe the name of the subject of his biography at the top of the page of a folio manuscript book. He would then note below all he could remember of the man's personal appearance and eccentricities, friendships, actions, or writings. If he could not recollect a name, a date, or the title of a book, he left a blank or put a mark of omission. Sometimes he wrote alternative words or phrases (he was for ever pursued by afterthoughts), transposed paragraphs, or added new material. It was not unknown—when the stress of the previous night's goodfellowship lay heavy on his brain—for this additional matter to appear in the wrong place in the text, to be inserted in the margin (so that it is not always clear to whom or to what the words are intended to apply), and even for cognate remarks to be scribbled in the middle of another Life or in a different volume.

In March 1680 he persuaded Petty 'to sit for his picture to Mr Loggan, the graver, whom I forthwith went for myselfe, and drew it just before his goeing into Ireland, and 'tis very like him.' On 25th of that month Sir Leoline (or Llewellyn) Jenkins, who had been tutor to Lewis Aubrey, son of Sir John Aubrey of Llantrithyd, was appointed 'Principall Secretary of Estate'. Aubrey had known his father, 'a good plaine countreyman', in Glamorgan, and waited on Sir Leoline to congratulate him. On this occasion Jenkins said 'it had pleased God to rayse-up a poore worme to do his majestie humble service'; but his humility appears to have resulted in no practical benefits so far as Aubrey was concerned.

However, Aubrey was deeply interested in his own work, in spite of obstacles to prolonged industry inherent in his way of life and unsystematic nature. On 27 March, 1680, he wrote to Wood: 'I have to my Booke of Lives made a Kalendar of 55 persons, and have donne 10 of them: 3 or 4 leaves a folio a piece. Pray doe your own your selfe, though I have you in W. 'Twill be a pretty thing, and I am glad you put me on it. I doe it playingly. This morning being up by ten, I writt two lives: one was Sir John Suckling of of whom I wrote a leafe and a halfe in folio.' On 22 May, 1680, he returned to this subject. 'I received your kind letter of April 9 which I have inserted into my Memoires of Lives (66) a booke of 2 quires close written, and after I had begun it I had such an impulse on my spirit that I could not be at quiett till I had donne it. I have lately been very ill of a cold, and being one day taken with a Lypothymie, fainting away, as soon as I came to myselfe in the first leave of the Booke aforesayd, I writt that my Will and Humble request was that these minutes should be safely transmitted to you.[1] They are fine things, but few fitt to be printed in my life or

---

[1] This refers to a note prefacing the first manuscript volume of the *Lives*: '*Tanquam tabulata naufragii, Sum Johannis Aubrii, R.S.S. Febr. 24, 1679/80.* My will and humble desire is that these minutes, which I have

yours. If you die, your papers will be all in the possession of Dr John Wallis (ex officio) as Keeper of the Archives, so there 'twill be stifled, for I am like Almansar in the Play, that spare neither friend nor Foe, but a religious John Tell-troth. . . . Pox take your orators and piets[1] that spoile lives and histories. The Doctor sayes I am too minute; but a hundred yeares hence that minuteness will be gratefull. Sir William Petty ordered me to be so. He would put it in the *High Style*. Upon better advertisement I have altered my title of *Monumenta Druydum* to *Monumenta Britannica*, for reasons I will tell you hereafter. So Olaus Wormius[2] called his *Monumenta Danica*. The next thing I goe about shall be to transcribe it faire, and print it, with my *Chorographia Antiquaria*.'

In fairness to Wood, and in view of the disagreeable light in which he was subsequently to appear, it should always be remembered that Aubrey embarked on the *Lives*, as such, only on Wood's suggestion. In at least the early stages of their composition, the manuscripts were kept sometimes by Aubrey and sometimes by Wood; so that the latter may have had some excuse for regarding the material as presented specifically for his use, to be treated in any manner he pleased as an editor. On the other hand, although Aubrey may or may not have accepted this view at the beginning of his labours, there can be no doubt that, as the work progressed, he realised that he was putting into the biographies something that no one else could supply; and, accordingly, felt that he had a right to receive from Wood not only the consideration due to a friend, but also the respect owed as a matter of course from one writer to another.

A letter dated 15 June, 1680, in formal terms accords Wood certain rights of censorship, and, incidentally, might to some extent be held to extenuate Clark's occasional prudishness as an editor:

hastily and scriblingly here sett downe, be delivered carefully to my deare and honoured friend Mr Anthony à Wood, antiquary, of Oxford.— *Ita obnixe obtestor, Jo. Aubrey, Ascenscione Domini, correptus lipothymiâ. circiter 3 P. M. 1680.*'

[1] *i.e.* magpies, chatterers.

[2] The Danish antiquary, author of *Danicorum monumentorum* (1643) and *Addimenta ad Monumenta Danica*.

'Sir!

'I have according, to your desire, putt in writing these minutes of *Lives*, tumultuarily, as they occur'd to my thoughts or as occasionally I had information of them. They may easily be reduced into order at your leisure by numbring them with red figures, according to time and place, &c. 'Tis a Taske that I never thought to have undertaken till you imposed it upon me, sayeing that I was fit for it by reason of my generall acquaintance, having now not only lived about halfe a Centurie of yeares in the worlde, but have also been much tumbled up and downe in it which hath made me much knowne: besides the modern advantage of Coffee-howses in this great Citie, before which men knew not how to be acquainted, but with their own Relations or Societies. I might add that I come of a longaevous race, by which meanes I have imped some feathers from the wings of Time, for several Generations; which does reach high. When I first began, I did not think I could have drawne it out to so long a Thread. I here lay-downe to you (out of the conjunct friendship between us) the Trueth; the naked and plain trueth: (and, as neer as I can and that religiously) as a Pœnitent to his Confessor, nothing but the trueth: which is here exposed so bare that the very *pudenda* are not hid, and affords many passages that would raise a Blush in a young Virgin's cheeke. So that after your perusall. I must desire you to make a Castration (as Raderus to Martial) and to sowe-on some Figge-leaves—*i.e.* to be my *Index expurgatorius*. What uncertainty doe we find in printed histories? they either treading too neer on the heeles of trueth that they dare not speake plaine, or else for want of intelligence (things being antiquated) become too obscure and darke! I doe not here repeat any thing already published (to the best of my remembrance) and I fancy my selfe all along discoursing with You; alledgeing those of my relations and acquaintance (as either you knew or have heard of) *ad faciendam fidem*: so that you make me to renew my acquaintance with my old and deceased friends, and to *rejuvenescere* (as it were) which is the pleasure of old men! 'Tis pitty that such minutes had not been taken 100 yeares since or more: for want thereof many worthy men's names and notions are swallowd-up in oblivion; as much of these also would, had it not been through your Instigation: and perhaps this is one of the usefullest pieces that I have scribbeld. I remember one saying of Generall Lambert's, "that *the best of men are but men at best*": of this, you will meet with divers examples in this rude and hastie collection. Now these *Arcana* are not fitt to lett flie abroad, till about 30 years hence; for the author and the Persons (like Medlars) ought first to be rotten. But in whose hands must they be deposited in the mean time? advise me, who am,

Sir,

Your very affectionate friend

to serve you,

JOHN AUBREY.'

This note is important as evidence upon which an apology for Wood could be based, as it clearly conveys permission to make at least minor alterations in, and excisions from, the manuscripts. But however much Wood's right to edit the *Lives* is recognised, his debt to Aubrey remained a great one, and his ultimate conduct sufficiently inexcusable. Their collaboration was described afterwards by Hearne (no enemy to Wood) in terms which show how indispensable Aubrey's help appeared to an antiquary of the next generation:

'[4 July, 1724] 'Tis almost incredible to see from Anthony's papers (which I have also often heard said) what Pains Mr Aubrey took to get Anthony Intelligence, which Anthony used to acknowledge in company, saying that he (Mr Aubrey) would go over fire and water to serve him, & yet, for all that, at last Anthony despised him, as I have spoken severall times.'

v

On 5 June, 1680, continuing his assistance in the work of research, Aubrey's brother William wrote from Kington St Michael, on the subject of Hobbes's pedigree and various ramifications of the Aubrey family tree which he had been verifying from parish registers in the neighbourhood: 'I was at Malmesbury but did see [neither] the church nor register but desired Mr Binnion the parson to doe against I come againe; but Francis Hobbes' widow's good memory did give me much satisfaction. The register at Westport is not 80 yeares old (not more): the paving is all new. The old vicar Hobs was a good fellow and had been at cards all Saturday night, and at church in his sleep he cries out "Trafells in troumps" (*viz*. Clubs). Then quoth the clerk, "Then, master, he that have ace doe rub." He was a collirice [choleric] man, and a parson (which I thinke succeeded him at Westport) provoked him (a purpose) at the church doore, soe Hobs stroke him and was forced to fly for it and . . .¹ in obscurity beyond London; died there, was about 80 yeares since . . . Mr William Gale² of Chipnam was buried yesterday. I was at Dracot, Wensday last; Sir J. and his lady was writing to you. They are in mourning for the earl of Marleborow. He died tomorrow will be three weeks. Sir J[ames] L[ong] is quatring his coat of arms.'³

Judging from his letters, William Aubrey's education does not appear to have been up to the standard of that of his elder brother; although the family touch is not entirely lacking. Aubrey mentions elsewhere that William was 'an excellent Herald', and, after Aubrey's death especially, he corresponded with Thomas Tanner and Edward Lhwyd from time to time. Later, as will be seen, there were differences about money which caused trouble between the brothers.

In spite of his irritating ways, Thomas Gore was still useful as a kind of heraldic encyclopaedia, and, on 8 September, 1680, after thanking Wood for 'great humanity, obligeingnesse and civility in your intimation of sending me a payre of gloves to my new cloathes', Aubrey added; 'Pray write to the cuckold at Alderton alias Aldrington to enquire . . . But he is *a yare man*⁴ and afraid of my queries as many people are and also of A.W. (the Devill does enter them I thinke) when we want to preserve the memories of their Relations.' Samuel Butler's funeral took place on 27 September, 1680, when he was buried, according to his own wish, in the churchyard of 'Convent Garden'. The coffin was covered with black bays, and there were present twenty-five of his old acquaintances. Aubrey, 'being one of the eldest helped to carry the pall with Tom Shadwell at the foot'. On 5 October in the same

¹ Letter mutilated.

² One of Joan Sumner's two counsels in her case against Aubrey had been called William Gale.

³ This was the 4th (and last) Earl of Marlborough of this creation, uncle of Sir James Long, whose mother, Lady Ann Ley, was the Earl's sister, in the absence of male issue a co-heir transmitting the Ley quartering to the Long shield.

⁴ 'Yare' means 'quick'; but the fact that the phrase is underlined may mean that this is a quotation.

year Hooke noted in his diary: 'Aubery impudent'; but we have
no clue as to the cause of offence given. On 22 November,
Izaac Walton (then eighty-seven) sent some information about
Ben Jonson to be incorporated in his biography in the *Lives*.

On 18 December, 1680, Aubrey wrote to Mary Miller, aunt of
Katherine Ryves, whom, had she not died twenty-three years
before, he might have married:

'Mris Miller. I wish you a happy Christmas, and New year: and
truly I wish it heartily being a good lady, and one from whom I have
received great kindness which I shall never forgett and shall ever acknowledge: and I have oftentime been thinking to write to you and thought
to have donne it by your mayd whom I met at Mris Ball's, but she was
too soon out of town. Mris Ball (whom I sometimes visitt) and I doe use
to talke of you; and that with much respect. I hope the next Summer to
see Sarum once more and then I shall not fail to enjoy your good Company. I am sorry (besides my ill fortune *et* in generall) that I am your
debtor[1] for some interest on a bond which was payd severall years
since: which I hope I may satisfy this Spring: for truly I doe but make
shift to live: and that in hopes: for I have been well promised for some
Employments. Having the opportunity now by Mr Hatchman (this
bearer) I could not but present my respects to you. Thus wishing your
health, with a thousand thanks for your many favours, I rest, Madame,
Your most affectionate & humble servant, Jo. Aubrey.'

Margaret Miller[2] lived on at 'the King's House' in Salisbury
Close until her death on 7 June, 1688. Her sister Mary, to whom
Aubrey wrote this letter, survived her. It seems not unlikely
that portions of this large house had been let to sub-tenants,
of whom Katherine Ryves may have been one. Mistress Ball was
possibly the wife of William Ball, of the Middle Temple,
one of the founders of the Royal Society, and an astronomer.
Probably it was of this same lady that Aubrey also wrote: 'I never
saw tinned-potts, *scil*. Brasse-potts tinned, till since the year 1660.

[1] A note of hand exists, dated 23 October, 1667, in respect of the
sum of thirty pounds borrowed by Aubrey from Mary Miller.

[2] The Miller family came from Nether Wallop in Hampshire.
Margaret Miller is commemorated in Salisbury Cathedral with a stone
bearing on a lozenge the canting Miller arms: *In pale a fer-de-moline*, *i.e.*
the iron fixed to the centre of a mill-stone.

'Tis not every Brazier that hath attained that mystery yet (1691). But Madame Ball doeth assure me that her Father had some Brasse-potts tinned thus, that were her grandfather's, Sir George Bond, Lord Mayor of London above an hundred years since.'

VI

In February 1681 Lord Norreys of Rycote wrote from Lavington, beginning 'Good Cosen', and, after thanking Aubrey for his letter, went on to say: 'if you please to call on Mr White (my Draper) in Paul's Churchyard hee hath an order to pay you ten pounds which I desire you to accept from your affectionate friend and kinsman.' This young nobleman (he was twenty-six) was married to Eleanor Lee, whose mother, Anne Danvers, was daughter of Sir John Danvers, 'the Regicide'. He was the husband, therefore, of Aubrey's fourth cousin, once removed, and the recognition of their relationship is a good illustration of seventeenth-century acceptance of remote family ties. In the following year, Norreys was created Earl of Abingdon. Burnet says that he was 'a gentleman of fine parts; makes a good figure in the counties of Oxon and Berks: is very high for Monarchy and Church, of a black complexion'. To this description Swift added that the earl was 'very covetous'. Aubrey no doubt felt that, with the death of Lord Thanet, it was necessary to find and to attach himself to another patron in high places.

On 19 March, 1681, Aubrey wrote to Wood, apologising for having failed to finish more of the *Lives*, and saying that he had 'only not ill spent my time in reading of French Romances, to rub up my French, which was almost grown rustie with me through desuetude'—an excuse that was not likely to meet with enthusiastic acceptance—' . . . if I had but either one to come to me in the morning or with a good Scourge, or did not sitt-up till one or two with Mr Wyld, I could doe a good deale of businesse'. On 28 April, Ralph Sheldon, who seems always to have regarded Aubrey as incurably eccentric, wrote to Wood: 'I have met our friend Mr Awbrey twice in the streete, talking to himselfe and passing forward without regarding anybody; I am really of the opinion that he is a little crazed.'

On 21 June, 1681, Aubrey wrote thanking Wood for returning some of the *Lives* 'by your pretty Niece: for whose goodness and Graces the Heavens (I presume) have a blessing in store. I could enlarge but you expect from me Antiq: and not compliments and amorous Elegies: but pray present my service and thankes to her.' He goes on to make recommendations for Wood's growing deafness. 'Mr Wyld sayes (from Dr Ridgely) that you must purge your head with Agaric-pills; 'twill cure your moistness and noise. An ancient Doctor commends the drinking of the Bath-water. Mris Bagshawe sayes, Take an Ivy-leafe, putt on each Eare when you goe to Bed, and againe when you dresse your selfe in the morning. You must warme it first in your hands: that cur'd her: and also one of eightie yeares old, lately . . . Mr High Sheriff of Wiltshire lies damnably as to his age; if he had sayde he came—very little—he had sayd true: but Chronologie is the prettiest trap or gin to catch a Lyer in that can be. 'Tis true he published a table of Blazon 10 severall wayes in halfe a sheete of paper. I have one pasted by chance in my *booke B* which you have seen. Good God! the impudence of some precise narrow-soul'd persons. Some yeares after I found this very Table, word for word, in Sir John Fern's *Glorie of Generosity*.'[1]

On 'the Vigil of St Peter and St Paul' (28 June), 1681, he again wrote about the *Lives*: 'I am glad my memoires please you so well. 'Tis pity they should have been buried in Oblivion. I intend to lay papers by me for the future. . . . You see the papers are altogether rude, indigested, and impolished, and many things frivolous, which I may tell you as my friend, that are not fitt to be published.' On 14 July, 1681, he returned to this matter of censoring the *Lives*, and, although still only in his middle fifties, to the question of his own death: Aubrey having himself removed some 'severe touches on the earle of Corke, Dr John Wallis, etc.' A note on the margin of the excised leaf, given on the authority of 'Mr A[nthony] E[ttrick]' seems to speak of the Earl's love affairs and bastards; while Wallis, as an antagonist of Hobbes, an unfriendly competitor in the fame of Aubrey's friend William Holder, and a divine who had taken advantage of the Parliamentarian ejections

[1] A book on heraldry published 1586. The passage refers, of course, to Thomas Gore.

from the universities, might expect sharp treatment—although Aubrey is, in fact, notably fair to Wallis as a mathematician. In the same letter he goes on to ask: 'If I die in London (as most likely) would you advise me to be buried in our parish Church (St Martin's Outwych) neere the dore, like a poor Penitent with a footsquare inscription: or els in the Fanatique church yard by Ned Bagshawe, under the brick wall with an inscription on the wall, as I have ordered in my will?' Edward Bagshawe was an old acquaintance, a nonconformist and violent controversialist, who had spent much of his time in prison for his intransigent opinions. He had died ten years before, and was buried in Bunhill Fields 'in the fanatique burying-place by the Artillery-ground in Moorfields', the last place in the world which one might have expected Aubrey to consider favourably in the choice of a resting-place for his bones.[1] Bagshaw's widow, who was blind, had recommended ivy leaves for Wood's deafness. He was certainly not one of Aubrey's more intimate friends, though, as former second master at Westminster (where he had tried to supplant Dr Busby), he had stories of the great antiquary Camden, once headmaster of the school. Possibly Bagshawe's grave enjoyed an unusually quiet and attractive situation which had taken Aubrey's fancy.

On 15 August, 1681, Aubrey's brother Tom (who had been born in 1645) died. Aubrey wrote to Charles Snell, the astrologer, to establish the documentation of his brother's decease; and received a reply, dated 3 September, saying 'I never heard Mr Aubrey was at Sarum or ill, till he was dead. He had no very learned physitian with him, old drunken Jack Chapman,[2] some tyme apothecary at Bath.'

[1] This ground had been set apart at the time of the Great Plague, and the landlord, one Tyndale (perhaps the 'Mr Tyndale at Bunhill, who makes several sorts of English wines and cyders'), charged 11s. 6d. for a grave and £8 for a vault. This was called Tyndale's ground. Aubrey says there was, however, another burying place by Bunhill Fields where graves were only 2s.: and, elsewhere, that Milton had died in 'Bunhill, opposite to the Artillery-garden wall'.

[2] Presumably the Chapman, apothecary, ex-Mayor of Bath, who gave evidence in Titus Oates' case that Fr Thimelby (pp. 140–142) had called on him: re charges against Sir G. Wakeman, the Queen's physician (see Lane, *Titus Oates*).

VII

On 20 December, 1681, Aubrey wrote to Wood saying that he had been informed by Sir John Saintloe, of Chalke, that the principal of Hart Hall, Oxford, Dr John Lamphire (Wood's physician, who had tried to cure his deafness), was dangerously ill, if not dead; and that Saintloe suggested that Aubrey should address himself to Sir Leoline Jenkins to obtain the place. It is not very likely that much would have come of such an application; but, as usual when faced with some more or less concrete proposal for taking a job, Aubrey found himself disinclined to commit his freedom. 'Now I say unto you *tali non sum dignus honore.* I am an ignote fellow and but of little learning. They will surely choose some worthy man. Dr Plott were a fitt person . . . if I should have it, I should be like the weaned child to leave Mr Wyld: who also are inseparable and dote together till 12 or 1, at night . . . after the opiating quality of the mince-pies is exhaled I will begin with old Mr Beeston,[1] about the Lives of the Poets. But what comfort have one to doe these things, for which one have generally but scorne and contempt.' On St John the Evangelist's Day (27 December) he wrote again, saying that he must be 'in his dotage' not to have thought of Wood himself for Dr Lamphire's place; adding that he would do his best with Jenkins and Petty ('to whom the Duke of Ormonde will deny nothing') to have his friend appointed.

He wrote again on 11 May, 1682, of effecting some revision in the manuscript of the *Lives*: 'When I come to Oxon I might make a castration in my first part: for besides *Scandalum Magnatum* there be other things reflecting on others.'[2] In the same letter he says: 'My Lord Norris comes to Ricot at Whitsuntide. I shall wayte on him. I doe not intend to lye-on him much. I have no

[1] William Beeston, whose father had been 'master of the playhouse', told Aubrey that Shakespeare had been a schoolmaster in Warwickshire. Aubrey's story about Shakespeare's 'killing a calfe in high style' may have reference to a traditional Mummers' performance.

[2] The following slip is pasted in the second volume of the *Lives*: 'Mr Aubrey, I beseech you as you have been civil in giving the book to me at Oxon in Sept. 1681, so I hope when you have done with it you'l returne every part of it againe to your servant, Ant. Wood.'

horse; and I suppose, if I stay there 3 weekes in a yeare 'tis no great businesse. I could there doe more than here . . . when I come to Ricot I'le bring my Surrey papers and putt them in order . . . I wish you could send to Mr Kelsey of Newton Tony. I lay at his house two severall nights, and [was] civilly entertained. I frankly and heartily promised to send him some Venison, and spake to my brother accordingly (for at Chalke you must knowe that we have the command of Venison enough, and the Fermour there is oftentime Ranger, for the Deer feed in our ground) the divil a Bucks foot did they ever send to him. Neither did I ever receive a piece of Venison here, to oblige a friend. Be so that I suspect he is disobliged, thinking that I did shamme him with what I never intended: but if you have no other way I will put on a bold face and write . . . I have Mars in the 3rd Howse which showes I should never receive any good from my relations, the neerer the worse.'

On St Anne's Day (26 July), 1682, he wrote: 'My old Friend Seigneur Wyld hath brought me to the old habit again. (They told me he wanted me exceedingly.) He hath made me loose two or three opportunities of sending these things inclosed to you.' He goes on to describe to Wood a visit to Eton, where he had gleaned further information about the 'ever-memorable' John Hales, from Mistress Powney,[1] in whose 'handsome darke old-fashioned howse' opposite the churchyard adjoining the Christopher Inn, Hales had lodged after his ejection from his fellowship. He had heard nothing but praise of Hales, and stories of his giving groats to the children from Mistress Powney, who said that his nephew, Mr Sloper, the vicar of Broad Chalke, had not 'sent him a token' after his sequestration; and was angry with her, thinking Hales had 'left her too much'.

On 15 August, 1682, he wrote to Wood: 'I'le shew you a trifle of mine writt in 1671 in my solitude at Sir R. Henley's in Hants and among the Beeches, being a description 13 or 14 sheets in verse and prose 30 miles round Easton *viz*. akin the Prospects.

---

[1] Mistress Powney ('she has been handsome: a good understanding, and cleanlie') had her hall 'after the old fashion, above the wainscot, painted cloath, with godly sentences out of the Psalmes'. She was, says Aubrey, 'a woman primitively good, and deserves to be remembered'.

I had not seen it these eleven yeares till my box was sent to mee a week before the Act. But that is only to show a friend.' This seems to refer to *Villa, or a description of the prospects from Easton Piers*, a manuscript numbered 16 in Aubrey's list of his own works, given later to Edward Lhwyd,[1] no doubt intended as the prose counterpart of the pictures Aubrey had drawn of the house and grounds. Unfortunately this piece is no longer to be found among the Aubrey manuscripts.

There was a severe blow in 1683, when 'it pleased God at Whitsuntide last to bereave me of a deare, usefull, and faithfull friend, Mr Johnson who had the place of Master of the Rolles;[2] who generously, for friendship and neighbourhood sake (we were borne the same week and within four miles and were educated together) gave me the graunt to be one of his secretaries—which place is worth 500*li* per annum. He was a strong lustie man and died of a malignant fever, infected by the Earl of Abington's brother, making of his will. It was such an opportunity that I shall never have the like again.'

There was a letter from William Penn, dated from Philadelphia 'the 13th of the 4th month called June', 1683, giving some description of the country, and saying: 'I have begun a vineyard by a French man of Languedock and another of Poictou'; and, in *Faber Fortunae*, Aubrey noted: 'William Penn, the Lord Proprietor of

---

On 18 November, 1692, see Appendix A.

[2] George Johnson, a judge on the North Wales circuit, Solicitor to the Treasury, and M.P. for Devizes in 1681, had lived at Bowdon Lodge in Wiltshire not far from Chippenham, and was therefore next door to the Aubreys at Easton Pierse. He had trebled his estate (upon which were the remains of a Roman iron forge) by finding marl under the soil. The reversion of the Mastership of the Rolls had been granted to Johnson in 1667, but the death of Sir Harbottle Grimston (appointed 1660) did not take place until January, 1685; although the latter had caused not a little scandal at St Albans in October, 1681, by removing the coffin of Francis Bacon to make room for his own, in anticipation of this event. Was George Johnson perhaps the 'G.J.' (if such are the initials) above the words '[I] was faine to make friendship with a strong boie to protect me' in a passage that refers to Blandford school in the *Education of a Young Gentleman*?

Pennsylvania, did, *ex meromotu et ex gratia speciali*, give me a graunt under his seale, of six hundred acres in Pennsylvania, without my seeking or dreaming of it. He adviseth me to plant it with French protestants for seaven yeares gratis and afterwards [they are] to pay such a rent. Also he tells me, for 200 acres ten pounds rent for ever, after three yeares.'

These plans for going overseas were vague enough, but they were not entirely without some sort of scientific preparation and thought to the future. *Faber Fortunae* also records that: 'Mr Robert Welsted, goldsmith and banquier, saies that Mr John Evelyn's bookes are the most proper for a plantation. Also Markham's husbandry and huswifry, etc. This is in order for Mr W. Penn and myself.—also let him carry with him Mr Haines book of Cydar Royall, which method will likewise serve for other fruits.—it is by distillation—*Quaere* of Mr Tyndale's at Bunhill, who makes severall sorts of English wines and cydars—Memorandum the great knack and criticism is to know when it comes to its sowrenesse; it must not be vinegar for then nothing will come—*quod N. B.*'

Meanwhile, Aubrey maintained an energetic correspondence. Andrew Paschall[1] (who had lived in Erasmus's rooms at Queens', Cambridge), like the Wadham don, Thomas Pigot, and Seth Ward, Bishop of Salisbury, was interested in 'the Universal language'. He wrote regularly between 1674 and 1693 painstaking if somewhat prosy letters; and in 1683 enclosed an account he had received from the incumbent of Barnstaple of the doings of 'a discontented daemon', which had been disturbing the neighbourhood, a description that closely accords with happenings now broadly documented as poltergeist phenomena. Paschall used to give news of Aubrey's mother, who, when not at Chalke, lived at Bridgwater in Somerset, and sometimes at Bristol. Aubrey was also trying to persuade the authorities of the University of Oxford, or, alternatively, those of Trinity College, to buy the mathematical library of his friend, Sir Jonas Moore ('sciatica he cured it, by boiling his buttock'), a mathematician and surveyor of some

---

[1] Possibly he had married Mary Wiseman's sister—see p. 69 n., and Appendix B. p. 308.

standing, who had built the dykes of East Anglia so that their out-line corresponded with (and, therefore, kept back) the uneven ingress of the sea. Moore had intended to leave his books to the Royal Society, but had died intestate. Sir Isaac Newton exchanged letters with Aubrey on this subject, telling him, on 23 December, 1683, that Trinity was unable to afford the books because of the heavy charges incurred for new buildings. The offer was passed on to the Vice-Chancellor; but not much hope was held out, 'their chest being at present very low'.

In June 1684 *The Idea of the Education of a Young Gentleman* was sent to Anthony Henley at Bramswell, at another of whose houses, some fifteen years earlier, Aubrey had first turned over in his mind that essay. In August of the same year Edmund Wyld gave a dinner-party attended by Aubrey, at which, before the guests were seated, seeds of plants were sown, which, inexplicably, flowered by the end of the meal, about an hour and a half later. This must have been the occasion which caused Roger North to describe Wyld as a 'gentleman of a superior order' who 'sowed salads in the morning to be cut for dinner'. Aubrey's account of the party is quoted later, when Wyld is considered among the *Amici*.

VIII

On Midsummer Day, 1684, Ralph Sheldon died (Thomas Gore of Aldrington *aliàs* Alderton had given up the ghost on Easter Monday of the same year), and Wood travelled up to Warwick-shire to arrange the funeral, and determine what pickings there might be. On his arrival he constituted ceremonial appropriate to the occasion, and left a description in his diary of the arrangements he had seen fit to make:

'In the afternoon, after I had caused the hall at Weston, stair-case, dining roome, room of state, to be hung with scocheons, Mr Sheldon's body laid in state and was viewed by above 500 country people . . . at six in the morning his body was carried from Wes-ton in a carriot hung with scutcheons and streamers, the six horses hung with scutcheons and shuffrons and about 8 couples of

¹ See p. 254.

blacks before, besides 4 streamers and myself. About 2 of the clock we arrived at Beoley church where he was buried.'

After this impressive journey to Worcestershire, there was the question of the will, and here Wood found that matters were not as satisfactory as he might have hoped. It will be remembered that as a reward for the cataloguing of his library, Sheldon had promised help towards the printing of the *Athenae*; although Wood had often to admit to himself that he did not always feel completely comfortable as to the manner in which this understanding was to be fulfilled. In 1682, for example, he had written: 'A. Wood received then 10 guineas of Mr R[alph] S[heldon] to stop my mouth; he acknowledged that he did promise to print my book; but the times are since altered and he is not able. Yet he is able enough to throw away 2 or 300*li* to alter his house for the sake of the M[aid] of H[onour] and he gives her and her brothers what they please.' The last sentence refers to the lady Aubrey calls 'faire Madam Frances Sheldon',[1] Ralph Sheldon's cousin, who was Maid of Honour to Charles II's Queen, Catherine of Braganza. Sheldon was a widower and childless, so that no doubt Wood was right in regarding her as a serious rival in extracting money from his friend; who was, after all, entitled to dispose of his wealth in his own way. The promise was referred to again in December 1683: 'Mr R. Sheldon with me to look at my transcript and papers which I had done for his sake and he said he would give me 100*li* to print my Bibliothecia.' A note follows this entry to the effect that Sheldon had himself recorded in his own diary this promise of assistance. However, when the will came to be read, it turned out that Sheldon had bequeathed £40 to Wood, asking that he would see all his pedigrees, manuscripts, and papers (except such as were written in his own handwriting) delivered 'into the Heralds' Office, near Paule's Wharf London that they be put in a cupboard apart from the others'.

[1] Frances Sheldon seems to have enjoyed teasing Wood, because when Sheldon wrote to him on 28 April, 1681, he adds: 'I have no more to say but to tell you from the Maid of honour that she read the letter which you writt to mee and did not find any commendation to herselfe from You; of this she bid me advertize you in a friendly manner.'

On 22 July, 1684, Aubrey wrote to Ashmole that Wood intended to 'doe his best with Mr Sheldon's heire to get the bookes for the Heralds' Office', where Sir William Dugdale was now Garter King of Arms and his son, John Dugdale, Windsor Herald. These two were anxious, naturally, to obtain for the College as much as possible of the Sheldon library. However, on 16 December, 1684, John Dugdale wrote to his father, then in Warwickshire: 'Mr Aubray this day told me (with trouble of mind) that Mr Parker, coming to the Executor of Mr Sheldon, when the books were all in hampers, and being told what they were, desired to see the catalogue; whereupon he caused all the books to be taken out, and advised the Executor to detain all such manuscripts as did not relate to Herauldrie: which he did accordingly; and how to get them will be hard to contrive I doubt.' After this, some acrimonious correspondence passed between Wood and Sir William, as the latter suspected that Wood (who had said there would be no trouble with executor or heir 'for one is a huntsman and the other a horseman') was in some degree a party to the removal of the books. Wood, in one of his furious letters (14 October, 1685), speaks of Dugdale as having been 'misinformed by some envious coxcombe'; but it may well be that there was something to be said on the herald's side, over and above Wood's protest that it was an endeavour 'againe to cut my throate with mine own Knife, which a man of generous spirit and breeding would scorne to do'.

IX

On 6 February, 1685, Charles II died, and, on the same day, the Duke of York was proclaimed king. When Aubrey watched the coronation procession on St George's Day, he noted that the canopy of cloth of gold carried over the new king's head by 'the Wardens of the Cinque Ports' was torn by a puff of wind (although it was not a windy day) as James came to Westminster Hall. 'It hung down very lamentably', he wrote; 'I saw it.' Storms were indeed gathering again, and it seemed as if the former days of strife and insecurity were likely to return. More personal and immediate problems had also to be faced. Sir James Long promised some cloth for a winter suit and four cheeses from Draycot, both products for which North Wiltshire was renowned, no doubt acceptable enough. There was also work to be done on the *Natural History of Wiltshire*, to which he continued to add, writing the title-page and preface, both of which bear the inscription, 'June 6, 1685, London; Gresham Coll:'. He dedicated the work to Lord Pembroke, then President of the Royal Society, and the Society was given a fair copy of the book, which, it will be remembered, the members had inspected in 1675. This was Thomas Herbert, 8th Earl of Pembroke, who had succeeded his brother Philip, in 1683. 'He is very hard in his bargaining:' wrote Aubrey, 'but as just a paymaster as lives'; and the change was advantageous.[1]

With his unvarying instinct for running into trouble Aubrey visited his friend Andrew Paschall in the West Country at the moment of Monmouth's insurrection. On 3 August, 1685, he wrote to Wood from Broad Chalke: 'I went from London tuesday in Whitsonweeke into Somerset to an ingeniose friend of mine; and I came just that night as Monmouth began his rebellion. It was not without danger that I came hither. Monmouth's soldiers came into my friend Mr Paschall's house and tooke away horses and armes and came into my chamber as I was abed: but *Deo gratias* that Clowd is overblown. . . . Pray remember me kindly to that worthy friend of yours and mine Mr Allam:[2] pray mind him of the markets in Oxfordshire. I sent him my *Naturall Historie of Wilts* by the Taunton Carrier, and have made much enquiry after it: and gave it up for lost, but by the last post Mr Paschall tells me he haz recovered it. You see what luck I have.'

x

On 2 January, 1686, he wrote to Wood from London: 'I returned hither about St Andrews tyde from Chalke, where

---

[1] Of the 7th Earl, Aubrey had written: 'This present Earl of Pembroke (1680) has at Wilton 52 mastives and 30 grey-hounds, some beares, and a lyon, and a matter of 60 fellows more bestiall than they.'

[2] Aubrey did not know that Andrew Allam (who had also given Wood much help with the *Athenae*) had died of smallpox a few weeks before, on 18 June, 1685, aged thirty.

my domestic troubles were so great that I was hardly able to sus-
tayne them: whether ever I shall shake off the grief I knowe not.
If it had not been for those troubles I would have willingly gonne
to Salisbury and have answered your questions. I have not been
able to reade or write these 6 weekes for griefe and this is the 3rd
letter that I have writt. My Tygre brother and I are at so great a
difference (too long here to relate) that I beleeve we shall never
close again.'

Soon after this, Mrs Aubrey died at the age of seventy-five, and,
on 11 May, Aubrey wrote to Wood:

'Deare Freind: In January last after a very great conflict of affliction I
rowsed up my spirits and writt a letter to you, and immediately fell to
work with my *Naturall History of Wilts*, which I had just donne Aprile 21
i.e. rough hewn, and finished the last chapter, when at the evening I
heard of the sad news of the Decease of my deare and ever honoured
Mother: who died at Chalke, but my brother buried her with my father
in North Wilts (Kington St Michael). My heart has been a fountaine of
teares, and this is the first letter (except of businesse) that I have writt
since my Griefe. I am now involved in a great deal of trouble: and Chalke
must be sold:[1] but I hope to make some reservation for myself: and I
hope before I dye to be able to make an honourable present to you: for I
am of the Spaniards way; *sc.* not to make my soul my Executor. I shall
shortly goe to Chalke to see how matters goe there: and as soon as I can
pick up a little money intend to see you at Oxon, and I think the time
very long till I am with you. Sir W. Dugdales's *Paules* is to be printed
at Oxon: there is a mistake in Dr A[ubrey]'s Inscription *sc. Atavus* for
Proavus.[2] Mr Ashmole and his wife is angry with him for making such

[1] There is a note: 'Possession of Chalke farm was given by Mr
Rich. Kitson to Mr J. Mawtus Dec. 9th 4h. P.M. 1688'; but in a letter
to Wood (24 April, 1690) Aubrey says: 'After Michaelmas I parted with
Chalke farm to Mr Kent to my great grief'. This last transaction seems
to have been connected with his quarrel with his brother William. See
p. 212.

[2] Dugdale had died 10 February, 1686. His *History of St Paul's
Cathedral in London* had appeared in 1658; but he had been working on a
continuation of this book, of which a new edition was published in 1716.
He left many of his papers to the Ashmolean. Ashmole was his son-in-
law, and had perhaps expected that these should have been bequeathed to
him. On p. 96 of Dugdale's book is an engraving of Dr William Aubrey's

a scandalous will. I shall bring severall memoranda with me to insert. God blesse you and comfort me, that I may but live to finish and publish my papers . . . My true love to Christopher Wase, of whom the Earl of Pembroke and I had much discourse at dinner, with much respect. Let me desire you to write to me by the next post, to let me know how you doe. Your letter will be a cordiall to me: therefore pray fail not. Fabian Philips is yours. I am sorry for the loss of our facetious friend Parson Hodges. I must make hast with my papers, for I am now sixty.'

Christopher Wase, was, of course, an old friend (rather addicted to the bottle) often mentioned by both Aubrey and Wood.[1] Years before, when Aubrey used to visit Wilton from Broad Chalke, Wase had been tutor there, and he was a favourite source of information on the subject of the Herbert family. For a time he had been a schoolmaster at Tonbridge and used to supply Wood with material about ancient manuscripts. Fabian Philips was an antiquary who belonged to the generation of Aubrey's father, and he was now more or less in his dotage. He was a 'filiser' (an official responsible for the filing of writs) for London and other districts, and his own writings had been chiefly devoted to Royalist apologetics. It was Philips who had assured Aubrey that Charles I's plain deal coffin had cost but six shillings. Parson Hodges, Rector of Wytham, had been usually referred to by Aubrey and Wood as 'the Bishop of Botley' in their letters.

Once more there was thought of emigration, though sixty was

memorial in St Paul's Cathedral, and on the shield in the top right-hand corner is the inscription:

P. M.
Atavi
posuit
IOH AVBRE
IVS: AR

'Atavus' means 'great-great-great-grandfather': 'Proavus' means 'great-great-grandfather', which would be correct.

[1] When James II visited Oxford in September 1687, Wase was 'Superior Bedle of Law', and, Wood says, 'being a meer scholar and troubled with shaking hands, could not get on horseback, but was helped up, and when he was, he could not hold his staff upright, which caused laughter in some, and anger in others'.

late to find a home in a new country. However: 'Captain Poyntz (for service that I did him to the earle of Pembroke and the earle of Abingdon)[1] did very kindly make me a grant of a thousand acres of land, in the island of Tobago, Anno Domini 1685/6, Feb. 2d. He advised me to send over people to plant and to gett sub-scribers to come in for a share of these 1000 acres, for 200 acres he sayes would be enough for me. In this delicate island is *lac lunae* (the mother of silver).'

XI

The danger of the loss or destruction of his papers was a worry that constantly occupied Aubrey's mind as he grew older. This was a very reasonable apprehension, and the fact that so large a proportion of his writings have been preserved can be directly at-tributed to the pains taken by their author in seeing that they should be given a fair chance of survival. He made arrangements for the disposal of his *Wiltshire Collections* in a draft will which he left; and these, with some other manuscripts, are the sole property mentioned.

'Whereas I John Aubrey R.S.S. doe intend shortly to take a journey into the West: and reflecting on the fate that Manuscripts use to have after the death of the author, I have thought good to signify my Last Will (as to this *Naturall History of Wilts*) that my will and desire is, that in case I should depart this life before my return to London again, to finish, if it pleaseth GOD, this Discourse; I say, and declare, that my will then is, that I bequeathe these papers to my worthy friend Mr Robert Hooke of Gresham College and R.S.S., and I doe also humbly desire him, & my will is, that the noble buildings and prospects should be engraven by my worthy friend Mr David Loggan, who hath drawn my picture already in order to do it. Witnesse hereunto my hand and seale the eighteenth day of August *Anno Domini* one thousand six hundred and eighty six.

Jo. Aubrey.

'Signed and sealed in the presence of us Francis Lodwik, Jo. Godfrey, sen., Saml. Meverell, Henry Spencer.

[1] 'The Earle of Abingdon to buy of Captain Poyntz the property of the island of Tobago, now *regnante Guilemo III*': *Faber Fortunae.*

'*Memorandum*, there are deposited in the hands of my honoured friend Elias Ashmole, Esq., two manuscripts of my writings, *viz: Templa Druidum, & Chronologia Antiquaria*: being both about three quires of paper: which doe belong to this historie and to be printed with. My *Chronologia Architectonica* is at the begining of the first part of my *Antiquities of Wilts*; which are deposited in the hands of my worthy friend Mr Anthony à Wood of Merton College in Oxford: & they will deliver the aforesayd Manuscripts to the sayd Mr Robert Hooke.'

There is a note on the manuscript of the *Natural History of Wiltshire*: '*Anno* 1686, *Ætatis* 60. Mr. David Loggan the graver drew my picture in black and white, in order to be engraved, which is still in his hands.' Of the witnesses, Francis Lodwyck was 'merchant of London' and a friend with whom Aubrey used to discuss such subjects as settlement of Flemings in Wiltshire or his project for a duty on Spanish wood. Lodwick was F.R.S. and is often mentioned in Hooke's diary, as are also Godfrey and Spencer. Samuel Meverell was a Russian merchant who had been in Moscow in 1653, or thereabouts, when the 'great bell' was cast, and where he reported 300,000 souls had died in the following year of plague.

On 5 February, 1687, he wrote to Wood: 'You may thinke it much that I have not writt to you thus long time: but this is to acquaint you that I have been so weekely perplext and plagued with letters from my brother; and with running up and down to Lawyers and Proctors, that I have had no time to thinke my owne Thoughts: or doe anything for you, or my *Naturall History*: but as soon as the Terme ends I will performe my promise to Sir W. Dugdale, *viz*. to make fitt for the Presse my *Templa Druidum*.'

He wrote on 28 July, 1687, to Wood: 'a friend of mine hath invited me into Yorkshire as far as Ripon'. This was probably the occasion when he saw the prehistoric stones called The Devil's Arrows at Burroughbrig in Yorkshire. He seems to have travelled as far as Durham, and noted: 'From Stamford to the bishoprick I sawe not one elme on the roads, whereas from London to Stamford they are in every hedge almost.' In this year and the next he worked on his *Remains of Gentilism and Judaism*, and dedicated these extracts from Greek and Roman writers (intended to prove that

many English customs were derived from classical times) to Edmund Wyld. He toyed with a number of other subjects, too, and
wrote to Wood on 27 October, 1687: 'I have dipped my fingers in
Inke this moneth and am about halfe way oversea: *sc.* to transcribe
all the British names I can find in the *Villare Anglicanum*,[1] and to
interpret them by the help of Dr Davies Dictionary (which is very
imperfect) and with the assistance of some of my Welsh friends
and am under the temptation to do the like for the old English
words out of Whelock's Saxon Dictionary . . . when I come to
Oxford I will bring a matter of 3*li* or more with me and stay there
for a fortnight, where I hope I shall be out of harmes way, and also
I would run over the marginall notes of *Holingshead Chronicle* for
some naturall philosophica¹l Remarques for my *Naturall History of
Wilts*, which I forgott to st.ew you, and I am under a temptation
since I sawe you to write Me.noires of that kind of *Gloucestershire,
Monmouthshire, Flyntshire,* and *Surrey*: having long since picked up
considerable Remarques: many whereof will be utterly lost to
posterity without I stitch them together. Now what shall I say, or
doe with these pretty collections? I thought to have made Mr R.
Hooke my Executor to publish them if I dye before I doe it myselfe: but he hath so much to doe of his owne that he will not be
able to finish: and you know how Dr Plott served me.'

On 16 December, 1687, Aubrey's old friend, Sir William Petty,
died 'at his house in Pecadilly-street, almost opposite St James
church.'

XII

The egregious Dr Plot had been appointed curator of the new
museum at Oxford, and, on 17 February, 1683, Ashmole had
noted in his diary: 'The last load of my rarities was sent to the
barge, and this afternoon I relapsed into the gout.' According to
Wood this gift for the 'new elaboratory at Oxon' had made up
twelve cart-loads; and the Ashmolean offered an acceptable solution to the problem of finding a secure depository for Aubrey's
writings. He had been in Oxford in June 1688 and had dined at

----

[1] *Villare Anglicanum,* by Sir Henry Spelman, London, 1656.

the Mermaid with Wood and Plot. On 23 October, 1688, he wrote to Wood: 'I am exceedingly glad that the Box has come safe to your hands. I shall now dye with the greater peace of mind. On Sunday last I went to Mr Ashmole, who shewed me a letter of October 18th to Dr Plott, but he received not any thing from you then, neither had seen the Catalogue. Mr Ashmole is much vext at my management of this business; but I must humbly beseech you to refraine your choler and passion for what I shall tell you. I told Mr Ashmole in May, before I came to Oxon, that you should have the perusall of all, in the first place. I expected (you knowe) the receipt of the Things when I was there: and now he tells me the reason: *sc.* because that You are looked upon as a P— and in these tumultuous Times your papers will be search't, which is like enough, for people grow mad by changes of — and so of leaving of any thing in your hands, it would be a means to have them lost; wherefore (in passion) he desires that those papers that I conceive fitt to be kept secret, should be all sealed-up (after you have donne with them) and then putt in the Museum; not to be opened till after my death: and I thinke his advice is very solid and sedate. You know that in my memorandum of *Lives* there are for me things that make me obnoxious to *Scandalum Magnatum*: and I have heretofore writt a letter or so which I wish were turned to ashes. New troubles arise upon me like Hydra's heads; and my poore brother whom I have injured is very violent and I must be faine shortly to take Sanctuary again at Oxon, or rather if I could at Bayworth with my cosen Baskerville.[1] When I was coming one time out of All Souls the Gape-abouts at the Gate pointed at me and one sayd a Roman-Catholicus: I pray God blesse you and deliver you from

[1] Bayworth, 'a private and lone house' (first visited by Wood in 1659) belonged to Thomas, son of Hannibal Baskerville, a recluse: both antiquaries and eccentrics. Apparently Aubrey arranged this visit, because he speaks elsewhere of 'when I was at Bayworth, seeing the earth was vitroliq and plenty of Irone-stone I sent for Galles, and tryed severall springes there which turned black: and my cosen Baskerville and I rode from thence to North Lye to a Clubb, beyond Bablak-hythe, through Wotton;' Baskerville is a Welsh border name, but Aubrey's connexion seems to be that Constance, dau. of Capt. Nicholas Baskerville, married her cousin Henry, son of Thomas Lyte of Lyte's Cary, the Herbalist.

affronts. . . . My heart is almost broke and I have much adoe to
keep up my poore spiritts. . . . I sent 4 or 5 yeares since (upon a
threatening of my brother to throw me into Gaole) those Things
to Mr Ashmole in a Deale-Box, which was bigger than the thing
required: but about a yeare since Mr Ashmole had occasion for a
Box of that bignes, and tumbled out my things into that lesser box
I sent downe: but I find it like a transfusion of Chymicall Spirits
out of one glass into another, they wast by it: and some papers I
am sure are miscarried . . . all my Bookes at Mr Kent's; so that if
I had leisure I cannot enjoy them. Since my returne, I have been in
Physick, or tumbling with porters upon my removall; which is at
present in an obscure place, to enjoy the society of an *old acquaintance* of mine, Mr Uniades,[1] of the family of the King of Hungarie,
that was Chymist to this Earl of Pembroke's father, who can (if he
will) tell me a hundred things more than Mr White (to whome
when you see him, pray remember me) or Mr Boyle, or any one
els . . . .For Godsake take no notice to Dr Plott, or anyone else of
Mr Ashmole's displeasure. I would have payd the postage but then
the delivery is more uncertaine. I will be responsible for it. A Barber's shop at Oxon is too publick for my circumstances. I wish I
had a lodgeing towards New-Inne in some of the Lanes there. . . .
To divert myself since the removall of my Bookes, I am perusing
Ovid's Works, and I have halfe gonne it over and have picked up a
sheet or more for my Gentilisme, even in his Epistles and Amores,
where one would not expect it; which I will either bring or send.
You see what strange distracted way of study my Fates give me.
When that is over I shall fall upon only my transcribing and finishing *Templa Druidum*: and the Camps.'

  Public events were now moving quickly. Early in November
1688 the Prince of Orange landed in England, and on the 17th of
that month Lord Abingdon, Aubrey's patron, with a party of
fifty horse, had ridden through Dorchester to join the invading
army. In December, some days before Christmas, King James set
sail for France. On 22 December, 1688, Aubrey had again written
about the papers for the Ashmolean:

  [1] Apparently Janos Bannfy Hunyadi, the younger, alchemist, *d.*
age 75, 1696, memorial Shoreditch Church (see letters in *Times Lit.
Supp.*, 17 Aug. 1951, 11 June, 2 July, 9 July, 1954, 15 Aug., 2 Sept.,
1955).

'Mr Wood! Last Tuesday I went to see Mr Ashmole, (whom I found ill). He lately received a letter from Dr Plott, about the things that I sent to Oxford; and says that he desired you to send to the Museum, but you denied it; and would not let him see the Catalogue I sent. Mr Ashmole desired to speak with me about it, and is most outrageously angry; and charg'd me to write to you as soon as I could, to put the Box in the Musaeum: for he looks upon you as a P. and sayeth so does the whole Universitie and there was present at this angry fitt of his, an Oxford scholar (I thinke his kinsman) who owned what Mr Ashmole sayd. Mr Ashmole says that now there is such care and good method taken, that the Bookes in the Musaeum are more safe than those in the Library or Archives: and he says he expects to hear of your being plunder'd, & papers burnt, as at the Spanish Ambassador's, at Wild House,[1] where were burnt MSS & antiquities invaluable, such as are not left in the world and he farther bids me tell you, that if you shall refuse to deliver the things sent downe by me, to Oxford, that he will never look on you as a Friend and will never give a farthing more to the University of Oxford. I am very glad to heare by Dr Plott's letter to him the great care that is taken at the Museum to preserve the bookes: and one, *viz.* that the Keeper of the Museum is to be present while the other party peruses the booke. Since therefore is it so order'd, I do desire and appoint you to send my Box forthwith (you may keep the Key), for fear that all my MSS &c should be rifled by the *mobile* (which God forbid but Mr E. Ashmole and I doe much feare it,) besides my Guift will make a better show in the Museum than when dispersed in two places. When you see Mr Christopher White pray remember me to him. Let him give my Laundresse, Mris Seacole, to keepe my Shirts &c safe, for I was to have returned in a fortnight; but the Times prevented me. I wish I could come to you in January or Febr. but some where I must retire about that time for fear of my Brother and other Creditors. I wish you a merry Christmas, Tuissimus,   J. Albericus.

I have several other MSS of my own and Mr Mercator's. That of mine

---

[1] Weld, or Wild, House, on the site of Little Wild Street, Lincoln's Inn, was the Spanish Embassy. It was pulled down *circa* 1695. Evelyn wrote on 9 December, 1688: 'The rabble demolished all popish chapels and several Papist lords and gentlemens' houses, especially that of the Spanish Ambassador, which they pillaged and burnt his library.' This was during the last few days before James II left England for France. The damage at Wild House was said to have been enormous, many people having taken their valuables there for safety.

that I most value is my *Idea of the Education of a Young Gentleman*, which is in a box as big as that I sent you; with choice Gramaticall bookes both ancient and moderne for the *Informators* to peruse and study. If I should die here they would be lost or seized upon by Mr Kent's sonnes. If I send them to the Museum the tutors would burn it for it crosses their interest exceedingly: if in your hands when you die your nephew will stop guns with them. I intended the Earl of Abingdon, but now he has other fish to fry. I think the Earl of Pembroke would do best, but had I the money to pay an amanuensis, I would leave a copy in the hands of both these two peers. I am very troubled and concerned for you, for feare of your writings being confounded by the *mobile*. *Vivas et valeas*.'

Aubrey's collections found their way into the Ashmolean soon after this, and a rough catalogue[1] was made of them; but this was a strong letter for Aubrey to write, and one that could have been called forth only by unusually obstructive behaviour on the part of Wood. It was not surprising that Aubrey, full of trepidation at the prevailing unrest, harassed by debt and the vagaries of his cantankerous and unreliable friend, felt increased anxiety for the security of his papers. The tone of his letter must have been somewhat disturbing to its recipient ('he looks upon you as a P.' means, of course, 'as a Papist'), who had good enough reason to feel uneasy with any such reminder. Activities at the court of the new rulers were naturally providing Lord Abingdon's 'other fish to fry'; as, in spite of being the first peer to join William of Orange's forces, he strongly opposed the Prince's acceptance of the Crown.

Mr (Matthew) Kent, mentioned in the postscript, seems to have been Aubrey's landlord in London. He became eventually the owner of Broad Chalke, and Aubrey's transactions with Kent were largely the cause of his brother's displeasure, and his own guilty feelings on this subject. A series of about half a dozen letters from

---

[1] The following contemporary entry appears in a manuscript Register of the Benefactors to the Museum: '*A.D. 1689. Johannes Aubrey, de Easton Piers apud Wiltoniensis Arm. e Soc. Reg. Socius, olim Alumnus, praeter Libellos, tum MSS tum impressos, plus minus octaginta, diversas illustrium virorum Effigies, Numismata Romana, Eorumque matrices lateritias. Operis item Musivi Teelati specimen.*'

William Aubrey belongs to this period, though only one is dated '1688'. They are addressed to Robert Hooke at his rooms (where Aubrey usually stayed), and begin 'D.B.' (Dear Brother), ending with a signature of illegible initials. Under the seal bearing the Aubrey arms (differenced with a mullet) the writer has drawn a small five-pointed star, no doubt to indicate that the letters were, in fact, intended for Aubrey (who would desire his whereabouts to be kept secret) and not for Hooke, to whom they were directed. In one of them, William Aubrey apologises for having forgotten to put the star on his previous letter, and he speaks of his money troubles and his efforts to find employment. Another of his letters is written from Chalke, where he seems to have farmed, as there is much talk of his sheep; but he was also occupied as some sort of agent locally, as he mentions the difficulties of controlling servants and preventing neighbours from despoiling the estates he was supervising. He says that Lady Raleigh had 'warned me out of the Lodge but I designe not to leave it before next Court day'. The 'Lord Warden'[1] is often mentioned as a possible patron. William Aubrey shows some anxiety to prove that he was not a Roman Catholic, saying:

'I took the Test one of the last Militia Officers in Wilts since Segemore battle, when K. James was at highest therefore unlikely to alter (for preferment) when he was declining.' There is also a mention of the rings left by their mother, which might have gone astray when the Dutch landed, and an assurance that these rings had been sold to him and were 'assets of hers', in case he or his brother might be sued on their account. He also refers to a neighbour mentioned several times by Aubrey, one Thomas Stokes,[2] with whom William seems to have boarded, and who might make difficulties about money owed to him. Stokes, who seems to have been specially interested in the records and privileges of the manor

---

[1] Perhaps John Granville, Earl of Bath, who was Lord Warden of the Stannaries, i.e. principal official of the tin mines of Devon and Cornwall.

[2] John Stokes, perhaps a brother, is also mentioned by Aubrey as a possible source (with William Aubrey) of information regarding the killing of Henry Long by Charles and Henry Danvers in 1594, an affray that held a long-remembered place in the annals of Wiltshire.

of Kington St Michael, was indeed William Aubrey's 'principle creditor' when he took out letters of administration for William Aubrey's goods and chattels on his death nearly twenty years later.

In these letters there is not much to indicate the seriousness with which Aubrey regarded his brother as a menace that might bring him to a debtors' prison. William Aubrey was certainly very keen to arrange a meeting between them, and says that he had been making efforts in this direction for two years or more, in order that they should discuss their difficulties together; otherwise there was danger that both of them would be imprisoned. He says that he is sorry for what he has 'at any time in passion said amiss'; but unfortunately this part of his letter—which speaks with affection of his brother—is badly mutilated, and only the general purport is conveyed by the words and phrases that remain. Aubrey no doubt wished to avoid an encounter as being somewhat ashamed of his own conduct (there had been, among other things, some altercation about William Aubrey's sheep) and there can be no doubt that his bad relations with his brother gravely disturbed him.

XIII

On St Peter's Day (29 June), 1689, he wrote to Wood:
'Oh the Happy life that the innocent poore Hermit does enjoy! You are not sensible of the load of Grief and dayly vexation that some lie under. Notwithstanding the which, considering my candle burns low, and that heartbreaking cares will shorten my life, I have forced myself from March 1st to transcribe, and on one day with another I transcribe at least halfe an hower. . . . You observe my desire in not letting Dr Plott see my Surrey papers. Between this and August Sir Edward Hungerford[1] and I, and another friend of mine (a very rich person) intend (by the grace of God) to make some profitable progress as to a secret there that you know.

[1] Sir Edward Hungerford was noted for his reckless extravagance. Aubrey had approached him on the subject of 'My discovery of nitrous Springs at Minetie in Wiltshire called the Gogges 1665 which is good Fuller's Earth and Sir Edward Hungerford will be engaged and help me get the ground from our friend George Pitt Esq.'

. . . I search't all Seth, *episcopus Sarum's*[1] papers that were at his house at Knightsbridge when he died. Of which I will give and bring you an account when I come to Oxon about the latter end of this month. I have taken care with his nephew and heir to looke over his papers in his study at Sarum. . . . I sent a letter to my cosen *Henry Vaughan* (Olor Iscanus) that very day that the Prince of Orange came to London: but never received an answer. He was wont to be free enough of his pen. I will write againe. I have sent two letters to my Landlord Mr Christopher White: but have received no answer. I am afrayd he is dead. A friend of mine (Mris Smyth at Mr Wyld's) wants a rare medicine that he hath for the stone. I desire to know the price, which I pray let me know *in your next*, unless he be alive to write himselfe. Now I conclude with an earnest Request that you would be pleased to enquire for a Colledge-lease, as you did for Edward Shirbourne[2] (whom no body can find). It is for that good obliging body Mris Smith, that lives with Mr Wyld. They cohabite as M[ary] Countess of Pembroke with Dr M[artin] L[ister]. I owe most of Mr Wyld's civility for her goodnesse and herein you will doe me the greatest kindnesse that you could imagine: for I am more obliged to her than to anybody. I beseech you for God's sake to mind this humble Request of mine. . . . Yesterday I sawe Mr Rushworth[3] which was a great mortification. He hath quite lost his memory with drinking Brandy. Remembered nothing of you, etc. His landlady wiped his nose like a child.'

On 15 July, 1689, Aubrey wrote to Wood: 'I doe give my hearty thanks for your care in my request about that good Gentlewoman at Mr Wyld's, also for goeing to Christopher White. . . .

---

[1] Aubrey's friend, Seth Ward, Bishop of Salisbury, had died in January 1689.

[2] Captain (Sir) Edward Shirburne, Clerk of the Ordnance of the Tower of London: writer and poet.

[3] This was John Rushworth, the historian, and author of *Historical Collections* and *The Earl of Strafford's Trial*, who had been brought by debt to the King's Bench Prison at Southwark. Rushworth had been Secretary to Fairfax, and there, and in other employments, he had played a part of some importance in the Civil Wars.

Mr Wyld will goe into the Countrey to see his Estate (for a moneth or 6 weekes): therefore I will deferre my coming to our English Athens till that time.' His own health was bad still, and writing to Wood of some papers, on 3 August, 1689, he said: 'I will send them to you for fear of Death's preventing me. For life is uncertain: and this morning I was anguishd and if I die before I send them to you all will be lost and there is no trust (hardly) to anybody: and I know you are so much a Gentleman, that you will not doe me wrong by putting out another's Labours under your own name—a thing too common in this world.' As well as these misgivings, there were new inconveniences to endure; and on 5 September he wrote again: 'One would be apt to thinke (God blesse me) that there was an evil Genius did haunt me. I came to my pleasant Lodgeing at the end of January last and a week after a writting schoolmaster takes the chamber above me: comes in at 12 or 1 and awakes me out of my sleep: and rises very early and falls a hammering for a quarter of an hour or more about his formes. The week after came a man and his wife and a child breeding Teeth, that cries day and night and the mother's shrill Tongue and singing to the cradle in the next roome is intolerable. But notwithstanding this I putt on a resolution to begin to transcribe, on the 1st of March. I had about a weekes worke left *sc.* to read over and correct and transcribe anew two Diatribes *when* the Chitt in the next chamber fell sick of the small-pox: and since the mother: so that I was fayne to lye at Innes &c. because Mris Smyth is afrayd never having had them, and fatt: but I carried my MSS out with me; but want my Plinys and Homers &c for quotations. I had the good luck lately to get a lodgeing in an empty house, where I have layne 5 daies, and am this day warnt out for a new Tenant to come-in. (I thought to have layn at M. Kent's and he haz two children sick of the same disease.) I intend by the middle of this moneth to come to Oxford, and bring my MSS with me: and there finish them: which I could doe in a fortnight. In the mean time pray consider where I should lye: whether at Mr White's and board there: or else at some other private place. I wish the windows might be South or East. I left with my laundresse Mrs Seacole, by Mr White's, a shirt, a cap, and cravat: for I intended to have returned in a fortnight, but then the Prince of Orange came in &c. I hope she has not lost it for I would not bring 2 shirts with me to stuff up my breeches and swelter me in the coach.'

On 16 September, 1689, he wrote again, in some excitement, enclosing a paper of Hooke's:

'Mr Wood! Mr Robert Hooke, R.S.S. did in anno 1670, write a discourse, called, *An attempt to prove the motion of the Earth*, which he then read to the Royal Society: but printed it in the begining of the year 1674, a *strena*[1] to Sir John Cutler to whom it is dedicate, wherein he had delivered the theorie of explaining the coelestial motions mechanically'. The letter goes on to describe how Hooke had discussed his views with Newton (who would 'run away with to glory of it', Aubrey feared) and closes with the words: 'Mr Wood! This is the greatest discovery in nature that ever was since the world's creation. It never was so much as hinted by any man before. I know you will doe him right. I hope you may read his hand. I wish he had writt plainer and afforded a little more paper.'

On 16 January, 1690, he wrote to Wood of his friend Dr Holder's controversy with Dr Wallis as to which of them could claim the credit of having cured the dumbness of Colonel Popham's son, adding: 'I have been extremely busy, and I much feare the next Term I shall be engaged in more trouble. I waived a Chancery Suite two terms when I was at Oxford; which was the reason I stayed there so long. . . . The Child in the next Chamber to me is of late much quieter, so that last month I writt faire and corrected the *Preface*.' This was work on the *Monumenta Britannica*.

In this year he was also collecting some biographies (now incorporated in the *Lives*) with the title *An Apparatus for the Lives of our English Mathematicall writers by Mr John Aubrey R.S.S. March 25, 1690*. This had been done at the suggestion of Dr Richard Blackbourne, to whom he had previously passed on the *Life of Thomas Hobbes*. In the index to this treatise on mathematicians, some names are mentioned of men of whom no account exists among Aubrey's biographical collections or elsewhere in his writings. These *Lives*,

[1] *i.e.* New Year's gift.

probably never written, were to be of: Thomas Blundeville, Henry
Bond, Robert Hues, Thomas Lidyate, Thomas Fale, and Edmund
Wingate. A project for a history of the mathematicians of England
had been anticipated, in some part, both by Selden and Sherburne,
as Aubrey noted: 'My purpose is, if God give me life, to make an
apparatus, for the lives of our English Mathematicians: which when
I have ended I would then desire Mr Anthony Wood to find out
one that is a good master of Latin Stile, and to add what is already
in his printed booke to the following minutes. I would not meddle with our own writers in mathematicks before the reigne of
King Henry VIII but prefix those excellent verses of Mr John
Selden (with a learned commentary on them) which are printed
before a book entitled [Arthur] Hopton's *Concordance of yeares*', and
he writes in another place, on the title page, 'Sir Edward Shir-
bourn somewhere in his translation and notes upon Manilius, has
enumerated our English Mathematicians, and hath given short
touches of their lives—which see.'

On 24 April, 1690, he wrote to Wood: 'By the begining of
October last I had made an end of my *Monumenta Britannica*, 3 volumes, and another vol. of *Miscellanea*, all which I will send you God
willing next weeke. After Michaelmas I parted with Chalke farm
to M. Kent, to my great griefe: which I putt off as well as I can:
and I cannot doe it better than by putting my papers in some
method before I dye; for I have a good deale of worke upon the
Loome. . . . About the middle of October M. Kent and all his
family went to Chalke: (and so I had no place for my letters till
our returne: for the postman hath left none at Mr Hooke's a great
while for he is seldom within: and so I have had letters lost and
miscarried.) And there we were to goe to settle matters and I
thought to have sent some good old Bookes to Oxon (V. Bede's
Works 2 Tom. &c.): but my brother in whose custody they were
would not be spoken with, and absented himselfe. At Christmas
I thought to have gone thither with Mr K[ent] but did not, and
then my brother and he mett: and I am afraid between my brother
and Mr Kent's son (a Westminster scholar) all my best things are
imbezilled. . . . For the three last months I have followed close
my *Naturall History* and have been ill two months of the time, with

stone and gowte but not very severe (except the stone two dayes).
. . . In March last it cost me 3 dayes paines to make a collection
of all my learned and Philos: letters which now make a fair volume. . . . I have sent 2 if not 3 letters to *Olor Iscanus*[1] and he
has not been so civil as to answer me: he is ingeniose but prowd
and humorous. . . . Pray consider where I should lye when I
come to you: for I shall stay but a little while and have but little
money to spare: and a great deale of businesse to do there: and I
never intend to see the place again for it seems I am a derision to
'em: and I will wash my hands of them and the place.'

This mood of depression continued, and on 10 May, 1690, he
wrote to Wood: 'Upon the receipt of yours I will by the next
waggon send down a box full of manuscripts and printed books.
The noble Earl of Pembroke gave me not long since as many good
books as cost him I beleive 5*li*. . . . In my next I shall send you
three or four obits. I wish heartily my papers were in your hands
for death seems to threaten. God blesse you and me in this in-and-
out world.' On 5 July he wrote again, almost resigned to Rules
Court Alley and the debtors' prison:

'I am fain to lye dormant for feare of an Arrest which will come
to a matter of 90*li* which my brother might have compounded for
twelve. His rough humour has put all my business so out of order,
that it hath also made me do him a great prejudice, and I have had
to do with odd people. . . . I hope to get a protection in a short
time. . . . John Rushworth of Lincolnes-Inne Esq (Historian)
died in the Rules-court in Southwarke, at the widow Bayley's
house (a good woman and who was very careful and tendfull of
him). . . . If I am caught by the Bayliffs, my brother having been
so unkind, I will end my daies with that good woman Mrs Baylie
. . . . Mr Kent's mayd is a giddy wench, and puttes my letters in
her Boxe of worke, that 'tis looking a needle in a bottle of hay, and
one letter she lost out of her breaste. I met the party afterwards,
'twas a cashiered Life-guard-man desired me to speake to the Earl
of Pembroke to prefer him. . . . (July 10) Since my former part of
the letter I met Dr Plott, who told me he would carry downe and

---

[1] Henry Vaughan, the poet.

see safe the things that I should send to the Museum, and to you. Accordingly on monday last, I brought him 2 boxes and a great bundle of Books. In the box I have this day sent downe to you by the Saracen's head carrier (carriage payd) I have put 4 volumes of MSS of my owne in folio, beside a thick folio of letters to me. But yesterday the Royal Society hearing of it, were all up-an-end, and would not have a denyall, but that I must stay the MSS and they will be at the charge of transcribing them. I could not disobey their order; and did not expect so great an honour from them. I thought to have enclosed my watch in the box for you, but 'tis out of order, and the Watchmaker hath not donne with it. I will be my owne Executor; it was the gift of my noble and deare Lord the Earl of Pembroke: and which I desire you to keep it as a memorial of me. I would willingly print my *Templa Druidum* in my life time; for that is finished; only wants an Aristarchus to polish the stile. . . . Pray let me heare from you by the next post. Vale. Without faile, for my satisfaction that the things are come safe to Oxon: for I heare there is exceeding robbing.'

On 4 January, 1691, he wrote to Wood once more about his domestic troubles: 'I am mightily discomposed about my brother. I intrusted him with my estate at Chalke (250*li* per annum) almost two yeares ago. I desired him to pay Captain Stumpe of Malmesbury a debt of 20*li* upon Bond borrowed in 1660 and he was so civill as to accept of the principall, and my brother never did it: also to take up a debt of 80*li* besides interest which was offered to him for 12*li* and he never did it: and I never received of him for all that time for that estate but 12*s*. 6*d*. which disgusted me so much that I threwe myself upon Mr K[ent] and he will appease my Creditors: and besides I shall be in danger of imprisonment. But nothing does wound me so much as my poor Creditors. Had my brother been but ordinarily civill to me I could have confirmed the estate upon him. . . . I suspect my brother (knowing the intimacy between you and me) may ask a trepanning question whether I have an Annuity from Mr Kent for Chalke. If he should know it, he would seize upon it. I expect the next terme to be engaged in a Suite in Chancery of which I shall never live to see the end.'

On 4 February, 1691, he wrote: 'Mr Kent had ill luck to put
Mr Ashton's life into Chalke farm. *sc.* the 3rd life. It does not
prosper.[1] At the later end of the Terme I expect my brother to
come like a Fury to fall upon me and Mr Kent: and very likely
I may be arrested.' These negotiations with Kent are obscure, but
it seems clear that Aubrey managed to get at least a small income
to the end of his days as a price for the farm at Broad Chalke.
There can be no doubt that William Aubrey had some right to
consider himself badly treated, but it is hard to say how unreasonable or dilatory he himself may have been; or what opportunities
he had been given by Aubrey to take matters in his own hands at
an earlier stage.

XIV

Meanwhile, he still shifted about, sometimes at Mr Thomas
Bridgeman's in Great Lincoln's Inn Fields 'near the Lord Powis
house, a large sun Dyal upon it'; sometimes at Mr Clarke's 'over
against the King's Head in Wardour Street at the upper end of the
old Soho'; with Robert Hooke at the Royal Society's rooms at
Gresham College in Bishopsgate; or at Mistress More's nearby in
Hammond Alley, or Mistress Byerlye's in Dirty-Lane in Bloomsbury near Holborn; or, again, at Oxford at Kit White's, the chymist in Holywell. The *Perambulation of Surrey* was revised, and received some additions, notably in regard to Southwark. There was
also work to be done on *An Interpretation of Villare Anglicanum*, a list
of English place names and words that 'had escaped the fury of the
Saxon conquest'. He wrote to Edward Lhwyd on 21 April, 1691,
asking his help in completing this study for publication, adding:
'Pray register my Strawe Tobacco-box and Mr Potter's little quadrant and agate-haft.' Difficulties of finding a publisher, or his usual

[1] This refers to a lease 'pur autre vie'—that is not for a period of
years but for a period of several lives. Apparently the life of Mr Ashton
was a poor one, which brought the date of the termination of the lease
nearer the end. In his next letter to Wood, dated 12 February, Aubrey
writes: 'Mr Ashton was of Lancashire, and paymaster and cashier to
King James Queen. I think he was a gent. yet 'tis sayd he was vallet de
chambre to Major-General Worden.'

inability to take action, prevented these works from being printed, in spite of enthusiasm on the part of readers to whom they were lent, that they should be speeded to the press. Apparently Wood complained that the watch presented to him by Aubrey kept bad time, because, on 29 April, 1691, Aubrey wrote: 'The watch went indifferently well with me: but the dayes of the moneth were faulty: which is not worth a chip. You were better to have it mended or changed here than at Oxon. I believe the watch cost at first not lesse than 10*li*. . . . My old acquaintance and deare friend T. Mariet Esq. deceased in Towne about 10 dayes since. His 3rd wife broke his heart.'

In May 1691 he paid a visit to the 2nd Lord Clarendon, who had been committed to prison at the beginning of the year, following the discovery of his correspondence with the exiled James II. Aubrey described this meeting to Wood (to whom the matter was of some significance in the light of future events) in a letter dated 12 May: 'I went to the Tower to the Earl of Clarendon and he received my Visit very kindly (I wonder that so few make visits to so great a person). I gave my Lord directions how to write to You: which he will: but he tells me he cannot doe his father's life till he is at liberty and to come to his papers.'

On 27 June, 1691, he wrote to Wood: 'I have lately received another kind invitation from the Earl of Abington, who goes the next week to his sister Carnarvon at Wing, for a moneth, and then returns to Ricot, where at my return from Oxon I will wayte on him, to be a sorry comforter in his sadnesse'—Lord Abingdon's wife Eleanor (daughter of Sir Henry Lee) having died suddenly at Lavington on 31 May that year. He tried to go to Oxford early in September, but, as he wrote to Wood on the 5th: 'I gave Earnest to come to Oxford on fryday last: but when I was to goe to the coach I found 5 Woemen: and two of them old and very sick: and no roome for my Bitch.[1] So I have deferred it till Monday but it would be hard if I should loose my Earnest . . . on Munday

---

[1] Aubrey wrote to Wood on 19 May, 1692: 'My pritty little Bitch is with puppy and I am much concerned to leave her behind me; she was lined by a most curious little Spannel. I could afford to bring her with me.'

night (God willing) I shall be at Oxford. I shall come weary. Pray consider where I shall lodge: for I shall stay but a weeke and perhaps Mr White would not foul his sheets for so little time. I ought to be pretty neer to you.'

John Ray, the botanist and zoologist, wrote to express his enjoyment of the *Natural History of Wiltshire*, on 22 September, 1691, questioning only the 'Hypothesis of the Terraqueous Globe' and taking the author to task for some 'new coyned' words, to which Aubrey was certainly addicted. He also sent his service to Mr [Jacob] Bobart.[1] Ray, son of a blacksmith, lived at his birthplace, a house called Dewlands at Black Notley, Essex. F.R.S., an old friend of Aubrey's, who as far back as 1676 had tried to arrange for him to tutor the son of Sir Francis Rolls during continental travels, Ray was a man of extraordinary gifts. Pre-eminent in the study of plants, birds, and insects, he was also a brilliant savant, concerned with wider issues such as the interpretation of religion in the light of science. He is perhaps the greatest of the early naturalists. Ray's contacts with Aubrey were close. To him on 22 October, 1691, Aubrey wrote of yet another untoward incident that had taken place:

'When I was lately at Oxford I gave several things to the Musaeum, which was lately robbed, since I wrote to you. Among other things my picture in miniature by Mr S. Cowper, (which at an auction yields 20 guineas,) and Archbishop Bancroft's, by Hillyard, the famous illuminer in Queen Elizabeth's time.'[2]

Ray replied from Black Notley on 27 October, 1691:

'You write that the musaem at Oxford was rob'd, but doe not say whether your noble present was any part of the losse. Your

---

[1] Keeper of the Physick Garden at Oxford, a naturalist of some eccentricity, remembered among other exploits for having 'made a dead rat resemble the common picture of a dragon. . . . The learned immediately pronounced it a dragon.' He had been preceded in his post by his father, also called Jacob, an unconventional figure, followed by a goat instead of a dog, and accustomed 'on rejoicing days to tag his beard with silver', who had clipped the yew-trees of the Physick Garden into the form of giants. There are many stories about him in Wood's diary, and ballads dedicated to his 'Yew-men of the Guard'.

[2] The receipt of both Aubrey's portrait and Bishop Bancroft's at the Museum was acknowledged by Dr Plot on 18 October, 1688.

picture done in miniature by Mr Cowper is a thing of great value. I remember so long agoe as I was in Italy, and while he was yet living, any piece of his was highly esteemed there: and for that kind of painting he was esteemed the best artist in Europe.'

Whether or not this is the portrait of Aubrey that had once belonged to the Seymours is uncertain. His biographer, Britton, seems on the whole to have believed that it was the same. If so, Lady Seymour of Trowbridge (or, as she was by that time, Lady Ernle) possessed the miniature in 1683, when William Aubrey had come over to Alington, who had afterwards written that there were a hundred quarterings of the Seymour family in the windows there—and his brother's 'picture in my Lord's parlour'. Lady Ernle died on 16 October, 1691. She may have given the painting to Aubrey between 1683 and 1689, when he made his gift to the Ashmolean; but there appears to be no evidence to suggest this. Neither the Cooper nor the portrait of Archbishop Bancroft is now in the Ashmolean; only the Faithorne has survived in Oxford, and now hangs in the Bodleian. There were, therefore, at least four portraits of Aubrey: the picture owned by the Seymours, which may have been the Cooper or the painting ascribed by Lodge to Lely; the Faithorne drawing; and the Loggan.[1]

On 27 October, 1691, Aubrey also wrote to Wood: 'In the first place I returne you my hearty Thanks for your Civilities to me and for my good Entertainment at Oxford: and for your kind token. I thanke God I have yet my Liberty. Mr Kent compounded the debt that I was arrested for: but I dread the end of this Terme. My Brother has been unkind to me (and God forgive me) I have undonne him and myselfe. Hereafter when your businesse is over, I will give you a state of the matter, but the trueth is, I was never made to manage an estate and was predestinated to be cosened and cheated.'

[1] There is a note in the MS. of the *Monumenta Brittanica* (f. 17): 'My brother hath my picture that Mr Faithorne drew in black and white *Ao* 1666, in order to engrave it for his booke: my Ld Ch: Seymor had my picture *Aetat* 30, which his Lady now hath. Quaere *Sir John Erneley* for it.'

XV

On 13 February, 1692, he wrote: 'Your advice to me was prophetique, viz not to lend my MSS. You remember Mr J. Ray sent me a very kind letter concerning my *Naturall History of Wilts*: only he misliked my Digression, which is Mr Hooke's Hypothesis of the terraquious Globe whom I name with respect. Mr Ray would have me (in the letter) leave it out. And now lately is come forth a booke of his in 8vo[1] which all Mr Hooke's hypothesis in my letter is published and without any mention of Mr Hooke or my booke. Mr Hooke is much troubled about it. 'Tis a right Presbyterian trick.' On 3 March he wrote to Wood: 'Yesterday my brother came to Towne, and this day is gonne into Sussex and I am served with a Subpoena and also Mr Kent—So that I have gott a new Suite that I never expect to weare out.'

Aubrey visited Black Notley in the Summer of 1692; leaving another manuscript, *Adversaria Physica*, for comment, on the subject of which Ray wrote on 24 August, 1692: 'Your *Adversaria Physica* I have read over once, but the variety and curiosity of the matter and observations is such that I cannot satisfy myself with a single reading.' Earlier in the year Aubrey had lent the *Education of a Young Gentleman* to Evelyn: and there had been correspondence with Dr James Garden, Professor of Theology at King's College, Aberdeen, on the subject of Celtic monuments and Scotch customs and traditions. Dr Garden sent information about stone circles, the Orkneys, second-sight, transportation by invisible power, and other matter to be incorporated into the *Remains of Gentilism* and the *Monumenta Britannica*. Material for the former of these works was also contributed by the rector of Stanton St Quintin in Wiltshire, John Byrom (a close friend of Aubrey's brother William), who wrote a letter about the curious custom of *Montem* at Eton, when the boys assumed fancy dress and demanded tribute of salt from passers-by. On 8 November, 1692, Aubrey wrote to Wood: 'Pray doe me the favour when you light upon

[1] Probably the *Three Discourses*, 1692. Ray's biographer, Dr C. E. Raven, thought the charge of plagiarism (which Hooke was always inclined to scent) most improbable.

My Verses of the Robin-red-breast to insert and pin it to my *Villa*. I should be very sorry to have it lost: and I see one is sure of nothing that is not in one's owne Custodie—and when one is dead, all is lost that is not deposited in some public Repository.' This, indeed, seems to have been the fate of the verses, for no trace of them remains.

CHAPTER SEVEN

The Quarrel and the Final Years (1692–1697)

I

IN 1692, TOWARDS the close of the year, an episode took place
which spoiled, utterly and irrevocably, his friendship with
Wood and filled Aubrey's heart with disappointment and
vexation. This came about as a result of the publication of the
Athenae, the first volume of which had appeared in June 1691, the
second volume following a year later. This work had excited not a
little irritation among its readers, especially those who found
themselves included in the biographies there set forth. Wood was
shown a letter in which the writer described how he was told in
London 'by severall that a great deal of ill-nature was expressed in
my book lately published'; and, having recorded this in his diary,
he commented: 'Who is ill-natured? Whether the author who
speaks the truth, or a company of idle fellowes that sit all day in an
Alehouse or taverne to pick holes in the coates of industrious men
who labour for the honour of the University.' This last point of
view was not one very generally accepted, and feeling ran so high
that 'in New College common-chamber severall of the fellowes
said that I had abused their relations and that when darke nights
come they will beat me'.

On 20 August, 1692, Aubrey, on his return from visiting Ray,
wrote a letter to Wood on this subject: 'Accidentally I spoke with
Mr Gadbury who is extremely incenst against you. He tells me
what you have wrote, and I am sorry for it, for he was civill to you
and was a very ingeniose loyall person. He sayes that you have
printed lyes concerning him, and he wonders that you should
meddle with him, having never been of the University.' This
refers to the sketch of John Gadbury's life given in the *Athenae*,
under the biography of Sir George Wharton, the astrologer and
Royalist Captain of Horse, which runs as follows:

221

'John Gadbury, born at Wheatley near to, and in the county of, Oxon, the thirty first of December 1627, son of William Gadbury of that place, farmer, by his stol'n wife the daughter of Sir John Curson of Waterperry knight, bound an apprentice to Thomas Nicholls a taylor living in the parish of St Peter in the Bayly in Oxon, left him, after the great fire hapned in that city 1644, and having a natural genius to the making of almanacks, improved it at London under William Lilly, then called the English Merlin, and afterwards set up the trade of almanack-making, and fortune-telling for himself; in which he became eminent.'

Gadbury[1] was annoyed, perhaps not unnaturally, at the publicity thus given to his origins and early employment, especially as he had not been educated at Oxford. This thumbnail sketch was gratuitously tacked on to the information that he had collected and published some of Wharton's astrological treatises. His activities in the last respect were the sole excuse for mentioning his name at all in the *Athenae*, and Wood can only have included him to gratify an uncontrollable taste for malicious gossip, although it must be admitted that this *curriculum vitae* was less provocative than the remarks in Lilly's *History of His Life and Times*, where the author speaks of 'that monster of ingratitude, my quondam taylor, John Gadbury'.

Characteristically, Wood was unable to see, or perhaps determined to ignore, anything to which exception might be taken in what he had printed. He replied at the end of November 1692: 'I wonder at nothing more than that Mr Gadbury should take it amiss of those things that I say of him: for whereas the generality of scholars did formally take him to have been bred an academician, because he was twice at Oxon, and so consequently, not to be much admir'd, now their eyes beinge opend and knowing that his education hath been mechanical they esteem him a prodigie of parts and therefore are much desirous that his picture may hang

---

[1] On 3 September, 1676, Robert Hooke had recorded in his *Journal* a visit paid with Aubrey to Gadbury, the astrologer, and Harrington of the Rota—Harrington, it will be remembered, suffered, by this time, from an obsession that his sweat turned to flies. Hooke had remarked of them: 'Both mad but of Divers humours.'

in the public gallery at the scholes. Pray recommend me to him, and desire him, that if I seek any things that are untrue, he may rectifie them: put them into your hands and to be sent to me.'

There were, however, other and more powerful elements at work than an exasperated astrologer to take offence at the uncompromising pages of the *Athenae*; and, on 16 November, 1692, Wood received a summons to appear in the Vice-Chancellor's Court. This was at the instigation of Henry Hyde, 2nd Earl of Clarendon, who complained that his father, Edward Hyde, 1st Earl of Clarendon, had been libelled by a statement to the effect that when Lord Chancellor he had sold offices at the Restoration. This implication was to be inferred from some of the information supplied to Wood by Aubrey, who had, for example, written in the *Life* of Judge David Jenkins: 'He would have taken it kindly to have been made one of the judges in Westminster Hall, but would give no money for it', the words that follow '*so the Lord Chancellor Hyde never preferred him*' being scored through in the manuscript.[1] This passage appeared in the *Athenae* as: 'After the Restoration of K. Charles II it was expected by all that he (Jenkyns) should be made one of the judges in Westminster Hall, and so might he have been, would he have given money to the then lord chancellor'; while another passage in that work, referring to Sir John Glynne (who had sentenced Colonel Penruddock to death), stated that 'after the restauration of K. Ch II he [Glynne] was made his eldest serjeant at law by the corrupt dealings of the then lord chancellor.'

Terror caused by this threat of prosecution was probably the cause of the action that Wood now took; for on the manuscript of the second part of the *Lives* the following words were written by Aubrey: 'Ingratitude! this *part the second* Mr Wood had gelded from page 1 to page 44 and other pages too are wanting wherein are contained trueths, but such as I entrusted nobody with

---

[1] The statement is repeated in a letter to Wood dated 16 January, 1671. Judge Jenkins had married a sister of Sir John Aubrey, 1st bt., of Llantrithyd. Aubrey first mentions him in a letter to Wood dated 17 November, 1670, in which he adds: 'If you wish I can further satisfye you.'

the sight of but himselfe (whom I thought I might have entrusted with my life). There are severall papers that may cutt my throate. I find too late *memento diffidere* was a saying worthy one of the sages. He hath also embezill'd the index of it—quod N.B. It was stich't up when I sent it to him. Novemb. 29, 1692.'

It is just possible that Wood, to save himself the trouble of the transcription, mutilated this manuscript of the *Lives* so that he could paste the cuttings into his rough copy of the *Athenae*; but it is far more probable that alarm at the thought of what might be the dire consequences of his indiscretion caused him to remove bodily all incriminating evidence. The names missing from the index to the *Lives*, made by Aubrey and presumably removed by Wood (who may have excised additional subjects of which no record remains) are those of: Richard Alcorne, Samuel Collins, D.D., Richard Blackbourne, M.D., John Flamsted, Sir John Hoskyns (one of Aubrey's special friends), Benjamin Ruddier, Captain Edward Sherburne, Captain Thomas Stumpe (whose adventures in Guiana are recorded in the *Natural History of Wiltshire*), and Richard White; the lives of some of whom may, of course, never have been completed by Aubrey, who had, as we know, himself removed a small amount of what he considered to be dangerous matter.

On 14 December, 1692, he wrote to Wood in a state of great alarm: 'All last week I was Ill, but on Sunday I went to my Lord Abington who saluted me with a sad aspect, and a sudden Intimation *sc.* that he was exceedingly greived for the Trouble that was coming upon me; I was mightily surprised. Say'd he the Earl of Clarendon hath told me, that Mr Wood had confessed to him, that he had the Libell (advice to the Painter)[1] from me: as also the other informations. I do admire that you should deal so unkindly with me, that have been so faithfull a friend to serve you ever since 1665, as to do so by me: the Libell was printed and not

---

[1] Aubrey says elsewhere : 'The verses called The Advice to the Painter were of Marvell's making.' The title became very popular for pamphlets, and some twenty or more appeared with this, or closely related name. The lines were a savage attack on the Court. Savile may have been the true author.

uncommon: could not you have sayd that you bought it? Or had it of George Ent, or someone that is dead? To be short my Lord is resolved to undoe me: pray let me know by the next post, what 'tis that you have donne against me, that I may be the better enabled to make my Defence. I must be faine to fly some whither ere long, but nothing greives me more than that I shall not be able to see my Booke printed. I much fear that I shall never see you or Oxford again, so I desire as a dying person to look out my papers for me and send to Dr Gale who is my faithful friend. My heart is ready to breake. . . . As to that of Judge Jenkins I told you, I could attest from his owne mouth. Thomas Shadwell Poet Laureat obiit Chilsey about 1 December.'

It will be remembered that Aubrey had visited Lord Clarendon in the Tower in May 1691, and had been pleased with the reception given him. His present fears, as will be seen, turned out to be groundless, but the situation certainly looked ominous. Thomas Gale,[1] the friend to whom the papers were to be sent, was headmaster of St Paul's school. He was F.R.S. and a person often mentioned by Aubrey as a source of information and advice.

II

Edward Lhwyd, who had become Keeper of the Ashmolean in 1690, wrote in March 1693 that he had made a catalogue of Aubrey's books there, and was making another of his manuscripts: 'I have got all your pamphlets in the museum bound, and in case you are disposed to dedicate your Collection of Letters to the Museum, I will take care to have them bound out of hand: unlesse you have been at that charge already yourselfe.'

On 4 April, 1693, Aubrey wrote to Wood from London:

'I told you I was invited into Hartfordshire to Dr Holder (who remembers him kindly to you) and my cosen Freeman (Sir J. Aubrey's sister) his neighbour. I have been here before March but never so much entangled and ingaged in businesse in my life:

---

[1] He was made Dean of York in 1697. He married Barbara, daughter of Thomas Pepys of Impington, and his daughter, Elizabeth, became the second wife of William Stukeley, the antiquary.

and partly in publishing my Booke. I am exceedingly obliged to my old Acquaintance Mr John Dreyden for his friendly advice and recommendation. He would have had his bookseller printed it: but *he* will print only Plays and Romances. So I am obliged to do it by Subscription, which doe begin pretty luckily. . . . I writt to you to send me the papers which you took out of my collection of Lives, or send them to Dr Gale. But he has heard nothing of them. March 20 I lighted upon Theives that robbed and wounded me sorely. I kept my chamber a weeke and have since been in a course of Physick. . . . I have been but thrice at the Royal Society since I sawe you. People are shy and afrayd to speek freely to me concerning your book lest I should tell you of it. The Peers (I can tell) are offended at your liberty, be it true or false. Mr Evelyn desired you to send him what you writ of him before you printed it: and takes it unkindly you did not doe it: but he sayes you call him a great *Virtuoso*: he had rather you had called him Coxcomb. The Mayd of Honour was here at dinner and her neice [Mary] Tuke,[1] and they are angry with you, that you disparag'd their Gentility and sayd that you sent it up to London for 2*d*. per pound: sayd I, that was only drollery and not disrespect: for he much honours the family.'

The book to which Aubrey refers was the *Miscellanies*, the only work to appear in his lifetime. The robbery, which took place between 10 and 11 o'clock at night, left him with fifteen wounds in his head, a serious enough misadventure at the best of times and disastrous to an elderly man in bad health. However, in spite of complaints about his constitution, Aubrey must have had remarkable recuperative powers. A correspondent with whom he was now in close touch was Thomas Tanner[2] (afterwards Bishop of St

---

[1] Mary Sheldon, daughter of Edward Sheldon, had married Samuel Tuke, the playwright. This was the Tukes' daughter Mary.

[2] Tanner (notwithstanding his assumption, of the arms of the Tanners of Cornwall) was the grandson of a poor man, probably a weaver, of Urchfont in Wiltshire; his father being vicar of Market Lavington, and his mother, daughter of Joseph Willoughby, sometime 'Foreman of the Homage' to the Manor of Sir John Danvers, 'the regicide', at Lavington. The Steward of the Court of this Jury of

Asaph and author of *Notitia Monastica; or a Short History of the Religious Houses in England and Wales*), a young antiquary, who used to borrow Aubrey's manuscripts; and, eventually, carried on some of his work. On 16 May, 1693, Tanner wrote to Aubrey: 'I was heartily sorry to hear of your affliction by that tormenting disease the Gout, but was more troubled that you told me at the bottom of your letter, *viz* that you were so far stricken in years. I have seen, heard and read of the notorious misfortunes that usually attend posthumous papers, so that I hope you will make haste, and yourself communicate the greatest and best part of your laborious collections to the world. . . . Your entire originals shall be deposited hereafter in the musaeum according to your desire, that posterity may see how just we have been to the memory of your pains.' Tanner asked for further loans of Aubrey's collection, and shows that Wood's demeanour must have been common gossip by the words: 'I shall scorn to be like Anthony Wood *viz* to make use of your papers and acquaintance, and at last not to afford you a good word.' On 1 June, 1693, Aubrey replied that his manuscripts would show how much Wood was indebted to him for the *Lives*, making a special request that Wood should not know that they had been placed in the Ashmolean.

III

Wood, haled before the Vice-Chancellor's Court to answer the *scandalum magnatum* proceedings, instead of pleading that there could be no case of libel against the dead, or that bribery was one of the misdemeanours alleged to have been the official reason for Clarendon's dismissal from office, made his defence the purely

freehold tenants of the manor was the same William Yorke, who, it will be recalled, was one of those who had undertaken to help in the compilation of a country history of Wiltshire at the meeting Aubrey had attended in 1659/60. The Lavington estate descended eventually to the 1st Earl of Abingdon, who was a friend of Dr Leopold Finch, Warden of All Souls, Oxford. The chaplaincy of that foundation was obtained for Tanner, setting his foot on the way to preferment. It can be seen that he was closely associated with many of Aubrey's connexions.

technical one that there was no proof that he, Wood, had written the offending passages. There was, perhaps, no alternative course in the case of an opponent belonging to so powerful a family, although not one in great favour at Court. In July 1693 he was found guilty of the libels alleged, fined forty pounds, and expelled the University. The entries in the *Athenae* to which objection had been taken were publicly burnt; while the Vice-Chancellor laid out the amount of the fine upon providing three statues to be placed in the niches of the gate of the Physick Garden.

No doubt Wood considered Aubrey largely to blame for his plight, and the denigratory account in his diary of their first meeting may date from this period. It is, however, difficult to feel great sympathy for Wood. The material was sent to him by Aubrey for general editing, full of personal comments such as might be written in a letter (indeed much of the information was passed in letters), and not necessarily intended for (at any rate contemporary) publication. Aubrey had said in so many words: 'I fancy myself all along discourseing with you.' If the remarks were of a kind likely to be dangerous in print, Wood was as good a judge as Aubrey of this; and it is clear from Wood's character and his works that discreditable statements about persons to be included in the *Athenae* would, to say the least, appeal to him as an editor no less strongly than those which showed the subject of a biography in a favourable light. His attitude to Gadbury alone makes this apparent enough. So far as the lost Aubrey material is concerned, Andrew Clark (whose opinion on the matter must be allowed much weight) had little doubt that the substance of the missing pages was all incorporated in the *Athenae*. On the other hand, Aubrey mentions lives of King James I and the Duke of Monmouth, with the other names of which no trace remains, so that it is not unlikely that controversial matter, now lost, was contained in some of these.

IV

On 19 July, 1693, Aubrey wrote to Tanner: 'I shall goe tomorrow towards Cambridge and shall returne about a fortnight hence or perhaps three weeks. . . . My brother went out of this town yesterday to Kington St Michael, two miles beyond Chippenham who had a great collection of Heraldry and Antiquities.'[1] On 30 August he wrote to Tanner again, from Cambridge: 'I reade the fate of our friend Anthony in the Gazette at the Coffee House and the Heads of Houses are offended with him. The Young Men are learned but no antiquarians.'

From Lavington on 21 October, 1693, Aubrey wrote to Wood: 'After my recovery of wounds by the Theives I fell most extremely ill of the Gowte for two moneths: above halfe the time keeping to my bed. It had almost carried me off. Then I tooke the fresh aire and good entertainment in Hartfordshire at my cosen Freeman's, marryed to Sir John Aubrey's sister, and Dr Holder who carried me to Cambridge and brought me acquainted with the Heads of Houses, who kindly entertained me. The newes of your book I found there in the *Gazette*: but which I admire at very much few there read your book. I told them 'tis pity somebody does not doe the like for Cambridge. They slighted the proposal *as a useless learning*. These are excellent Philologists &c: but the worst Antiquaries that ever I conversed with. I had the honour to be acquainted in these parts with a matter of 3 Bishops: but both Bishops and Clergie (except the Bishop of London,[2] whom I saw every day—half a mile from Dr Holder) *are spightful at your great Labours*. I am not acquainted with the London Ministers, but I believe the same humour reinges amongst them all; but on the other side, all the Gentry of Hartfordshire, (and 'tis very full) *mightily applaud your Book* as most of the Royal Society (except Grandees) . . . I after met with one of the *Young Heralds* who tells me that all the Young Heralds are extremely incenst against you for your handling of Sir W. Dugdale *so roughly*. . . . I shewed your letter to Mr Gadbury, wherein you tell him what he desires shall

[1] On 10 August, 1693, William Aubrey wrote to Tanner from Kington House, denying that he had any of his brother's MSS.

[2] Henry Compton, Bishop of London. In his youth he had served as a cornet in the Royal Horse Guards, and James II complained that he 'talked more like a colonel than a bishop'. He was a good botanist, quoted by Ray in his *History of Plants*.

be done in the Appendix[1] to be printed: but he huft and pish't, saying *that your copies are flown abroad and the scandals are irrevocable and that he will have a fling at you* in Print to vindicate himselfe. I have here retirement and leisure enough, and have read over Mr Lock's book:[2] but when I come to London I shall be ready to sinke under the trouble I am coming into—*viz* Mr Kent and my brother are up to their eares in Chancery and I shall be drawn-in: but though my brother hath not been so kind to mé as he ought to have been, which has happened exceedingly to his prejudice for he might have had Chalke farm (now) let for 2 50*li* per annum yet when I come upon my oath I must doe him right though to my owne hindrance. I have had much ado to satisfye the E[arl] of Ab[ingdon] concerning—but I did affirm to him that you will take your oath that &c. . . . I forgot to tell you I just called upon Mr Coley as I was goeing out of Town and he is very angry with you because you terme *Astrologers Conjurors*. . . . My cosen *Freeman* haz a pretty good Library, and he is obliged to you for vindicating his wives uncle Judge Jenkins.'

On 26 December, 1693, Tanner wrote to Aubrey: 'You need not fear my playing plagiary with your MSS, tho' I must excuse your jealousy of such a thing, Antony Wood having dealt so ungenteely by you.'

V

Aubrey suffered a fit of apoplexy on 5 January, 1694. He wrote to Anthony Henley on 27 February of the *Education of a Young Gentleman*: 'I hope this child of mine will be presented to you in a lucky house. I am much joy'd to heare what excellent character you give of the Earle of Leicester. He may be a meanes to promote the Designe. The Earle of Pembroke hath read it over and excerpted some things. He approves of it, but is not active. I wish I may live to transcribe a fair copie from which others may be transcribed. I

---

[1] The third volume of the *Athenae*, upon which Wood was then at work.

[2] Probably *Some Thoughts concerning Education*, 1693. For Locke's acquaintance with Aubrey, see Cranston's *John Locke* and *Notes & Queries* 23 Dec. 1950, 30 Aug. 1951.

have some hopes that the Marquess of Worcester (to whom my brother is well known) may propagate the designe in Wales. I am not over confident of my Lord Weymouth. It would be but, as it were, saying *fiat* to the E[arl] of P [embroke] Lord W[orcester], and Lord Ashley, to have established it at Cranbourne. But God's will be done. If the noblesse have a mind to have their children put in the Clergie's pockets, much good may it do 'em.' Aubrey goes on to ask that the manuscript may be returned to him, or to Robert Hooke, in the event of his own death; and adds: 'But I foresee that it will lie there coffined up, and nobody have the generosity to set afloat this noble designe.'

He was again with Holder in Hertfordshire when he wrote, on 22 April, 1694, to Wood, sullenly continuing his labours in exile: 'Sir John Aubrey sent me a letter dated 5 March desiring me to come to Borstall by the last week in April: but at Easter I received another in this country, that informs me he haz not been well, and shall not be at Borstall till the middle of May. Els I had been with you this weeke. This is a country of Harmony, and I have been at severall good Music meetings which have hindred me from writing sooner.' On St John's Day (24 June), 1694, he wrote again to Wood: 'I returne to London with the Earl of Abingdon ten dayes since. . . . I have not above half a dozen of your letters to me which at present I cannot come at. I sent you all the letters before. I expect that you shall deliver your letters to me. About March I intend to be at Oxford a month and desire you to restore the ten pages you have cutt out of my Collections, and then you may peruse all the rest. Mr Lloyd [Lhwyd] tells me you have not restored them as yet.'

He continued to take his habitual interest in the eccentricities of human behaviour and recorded of the day upon which he wrote this letter: 'On the day of St John the Baptist, 1694, I accidentally was walking in the pasture behind Montague House.[1] It was 12 o'clock. I sawe there about two or three and twenty young women, most of them well habited, on their knees very busy, as if they had been weeding. I could not presently learn what the

<hr>

[1] Where the British Museum now stands.

matter was. At last a young man told me that they were looking
for a coal under the root of a plantain, to put under their head that
night, and they should dream who should be their husbands. It was
to be sought for that day and hour.'

On 6 July, 1694, he wrote to Wood from London: 'I sent a
letter to you lately and told you that I should be at Borstall last
night. I gave earnest 3s. 6d. to the Alesbury coach a week since:
but man proposeth and God disposeth. On Wednesday I went to
take leave of my shee cosen Montagu (Sir John Aubrey's sister)
whom I saw but a fortnight since, and she lay in a dying condition
and sent to her brother to come and see her. He is expected this
night. She is yet living: and some hope she may master this feaver.
Sir J.A. does not love London: and will stay as short a time as he
can, and so I shall come downe with him: but he wonders that I
stayd here so long. My Lord of Pembroke's scrupulosities made
me loose a whole moneth about March last. Being with his Lordship lately, my Lord and Mr Locke speaking of my *Templa
Druidum* (which his Lordship will have dedicated to him) Mr
Lock sayd that there is an excellent and learned booke published
by Mr Dickinson where are discourses of Druids and Delphi[1] &c
which is thought to be writ by the learned H. Jacob. . . . I shewed
your paper to Dr Gale as he came out of the schoole; he was so
peevish he would not read it over: and was positive it was donne
by the University. I shewed him the begining of your letter where
his name was first placed. Pedants are froward persons.'

He wrote to Wood on 2 September, 1694, from Boarstall, where
Sir John Aubrey, too, seems to have been mildly interested in
antiquarian matters: 'I thought I should have heard from you ere
this time. I have been ill ever since I came from Oxford, till within
these five days, of a surfeit of peaches &c: so that I was faine to
send to Kit White for a good lusty vomit. I could not eatt a bitt of
flesh for six days, but abstinence hath pretty well settled me
againe. Your unkindness and choleric humour was a great addition

---

[1] Edmund Dickinson, M.D. (1624–1707), alchemist and physician
to Charles II and James II: Henry Jacob (1608–1652): Fellows of
Merton: *Delphi Phoenicazantes*, Oxon 1655, is said to have been written
by Jacob, though published under Dickinson's name.

to my illness. You know I always loved you, and never thought I took paines enough to serve you; and was told by severall at Oxford, and so the last yeare, that you can never afford me a good word.[1] I desired you to give to the museum my draught of Osney, which cost XXs when I was of Trin: Coll: 'Twas donne by one Hesketh, a Hedge-Priest, who painted under Mr Dobson. Also I desired you to give me the entertainments to the Queen at Bushell's Rocks.[2] Your Nephews and Neices will not value them. You have cutt out a matter of forty pages out of one of my volumes, as also the index (was ever any body so unkind?) and I remembered you told me coming from Heddington, that there were some things in it that *would cutt my throat*. I thought you so deare a friende that I might have entrusted my life in your hands; and now your unkindnes doth almost break my heart. If you will returne these papers to me and the other 3 things to the . . . [you may then] have the *Lives*. I tooke Dr Gale's life from his own [mouth] . . . writings under his own hand. I should be glad . . . you shall be heartily welcome, and I will . . . booke of this house in parchment done in H.6. and . . . this estate granted to him by Edward Confessor. This place . . . I want Mr Lilly's epitaph. I would have you come the next week for . . . fortnight hence Sir J. A. goes into Glamorganshire and will have me . . . I have not been very fitt for riding, but I intend to spend two or three dayes . . . before Sir John goes away. You cannot imagine how much your unkindnesse vext and discomposed me. So God blesse you. Tuissimus, J.A. . . . I think I told you that my Lord Abington told me that Lord Clarendon never sayd any such thing—but he only spoke it to me to banter me and putt me in a fright. I would have you come hither as early as you can, because of perusing the MS and seeing the gardens, for the afternoon will be taken up with good fellowship.'

This letter is mutilated in a number of places; but the sense seems fairly clear. Dr Gale's life was apparently one of those

[1] Tanner's phrase in his letter quoted p. 227, *supra*.
[2] *The Severall Speeches and Songs at the presentment of Mr Bushell's Rock to the Queen's most excellent Majesty*. Oxford. 1636, copy given to Aubrey's grandfather by the 'graceful' Jack Sydenham, Thomas Bushell's servant.

removed by Wood, as only a list of Gale's works is extant, drawn
up in a hand other than Aubrey's. Wood had in fact visited Boarstall as far back as 1646, and again in 1668, when Penelope, Lady
Dynham had been living there[1]; and he had also examined the
manuscript, which referred to the grant of the property to one
Nigel or Niel, who had slain a formidable boar that infested the
adjacent royal forest of Bernwood. On the same day (2 September,
1694) Aubrey wrote to Lhwyd: 'I would desire your prudent and
friendly advice and Mr Tanner's. Mr Anthony Wood is peevish
and froward and angry with me that he hath not my *Lives*. He
is writing of a 3rd volume where he sayes he shall make an honourable mention of me: but he speakes ill of me and bespatters me
wherever he goes: and haz betrayed me to Dr Plott who is angry
with me: but I value not his pride, nor his tuff't gowne, nor his
Hornes. Mr Wood has cut out of one of the Volumes ten leaves
or more and also the Index, and keepes it by him . . . now if I
could get out of his hands those papers which he cutt-out, and the
2 other things I could be contented he should have the perusall of
my *Idea* [*of the Education of a Young Gentleman*]: if he hath them not
he will abuse and — me damnably in his next volume.' On the following day (3 September, 1694) he wrote again to Wood: 'Mr
Wood, I sent a letter lately to you, and to desire you to come hither
to dinner where you should be very welcome, and see the antiquities and MSS of this old seate. This is to acquaint you that
either next fryday or Saterday (to morrow Mr Kennet will bring us
word) Sir William Glyn and his brother dine here: who would not
looke upon you with a good eie.[2] Any day else Sir John and I shall
be glad to see you!'

[1] Daughter of Sir Richard Wenman and widow of Sir John Dynham, a lady who was a strong Parliamentarian and had held Boarstall
against the King's troops in the Civil Wars. The estate held '*per unum
cornu, quod est charta praedictae forestae*' had descended to the Aubreys
through several heirs female. The story of the slaying of the boar is
partially corroborated by the confirmation, in 1266, by Henry III to the
heir of the Fitz-Neils, of the 'bailwick and Derhyde' (the nucleus of the
manor), the former of which is described as held by an ancestor from the
Conquest.

[2] On account of the biography in the *Athenae* of Sir John Glynne (who

A furious reply came from Wood, dated 15 September, 1694. He quotes much of Aubrey's letter of the 2 September, and goes on to complain of this and others that Aubrey had written to him: 'that you forward to plague and disturb my thoughts without examination. At length when you came to towne one year after you told me it was a *Banter*. Now I appeal to all the world whether this was not an unworthy thing in you as to those particulars—first that which was bad you let me know in your letter to disturb my thoughts and rest: but that which proved good (the *Banter*) you never did let me know it by your Letter to comfort my thoughts, only by word of mouth a yeare after and that by accident. Another thing since this happens, that when I was in your company last at Oxon you told me I had yett your book and so in your most wicked and silly letter of the 2nd of September You tell me so againe: as you did in another letter last week to Mr Lloyd of the musaeum, and perhaps to others. Now I must let you know that before you did disturb my mind by word of mouth and by letters, especially by that rascally letter that had been soaked in a bucket of ale, you should have examined this matter and brought the book with you to shew me where the Leaves were cut out, and to prove those to be cut out, but this you have not done, but go on with stuff and tattle to abuse without end, before I can prove whether the matter be true, or whether such a thing be done.

'Another thing is that when a suit was commenc'd against me by the Earl of Clarendon, your poore spiritt was so much affrighted, that after about 20 yeares acquaintance you took away your books in your Kodpiece, left your freind to seek and to shift for your self.

'You talk of freindship and acquaintance ever since 1665 and now when a little affliction comes upon your friend you leave him—Is this handsome?

had sentenced Penruddock), where Wood had quoted the suppressed lines from *Hudibras*:

'Did not the learned Glynne and Maynard,
    To make good subjects traytors strain hard?'

and stated that Glynne owed his preferment to Clarendon's corrupt dealings. His son, Sir William, was White Kennett's patron.

'Suppose your brother or any body else goes to lawe with you, must I therefore leave you ? Must I foresake you and afterwards terrifie you with unworthy letters relating to the Earl of Abington and cutting out leaves of my books. Have not my troubles been great enough but you must trouble me with more ? Apage !

'Twenty yeares agoe you left in my hands Hobbs Leviathan, which I took for a gift. Now at last you take it from me and give it to New Inn Library; which they will not take. Doe you think that that it is a booke for young students to study in ? No, rather to make them Hobbists and confound them. You think you have shew'd yourself very wise in this matter.

'There is a little pamphlet of a Sh[eet] of paper called Bushell's rocks I think. This, with your prospect of Osney which is printed in Monast. Angl. I have had long and now they must be given to the Museum. This is like a child, *give a thing and take a thing*.[1] . . . Mr Aubrey, next Munday about two in the Afternoon I shall be at Beckley about 2 or 3 miles on this side of Borstall, and therefore this is to desire you that you would take a horse and come by yourself there to meet me at an Alehouse called the Earl of Abendon's Armes (the Battering rams).[2]

'I shall bring some queries with me for you to do at London for me when you goe to that place. I perceive that you will not come to Oxon before you come to London, or if you do will not call upon me, and therefore I had as good be sure of something.

'Last year you slipt from Borstall to Ricot and I did not see you and so you may do the same now. If you bring anybody with you let him be only a servant, because I have severall things to say to you. A.W.

[1] Aubrey's letter to Wood dated 18 August, 1674, in which he writes that he is sending these papers by George Ent, makes it clear that they were intended to be lent to Wood for his use, and were not gifts. In another letter dated 6 June, 1678, he specifically mentions that they are to be bound up with pamphlets for the 'Publiq Library'; and again on 3 November, 1680.

[2] The Bertie coat is *Argent, three battering rams proper headed and garnished azure*. Aubrey, of course, knew this perfectly well; but, in spite of his bad temper, Wood cannot resist, as it were, dwelling on their common pleasure in heraldry.

'If I am at Beckley before you make no noise in enquiring after me, nor name my name.'

Wood's point of view must be considered impartially. He had behaved badly in a number of ways, but he had not gone to Lord Clarendon and pleaded that Aubrey was to blame for the matter which had caused so much trouble. Little as we may approve Lord Abingdon's sense of humour in inventing this story, it was an obvious enough teasing statement, a joke not even specially brutal by the standards of the time; and there was certainly something to be said for Wood's contention that he should have received an apology as soon as Aubrey discovered that the news was untrue. On the other hand, Wood had only himself to blame for the situation in which, after twenty-five years of friendship, even so unsuspicious a character as Aubrey found it perfectly possible to believe that he had incriminated an old friend to save himself. Nor could anything be less candid than Wood's reference to the pages taken from the *Lives*. He must have known whether or not he had removed them. He does not even deny having done so. He employs, in fact, the same defence that he used in his case before the Vice-Chancellor's Court—that there is no proof that the act was his. Dual personal relationships have a way of taking a masculine and feminine form; and Wood's letter strangely suggests that of a nagging, shrewish woman, detected in a fault, but determined by the sharpness of her tongue to subdue a hardworking, long-suffering partner. 'Mr Aubrey was his very great Friende,' says Hearne, 'and helped him exceedingly. Indeed, he could not have done without him. Yet he us'd Mr Aubrey scurvily.'

VI

On 9 October, 1694, the poet, Henry Vaughan,[1] 'the Silurist', of whose delays in answering letters Aubrey had often complained,

---

[1] Of the two Vaughan brothers, Aubrey had written to Wood on 14 March, 1672: 'Their grandmother was an Aubrey: their father, a coxcomb, and no honester than he should be—he cosened me of 50s. once.' The relationship existed but was not, in fact, so close as this.

wrote, from Newton in Breconshire (beginning his letter 'Honoured Cousin'), about Welsh bards and their connexion with the Druids. He was seventy-three and died six months later.

'I was told by a very sober and knowing person (now dead) that in his time there was a young Lad father and motherless, and so very poor that he was forced to beg, but at last was taken by a rich man, that kept a great stock of Sheep upon the mountains not far from the place where I now dwell who cloathed him and sent him into the mountains to keep his sheep. There in summertime following the sheep and looking to their lambs, he fell into a deep sleep; in which he dream't that he saw a beautiful young man with a garland of green leaves upon his head, and a hawk upon his fist: with a quiver full of arrows at his back, coming towards him (whistling several measures or tunes all the way) and at last let the hawk fly at him, which he dream't got into his mouth and inward parts, and suddenly awakened in a great fear and consternation; but possessed with such a vein or gift of poetrie, that he left the sheep, and went about the Country, making songs upon all occasions, and came to be the most famous bard in all the Countrey of his time.'

A similar letter, dated 25 March, 1695, giving details of wonderful happenings, came from Dr Garden in Scotland, the subject of which was the use of the mysterious words 'Horse and Hattock', which one Lord Duffus[1] was reported to have employed with the startling result that 'he was suddenly carried away, and found the next day at Paris in the French King's cellar, with a silver cup in his hand'.

Aubrey wrote to Wood on 2 March, 1695: 'I have been ill of a great cold ever since St Paul's tyde: and have been but about a week abroad. Your angry letter did very much discompose me and add to my illness. I came to this lodging on a Saturday night, and the next morning Mr Tanner came to me who was in haste. . . . He is a very good man, and I could not but confide in his integrity. . . . I have been ever ready to serve you but have gott neither thanks nor credit for it.'

[1] Presumably Alexander Sutherland, 1st Lord Duffus, a peerage created by Charles II when in exile.

On St Mark's Day (25 April), 1695, Aubrey travelled to Oxford and, coming through Bagley Wood on his way there, discovered 'two Chalybiate springs' in the highway, which on 10 May he tried with 'powder of galls and they gave as black a Tincture as ever I saw of such waters'.

VII

Wood was pardoned in June 1695, and allowed to return to the University. On 18 July Aubrey wrote to Lhwyd, who had to some extent taken Wood's place as his regular correspondent: 'I had writ sooner to you but that ever since I came from Oxon I have a *mist* in my eies: some vapours I suppose rising from the Spleen upon my so soon leaving of the good company at Oxon which did very much vex me. I drinke by the advise of a Doctor, Stretham waters. My Lady Russell's French Doctor sayth it will weare off: but I must forebare reading. Indeed I can hardly reade a letter, but I write by guess.' He spoke of this infirmity of the sight to the bookseller, Awnsham Churchill, who was considering the publication of *Monumenta Britannica* (which he had kept 'shamefully long'); and to Wood, to whom he wrote on 11 August, 1695: 'My eies are hardly any thing mending but I can write by guess. Mr Toland[1] is not unmindfull of you and you have (I presume) heard from him by this time. Dr Goodall would have you undertake the Antiquities of Cambridge. He tells me he hath an interest with halfe the Heads of Houses of the University. . . . Mr President of St John's[2] is now pretty well recovered, and goes to Oxford on Monday next. I told him I would have a Fayre in that lovely pleasant Wood in the Summer-time: for Finery &c. It would certainly concenter all the young people of both sexes 20 miles round. A gentlewoman that was sowing sayd, but what

[1] John Toland, the deist, who wrote of Aubrey: 'Tho' he was extremely superstitious, or seem'd to be so: yet he was a very honest man, and most accurate in his accounts of matters of fact.' In the course of his stormy career, Toland had arrived in Oxford in January 1694. Amongst many other works he wrote the *History of the Druids,* and edited Harrington's *Oceana.*

[2] Dr Edward Bernard.

profit will that be to the Coll:? I sayd what profitt do Faires bring
to other Proprietors. The standing will be considerate. I told him
that I am acquainted with foure of the seaven Vice-Roys, and
should if the Coll: pleased be ready to promote it. My friend Mr
Secretary Trumball[1] was of St John's Coll and loves it. But I
leave it to the Coll: to consider their own Interest. It does not concerne me. I should be glad to promote any thing that might be
usefull to the University. . . . The Booksellers are a sort of Jewes.
I know not yet what to resolve on. They will give almost nothing
for a copy. . . . On Saterday morning I was hot, in a sweate, etc.,
and went to the Barber's to have my head shaved. He had no hot
water. I was in haste and was shaved with cold water. On Monday
I was in the coach by 5 o'clock and 'twas a very cold morning. I
rode with woemen: and in respect sate on the cold side. I was vext
to be torn from Oxford about business. All things concurd to rayse
up ever since a Mist into my eies. How 'twill end God knowes.'

On 24 August, 1695, he wrote to Lhwyd: 'My eies do not
mend but very slowly. My candle growes lowe. My dear Friend
Mr Edmund Wyld growes very weake and I feare cannot long
continue.' On 2 September he wrote again to Wood: 'Mr Wood,
I take your advertisement about the Springs extremely kindly.
The St John's men are slow, and mind not the running of the
spring. They are to digg and draine in the little Bogge above it and
to trace it to the spring and then they would have water enough.
The Woodman told us at the Coll: that it is never dry in the driest
Sommer, nor freezes in the hardest Frost. . . . The Earl of Abingdon haz told me 20 times, cosen, thou hast donne me the greatest
disobligation by discovering the well at Seen[d], that could be
4 miles from here it will bring company, which will disturb my
Game.[2] Sir William Trumbull sayes that the charter for a faire

---

[1] Sir William Trumbull, Secretary of State, who had assisted Aubrey
with the *Monumenta Britannica*. Trumbull was later a friend of Pope as
a young man.

[2] This was also Sir John Aubrey's view, for Aubrey had discovered
that the 'old house' at Boarstall was built partly of 'iron-stone' and there
were springs there which 'would draw too much company to his House'
if made known.

in Bagley Wood will cost about 60*li*: and he bids me tell them that what Fees belong to him, he will doe it gratis for his respect to the College. . . . On Monday I am for Llantrithed with Sir J[ohn] A[ubrey]. There has been a great controversy not yet decided between the Heralds and the Church of Westminster about the velvet of the Mausoleum for the Queen. The Heralds claim it as their Vailes:[1] and can show records for it ever since Hen. 7.'

Aubrey went to Glamorgan with his cousin and, on 29 October, 1695, wrote to Lhwyd from Llantrithyd: 'I am extremely caressed here by my noble Chief Sir J[ohn] A[ubrey] where I am treated with all the varieties that Sea and Land affords: but I declare that I am near so well pleased as with a College Commons or at the Confectioners in your good company. In the afternoon we shove the Tankard and the Bottle one to another in the bond of peace and frequently drinke your good health.'

That October Wood had an opportunity to tell Lord Clarendon what he thought of him and his libel action.[2] In November King William III visited Oxford, and an incident took place which furnished the last and most bitter comment in Wood's diary: 'The University was at a great charge in providing a banquet for the king: but the king would not eat anything but went out, and some rabble and townsmen that had got in by the connivance of the stairers (and some when the king went in and out), they seyzed upon the banquet in the face of the whole Universitie, and in spite of their teeth, all looking on and would not or could not help themselves; and soon after this the University caused this collation to be put into the Gazett.—This is partly my case. I have spent all my time in providing a banquet for the honour of the Universitie. Which being done and applauded by the generalitie of the Universitie, come some barbarous people of the Universitie and spoyle that banquet, even in the face of the Universitie, undoe the preparer of the banquer in the Universite and

---

[1] Perquisites.

[2] 'I was with the earl of Clarendon at Mr Turner's lodgings, and there I began to ripe up all the matter, how unworthily he had dealt with me against the law . . . company came and stopp't our farther progres.'

before and in the face of the Universitie, and they make public proclamation of their excellent dinner.'

On 28 November, 1695, Anthony Wood died, his malady—'a Total Suppression of the Urine'—having prompted the acid remark of his acquaintance, Robert South, that 'if he could not make water he would have to make earth': one of those pleasantries that the victim remembered, and one that certainly did nothing to ameliorate the somewhat caustic biography accorded in the *Athenae* to Dr South.[1]

Wood had some cause to be bitter. He was sixty-three years of age, an unhappy, unhealthy, malicious, frustrated old man; but one to whom all 'pretenders to antiquity' owe a great debt. Oxford, suffering him far from willingly during his lifetime, owes him something too. He was not, on the whole, an attractive figure, but he did not lack qualities of courage and perseverance. He had worked on at his projects in spite of his deafness (ridiculed by ill-mannered dons), 'the great noises in his eares', and the weakness in his joints. Aubrey had found in him something that was intensely sympathetic, and Wood is yet another instance in the strange annals of friendship of the unlikely human beings who can inspire deep affection.

He bequeathed his books and papers to the University, to be placed next to Sir William Dugdale's manuscripts, 'which are very valuable to any of his own Temper'. His friends, Dr Arthur Charlet, James Bisse of Wadham, and Thomas Tanner (who, where Aubrey and Wood were concerned, had contrived to run with the hare and hunt with the hounds) were to oversee the disposal of the very extensive Wood collections.

On 19 March, 1696, Aubrey wrote from Llantrithyd to Tanner: 'I am extremely sorrowful for the death of my deare Freinde and old correspondent Mr Anthony Wood: who (though his spleen used to make him chagrin and to chide me) yet we could not be asunder, and he would always see me at my Lodgeing, with his darke Lanthorne, which should be a Relick. I hoped that

---

[1] South's disapproval of the Royal Society has been referred to on p. 105.

he would have lived to have given me a cast of his office in naming
the place of my obit and grave: which I hope will be here: here is
a fine red earth but not deep. I am glad that you have all his papers
and will be faithfull to him and finish what is left undon.'

VIII

In 1695 Edmund Gibson's first edition in English of Camden's
Britannia appeared, containing references to Aubrey and his
work; and, in 1696, Edward Castle published Aubrey's *Miscellanies*. This volume was dedicated to 'the Right Honourable
James, Earl of Abingdon, Lord Chief Justice in Eyre of all his
Majesty's Forests and Chaces on this side of Trent'. The dedication goes on to recite some of the literary arrangements Aubrey
had made: 'My Lord, when I enjoyed the contentment of solitude
in your pleasant walks and gardens at Lavington the last summer,
I reviewed several scattered papers which had lain by me for
several years; and then presumed to think, that if they were put
together they might be somewhat entertaining: I therefore di-
gested them in this order, in which I now present them to your
Lordship. . . . It was my intention to have finished my *Description
of Wiltshire* (half finished already) and to have dedicated it to your
Lordship: but my age is too far spent for much undertakings: I
have therefore devolved that task on my countryman, Mr Thomas
Tanner, who hath youth to go through with it, and a genius proper
for such an undertaking. Wherefor, I humbly beseech your Lordship to accept of this small offering, as a grateful memorial of the
profound respect I have for you, who have for many years taken
me into your favour and protection. My Lord, may the blessed
angels be your careful guardians: such are the prayers of your
Lordship's most obliged and humble servant, John Aubrey.'

On 13 July, 1696, Aubrey wrote to Tanner from Llantrithyd:
'I am to goe this night from Cardiff to Bristoll by Sea; and there
Sir John Aubrey and I take coach to London, and shall be at
Oxon or Borstall by or before the latter end of August and I believe
my brother will meet us.'

The *Miscellanies* achieved some success, and a second edition was
reprinted, with alterations and additions, in 1721. In this later

volume, a letter from Aubrey to Awnsham Churchill was included,
originally written on the fly-leaf of the corrected copy of the first
edition: 'Mr Churchill—There is a very pretty remarque in the
Athenian Mercury, concerning apparitions, which I would have inserted under this head. It is in vol 17, numb. 25, Tuesday, June
1695. Mr Dunton,[1] at *the Raven* in Jewin Street, will help you to
this Mercury, but yesterday he would not, his wife being newly
departed. J.A. 1st June, 1697.'

But the sands were running out. Aubrey too (although his intellectual vigour never flagged) had in his own words 'been surprized
by age'; and within a week he was buried, in his seventy-second
year, in the parish church of St Mary Magdalene at Oxford, probably in the south aisle, where it was the custom to inter Trinity
men. The register records:

'1697. John Aubery A stranger was Buryed Jun 7th.'

The word 'stranger' implies merely an out-parishioner, for
whose burial an additional fee was charged. Wood's friend, Dr
Charlett, was invited to the funeral, or so, at least, he told Hearne;
but as, in 1720, he asked the latter where Aubrey was buried, he
presumably did not attend the ceremony. Hearne himself had
also been anxious to find out the whereabouts of Aubrey's grave,
information which he eventually acquired from Thomas Collins,
master of Magdalen School. Dr Rawlinson, in his far from reliable
memoir, says that Aubrey died when on a journey to Draycot
to stay with his old friend, the widow of Sir James Long. This may
well have been true, as Lady Long certainly did what she could to
help him in his later days; but there is no supporting evidence to
prove that he was on his way to Wiltshire at the moment of his
death. The fit of apoplexy suffered in 1694 was perhaps repeated
and the final cause of his end.

At the last, in spite of several drafts of wills, he died intestate;
and Letters of Administration (Probate Inventory, PRO Prob.
4/8868) were granted in respect of the effects of John Aubrey, 'late
of Broad Chalke, in the County of Wilts., Bachelor', at Doctors'
Commons on 18 December, 1697, to his brother, William.

[1] John Dunton (1659–1733), bookseller and eccentric.

IX

On 29 October, 1698, Gadbury wrote to Tanner, thanking him for his account of Aubrey's death and funeral, adding that it was too late to include an obituary notice in the current year's *Diary*; but that he hoped to speak of him 'in a more durable work'. The astrologer goes on to say: 'He was a learned honest gentleman and a true friend, whose loss I really mourne, as having had a more than XXX years acquaintance with him, a time sufficient to experience any man's integrity.' William Aubrey had some correspondence with Edward Lhwyd, who had sold books for him in Oxford, and at first he seems to have been a little resentful of the small part allotted to him in connexion with the disposal of his brother's literary remains. He points out that he made no difficulties at all about Aubrey's books and papers going to the Museum. However, any discord that there may have been was satisfactorily removed by Lhwyd, for whom the later letters are full of thanks. On 27 October, 1699, William Aubrey wrote to Tanner, apologising for delay in replying to an enquiry about some antiquarian matters, and saying: 'I am in hopes to get possession of Chalke farm.' He speaks of his regret that his brother's picture should have been stolen from the Ashmolean, as he had intended to have had it engraved and sent round to some friends.

William Aubrey himself died in 1707 and was buried on 29 October at Kington St Michael. Administration of his goods and chattels was taken out on 24 November by his 'principal creditor', Thomas Stokes, the neighbour in whose house he seems to have lived.

X

Amongst his papers, Aubrey left two suggestions for an inscription to be placed on his tomb. In the first of these (contained in the *Wiltshire Collections*) he describes himself briefly as son and heir of John Aubrey of Easton Pierse:

'*Heic situs est, Johannes Awbrey, Filius et haeres Rich. Awbrey de Easton Piers in agro Wilt. armig. Reg. Soc. Socii. Obiit Ao. Dni. 168. . . Die mensis. . . . Ao. Ætatis suae 6. . . .*'

This memorial was to be surmounted with a shield, quartering Aubrey, Einon, Morgan, Blount of Mangotsfield, and Lyte; or, alternatively, four coats only—Aubrey, Danvers, Blount, and Lyte. On this final heraldic point Wood was to have been consulted. The tablet was to have been set up 'just over the Holy water nich' in St Martin Outwich, 'as I was wont to be a peeper at the Church doors like a devout Poenitent to hearken for halfe an hour'. The epitaph shows that he expected death sooner than at last it came.

The second draft (written on the fly-leaf at the end of *Villare Anglicanum*) gives fuller details of the form that the memorial was to take: 'I would desire that the inscription should be a stone of white marble about the bigness of a Royal sheet of paper, *scilicet* about two foot square. Mr Reynolds of Lambeth, a Stonecutter, (Foxhall) who married Mr Elias Ashmole's widow will help me to a marble as square as an imperial sheet of paper for eight shillings.' The alternative inscription was to run:

'*M. S. Johannes Aubrey de Easton-Piers in Agro Wiltoñ Arm: Regalis Societatis Socius infra situs est. Obiit Anno Dni. . . . Ætat. . . .*'

Above was to be the escutcheon (held up by an angel) bearing the Aubrey coat: *azure, a chevron between three eagles' heads erased or, a crescent for difference.* Below the inscription, the crest was tricked large: *an eagle's head erased or.*

It was right that Aubrey's bones should lie at Oxford—the place that he used to long to see 'with the longing of a woman'; better on the whole than St Martin Outwich (where Mary Wiseman had married another) or the Fanatick burial ground, surrounded for ever by the smoke and traffic and commerce of the City; better, too, than the red earth of Glamorgan, among those Welsh lands won with an admixture of force and prudent marriage by ancestors from whom the generations had left him separate and strangely remote. Wiltshire, it is true, might have claimed him. He had, indeed, toyed with the thought of a resting-place there, by Broad Chalke; and, speaking of a little burial mound on the downs called Gawen's Barrow, he had written: 'I never was so sacralegious as to disturbe or rob his urne: let his Ashes rest in peace: but I have oftentimes wished that my Corpse might be interred by it: but the Lawes Ecclesiastique denie it. Our bones in consecrated ground never lie quiet: and in London once in ten years (or thereabouts) the earth is carried to the Dung-wharfe.'

CHAPTER EIGHT

The Amici

I

It would not be an easy task to decide, from out of the mass of names of contemporaries with whom he was familiar, who should be considered Aubrey's 'friends', had he not himself composed a list of 'amici'. This register is in itself of some interest, because, although any biographer might have marked down more than half of those inscribed—from the warmth or frequency with which they are mentioned in Aubrey's writings—the remainder include names impossible to guess that he considered in such a light, some indeed scarcely mentioned by him elsewhere in his papers. That Aubrey felt it possible to draw up a list of this kind shows that he regarded neither death nor prolonged absence as altering the relationship; any more than daily and close contact with other persons turned them necessarily into friends. Perhaps it is not surprising that the account he gives of these men sometimes lacks the incisive character of mere acquaintances' biographies. The list comes from the autobiographical notes contained in the second manuscript volume of the *Lives*:

> ### Amici
>
> A[nthony] Ettrick, Trin. Coll.
> M[iddle] T[emple]—John Lydall.
> Francis Potter, of 666, C[1] letters.
> Sir J[ohn] Hoskyns, baronet.
> Ed[mund] Wyld, esq., of Glasley Hall, *quem summae
> gratitudinis ergo nomino.*
> Mr. Robert Hooke, Gresham College.
> Mr [Thomas] Hobbes, 165—
> A[nthony] Wood, 1665.
> Sir William Petty, my singular Friend.
> Sir James Long, baronet, of Draycot, χρονογραφία, etc.

---

[1] *i.e.* one hundred.

Mr Ch[arles] Seymour, father of the d[uke] of S[omerset].
Sir Jo[hn] Stawell M[iddle] T[emple].
Bishop of Sarum [Seth Ward].
Dr W[illiam] Holder.

II

Of the fourteen names, only Ettrick, Lydall, Wyld, and Stawell
are not accorded places in the *Dictionary of National Biography*. The
two former are named in Aubrey's draft will, made about 1654, in
which they were to have been responsible for the disposal of
Aubrey's books, and each was to have received 'a ring of 50s. with
a stone in it'. John Lydall was 'of Uxmore, Oxon' and was elected
a scholar of Trinity in 1640. When he was fifteen Dr Kettle had
appealed to him for the declension of *Tondeo*, after his onslaught
on William Radford's hair with the bread-knife. Later he became
a Fellow of that college and tutor to Aubrey's other friend, Tom
Mariet. When the latter had made his 'sharpe returne' to the
Parliamentarian Visitors, Dr John Wilkinson had asked whose
scholar he was 'and told him his Tutor might have taught him
better manners'. Aubrey often refers to Lydall in his letters,
usually speaking with deep regret of his friend, who died at the
age of thirty-two on 12 October, 1657.

Anthony Ettrick (*c.* 1622–1703), son of William Ettrick of
Barford by Anne, daughter of William Willis, Fellow of Trinity,
came of a family (by tradition from Scotland) settled in Dorset
since the middle of the sixteenth century. He was born on Sunday,
'for which reason his mother would say he was a Sundaye's bird'.
At Trinity (to the Fellows of which he devised an annual £2 'to be
spent on wines and tobacco on the fifth of November, yearly'),
says Aubrey, 'Mr Anthony Ettrick and some others frightened a
poor young freshman of Magdalen Hall with conjuring, which
when the old Doctor heard of it: on the next Tuesday, sayd he,
"Mr Ettrick"—who is a very little man—"will conjure up a
jackanapes to be his great-grand-father."' Ettrick had accompanied Aubrey on his journey to Ireland in 1660. He was admitted
to the Middle Temple, 1641; called, 1652; and became Bencher,
Reader, and Treasurer, often sitting on committees appointed to

consider such subjects as erection of new buildings, or 'touching the beautifying of the great gate' (above which he lived). He was Recorder of Poole, 1662–82. Monmouth was brought to his house, Holt Lodge, Wimborne, after Sedgemoor, and committed by him—to which Aubrey's lost *Life* of the Duke may have owed something. He sat as M.P. for Christ Church, Hants, 1685–87, with Sir Thomas Clarges, Monk's brother-in-law. As an antiquary, he contributed to Gibson's edition of Camden; and Ettrick's papers and those of his father-in-law, Davenant, appear to have provided the foundation of Hutchins's *Dorset*. Like Aubrey, who calls him 'a very judicious gentleman', he took a keen interest in occult matters, and was dissatisfied with the procedure at a witch trial before Chief Baron Wyld at Salisbury in 1649. He had also lain all night at Mr Mompesson's house at North Tidworth, where in 1661 mysterious drummings had occurred. 'They did heare sometimes knockings: and if they said, "Devill, knock so many knocks" so many knocks would be answered. But Mr Ettrick sometimes whispered the words, and there would be no returne.' As he aged, Ettrick 'grew very humoursome, phlegmatic and credulous', and on account, it is said, of a quarrel with the inhabitants of Wimborne, swore that he would be buried neither in their church nor churchyard. Later he longed to be laid with his ancestors, and, to evade his oath, a sarcophagus was built in his lifetime in a recess of the wall—neither in nor out of the Minster. '1691', the year he foretold his death, is still legible under '1703', when he finally deceased.

III

Something has already been said of Francis Potter (1594–1678). His work on 666, *the Number of the Beast* brought him a certain amount of fame in his own time and, as Joseph Mead wrote to Hartlib, was calculated to 'make some of your German speculatives half wild'. He had high mechanical skill and made quadrants with a graduated compass of his own invention. He also drew and painted, theorised as to the transfusion of the blood, and experimented with bees, showing Aubrey their thighs through a microscope. Aubrey adds that Potter was fond of chess and used to play with Colonel Bishop, his contemporary at Trinity, accounted 'the best of England', but though they used to play for two days together, 'neither gott the maistery'. Aubrey wrote of him:

'Francis Potter was hospitable, virtuous, and temperate; and, as I sayd before, very contemplative. He lookt the most like a monk or one of the pastours of the oldtime that I ever sawe one. He was pretty long visaged and pale cleare skin, gray eie. His discourse was admirable, and all new and unvulgar. . . . On the butterydore in his parlour he drew his father's picture at length, with his booke (fore-shortened), and on the spectacles in his hand is the reflection of the Gothique south windowe. I mention this picture the rather, because in process of time it may be mistaken by tradition for his son Francis's picture, the author of the book aforesayd. I never have enjoyed so much pleasure, nor ever so much pleased with such philosophicall and heartie entertainment as from him. His booke was in the presse at Oxford, and he there, when I was admitted of the College, but I had not the honour and happinesse to be acquainted with him till 1649 (Epiphanie) since which time I had a conjunct friendship with him to his death, and corresponded frequently with him. I have all his letters by me, which are very good, and I believe neer 200, and most of them philosophicall. I have many excellent good notes from him as to mechaniques etc; and I never was with him but I learn't and always tooke notes: but now indeed the Royal Society haz outdonne most of his things, as having a better apparatus and more spare money.' After his father Richard Potter's death, Francis Potter had succeeded him as rector of Kilmington, in Somerset, but he seems to have spent a good deal of his time away from his parish. In 1663 he became a member of the Royal Society. His health had never been good, and it will be remembered that, when Aubrey visited him a few years before his death, he had become almost blind.

IV

Sir John Hoskyns (1634–1705) was the son of Sir Bennet Hoskyns, 1st baronet, of Harewood and Morehampton in Herefordshire. He was the grandson of John Hoskyns, the famous wit and lawyer, whose bitter satires had more than once involved him in trouble with the authorities in the time of James I—notably in connexion with his speech against that king's Scotch favourites, whom he reminded in no uncertain terms of the Sicilian Vespers. Wood possessed a volume of the epigrams and epitaphs of the elder John Hoskyns, who had been a friend of Raleigh and Jonson, and is said by Aubrey to have composed the lines on 'the Trusty Servant', 'with asses eares and hind's feet, a lock on the mouth, etc.' at Winchester, where he had been at school. He had also arranged the meeting of the 'nest of Nestors', the ten veteran morris dancers who had performed at Hereford races in 1609, whose accumulated ages exceeded a thousand years. By unsubstantiated tradition, this entertainment was put on for James I, said to be visiting Serjeant Hoskyns at that time.

John Hoskyns, the grandson, Aubrey's friend, had been at Westminster under Busby, later at Trinity, and of the Middle Temple. He was a Master in Chancery, Member of Parliament for Herefordshire, and had been one of members of the Rota. In 1682 he was elected President of the Royal Society, but he resigned in the following year, and filled the post of secretary to the Society from 1685 to 1687. Hoskyns was a friend of Roger North's, who described him as 'one of the most hard-featured men of his time'—in the sense that North considered him very ugly. Like Edmund Wyld, Hoskyns is often mentioned in Hooke's diary as forming one of the party with Aubrey and Hooke. Aubrey intended to have written Hoskyns's biography, for the name is included in the index to one of the volumes of the *Lives*; but, as it no longer exists, it was removed by Wood or never completed. The letters that remain show Aubrey and Hoskyns as on the most friendly terms. There were jokes about Aubrey's love affairs and the courtesans of Venice. They had gone together to see Mr Lee's ingeniose contrivance for weaving stockings; and, when they had been undergraduates at Trinity, Hoskyns had teased Dr Kettle by singing a higher note in chapel than even the President could reach. He married Jane, daughter of Sir Gabriel Lowe of Newark.[1]

[1] See p. 45.

V

Edmund Wyld (1618—1696) is a friend of whom little is known, but enough to suggest a character of some interest. He was the elder of the two sons of the judge, Sir Edmund Wyld, of Kemsey in Worcestershire, where there is a monument in the church in which Edmund and his brother Walter kneel before the effigy of their father. The Wylds, several of whom had been distinguished in the law, had lived for some generations at the house called the Commandery on the outskirts of Worcester.[1] Sir Edmund Wyld, who, according to Aubrey, had kept as his mistress Venetia Stanley (whose portrait he owned and whose gilt bust Aubrey had seen), had married Dorothy, daughter and heir of Sir Francis Clarke of Houghton Conquest in Bedfordshire, where his son Edmund had been born, probably at the house called Britens, or Grove Manor. Aubrey says that Wyld's birth took place on 10 October, 1616; but the parish register records his parents' marriage in 1617 and his baptism in the following year.

Wyld matriculated at Christ Church, Oxford, in 1633 (having become a King's Ward in the previous year), and in 1644 he was barrister-at-law of the Middle Temple, at about which time 'he had the misfortune to kill a man in London, upon a great provocation'; but Aubrey gives no details of this unfortunate incident. He was a member of the Royal Society. Roger North, not much at ease outside the circle of his fellow lawyers and their circumscribed preoccupations, adds his impressions of Wyld, after speaking of Aubrey's visits[2] to the writer's brother, Lord Guilford:

'One Mr Weld [Wyld] a rich philosopher, lived in Bloomsbury. He was single and his house a sort of knick-knackatory. Most of the ingeniose persons about the town sometimes visited him: and

[1] Margaret, daughter of Thomas Wyld 'of the Commandery', was mother of Dr John Fell, Dean of Christ Church.

[2] 'There was one Mr Aubrey of Surrey, a professed virtuoso, and always replete with new discoveries. He often visited his Lordship who encouraged him by his attention and asking many questions: and his answers served well enough in order to a farther enquiry.' North's *Lives of the Norths.*

among the rest, his lordship [Guilford] did suit and service there. This gentleman was of a superior order and valued himself upon new inventions of his own. He sowed salads in the morning to be cut for dinner, and claimed the invention of painted curtains in varnish upon silk which would bend and not crack; and his house was furnished with them: and he delighted in nothing more than in showing his multifarious contrivances.'

A note of Aubrey's explains North's remarks about salads which refer to a dinner-party mentioned earlier[1] in this book. 'London. Bloomsbury, August 12, 1684, my ever honoured friend Edmund Wyld Esq, did, just before he sate downe to dinner, sow in an earthen porringer of prepared earth, seeds of Parsely, Purslane, Balme, etc. The porringer was set on a Chafing dish of coales: and by the time we had ended dinner (which was about an hour and a halfe) seedes sprang visibly up: *scilicet* nineteen or twenty young plants. Their leaves as big as common pinnes heads: by and by appeared more, so that the dish was full; some of the plantes being drawne out with a paire of pliers, the stalkes were about half an inch long. About two or three hours after the sowing, the dish was exposed in the garden *sub die*: that night it happened to rain very hard all night yet all lived and flourished till about the middle of September: and then they began to wither. Some of them lived till Michaelmas, some till the 8th or 10th of October following. I was one of the fower (besides Mr Wyld) that was an eie-witness of the experiment. The dish remains in the garden to this day (Feb. 7, 1689/90) but no vegetables at all ever did grow in it since.'

Wyld owned Glasely Hall in Shropshire (*sed in margine*, adds Aubrey) as well as property inherited from his mother at Houghton Conquest and the house in Bloomsbury. He also had the manor of Totham in Essex, where, says Aubrey, various 'mischiefs' had befallen him and made him liable for 'deodands', probably from killing a man. When Aubrey finally lost his money, he wrote that Wyld 'tooke me in his armes, with whom I most commonly take my diet and sweet otiums'; and he frequently refers to Wyld as a source of information, notably on horticultural subjects.

[1] See p. 194.

As we have seen, Aubrey said that he owed 'most of Mr Wyld's civility' to Wyld's mistress, Jane Smyth, 'that obliging body'. He has some notes on this lady's life in the *Collection of Genitures*. She had been born in 1649: 'it was the April after the beheading King Charles the first. It thundred and lightened and the house was on fire then'; and there are some details (for astrological documentation) of various illnesses suffered in the course of her life. In the *Remains of Gentilism* he writes: 'Mris Smyth's notion of men being metamorphosed into Trees, and Flowers is ingeniose; *sc.* they planted a Tree, or a flower in the grave of a friend, and they thought the sould of the party deceased went into the tree or plant.' She had come to London 'about half a year' before the Great Plague in 1665, and her name often occurs in Hooke's *Journal* as accompanying Wyld to coffee-houses such as the Cardinal's Cap, an unusual diversion for a woman to share.

Wyld's gardens, and his care of them, provide a subject to which Aubrey often returns. 'In the court of my honoured friend Edmund Wyld Esq of Houghton in Bedfordshire, in twenty-four years, *viz.* 1656–1680, the ground increased nine inches, only by rotting grasse upon grasse. 'Tis a rich soil and reddish; worth XXs per acre.' Wyld also 'had a pott of composition in his garden these seven yeares that beares nothing at all, not so much as a grasse or mosse. He makes his challenge if any man will give him XX*li* he will give him an hundred if it doth not beare wheate *spontaneously*: and the party shall keep the key, and shall sift the earth composition through a fine sieve, so that he may be sure there are no graines of wheat in it. He hath also a composition for pease; but that he will not warrant, not having yet tryed it. John Tradescant had in his garden at South Lambeth the Balm of Gilead tree, and Edmund Wyld Esq had some Layers of it, which grew very well at Houghton Conquest in Bedfordshire, 'till in the hard Winter the mice killed it. I do not heare of any other now in England.' Aubrey also noted that: 'When an oake is felling, before it falls, it gives a kind of shriekes or groanes, that may be heard a mile off, as if it were the genius of the oake lamenting. E. Wyld Esq hath heard it many times.'

Wyld had sat in the Long Parliament and appears to have been fairly active as a Parliamentarian supporter during the Civil Wars.[1] In 1652 he helped to have Petty nominated for the Irish survey, 'although he only knew of him by common fame.' He was also the possessor of 'a modell of a citadell for Oliver Cromwell, to bridle the city of London', constructed for Cromwell by Sir Jonas Moore, who had been helped in early life by Wyld. The citadel 'was to have been the crosse building of St Paule's church'. Wyld had scientific and mathematical interests as well, and Aubrey had given him 'a paire of compasses, which will divide an inch into a hundred or a thousand parts', invented by his other friend, Francis Potter, who had made them with his own hands.

Wyld's stock of stories of people he had known was a source often used by Aubrey for illustration or verification. He had been one of the witnesses when Colonel Betridge, 'one of the handsomest men about the towne', was bragging of how the women loved him, and Sir Henry Blount (who had married a daughter of Christopher Wase) laid a wager 'that let them goe together to a bordello: he only (without money) with his handsome person, and Sir Henry with a XXs. piece on his bald crowne, that the wenches should choose Sir Henry before Betridge; and Sir Henry won the wager.'[2]

Wyld had known Captain Roger North, Raleigh's companion on the voyage to Guiana, and said 'he was a learned and sober Gentleman and good mathematician, but if you happened to

[1] Wyld was M.P. for Droitwich, where he sat with Major-General Thomas Rainsborough, with whom he was probably elected *vice* Endymion Porter and Samuel Sandys, disabled to sit, 11 November, 1646. Sir William Dugdale's son, John Dugdale, wrote to his father on 5 January, 1695, on the subject of a book dealing with the Regicides: 'I perceive by my brother Ashmole that one Mr Edmund Wild, who served for Droitwyche, hearing you are upon a work wherein you mention them, [the Regicides] and him particularly, hints that if you write more than you can make out, he will bring his action against you, as may any other.'

[2] It may be mentioned in parenthesis that Aubrey records that Sir Henry was called to account for his cynicism, when Henry Nevile wrote a pamphlet *The Parliament of Ladies*, 'Wherein Sir Henry Blount was first to be called to the barre for spreading abroad that abominable and dangerous doctrine that it was far cheaper and safer to lye with common wenches than with ladies of quality.'

speak of Guiana he would be strangely passionate and say "'Twas the blessedest countrey under the sun" etc, reflecting on the spoyling of that brave designe.' Another acquaintance of Wyld's was a disreputable Continental figure, described by Aubrey in the *Remains of Gentilism*:

'Captain Carlo Fantom (a Croatian) spake 13 languages, was a Captaine under the Earle of Essex. Sir Robert Pye was his Colonel, who shot at him for not returning a horse which he tooke away before the Regiment. This was donne in a field neare Bedford, where the army then was, as they were marching to the relief of Gainsborough. Many are yet living that sawe it. Captain Hamden was by: the 2 bullets went through his Buff coate, and the Captain H. sawe his shirt on fire. Captain Carlo Fantom tooke the bullets out and said to Sir Rob[ert]—Here take your bullets again—None of the soldiers would dare to fight with him, they said they would not fight with the Devill. E. W[yld] Esq was very well acquainted with him, and gave me many a Treat: and at last he prevailed with him so far, towards the knowledge of this secret, that Fantom told him, that the keepers in their Forests did know a certain herb, which they gave to children, which made them to be Shott-free (they call them Hard-men). He had a world of cutts about his body with swords. He was very quarrelsome, and a great Ravisher. He left the Parliament party, and went to the King Ch[arles] the first at Oxford, where he was hanged for Ravishing. R[obert] E[arl] of Essex General for the Parliament, had this Captain Fantom in high esteem: for he was an admirable Horse-officer, and taught the cavalry of the army the way of fighting with Horse; the General saved him from hanging twice for Ravishing, once at Winchester, 2ndly at St Albans, and he was not content only to ravish himselfe, but he would make his soldiers do it too, and he would stand by and looke on. He met (coming, late at night, out of the Horseshoe Taverne in Drury Lane) with a Lieutenant of Colonel Rossiter,[1] who had great jingling spurres on; said he, the noise of your spurres doe offend me, you must come over the Kennel and give me satisfaction. They drew and passt at each other

---

[1] One of Cromwell's cavalry colonels, of Presbyterian sympathies.

& the lieutenant was runne through & died within an hour or two; and 'twas not knowne who killed him. Said he, I care not for your Cause, I come to fight for your halfe-crown & your handsome woemen; My father was R. Catholiq and so was my grandfather. I have fought for the Christians against the Turkes, and for the Turkes against the Christians.'

Another memory of the Civil Wars is contained in the note: 'Mr Wyld saies, that in the ditches about Worcester, where the great fight was anno 165[1] (wherein the bodies of the slaine lye buried), doe growe great thistles.' Perhaps, however, the incident of Dean Colet's coffin, after the Great Fire, shows Wyld at his most inquisitive. 'After the conflagration his [Colet's] monument being broken, his coffin, which was of lead, was full of a liquor which conserved the body. Mr Wyld and Mr Ralph Greatorex tasted it and 'twas of a kind of insipid taste, something of an ironish taste. The body felt, to the probe of a stick which they thrust into a chinke, like brawne.' There were moments, on the other hand, when Wyld could be bored. Hooke records one of these occasions in his diary (16 December, 1675): 'Discoursed about Universal Character, about preadamits and of creation. About insects. I mentioned all vegetables to be females. I told Wild and Aubery of flying. Wild cold. Drank port.' Hooke's *Journal* shows this trio—Hooke, Wyld, and Aubrey—as seeing a good deal of one another. It was at Wyld's house (on 3 August, 1676) that Aubrey had told Hooke 'of his living and of bouncing Pru'; and in the same year (14 June) Hooke had noted his opinion: 'Aubery a fool about Wild'.

Wyld had also been suitor to Dorothy Osborne, the letter-writer, organised a collection for Richard Lovelace, the poet, and, when John Bunyan was in prison, helped his wife. He was buried at Glasely, 15 December, 1695.

VI

Robert Hooke (1635–1703) was the son of the Rev. John Hooke, incumbent of Freshwater in the Isle of Wight. His father had died in 1648, and left him £100, with which he came to London, where for a time he was pupil to the painter Lely, also working for a period with Aubrey's friend, Samuel Cooper. Then he entered Westminster School, and lived in the house of Dr Busby, where he caused some stir by mastering in a week the six books of Euclid. Later, he went up to Christ Church, Oxford, as a chorister or servitor. Mechanical skill brought Hooke to the notice of Seth Ward, Robert Boyle, and the rest of that learned circle about 1655. In 1662, he was appointed curator of experiments to the Royal Society, and elected a Fellow in 1663, at the same time exempted from all charges; and in the following year Sir John Cutler founded a lectureship of £50 a year for Hooke's benefit, leaving the number of lectures and the subjects under discussion to the discretion of the Society. In 1665, he was made perpetual curator of the Royal Society, with a salary of £30 a year, and Gresham Professor of Geometry. Aubrey used often to stay in Hooke's rooms at Gresham College in Bishopsgate Street.

Hooke spent the period of the Plague in association with Dr John Wilkins and Sir William Petty at Durdans, Lord Berkeley's seat near Epsom; and in September 1666, after the Great Fire, he exhibited a model for the rebuilding of London. This design was not adopted, but on account of it he was given employment as City Surveyor. While holding this appointment he accumulated some thousands of pounds, which were found in an iron chest after his death, and which had remained unopened for thirty years. He designed Bedlam, Montagu House, the College of Physicians, and 'the piller on Fish-street-hill'—the Monument. Respiration, combustion, falling bodies, diving bells, telegraphy, barometrical readings, astronomy—all occupied his attention. His diary (1672–1680, and 1681–1693) is full of interesting information about his own life and those of his contemporaries, Aubrey's name recurring there repeatedly.

'As to his person he was but despicable,' says his biographer, Richard Waller, 'being very crooked . . . low of stature . . . He was always very pale and lean, and laterly nothing but skin and bone, with a meagre aspect, his eyes grey and full, with a sharp ingenious look whilst younger . . . He wore his own hair of a dark brown colour, very long, and hanging neglected over his face uncut and lank, which about three years before his death he cut off, and wore a periwig. He went stooping and very fast . . . having but a light body to carry, and a great deal of spirits and activity especially in his youth. He was of an active, restless, indefatigable genius, even almost to the last, and always slept little to his death . . . oftener continuing his studies all night and taking a short nap in the day. His temper was melancholy, mistrustful, and jealous, which more increas'd upon him with his years.'

To the kind-hearted Aubrey, however, Hooke was 'a person of great suavity and goodness', and there is plenty of evidence from the diary that he often helped Aubrey with small loans of money. Sometimes, like all friends, they irritated each other, and Hooke wrote that Wyld and Aubrey were 'sottish company' (18 May, 1676); and, on 5 October, 1680, he noted 'Aubery impudent'; but in spite of such occasional differences, they met perpetually and discussed all manner of subjects together, often over a bottle.

' 'Twas Mr Robert Hooke', says Aubrey, 'that invented the Pendulum watches, so much more useful than the other watches', and he speaks of his friend's prodigious inventive head. Hooke was, indeed, a figure of unquestionable genius. The energy in his small frame was colossal and there seems to have been scarcely a limit to the range of his scientific abilities.

VII

Of the next two *Amici* on Aubrey's list, Thomas Hobbes (1588–1679) and Anthony Wood (1632–1695), much has been said already, so far as their careers touch that of Aubrey. They are followed by Sir William Petty (1623–1687), 'My singular friend', as Aubrey called him, one of the most remarkable men of his time, and one whose name is perhaps less widely known than might be expected from his many attainments. This ancestor of the Houses of Shelburne, and of Lansdowne, was the son of a poor clothier of Romsey in Hampshire. He had some sort of an education at the village school, and 'a competent smattering' of Latin and Greek by the age of fifteen. While still a boy, he wandered about France, where the Jesuit fathers of Caen took him into their college. He studied mathematics and medicine, and in 1645 he was reading with Hobbes in Paris, where, says Aubrey, 'one time it happened that he was driven to a great streight for money, and I have heard him say, that he lived a weeke on two peniworth (or 3, I have forgott which, but I thinke the former) of walnutts.' Three or four years later he became a Fellow, and Vice-Principal, of Brasenose College, Oxford, where in 1650 he achieved considerable notoriety by reviving Nan Green, a woman who had been hanged for the murder of her bastard child. Soon after this he was appointed Professor of Anatomy at Oxford. Two years later he went with the Cromwellian army to Ireland, as physician to General Fleetwood. There he made his famous 'Survey'; and was rewarded with broad estates in that island, where for the rest of his life his chief interests lay.

Petty was perhaps the first person in England to appreciate the value of 'number, weight, and measure' where 'ratiocination' was concerned. This great man cannot, indeed, be absolved from being considered the progenitor of the multitudinous and equivocal tribe of statisticians. His interests were legion. He was the inventor of a *Sluice-Boat*, or *Double-bottom Ship*, a project which did not achieve success until nearly two hundred years later. He also made excursions in the sphere of military logistics, one of these in connexion with a 'War Chariot' to economise the use of infantry and cavalry. This contrivance could be used singly or in formations, and was intended to co-operate with other arms, and 'to run or push with great violence against any object'. When opposition was overcome the engine was to act as a *'Fort Royal'*. This precursor of the tank was to carry its own arms and equipment, but, naturally, was horse-drawn. Isolation hospitals, a ministry of health, a medical research council, lying-in hospitals for women, and an Act of Union with Ireland were all projects advocated by Petty. He had no illusions about the last of these, which was to be assisted by wholesale transference of the populations between England and Ireland. A House of Lords strengthened with life Peers to hold its own against a too powerful House of Commons, manhood suffrage, a general land register, undenominational teaching, and decimal coinage were other schemes which attracted him.

'To be short,' wrote Aubrey, 'he is a person of so great worth and learning, and haz such a prodigous working witt, that he is both fitt for, and an honour to, the highest preferment.' Evelyn, after rehearsing Petty's attainments, says, 'Having never known such another genius I cannot but mention these particulars among a multitude of others.' Pepys was equally enthusiastic on Petty's account, and there were few, indeed, who did not speak of him in glowing terms. Among the latter may be included Sir Hieronyme Sankey, 'one of Oliver's knights', who challenged him to a duel, an invitation accepted by Petty (who was short-sighted) on condition that they fought with axes in a cellar. To his qualities of mind, he added a less serious side, and Aubrey noted: 'He can be an excellent droll (if he haz the mind to it) and will preach extempore incomparably, either the Presbyterian way, Independent, Cappucin friar, or Jesuit.'

VIII

Of Sir James Long, of Draycot (1613–1692), Aubrey wrote: 'I should now be both orator and soldier to give to this honoured friend of mine, "a gentleman absolute in all his numbers",[1] his due character.' He goes on to say, 'In the civill warres, a colonel of horse in Sir Fr: Dodington's brigade. Good sword-man; horse-man; admirable extempore orator pro harangue; great memorie; great historian and romancer; great falkoner and for horseman-ship; for insects, exceeding curious and searching long since, in naturall things. Oliver, Protector, hawking at Howneslowe heath, discoursing with him, fell in love with his company, and com-manded him to weare his sword, and to meete him a hawkeing, which made the strict cavaliers look on him with an evill eye.'

Long had been born at South Wraxall, son of Sir Walter Long of Draycot, a close friend of Raleigh, and one who had brought smoking into Wiltshire, where the Longs were an ancient and

---

[1] The phrase was Ben Jonson's and used of Sir Kenelm Digby.

eminent family. In their own country, the Longs looked with no very friendly eye on the Herberts, as a recently arrived Welsh clan with a somewhat disreputable background; and considered themselves to represent a far older and more dignified tradition. James Long had been educated at home and in France (not at Westminster and Magdalen, Oxford, as Aubrey says), and had married Dorothy, daughter of Sir Edward Leech,[1] of Shipley, in Derbyshire, 'a most elegant beautie and witt', who remained a friend and patroness of Aubrey long after her husband died.

In 1645 Long had escorted the Prince of Wales to Bristol, and on his return, 'in the basest weather', was attacked and captured by Cromwell's troops, who had laid an ambush for him in the Wiltshire lanes. This disaster was attributed by Clarendon, whether or not justly, to Long's 'great defect of courage and conduct'. The Parliamentarian force appears to have been much stronger in point of numbers, and the general opinion of his contemporaries certainly did not impute to Long any lack of personal courage. He himself was exchanged soon after falling into the hands of the enemy; later, he compounded for his estates, and seems to have been left in comparative peace during the period of the Commonwealth. He was F.R.S., wrote on genealogical and antiquarian subjects, about the causes of the Civil Wars, and of examination of witches at Malmesbury.

IX

Charles Seymour, 2nd Lord Seymour of Trowbridge (1621–1665), 'father of the Duke of Somerset', was another Wiltshire friend, of whom something has already been said. He was the eldest son of the 1st Lord Seymour of Trowbridge, by his first wife, Frances, daughter and heir of Sir Gilbert Prinne, of Alington, where, says Aubrey, Charles Seymour was living at the time of the hunt at Avebury. He succeeded his father in 1664, dying

[1] When Aubrey notes of himself that he was 'never riotous or prodigall', he quotes Sir E. Leech as remarking that 'sloath and carelessness' are 'equivalent to all other vices'.

himself in the August of the following year. He was M.P. for
Bedwyn in 1640, and married, first Mary, daughter of Thomas
Smith, of Soley Chilton in Wiltshire. His second wife was
Elizabeth, daughter of William Alington, 1st Lord Alington,
whom he married in 1654. On Charles Seymour's death, his
widow married (on 16 September, 1672) Sir John Ernle, of Whetham, sometime Chancellor of the Exchequer, who had agreed to
help Aubrey in the history of North Wilts at the Knights of the
Shire meeting in 1659/60. She was buried on 30 October, 1691.

Little is known of Seymour's personal character, but the stormy
history of the Seymour family (who had on more than one occasion, in different generations, made secret marriages with members
of the Royal Family, causing great disturbance) must have given
Aubrey plenty of opportunity for hearing the sort of stories of the
past that he loved. They may well have talked of such things,
since Aubrey knew that his own great-grandfather, Dr William
Aubrey, had acted as a legal authority in the case of Edward
Seymour, Earl of Hertford, who had secretly married Katherine,
daughter of Henry Grey, Duke of Suffolk. Queen Elizabeth
had sent both of them to the Tower, and the legality of their
marriage had been disputed in the courts of law. Aubrey was,
indeed, inclined to wonder whether Dr Aubrey had not personally taken part in the case of Lady Arabella Stuart and
William Seymour; but the Doctor had, in fact, died some fifteen
years before that episode took place.

x

Sir John Stawell (1625–1669) appears among the *Amici*, but is
scarcely mentioned elsewhere by Aubrey, though there exists a
letter addressed to 'his old friend John Aubrey Esq.', but without
date as to year, arranging for Aubrey to have a place in the
Salisbury coach, saying Stawell will 'not admit a deniall, let no
slovenly, paultry, pittiful excuse be invented'. He came from
Devon, and was a distant relative of the well-known royalist of the
same name and title, who belonged to the previous generation—
Sir John Stawell, Knight of the Bath, of Cothelstone. Aubrey's Sir

John Stawell, of Parke and Indiho, Bovey Tracey, was a younger
son of William Stawell of Herebeare, Bickington, and Joan,
daughter of Hugh Wotton of Herebeare. He married first Sarah,
daughter of Nathaniel Stephens of Eastington, Gloucestershire;
and secondly Jane, daughter of Sir Edward Rodney of Stoke
Rodney, Somerset. He was knighted in 1663. Aubrey had known
Stawell, with Ettrick, at the Middle Temple, where a note in the
records for 1657 reads: 'May 6, Mr Anthony Ettoricke of the
Utter Bar to the chamber of Messrs John Stowell and Edward
Wallis, both of the Utter Bar, in the S.W. corner of Elme Court,
up one pair of steps, on surrender of the latter; fine £3.' The
friendship with Ettrick lasted until Stawell's death at the age of
forty-four in 1669; and in his will (which speaks of 'my house and
seat called Judes') 'my friend Anthony Ettrick of Holt Park,
Dorset, Esq' was to be a trustee. Stawell's sister and uncle had
married members of the West Country family of Ball, to which
belonged Aubrey's friend William Ball, F.R.S., the astronomer,
also a member of the Middle Temple. Aubrey refers several times
to a 'Mrs Ball'. Stawell's early death would partly account for the
absence of his name from Aubrey's writings.

XI

Seth Ward, Bishop of Salisbury (1617–1689), was the son of an
attorney 'of very honest repute' at Buntingford in Hertfordshire.
'His genius', says Aubrey, like Petty's, 'lay much to the mathematiques, which being naturall to him, he quickly and easily
attained.' He went up to Cambridge as a sizar, where his youthful
and engaging appearance seems to have attracted, more than
usually in an undergraduate, the attention of the dons there.
From an early age he was marked out for a brilliant career, but
the persecution of the Universities by the Roundheads made his
path difficult. It was arranged that he should have the Savilian
Chair of Astronomy at Oxford (from which its holder had been
ejected) without taking the covenant. Ward lived at Wadham
College, where, among others, he taught Sir Christopher Wren,
who became his great friend. Ward's reputation for learning

appears to have been too great for political objections against him
to be sustained, and he was appointed President of Trinity, from
which Hannibal Potter (brother of Francis Potter of '666') had
been ejected. At Wadham he was associated with the group that
formed the nucleus of what was to become the Royal Society.
He can, therefore, be considered to have weathered the period of
the Commonwealth with success. In 1662 he was elected Bishop
of Exeter and in 1667 translated to the see of Sarum.

'He is (without all manner of flattery) so prudent, learned, and
good a man, that he honours his preferment as much as the preferment does him', wrote Aubrey; 'and such a one that cannot be
advanced too high. My lord (Lucius) Falkland was wont to say
that he never knew anyone that a paire of lawne sleeves had not
altered from himself, but only Bishop Juxon; had he known this
excellent prelate, he would have sayd he had knowne one more.
As he is the patterne of humility and courtesie, so he knows when
to be severe and austere; and he is not one to be trampled or
worked upon. He is a batchelour, and one of a most magnificent
and munificent mind.'

Pepys wrote in his diary that Dr Ward was 'one of the two
bishops that the King do say he can not have bad sermons from'.
At one moment Ward became involved in a controversy with
Hobbes, but according to Aubrey, this did not destroy the regard
each held for the other. There is a note: '*Quaere* bp. Sarum (Seth
Ward) who and when (*annum*) the motion in parliament was to
have Mr Hobbes burnt.' Wood, as usual, found something disagreeable to say, and wrote in the *Athenae*: 'The said Dr Ward did
about his majesty's restoration 1660, endeavour to make his loyalty known by being imprison'd at Cambridge, by his ejection, his
writing against the covenant, and I know not what, but not a word
of his cowardly wavering for lucre and honour sake, of his putting
in and out, and occupying other mens place for several years, etc.':
all of which was no doubt a tenable point of view so far as the
Bishop's conduct was concerned.

Aubrey was irritated by Ward in 1671 for leaving unanswered
a letter enquiring after Sir Walter Raleigh's epitaph, and he wrote
to Wood: 'I writt to his Lordship as upon the public account for

your book, with great apologizing etc: that I did not expect that a person of his greatness should write himself about these matters, but tell his secretary, chaplaine, etc., of it. *Fac hoc et facit*. The Devill an answer have I received. He scornes it. I am confident never a one of the Cardinalls would have served me thus.' However, Aubrey dined with the Bishop about two months later and all seems to have been forgiven. They had a common interest in the project (which Aubrey used to discuss with Paschall and Pigott) for 'a Universal Language'.

Ward appears to have been something of a valetudinarian, and amongst the papers he left were many nostrums for this or that minor complaint. Towards the end of his life his mind and memory failed him, aggravated by the 'black malice' of Thomas Pierce, Dean of Salisbury, who, disappointed in a place sought for his son, attacked the Bishop for nepotism. This charge was not entirely without foundation, but in the light of contemporary practice certainly did not justify the Dean's malignant scurrilities. Ward died in 1689 at his house in Knightsbridge. He had made very considerable benefactions to Salisbury and other places with which he had been associated. Aubrey visited the house after his death and rescued the Bishop's papers 'from being used by the cooke'.

XII

William Holder (1661–1698) occurs in the *Lives*, and figures fairly often in Hooke's *Journal*. He was a friend who belonged to the latter part of Aubrey's life, when Aubrey used to stay with him, and visited Cambridge in his company. He had matriculated at Pembroke Hall, Cambridge, and became rector of Bletchington in Oxfordshire. In 1655 he gained some fame by teaching a deaf-mute, son of Colonel Edward Popham, 'admirall for the Parliament', to speak. Young Popham afterwards relapsed into dumbness and was sent to Hobbes's violent adversary Dr John Wallis, who restored his speech; so that afterwards there was some difference of opinion between Holder and Wallis (whom Aubrey considered a capable but envious and contentious man) as to which of them deserved the credit for the cure. Holder was 'very

musicalle both theorically and practically, and hath a sweet voyce',
says Aubrey. 'He hath writt an excellent treatise of musique, in
English, which is writt both *doctis* and *indoctis*, and readie for the
presse.' In 1674 he was sworn sub-dean of the Chapel Royal,
where he was a great disciplinarian, and Michael Wise, the convivial Wiltshire musician, who was one of the 'Gentlemen of the
Chapel Royal' used to call him 'Mr Snub-Dean', though Aubrey
found Holder's 'discourse so gent. and obligeing'. In 1687 he became rector of Therfield in Hertfordshire.

Holder (who was F.R.S.) married Susanna, only daughter of
Christopher Wren, Dean of Windsor, and sister of Sir Christopher
Wren. This lady, says Aubrey, had 'a strange sagacity as to curing
of wounds'. Charles II had hurt his hand, which had swollen
and pained him up to his shoulder. Mrs Holder made a poultice
and cured the King 'to the great greife of all the surgeons who
envy and hate her'. Aubrey adds that Holder 'was very helpful in
the education of his brother-in-law, Mr Christopher Wren (now
knighted), a youth of a prodigious inventive witt'. On 2 January,
1693, Aubrey wrote thanking Holder for 7s. 6d., spent on 'a
couple of as good fowles as ever I did eate and we had the rest in
wine (very good) . . . and had no single jingle jingle of the Barr,
or profane hoarse swearing to interrupt or disturb sacrifice of your
Freewill offering'.

                              XIII

Speaking of himself, Aubrey wrote, '*Cos*, a wheatstone, *exors
ipse secandi, e.g.* [my] universall character'. This judgment gives
some clue to his popularity; he was the whetstone against which
others sharpened their wits, and, whatever was brought to him,
he had something in the way of sympathy or interest to offer in
return, although he could never materially exploit his own gift.
Friendship was the essential basis of his life. The *Amici* were the
roll of his special friends, but there were many others with whom
he was clearly very intimate; while the persons in the *Lives*
described as 'my old friend' or 'my honour'd acquaintance' are
legion in number. Christopher Wase, Edward Bagshaw, Major

John Graunt were old cronies: Thanet, Abingdon, Anthony Henley, Edward Davenant, Christopher Wren, George Johnson, and countless others were kind to him when he was in distress. We know little of them; and even less of 'my old father, Colonel Sharington Talbot' (whose grandmother leapt from the battlements of Laycock Abbey into the arms of her lover, striking him dead, but later marrying him when 'with great difficulty' he was brought to life), who had been at Nottingham when the King's standard had, in ill omen, been blown down by the wind. His name is followed by the note: 'He had, I believe, 200 adopted sons.'

Sack in their shoppes. My Grandfather, & severall others,
that I knew heretofore, did remember it.

J'aime mon Honneur que ma vie.

1. Aubrey - 2 Danvers.
3. Lyte. 4. as the first

at Christnings & Feasts.
When I was a Boy (before the Civill-warres) y Tabor & Pipe
especially Sundayes & Holydayes were commonly used in the Marches of Wales (& in all Wales)
it is almost lost. The Drumme & Trumpet have put that
able Musiq to silence. I believe 'tis derived from the
Sistrum: [a brasen, or iron Timbrel] Cratalus
Ring of brasse struck with an iron rod: so we play with the
and Tongs.
The first point-band worne in England, was that

AUBREY'S BOOKPLATE displaying the Aubrey coat of arms, quartering *Danvers* and
Lyte: from one of the *Lives* MSS., showing Aubrey's habit of jotting down odds
and ends of reminiscence.

APPENDIX A

Aubrey's Works

I

To give an intelligible and businesslike account of Aubrey's literary remains is not easy (see p. 310). Although almost all the manuscripts still available have been collected under the author's name in the Bodleian Library at Oxford, Aubrey's method of writing, on some scrap of paper that came to hand, any item of interest that might at a given moment drift into his head—combined with his inability to stick to the point and habit of toying with a piece of work for thirty-five or more years—of necessity makes any brief attempt to describe the final accumulation of his work somewhat irregular in form. A list of his manuscripts given in his own handwriting at the end of *Villare Anglicanum* is headed: 'A Catalogue of Books written by Mr Aubrey; inserted here by himself, at my request. Nov. 18. 1692. Edw. Lhwyd.' Some of these items appear to have been withdrawn or at a later date altered in arrangement, perhaps after the publication of the *Miscellanies*; and it seems most convenient to comment on the manuscripts in the order in which they are now catalogued in the Library rather than to follow Aubrey's own list, which is given below:

1. Antiquities of Wiltshire, after the method of Sir W. Dugdale's Description of Warwickshire. 2 parts in fol.
2. Monumenta Britannica. 3 parts fol. With Mr Secretary Trumbull.
3. Memoires of Naturall Remarques in Wilts. 2 parts fol.
4. Perambulation of halfe the Country of Surrey. Fol. with Mr J. Evelyn. [The last phrase erased.]
5. Miscellanea. Fol.
6. Lives. 3 parts.
7. Mr Thomas Hobbes' Life in English.
8. An apparatus of the lives of English Mathematicians. A qr. At Gresham Colledge.
9. Idea of Education of Young Gentlemen from 9 to 18. Fol. The correct copie is with Anthony Henley, Esq. at the Grange in Hantshire.
10. Remaines of Gentilisme. 3 parts *sc.* about 3 qrs. With Dr Kennet.

11. Villare Anglicanum (to be) interpreted. Fol.
12. A Collection of Divine Dreams from Persons of my acquaintance worthy of beliefe. 8vo.
13. Hypothesis Ethic and Scala Religionis. With Dr Waple, Minister of Sepulchres by Newgate.
14. A Collection of Geniture well attested. 4to.
15. Easton Piers delineated.
16. Villa, or a description of the prospects from Easton Piers.
17. Faber Fortunae, a private essay.
18. A Collection of Approved Receipts.
19. A Collection of Letters, writt to me from about 100 ingeniose persons inch and half thick. This I designe for the Musaeum.
20. Adversaria Physica.
21. An Introduction to Architecture.
22. Some Strictures of Hermetick Philosophy, collected by J. Aubrey.

In so much as they still exist, the above works, with the exception of the *Remains of Gentilism* (which is in the British Museum) are now to be found in the Bodleian, in the order that follows.

II

The Naturall Historie of Wiltshire, 1685, may be looked upon as Aubrey's first serious work. It was begun in 1656 and he seems to have continued to add to it until 1691, when the rough draft in two volumes was given to the Ashmolean. A fuller copy, in one volume, was formerly in the library of the Royal Society, to the members of which it had been submitted in 1675. Later this copy was in the possession of George Poulett Scrope, of Castle Combe. The manuscript was in part edited by John Britton and printed (very inadequately) for the Wiltshire Topographical Society in 1847. The Bodleian copy lacks certain chapters, but contains notes by Ray, Evelyn, Tanner, and Gale, which were not copied into the Royal Society's volume.

This work (which was quoted by Horace Walpole in his *Anecdotes of Painting*) has all the characteristic features of Aubrey's compositions, in its muddle, striking phraseology, flashes of good sense, and curiously nostalgic quality. There is a great deal that is of interest to county historians in its chapters, which stray this way and that, from the minerals, beasts, and plants, to the grandeur of the Earls of Pembroke, Things Praeternatural, and the falling of rents. Architecture, agriculture, and the rise of the clothiers are considered; the number of attorneys, the price of corn, and Salisbury races; markets, Roman coins, and gardens; Chitterne, where lies the clay-pit from which Mr Gauntlet made his famous pipes, marking the heel with a gauntlet; the incomparable eels of Marlborough, and the Devizes metheglyn, find a place with the Burbage turnips, of which last Aubrey says: 'They are the best that ever I did eat. They are sent for far and near. They are not tough and stringy like other turnips, but cutt like marmelad. Burbidge is also remarkable for excellent Pease.'

There are some shrewd remarks, such as these: 'I have oftentimes wished for a mappe of England coloured according to the colours of the earth; with markes of the fossiles and minerals'; or: 'As the motion caused by a stone lett fall into the water is by circles, so sound moves by spheres in the same manner; which, though obvious enough, I doe not remember to have seen in any booke.'

On the subject of *Draughts of the Seates and Prospects* he writes: 'If these views were well donn, they would make a glorious volume by itselfe, and like enough it might take well in the world. It were an inconsiderable expence to those persons of qualitie, and it would remain to posterity when their families are gonn and their buildings ruined by time or fire, as we have seen that stupendous fabric of Paul's Church, not a stone left on stone, and lives now only in Mr Hollar's Etchings in Sir William Dugdale's *History of Paul's*. I am not displeased with this thought as a desideratum but I do never expect to see it donn; so few men have the heart to do public good to give 4 or 5 pounds for a copper plate.' He quotes Sir Walter Raleigh as having said: 'There are stranger things to be seen in the world than are between London and Stanes'; and there is an apt description of the litigious inhabitants of Norfolk, 'who carry Littleton's *Tenures* at the plough's taile'. There are remarks like 'I never saw Snail-shells so beautifull anywhere as on the Hedges in Somersetshire'; and he confirms that the famous lines so often attributed to Ben Jonson,

> *Underneath this sable hearse*
> *Lies the subject of all verse,*
> *Sidney's sister, Pembroke's mother . . .*

were 'made by Mr [William] Browne who wrote the Pastoralls'.

On the title-page of the manuscript is the note: 'Mr David Loggan drew my picture anno 1686, which is in his hands, to be engraven for this book.'

III

An Essay towards the Description of the North Division of Wiltshire, by me John Aubrey of Easton Piers. This is called on the outside of the original parchment cover, *Hypomnemata Antiquaria A*, and was put together between 1659 and 1670. 'I was much inclined by my Genius from childhood, to the love of antiquities,' wrote Aubrey; 'and my Fate dropt me in a countrey most suitable for such enquiries.' Unfortunately, he set to work, as usual, without any very decided programme, and these collections are really notebooks from which a county history (for the work spreads out beyond its original northern limits) might have grown in the course of time. At first these Wiltshire notes were to have been handed over to Wood, but after their estrangement Aubrey decided to 'reposit' in the recently founded Ashmolean this manuscript, then contained in two volumes called *Hypomnemata Antiquaria 'A'* and *'B'.* Of these two books, only the former can be found, because Aubrey's brother William borrowed[1] *'Liber B'* in 1703, some years after Aubrey's death; and, with the inconsequence of his family, failed to return it to the library.

A note to Warton's *History of Kiddington*, published in 1783 and quoted in Jackson's edition of Aubrey's *Wiltshire Collections*, states that the manuscript was at that time preserved partly in the Ashmolean and partly in the library of Alderton (seat of Aubrey's tedious friend, Thomas Gore, of 'Aldrington *aliàs* Alderton'), which then belonged to the Montagu family, one of whom had married the heiress of the Gores. This library was probably disposed of at the sale of the Montagu belongings at Lackham, near Chippenham, in 1815 or 1816, when many of Thomas Gore's heraldic papers were dispersed.

Subsequently the lost manuscript seems to have found its way into the sale of the Heber Library, in 1834/5, where it was described in the catalogue as: 'No 48, Aubrey. Extracts from Aubrey's papers in the Ashmolean Museum. It appears to be only the second volume.' From Sotheby's auction rooms the manuscript went to Thorpe, the bookseller; but this is the last stage to which it has been traced. One day, no doubt, it will reappear again, and more will be added to what is known of the

[1] 'August 14, 1703. Borrowed then of Mr Edw. Lhwyd, the Keeper of the Ashmolean Library, the Second Volume of my brothers "Hypomnemata Antiquaria" which I shall restore upon demand. Wm. Aubrey' is noted at the back of page Z in the index to volume A.

history of Wiltshire and its life in the seventeenth century. There will also be a few more autobiographical details about Aubrey himself.

The surviving volume, *Hypomnemata Antiquaria A*, consists of two parts bound together, small folio in size, written in Aubrey's hand and illustrated by him with coloured escutcheons of coats of arms and some rough drawings of ancient houses. The arrangement is irregular, but the places of each hundred are grouped together. With all its disorder, the information contained in this manuscript is of great topographical value, while the anecdotes quoted on the authority of 'the parish clerk's wife' or 'old Hughes the gunsmith' sometimes give local allusions of considerable interest. Aubrey complains more than once of the difficulties of research: 'Desire my brother to see it, for 'twas a dimm day, and winter'; or that he could not read the inscriptions on the high windows 'for want of a short telescope', so that the tricking of the charges on the shields are not always the same as his written descriptions of them. However, Canon Jackson, who edited a corrected and enlarged edition of the *North Wiltshire Collections* in 1862 (incomplete editions had already appeared in 1821 and 1838, under the direction of Sir Thomas Phillips), says that it is 'neither easy nor safe' to correct Aubrey on points of heraldry, more especially since unskilful retouching of the achievements, at a later date, may sometimes be the cause of the author seeming to be at fault. Canon Jackson, sometime Rector of Leigh Delamere, is one of Aubrey's most sympathetic editors. He is appreciative of Aubrey's character and qualities without being patronising, while the rearrangement he has made of the material at hand (which is set down in Aubrey's most confused and illegible manner) is both painstaking and sagacious.

Aubrey's preface to this book (which he intended to dedicate to James Bertie, 1st Earl of Abingdon) includes a summary of the history of England, which is one of his best pieces of sustained writing. Having touched on the characteristics of the land in those parts, he speaks of what had gone before:

'Let us imagine then what kind of a countrie this was in the time of the ancient Britons. By the nature of the soil, which is a sour woodsere land, very natural for the production of oakes especially, one may conclude that this North Division was a shady dismal wood: and the inhabitants almost as savage as the Beasts whose skins were their only rayment. The language British, which for the honour of it was in those dayes spoken from the Orcades to Italie and Spain. The Boats on the Avon (which signifies River) were basketts of twigges covered with an oxe skin: which the poore people in Wales use to this day. They call them *curricles*. Within this Shire I believe that there were several *Reguli* which often made war upon another: and the great Ditches which run on the plaines and elsewhere so many miles (not unlikely) their boundaries: and withall served for defence against the incursions of their enemies, as the Pict's wall, Offa's Ditch: and that in China, to compare things small to great. Their religion is at large described by Caesar. Their priests were Druids: some of their temples I pretend to have restored, as Avbury, Stonehenge, &c, as also British sepulchres. Their waie of fighting is lively sett down by Caesar.

'Their camps with their way of meeting their antagonists I have sett down in another place. They knew the use of Iron: and about Hedington fields, Bromham, Bowden, &c., are still ploughed up cinders, the Scoria of melted iron. (In Herefordshire, towards Monmouthshire, are many old Roman cinders found: which they use in their Blomeries[1] now to make their oare runne better). They were two or three degrees I suppose less savage than the Americans. Till King John's time wolves were in this Island: and in our grandfather's dayes more Foxes than now, and marterns (a beast of brown rich Furre) at Stanton Parke, &c: the race now extinct thereabout.

'The Romans subdued and civilized them. At Lackham, Mr Camden saith, was a Colonie of them, as appears by the Roman coine found there. About 1654 in Week-field in the Parish of Heddington digging up the ground deeper than the plough went, they found for a great way together foundations of howses, hearthes, coles, and a great deale of Romane coine, silver and brasse; whereof I had a pint: some little copper pieces no bigger than silver halfpence—*quaere*, if they were not the Roman Denarii—the pott in which a good deale was found, I had.[2] I presented it to the Royal Society's Repositorie: it resembles an apprentice's earthen Christmas boxe. At Sherston hath severall times been found Roman money in ploughing. I have one silver piece found there not long since (1653), of Constantine the Great. Among other arts, that of architecture was introduced by them, and no doubt but here as well as in other parts were there good buildings, here being so good stone. . . .

[1] A 'blomary' is the first forge in the iron mills, through which the metal passes, after it has been melted from the mine. The 'scoria' is slag. Bowden was the seat of Aubrey's friend, George Johnson, who was to have employed him if Johnson had become Master of the Rolls.

[2] The money was 'stolen by a servant from me'.

'The Britons received the knowledge of husbandrie from the Romans; the foot and the acre which we yet use is the nearest to them. In our West Countrie (and I believe so in the North) they give no wages to the shepherd, but he has the keeping so many sheep with his Master's flock. Plautus hints at this in his *Asinaria*, Act III, Scene I. 1.36:

> *Etiam opilio, qui pascit, mater, alienas oves,*
> *Alignum habet peculiarem, quâ spem soletur suam.*

'The Saxons succeeded them, and driving them away to Ireland, Cornewall, &c., these Roman Britaines left here:—(for they use the best of them in their warres, being their best soldiers). Here was a mist of ignorance for six hundred yeares. They were so far from knowing Arts that they could not build wall with stone. The church of Glaston was thatched.

'They lived sluttishly in poor howses, where they ate a great deale of beefe and mutton and dranke good Ale in a brown mazard: and their very kings were but a sort of Farmers. After the Christian Religion was planted here it gave a great shoote; and the Kings and great men gave vast revenues to the Church who were ignorant enough in those days. The Normans then came and taught them civility and building: which though it was Gothique as also their Policy (*Feudalis Lex*) yet they were magnificent. For the Government till the time of Henry VIII, it was like a Nest of Boxes: for the Copy-holders, (who till then were Villaines) held of the Lords of the Manor, who held perhaps of another superior Lord or Duke, who held of the King. Upon any occasion of Bustling in those dayes, one of the greate Lords sounded his Trumpet (all Lords then kept Trumpeters, even to King James) and summoned those that held under them: those again sounded their Trumpets, and so on downwards to the Copy-holders. Old Sir Walter Long, grandfather to Colonel Long, kept a Trumpeter: and rode with thirty servants and retainers to Marlborough [Sessions] and so for others of his ranke and time.'

Aubrey goes on to praise much of what had been already lost by the age in which he was writing, although he admits that in the past, too, there had been things that were evil and foolish:

'From the time of Erasmus till about twenty years past, the learning was downright pedantry. The conversation and habits of those times were as starcht as their bands and square beards; and gravity was then taken for wisdom. The doctors in those days were but old boys, when quibbles past for wit even in their sermons. The gentry and citizens had little learning of any kind, and their way of breeding of their children was suitable to the rest. They were as severe to their children as their schoolmasters; and their schoolmasters as masters of the house of correction. The child perfectly loathed the sight of his parents as the slave his torture. Gentlemen of thirty and forty years old were to stand like mutes and fools bareheaded before their parents; and the daughters (grown woemen) were to stand at the cupboard-side during the whole time of their proud Mother's visit, unless (as the fashion was) leave was desired, forsooth, that a cushion should be given them to kneel upon, brought them by the serving man, after they had done sufficient penance in standing. The boys (I mean the young fellows) had their foreheads turned up, and stiffened with spittle: they were to stand mannerly forsooth thus: the foretop ordered as before, with one hand at the band-string: the other behind them. The gentlewomen had prodigious fans, as is to be seen in old pictures, like that instrument which is used to drive feathers: and in it had a handle at least half a yard long: with these the daughters were often times corrected.'

The preface (which is strangely reminiscent of some of Carlyle's passages of historical description) closes in that personal manner, which is at once Aubrey's strength and weakness, giving his writing vitality, but preventing him from ever approaching his work in a wholly serious manner:

'This searching after Antiquities is a wearisom taske. I wish I had gone through all the Church monuments. The records at London I can search gratis. Though of all studies I take the least delight in this, yet methinkes I am carried on with a kind of divine Œstrum: for nobody els hereabouts hardly cares for it, but rather makes a scorn of it. But methinkes it shewes a kind of gratitude to revise the memories and memorialls of the pious and charitable Benefactors since dead and gonne.'

IV

A Perambulation of the County of Surrey, or, to give the work its alternative title, *The Natural History and Antiquities of the County of Surrey*, was written by Aubrey in 1673, when he had been appointed by 'His Majesty's Cosmographer', John Ogilby, as deputy for the survey of that county. Aubrey continued to revise the manuscript until 1692, when he left it unfinished. It was printed in 1718/19 by Curll, with Dr Richard Rawlinson's memoir, which contains a number of misleading statements on the subject of Aubrey's career, Rawlinson made many minor, but wholly unnecessary, emendations in Aubrey's text. Unlike his connexion with Wiltshire, Aubrey could claim only a remote family association with Surrey. 'Willey is a hamlet within the parish of Chaldon. Here is a fine Grove of Ashes; now [belonging to] Mr Beteston on the top of a hill, from whence is a prospect Southward to the Vale of Surrey, and so to the South Downs (which seem azure colour) to Hampshire West, to Kent East, and Middlesex Northwards. This pleasant seat was heretofore belonging to — Browne Esq., who married my Great-Grandmother Wilgiford, the relict of William Aubrey, Doctor of Lawes and one of the Masters of Requests etc. In anno 1656 I came to search the Register here for her obit to have it attested at the Great Sessions at Brecknock when my Triall was concerning the Estate entailed upon me by Dr Aubrey (six hundred pounds in Brecknockshire, mostly and some in Monmouthshire), I little thought of writing this description.'

The result of his labours was a very creditable collection of information, suitable to form the basis of a county history, and comparable in method to Ashmole's *History and Antiquities of Berkshire*. Aubrey must have worked hard while occupied in the survey, the transcription of memorial tablets in the churches alone being very numerous, and constituting an important contribution towards co-ordinating material for the genealogist and county historian. There are also a number of coats of arms tricked out, together with a few drawings of houses. These Surrey inscriptions are remarkable for the number of minor officials of the Court who are commemorated: 'Serjeant of the Wine Cellar . . . Serjeant of His Majestie's Wood Yard . . . Serjeant of His Majestie's carriage . . . Serjeant of the Larder . . . Officer of the remooving Wardroppe of Bedds . . . Serjeant of the Confectionary . . . Yeoman of His Majestie's Sculery . . . Pensioner and Groome-Porter unto Queen Elizabeth of blessed memory . . .', so the list continues endlessly.

There is the usual flow of unconventional comment on Aubrey's part. At Wandsworth 'is a Manufacture of Brass Plates, for Kettles, Skellets, Frying-Pans, &c by Dutch-men, who keep it as a Mystery; here is a bridge called *the Sink of the Countrey*'.

'East of Kingston, on the rising of the Hill, stands the gallows, in dry gravelly ground, where they often find Roman urns.'

At Ockley: 'Dog Smyth gave to the Poor of this Parish 6*li per annum*: he gave to every of the parishes of this county, except Micham, where he had been formerly whipped for a vagabond. See his will at the Prerogative Office. He had the nick-name *Dog Smyth* because he kept no house, but dined at friends houses, and then, desired a Bitt for his Dog: which was to refect himself.'

At Godalming 'is a manor called Catteshal, which is held of the King, as *Master of the King's concubines*: a chapelle belongeth to it'.

At Lingfield: 'The inhabitants are very fond of *ghirlands* or garlands made of Midsummer silver, a little herb which continues all the year of a bright ash colour, and have crowded the Church and their own houses with them.'

At Dorking (or Darking, as it was then called) 'is a great plenty of cherries, that Mr John Evelyn tells me, makes a most excellent wine, little inferior to the best French, and keeps many years'.

On the other hand, at Worplesdon 'the cheese of this country is very bad and poore: they robbe their Cheese by taking out the Butter which they sell to London, and they are miserably ignorant to Dairy (except for Butter). A gentlewoman of Cheshire, married into these parts (near Albury) and misliking the cheese here, sent for a Dairy-maid, a good housewife, out of her own Countrey, but she could not with all her Cheshire skill make any good cheese here. *Quippe solo natura subest*. But John Shakespeare's wife (Parson Blanchard's housekeeper) an excellent house wife, whom he brought with him from North Wiltshire, makes as good cheese as ever she did in her own Country, (*i.e.* that sort of cheese which is called in London Marleborough cheese, about an inch thick) and tells me it is only want of art.'

He has a good story of East Clandon. 'Thomas Goffe the Poet was Rector here, he was buried in the middle of the chancel, but there is nothing in remembrance of him; his wife, it seems was not so kind. I found by the register book that he was buried, July 27, 1629. His wife pretended to fall in love with him by hearing of him preach; upon which said one Thomas Thimble (one of the Squire Bedells in Oxford, and his confidant) to him: *Do not marry her : If thou dost, she will break thy heart*. He was not obsequious to his freind's sober advice, but for her sake altered his condition; and cast anchor here. One time some of his Oxford freinds made a visit to him; she looked upon them with an ill eye, as if they had come *to eat her out of her House and Home*, (as they say) she provided a dish of milk and some eggs for supper, and no more: They perceived her niggardliness, and that her Husband was inwardly troubled at it, (she wearing the breeches) so they were resolved to be merry at supper, and talk all in Latine, and laugh'd exceedingly. She was so vex'd at their speaking Latine, that she could not hold, but fell out a weeping, and rose from the table. The next day, Mr Goffe order'd a better dinner for them, and sent for some wine. They were merry and his freinds took their final leave of him. 'Twas not long before this

Xantippe made Mr Thimble's prediction good; and when he died the last words he spake were: *Oracle, Oracle, Tom Thimble,* and so he gave up the Ghost. Had not he been much happier at Christchurch in Oxford with his Student's place, than thus to be tyed to such a Snip-cheese, a curst Shrew.'

V

An interpretation of Villare Anglicanum is an unfinished piece of work, written by Aubrey between 1670 and 1690, consisting of a preface and a list of place names in England—'that had escaped the fury of the Saxon Conquest'—with an occasional note as to their meaning. Meredith Lloyd (often quoted by Aubrey as an authority on scientific and historical subjects), supplied a list of Welsh words; and Edward Lhwyd, Keeper of the Ashmolean, a Welsh glossary. There are also lists forming a *Villare Scoticum* and *Villare Hibernicum,* together with some odds and ends of notes, including the already quoted list of Aubrey's writings, and his epitaph written by himself. This book was to have been dedicated to Edmund Wyld, another example of Aubrey's originality and prescience.

VI

The *Lives* or Σχεδιάσματα, set down by Aubrey between 1669 and 1696, are for the most part contained in four folio volumes of manuscript, and much has already been said, in the course of describing Aubrey's career, on the subject of their composition and content. Andrew Clark edited an edition of the *Lives* in 1898, which, so far as the difficulties of transcription are concerned, provides as faithful a version as could reasonably be expected, no easy achievement in view of the chaos which prevails in many of the four hundred or more biographies. There are, it is true, a few omissions in the case of anecdotes which Clark considered too outspoken, all of which have been made available in subsequent selections. However, a complete and scholarly edition of all existent 'lives' to be elicited from the Aubrey MSS remains to be made. Although we may regret Clark's squeamishness, the absence of these passages can scarcely be held to effect seriously the appreciation of the *Lives,* to which he added many compact fragments of biography from the rest of Aubrey's works. In the introduction, Clark gives an account of his method in compiling this edition, the difficulties involved, and a description of the manuscripts. He points out that, whenever he can, Aubrey gives the exact nativity of each of his subjects, to assist in the accumulation of astrological data, and that when he notes a coat of arms he has often done no more than extract it from a Dictionary of Arms, not necessarily seen the arms borne in some manner by the persons concerned.

After the manuscript of the *Lives* had been placed in the Ashmolean by Aubrey in 1693, it was a century before there was any suggestion that they should be published. Then, in 1792, Edmund Malone made a transcript of 174 of them, adding notes with a view to publication. Some years later James Caulfield, a London publisher, employed his representative, Curtis, to transcribe some of the *Lives*; and in 1797 issued the first part of a volume called *The Oxford Cabinet*, illustrated with engravings from pictures in the Ashmolean. Before any further parts of this publication could appear, the Keeper of the Ashmolean, at Malone's instigation, withdrew permission from Curtis to continue his transcriptions—on the grounds that he had taken away papers and title-pages from libraries in Oxford, and was, accordingly, not fit to be trusted in the Ashmolean. It seems probable that Malone contrived to remove this source of competition in order to pursue his own projects[1]; but this dispute belongs to the history of late eighteenth-century literary quarrels rather than to the story of Aubrey. So far as it went, the Caulfield edition was superior in editing to *Letters of Eminent Persons . . . and Lives of Eminent Men by John Aubrey Esq.* which appeared in 1813 but had many faults of inaccuracy and omission, although the first edition to present the bulk of the interesting material.

VII

'No Nobleman's son in England,' wrote Aubrey, 'is so well bred (nor could have such good breeding) as the King's Mathematicall Boys at Christchurch Hospitall in London.' It was, therefore, with some thought of remedying the defects of English upper-class education, as these appeared to him from his memories of Blandford, and from the chance remarks of friends, that he set himself to compose *An Idea of the Education of a Young Gentleman viz from the age of nine or ten years; till seventeen or eighteen*, a scheme which, he says, had its conception in 1669, at the Grange, the seat of the Henleys, at Alresford in Hampshire, and was completed in 1684. This manuscript, about one hundred leaves of folio

---

[1] Malone noted 10 July, 1792: 'These Lives having taken seven days in the *perusal* alone, I cannot now make extracts from them, but at some future time will transcribe and publish them, with a vindication of Aubrey from A. Wood's *Calumny.*'

foolscap, written on one side only, was put for safety by its author in the hands of Ashmole, and has never been printed. Like the rest of Aubrey's work it contains eccentricities of style, imperfections of form, and a number of repetitions, but even a reader who knew nothing of its originator would be struck by some of the suggestions in so curious a contribution to educational theory. Although such essays were at that time by no means unusual, Aubrey's empirical approach to any subject in which he was interested brings an uncommon liveliness to the writing. He himself considered it his best and most important work, and the one that was most likely to bring him credit and fame.

Much of the material for the essay is drawn, naturally, from the existing stock of contemporary views and prejudices, and Aubrey's acquaintance with Hartlib, the friend of Comenius (Johann Amos Komensky), John Dury, and other educational reformers, would explain his familiarity with Continental systems. General education, by its very nature, must be peculiarly exposed to the accusation that it is obsolete; and the schools and universities of the seventeenth century were in an uneasy state of transition, in which the old Latin, monkish traditions had not yet contrived to adapt themselves to the needs of a fast changing, more commercial, more critical world. Montaigne and Castiglione in the previous century had been for a training that would be a preparation for active public life, and Sir Thomas Elyot in *The Boke called the Governour* wrote on similar lines, deriving much of his theory from Erasmus and Continental models.

A hundred years later, in *The Great Didactic*, Comenius criticised current methods of teaching, but his book and principles do not appear to have aroused much interest in England, although he visited this country in 1641, leaving hurriedly on account of the disturbed state of political affairs and imminence of war. Meanwhile in France the courtly academies were growing up, where French was given at least an equal place with the classics, and these schools, well spoken of by Milton in his tractate *Of Education*, were soon copied in Germany by the *Ritter-akademien*. In England, there was a growing feeling that the universities were unsuitable places for the education of a young gentleman destined to hold a high position in the world. The Grand Tour was an educational conception intended to supply an alternative approach. Aubrey shows himself in sympathy with this inclination to distrust the universities, and, no doubt, he was also familiar with the ideas of Descartes, who was an effective influence to bring education more into line with contemporary life.

In Aubrey's immediate circle, Petty had made suggestions in favour of trade schools and Cowley proposed to establish a college devoted to research. Aubrey's own plans seem to have had a little in common with those of Sir Francis Kynaston (whose family, like Aubrey's, came from the Welsh border), a poet, and Esquire of the Body to Charles I. In 1635 Kynaston was licensed to maintain in his house a *Musaeum Minervae*, where an immense variety of subjects could be studied. Physical training of the pupil was attended to, as well as intellectual, and the aim, like Aubrey's, was to produce suitable men to show skill and elegance in their position at the head of affairs, an admirable goal which modern education seems further than ever from achieving. To what extent this institution ever established itself is uncertain, but it seems to have ceased to exist, either when Kynaston died in 1642, or earlier, on account of opposition from the universities.

Aubrey begins his thesis by recording his objection to private tutors on the grounds of their servility; and to local schools because (a perspicacious opinion) at these, men living in the same part of the country came to know each other too well in their youth. Aubrey thought that in this way their view of each other was for ever prejudiced by memories of their schooldays, which made for difficulties in such matters as the administration of the law by a Justice of the Peace. His kinsman, Sir John Danvers, 'the regicide', had told him that the principal reason, when he was a young man, for parents sending their sons to travel 'was to wean them from their acquaintance and familiarity with servingmen: for the parents were so austere and grave, that the sonnes must not be company for their Fathers: and some company man must have—so, contracted a familiarity with the servingmen who got a hank upon them they could hardly claw off.' Of French educational methods, admired by some, Aubrey says; 'Like the shearing of Hogges they make a great crie and little wool . . . their mindes do chiefly run on the propagation of their race.'

There were to be seven or eight of Aubrey's schools, each containing fifty, or at the most sixty, boys, so that it appears that under five hundred men were all he felt it necessary to consider as candidates for his form of education, the future rulers of the country. At the head was to be the Provost, a gentleman, well-educated, travelled, a layman, and unmarried. There was, indeed, to be an irrevocable order that neither the Provost nor any of the 'Informators'—the ushers, who were to have £100 a year and all found—should marry, 'for if they did their daughters would debauch the young gents, not to say worse to become their wives.'

None of the Informators were to be English, but were 'to be chosen from Switzerland or Scotland—men of presence and bôn mine . . . not little contemptible Râttons'. Moreover, the tempers of these masters were to be good. Ten or twelve Swiss, Dutch, or Scotch boys of about fifteen, speaking Latin well, were to be included in the school to provide a ready-made form of prefects, to be replaced in four or five years by boys themselves brought up in the school. The Governess was to be a well-bred gentlewoman, unmarried, with no daughter. The Cook, a Frenchman or Swiss; as also the Scullion, both of whom were to speak Latin. The Butler was to be Swiss, too, and skilled as a barber to shave the boys' heads 'to keep them from lice'. The Porter 'should not be an old fellow in a gowne, like an old fool to forget men's lives and errands nor a scabby old sneaking servitor with a tattered gowne . . . but a lusty young Swiss with a decent livery and long sword'.

The curriculum was to include a certain amount of the classics, mathematics, and English, especially the writing of blank verse on such subjects as 'of a Prospect: Of a Faire: Of a Frigit'. As to Latin, 'Dr Pell[1] would have the boys sometimes to practice the Foreign pronunciation: but all the pronunciations are false'—the echo of a controversy that time has not stilled. The boys were taught to keep accounts, and there was to be an Army Class, for 'Valour alone will not advance a Soldier to a Great Command, without art. He may have the favour to play at Trictrac in the General's ante-chambre, but never to be elected one of the Councell: or to be made a Man of Conduct'. Drawing was to be studied, 'though I doe not intend or expect to have them Titians and Van dyks'. Shorthand (connected always in the seventeenth century mind with the useful art of cypher) was to be a potential subject, as were oratory, law, swimming, cookery, cards, chess, dancing, and also 'to know about timber'.

There was to be plenty of light in the rooms, and good food was to be provided. To supervise the latter, two of the young gentlemen would go to the kitchen as Stewards. There was also to be a 'modicum of good wine, French and Rhenish for this wine does clear the braine and refreshes the spirit and is good medicine against the Wormes'. Wine

---

[1] Dr. John Pell was a friend of Aubrey's, who had been professor of mathematics at Amsterdam, and at the Prince of Orange's *Schola Illustris* at Breda. Pell had also been Cromwell's envoy to the Protestant cantons of Switzerland; and it may have been his recommendations that made the natives of Holland and Switzerland appear to Aubrey so eligible for training the young.

was generally—and, one might add, rightly—considered preferable to
beer in its effect on the senses, for even Dr Fell if he 'found a young
gentleman in a Taverne he would chide him very mildly: but if he
caught him in an Alehouse he would be very severe with him'.

But the essential reform that Aubrey demanded, as others had done
before him and more were to do after him, was for a more humane
approach to the whole matter of pedagogy. Over and over again he
complains of 'the tedious effects of grammar and beside them, tyrannical
beating and dispiriting of children, [from] which many tender and
ingeniose children doe never recover againe'. Learning was to be made
attractive, not a horrible memory to cast a cloud over later life. 'For the
honour of this school', he says that he would have 'nothing of terror
or Gehenne to frighten youths from the love of learning. I would have
no such thing as the turning up of bare buttocks for pedants to exercise
their cruel lusts'. Instead, punishments were to be finger-stocks, keeping-
in, and the docking of wine, tarts, and fruit.

Another innovation was to be that no lecture was to last more than
half an hour, an important reform, for the question of how long the
attention of pupils might reasonably be held was one that was scarcely
regarded for many years to come. In addition, the boys were to have
enough sleep, and were not to be set to work at six o'clock in the morning.
At the age of eighteen, they were to be sent to Leyden, rather than an
English university. Aubrey seems uncertain whether this is not keeping
them at school too late, quoting Sir Thomas Overbury as complaining
that the English hang too long over their books, an early reference to
what has become a traditional criticism of English educational methods.

As the book progresses, Aubrey, as his custom was, slackens his hold
on his subject; and, although more than once he shows signs of wishing
to approach the question of training in matters of sex, he never manages
to persuade himself to come to grips with this problem. In several
places he remarks that the fact must not be forgotten that the older boys
have already become men; and he notes a proverb to the effect that:
'He that looseth his maidenhead with a bare-legged wench will never
run after a silk stocking.' He also records that 'Mr Hobbes told me that
George 2nd Duke of Buckingham at Paris when he was about twenty
years old desired him to read Geometrie to him; his Grace had great
natural parts and quicknesse of witt; Mr Hobbes read and his Grace did
not apprehend, which Mr Hobbes wondered at: at last Mr Hobbes
observed that his grace was at mastrupation (his hand in his codpiece).
That is a very improper age, for that reason for learning.' However,

Aubrey's preoccupation remains set on the danger of a young man with prospects making an unsuitable marriage, and it is to be regretted that he was too indolent, or unwilling, to apply himself to the question of what preparation should be given in this respect for the ways of life. His unprejudiced view of so many matters might have resulted in some interesting pronouncement on this one.

The situations suggested by Aubrey for his schools were: at 'Kensington in Surrey, neare the roade and Hyde Parke'; in Lancashire; at Merton in Wiltshire, under the eye of Lord Shaftesbury; at Cranborne in Dorset by Lord Salisbury's, 'the finest place in England'; at Gloucester Hall in Oxford, 'but it would be envied by the Colleges'; in North Wales; and in Glamorgan.

Such is Aubrey's treatise on education, which contains some good ideas. There is a freshness of approach, while the essential point—that pupils are sent to school to be trained and taught—is never, as in some other educational utopias, lost sight of. At the end of the manuscript the author has written: 'But now (methinkes) I see a black squadron marching from Oxford, led up by a crossier staffe to discomfort this pretty little Flock: and so this my pleasing Dream is all at an End.' Below, as a postscript, he has added the ominous name—'Dr Fell'.

VIII

The *Monumenta Britannica or a Miscellanie of British Antiquities* is in four parts, mainly written between 1665 and 1693. Aubrey notes of it in the manuscript: '*Historia quoque modo scripta bona est*:[1] and though this be writt, as I rode, a gallop: yet the novelty of it, and the faithfulness of the delivery, may make some amends for the uncorrectness of the Stile: the first draught was worn-out with time and handling: and now, methinkes, after many years lying dormant, I come abroad like the Ghost of one of those Druids.' It appears that the *Monumenta* was originally intended to have been dedicated to Charles II, no doubt in compliment to the interest the King had shown in Aubrey's 'restoration' of Avebury; though the second volume of the manuscript is dedicated to 'the Rt. Hon. Sir William Trumbull, Principall Secretary of Estate', another dedication to Sir Walter Long having been erased. Part I, *Templa Druidum*, deals with the Druids and supposed Druidical temples, especially Avebury and Stonehenge, plans of each of which are given. *Monumenta*, part 2, deals with camps, Roman towns, walls, etc. *Monumenta*, part 3, is concerned with sepulchral monuments, roads, dykes,

[1] Pliny's *Epistles*.

pavements, coins, etc. *Monumenta*, part 4, including *Chronologia Architectonica* (dedicated to Sir John Aubrey of Llantrithyd), 1671, is an early
and interesting attempt to trace a sequence of styles. Mixed up with this
treatise are notes on escutcheons, a study of palaeography, a history of
costume, notes on prices, weights and measures, a copy of the *Assize of
Beer and Bread* from the *Red Book of Bath*, 1428, and several letters. There
is a great deal of curious information and original work in the manuscripts of the *Monumenta*, which were deposited by Aubrey with Robert
Hooke, on 11 August, 1690. On Aubrey's death, these papers were in
the possession of Awnsham Churchill, a rich London bookseller. In
1755 and 1780 they were owned by a nephew of the same name; and,
in 1817, by William Churchill, son of the latter, from whom they passed
to a cousin, Colonel Sir William Greville, who sold them to the Bodleian.
(See p. 310.)

IX

*Designatio de Easton-Piers in Com: Wilts. Per me (heu!) infortunatum
Johannem Awbrey R. S. Socium . . . Anno Domini 1669*, is a series of coloured
drawings of the house and grounds at Easton Pierse, made by Aubrey
when he knew that the property must pass out of his possession. They
give a good impression of the beauty of the place (if the house was ever
completed) and show Aubrey's pleasant gift as a draughtsman.

X

*Country Revell, or the Revell of Alford, a comedy by and in the hand of John
Aubrey*, is Aubrey's surviving dramatic fragment. This play was begun by
him when he was at Broad Chalke in 1671, trying to avoid his creditors.
It is no more than a rough draft, chiefly written on some interrogatories
and depositions (taken in 1635, in which Roger Aubrey was concerned),
and the draft is written between the lines and in every available blank
space of these legal documents. Although its form is sketchy in the
extreme, some idea of the scope and plot of the *Country Revel* may be
formed from the more elaborate scenes, which show most of the
characteristic features of Restoration comedy. The play is loosely put
together, the dialogue representing what must have been the everyday
speech, more or less, of Aubrey's world. Its thesis is the decay of manners
and morals in comparison with those of the 'Good Old Times'. This
was, of course, a favourite theme so far as Aubrey was concerned, and
not merely the literary convention that it might have been to other
contemporary playwrights.

Gentlemen and ladies of the old school are contrasted with the bad-mannered, drunken, irresponsible louts whom Aubrey considered to mirror his neighbours. Sow-gelders, carters, dairymaids, and gypsies, by their speech and song, indicate in no uncertain terms that his criticism of the upper ranks of society was intended to imply no sentimental idealisation of the lower class. Squires who have left their wives and co-habit with scullery-maids stagger through the acts in the company of heiresses who have succumbed to the physical attraction of grooms. The plot has two threads: the first, the innocent loves of a boy and girl, living in disguise as shepherd and dairymaid; the second, the adventures of a married woman disguised as a page, pursued by her husband, and following her lover in a fruitless effort to prevent the latter from paying attentions to other women.

The scene as set out on the title-page is 'Alford in Cheshire, by the river Dee, St Peter's Day, 1669', but in Act I Aubrey feels himself unable to keep up the pretence, and places Scene I on 'Christian Malford Green', a village not far from Kington St Michael; while, over the names of a number of the *Dramatis Personae*, he has noted the names, or initials, of their prototypes among his acquaintances. These notes are, on the whole, the most interesting aspect of the *Country Revel*, because, although Aubrey was incapable of writing in a dull manner, he did not possess the ingenuity in literary mechanics necessary to galvanise into movement even so ramshackle a vehicle as the average play of his time. It is tempt-ing to speculate whether or not he might have achieved something in the form of a novel, along somewhat similar lines.

Some of the characters are: Sir Eglamore, Lady Euphrasia (wife of Sir Libidinous Gourmand), Sir Eubule Nestor, Squire Fitz-Ale, Sir Fastidious Overween, Captain Exceptious Quarrellsome, Sir Surly Chagrin, and Justice Wagstaffe. The last of these apparently represented Sir John Dunstable, of whom Aubrey writes elsewhere: 'Sir John Dunstable:—the cellar he calls his library.—Parliament men prepare themselves for the business of the nation with ale in the morning. Some justices doe sleepe on the bench every assize. At Chippenham the Deputye Lieutenants mett to see the order of the militia, but *quales D : Lieutenants tales officarii*. After a taedious setting (at dinner, and drinking after dinner) the drummes beat and the soldiers to march before the window to be seen by the Deputy Lieutenants. Justice Wagstaffe (Colonell) had not marcht before 'em many yardes but down a falls all along in the dirt. His myrmidons, *multâ vi*, heav'd him up and then cryd out " Some drinke, ho! " and so there was an end of that businesse.'

In the play, this country Justice also remarks: 'Your London Aldermen take great lechery to see poor wretches whipt at the court at Bridewell', and Aubrey comments, 'Old Justice Hooke gave [so much] per lash to wenches; as also my old friend George Pott, esq. *Vide* Animadversions Philosophicall on that ugly kind of pleasure and of cruelties—were it not for the law there were no living; some would take delight in killing of men', the last sentence echoing a saying of Hobbes recorded by Aubrey in the philosopher's biography.

Another figure, who was to be excoriated as Sir Fastidious Overween, was Gwyn, Lord Oxford's secretary, whose disagreeable demeanour is conveyed across the years as keenly by Aubrey's description as if we had encountered him only a few hours ago. 'Surlinesse and inurbanitie too common in England: chastise these very severly. A better instance of a squeamish and disobligeing, slighting, insolent, prowd fellow, perhaps cant be found than in Gwin, the earl of Oxford's secretary. No reason satisfies him, but he overweens and cuts some sower faces that would turne the milke in a faire ladie's breast.'

The other side of the picture was Sir Eubule Nestor, the old courtier, who was to be delineated from Thomas Tyndale (a friend and Wiltshire neighbour, mentioned earlier, who had been born in 1588, and was buried at Kington St Michael in 1671). Aubrey gives a sample of his conversation from which we can envisage the old gentleman's sterling qualities without experiencing at the same time any strong desire to have been part of the audience who heard his strictures on contemporary manners. 'He hath seen much in his time both at home and abroade,' says Aubrey, of Mr Tyndale, 'and with much choler inveighes against things new:—"Alas! O' God's will! Now-a-dayes everyone, forsooth! must have 8 coaches, forsooth! In those dayes Gentlemen kept horses for a man-at-armes, besides their hackney and hunting horses. This made the Gentry robust and hardy and fitt for service; were able to be their own guides in the case of a rout or so when occasion should be required. Our Gentry forsooth in these dayes are so effeminated that they know not how to ride on horseback—Tho when the Gentry mett it was not at a poor blind sordid alehouse, to drinke up a barrell of drinke and lie drunke there for two or three dayes together; fall together by the eares. They mett tho in the fields, well-appointed, with their hounds and their hawkes; kept up good hospitality; and kept a good retinue that would venture that bloud and spirit that filled their vaines which their master's tables nourisht; kept their tenants in due respect of them. We had no depopulacion in those dayse. You see in me the ruines of time. The day is almost at an end with me, and truly I am glad of it: I desire not to live in this corrupt age. I foresaw and foretold the late changes, and now easily foresee what will follow after. Alas! O' God's will! It was not so in Queen Elizabeth's time: then youth had respect to old age." '

This was, no doubt, all true enough; but it is hard to believe that Thomas Tyndale ever had his wish and, in fact, made an end of things, and passed on to the fields of asphodel, so persistently does the expression of his convictions continue to this very hour the familiar burden of the Mr Tyndales of all time.

In another note for the play, Sir Eglamore and Fitz-Ale 'discourse of the Gothique manner of living of then gentlemen, of their ignorance, and envy of civilised and ingeniose men; of the promising growth of civility and knowledge in the next generation (in our grandfather's or great Grandfather's dayes few gentlemen could write a letter: then "the clarke made the justice"); that there is a sort of provincial witt, *e.g.* in the west, which if used in the north, or elsewhere, seems strange and ridiculous.' The *Country Revel* is, in short, a useful corrective to the view that Aubrey's tolerance and good-nature made him uncritical of the things that were going on round him. He was, on the contrary, well aware that country life in the seventeenth century was not a romantic idyll; and that the goings-on of his neighbours often left much to be desired from many points of view.

XI

The *Miscellanies*, considered by John Britton to be Aubrey's 'most objectionable work', was the only book of his to be printed in his lifetime. Lord Oxford's chaplain,[1] as we have seen, considered it a 'mad book'. It is mentioned by Scott in *The Antiquary*, where Oldbuck, the antiquary, refers to 'the concise style of Old Aubrey' and quotes from the *Miscellanies* what is perhaps Aubrey's best-known anecdote. '*Anno*

---

[1] Dr Stratford (whose letter is quoted in the Introduction) referred to a passage in the chapter on Magic: '*To staunch Bleeding*: Cut an ash of one, two, or three years growth, at the very hour and minute of the Sun's entring Taurus: a chip of this applied will stop it: if it is a shoot, it must be cut from the ground. Mr Nicholas Mercator, astronomer, told me that he had tried it with effect. . . . When King James II was at Salisbury, 1688, his nose bled neer two days; and after many essays in vain, was stopped by this sympathetic ash.' Whether Dr. Stratford's 'elderstick' would have proved equally efficacious must remain a matter of opinion.

1670, not far from Cirencester, was an apparition: being demanded, whether a good spirit or bad? returned no answer, but disappeared with a curious perfume and most melodious twang. Mr W. Lilly believes it was a fairy.' This story was evidently familiar to Byron, who wrote in the *Vision of Judgment* that, when Southey began to read his MS., the devils, saints and angels vanished;

> . . . . *as they sprang,*
> *Like lightning, off from his 'melodious twang.'*

The *Miscellanies* are described as *A Collection of Hermetic Philosophy* and the subjects with which the book deals are: 'Day-fatality, Local Impulses, Knocking, Blows invisible, Prophesies, Marvels, Magick, Transportations in the Air, Visions in the Beril, or Glass, fatality, Ostenta (or portents), Omens, Dreams, Apparitions, Voices, Converse with Angels and Spirits, Corpse Candles in Wales, Oracles, Extasie, Glances of Love and Envy, Second Sighted Men in Scotland, and the Discovery of Two Murders by Apparition.' The volume first appeared in 1696, and was reprinted in 1721 and 1784, a fourth edition appearing in 1857. There are a number of entertaining anecdotes, such as: 'Arise Evans had a fungous nose, and said it was revealed to him that the King's hand would cure him, and at the first coming of King Charles II into St James's Park he kissed the King's hand and rubbed his nose with it, which disturbed the King, but cured him.' The usual scraps of autobiography also occur, together with a certain number of local and other traditions which are not without interest. The *Miscellanies* make a pleasant bedside book, which the passing of two hundred and fifty years has not made dull. They are also full of material of anthropological interest.

XII

'To his ever honoured Friend Edmund Wyld of Glasly Hall in the County of Salop, Esquier, these *Remaines of Gentilisme* are dedicated as a small Token of ancient Friendship by his affectionate & humble servant J. Aubrey.' The manuscript is marked 'London, St Bartholomew's Close, Octob. Novemb. Decemb. 1688'. It was written in collaboration with Dr White Kennett, Bishop of Peterborough (see p. 234), in three parts, the last of which was collected by Aubrey. *The Remaines of Gentilism and Judaism*, the book for which these notes were a draft, was intended to trace the customs and superstitions of seventeenth-century England from those of Classical and Biblical times. The result is an interesting hotch-potch in the Aubrey manner, which was, in part, reprinted more than once in the nineteenth century; and, eventually, *in toto* by the Folk-Lore Society in 1881, edited and annotated by James Britten (not to be confused with Aubrey's earlier biographer, John Britton), who remarks that not the least striking comment on the changing times in which Aubrey lived is the frequency with which the phrase 'before the Civil Wars' is used by the author, with the implication that the sayings or customs in question no longer existed.

The Remains of Gentilism, as a collection, is comparable with the *Miscellanies*, not only as a rich field for the student of folklore, but also as an admirable bedside book. Some of the following quotations give an indication of the material the volume contains. '*From my old cosen Ambrose Brown*:[1] Old Symon Brunsdon of Winterborne Basset, in Wilts: he had been parish clarke there *tpe. Mariae Reginae*. The Tutelar Saint of that Church is Saint Katherine; he lived doune till the begining of King James the first: When the Gad-flye had happened to sting his Oxen, or Cowes, he would run after them, crying out, Praying Good St Katherine of Winterborne stay my Oxen, &c. This old Brunsdon was wont in the summer-time to leave his Oxen in the field, and goe to the church to pray to Saint Katherine.'

Then there were the sin-eaters. 'In the County of Hereford was an old Custome at funeralls to hire poor people, who were to take upon them all the sinnes of the party deceased. One of them I remember lived in a cottage on Rosse-highway. (He was a long, leane, ugly, lamentable poor raskal.) The manner was that when the Corps was brought out of the house and layd on the Biere; a Loafe of bread was brought out, and delivered to the Sinne-eater over the corps, as also a mazar-bowle of maple (Gossips bowle) full of beer, which was to drinke up, and six-pence in money, in consideration whereof he took upon himself (*ipso facto*) all the Sinnes of the Defunct, and freed him (or her) from walking after they were dead. . . . This Custome (though rarely used in our dayes) yet by some people was observed even in the strictest time of the Presbyterian Government: as at Dynder, *volens nolens* the Parson of the Parish, the kindred of a woman deceased there had this ceremonie punctually performed according to her Will: and also the like was donne at the City of Hereford in these times, when a woman kept many yeares before her death a Mazard-bowle for the sinne-eater: and the

[1] Possibly Sir Ambrose Brown of Betchworth Castle, Dorking, d. *circa* 1661, or another of this family. (See p. 80.)

like in other places in this Countie; as also in Brecon *e.g.* Llangors, where Mr Gwin the minister about 1640 could not hinder the performing of this ancient custome. I believe this custome was heretofore used over all Wales.'

There was a story from Mr Wyld Clarke (perhaps a kinsman of Edmund Wyld, whose mother's name was Clarke). 'The Jewes have strange fancies concerning the Invisible beane *sc* Take the head of a man that dies of a natural death, and set it in the ground, and in his eie, set a Beane, cover it with earth, and enclose it about, that nobody make look into it, and without the enclosure set another Beane, or two; when those without the enclosure are ripe, that within will be ripe also; then take the Beane-stalke within the Inclosure, and take a Child, which hold fast by the hand, and the child must shell the Beanes; there will be but one invisible beane of them all, which when the child has, the other party cannot see her—*credat Judeus apella, non ego*—but this much I am morally certain of, that about 1680 two (or three) Jews, merchants, did desire Mr Wyld Clarke merchant of London, leave to make this following experiment in his garden at Mile-end; which he saw them doe, and who told me of it. As I remember, 'twas much after this manner. They took a Black Catt, and cutt off it's head, at a certain aspect of the Planets, and buryed it in his garden by night with some ceremonies, yet I have forgot, and put a Beane in the braine of the Catt; but about a day or two after, a Cock came and scratched it all up. Mr Clarke told me, that they did believe it, and yet they were crafty, subtile merchants.'

Among the changes after the Civil War: 'I have heard some of Ol. Cromwel's army say, that the Highlanders ate only oate-meale and water and milke: that their Rivers did abound with Trowtes but they had not the witt to take them till the English taught 'em.'

On the effects of music: 'At Leghorn, and other Ports in Italie, when shippes arrive, the Courtizans runne to the Mariners with Lutes and Ghitarres, playing and singing, with their haire dissheveld and Breasts naked, to allure them and gett fine things of them. In like manner at Gosprit, neer Portsmouth, where the Seamen lye, the towne is full of wanton wenches, and there is never a house but hath a virginall in it, and (they say) scarce three honest women in the Towne.'

And, perhaps most surprising of all: 'Periwigges were worne by Hannibal for a disguise—from Polybius.'

There are many other stories and traditions of this sort throughout the *Remains of Gentilism*, to which a number of Aubrey's acquaintances contributed their experiences.

The Aubreys, a family of Norman origin, believed themselves descended
Conqueror, whose descendants had come to Wales at the time of Bernard
pedigree is unreliable until the time of Hopkin Aubrey, of Abercynfrig, ir
Aubreys are described as constable or ranger of Brecknock Forest.

HOPKIN AUB
of Abercynfri
Brecon, who
in the latter
of the fifteen
century

THOMAS AUE
4th son

WILLIAM AU
2nd son: LL
Regius Profe
Oxon, etc., b
1529, d. 15

SIR EDWARD AUBREY, of Brecon=Joan Havard, d. of William Havard: and had issue 6 sons, the eldest of whom had issue 7 sons.	SIR THOMAS AUBREY, of Glamorgan = Mary Mansell, d. of Anthony Mansell of Llantrithyd, Glamorgan.	JOHN AUBREY, of Burlton, Hereford, b. c. 1578, d. 1616.	= (1) RACHE DANVERS, Richard D of Tockenl Wilts, d. *See* Chart

MARY SOUTH, d. and heir of Sir Richard South.	= SIR JOHN AUBREY, 1st Bt., b. c. 1606, d. 1679.	RICHARD AUBREY, = of Burlton, Hereford and Broad Chalke, Wilts, b. 1603, d. 1652.

LEWIS AUBREY, o.s.p.	SIR JOHN AUBREY, 2nd Bt., d. Sept. 1700. =(1) MARGARET LOWTHER, d. of 1st Lord Lonsdale. (2) MARY LEWIS, d. and heir of William Lewis, of Boarstall.	JOHN AUBREY, F.R.S., author of the *Lives*, etc.: of Easton Pierse, and Broad Chalke, Wilts, b. 1626, d. unmarried, 1697. W b. m

MARY AUBREY = WILLIAM MONT.
('My she-cosen   Lord Chief Baro
Montague'.)   the Exchequer.

nders de Sancto Alberico, or de Alba Ripa, a companion of William the
h, when the family had settled at Slwch and Abercynfrig as *Advenae*. The
who lived in the latter half of the fifteenth century. Several of the earlier

(1) WILGIFORD (2) = BROWNE, of
d. of John   Willey, Surrey,
Williams, of   whose estate there
Teynton, Oxon.   Aubrey saw in
             1673 when making
             his survey of
             Surrey.

JOHN WHITSON,   —ELIZABETH = THOMAS NORTON,
Alderman of   AUBREY   of Norwood, Kent
Bristol, b. 1557,   —MARY = WILLIAM HERBERT,
d. 1629, Aubrey's   AUBREY   of Crickhowell,
godfather.   Brecon.
          —JOAN = SIR DANIEL DUN, LL.D.   and
           AUBREY   had
         —WILGIFORD = RISE KEMIS, of   issue.
           AUBREY   Llanvery, Mon-
                     mouth.
         —LUCY AUBREY = HUGH POWELL.
        —ANNE AUBREY = JOHN PARTRIDGE
                     of Wishanger, Glos.

H LYTE,
eir of Isaac
Easton
Lington St.
Wilts.
t II.

UBREY,   THOMAS AUBREY,   —ANNE, b. 1628.   died in
un-   b. 1645, d. un-   —ISAAC, b. 1630.   infancy.
07.   married, 1681.   —ISAAC, b. 1631.

IZABETH AUBREY = RALPH FREEMAN, M.P.
osen Freeman'   of Aspeden Hall, Herts, 'a virtuous and hospitable
                 gentleman' (Aubrey)

This chart is intended to show only certain persons related to Aubrey, and

SIR JOHN DANVERS,=ANNE STRADLING,
of Dauntsey, | d. of John
Wilts, b. *c.* 1455, | Stradling, d.
d. 1514. | *c.* 1539.

THOMAS DANVERS, d. 1532.	=MARGARET COURTENAY, d. of Sir William Courtenay.	JOHN DANVERS, of Tockenham	= MARGARET of Mangotsf Glos. Aubre a right to q the arms of family.
SILVESTER DANVERS, b. 1518, d. 1555.	=ELIZABETH MORDAUNT, d. of Lord Mordaunt.	RICHARD DANVERS, of Tockenham.	=MARIA.
SIR JOHN DANVERS, b. 1540, d. 1594.	=ELIZABETH NEVILL, d. of John, Lord Latimer. 'Prodigious parts for a woman . . . a great politician' (Aubrey).	RACHEL DANVERS	=JOHN AU of Burlet Hereford. Chart I, b d. 1616

SIR CHARLES DANVERS, beheaded for complicity in Essex's Rising, 1600: involved, with his brother Henry, in the killing of Henry Long in 1594, and consequent feud with the Long family of Wilts.	SIR HENRY DANVERS, Earl of Danby, K.G., 'Page to Sir Philip Sydney' (Aubrey).	MAGDALEN HERBERT, (1) d. of Sir Robert Newport, a widow 'Old enough to have been his mother' (Aubrey), and mother of Lord Herbert of Cherbery and George Herbert, the poet.	=SIR JOHN D of Chelsea, West Lavin 'The Regici d. 1655.
ELIZABETH DANVERS, 'My Cosen Elizabeth Villiers, Viscountess Purbec'.	= ROBERT WRIGHT, or VILLIERS, who took the name of Danvers, and styled himself Viscount Purbeck.	ANNE DANVERS, m. 1655, d. 1659.	= SIR HENRY I of Ditchley, C 'Descended fr keeper's son one eie' (Aub

ELEANOR LEE, =JAM
d. 1691. of
pat

...ed by him, or of general interest. It is not in any sense a complete pedigree.

JOAN GALE, of = RICHARD LYTE,
Sutton Benger.   'of the Ancient Family
of Lyte of Lytescary in
Somerset', possibly s. of John
Lyte and Joan Ilberd
(Som. Arch. Soc. 1892 and 1931).

ELEANOR TAYLOR = THOMAS LYTE
d. of John Taylor, of   of Easton Pierse,
Kington Priory,   Kington St.
Wilts, m. 1568,   Michael, Wilts,
1568, d. 1582.   b. 1531, d. 1627.

MARGARET DANVERS=ANTHONY BROWN, ISRAEL BROWNE, =ISAAC LYTE, b. 1577,
   of Broad Chalke.   of Winter-   d. 1660. 'my old
   'My Uncle   bourne Bassett,   grandfather Lyte', who
   Anthony Browne',   b. 1578,   wore a dagger, and had
   who had stories of   d. 1662.   known the Raleighs.
   the early days of
   the Pembrokes at
   Wilton.

=(2) ELIZABETH DAUNTSEY, DOROTHY DANVERS RICHARD AUBREY = DEBORAH LYTE,
d. of Ambrose Dauntsey, =SIR PETER OSBORN,   *See* Chart I.   b. 1610, m. 1625,
by Gertrude, d. of Henry of Chicksands.   d. 1686.
Sadler, and Relict of
Henry Brouncker.

DOROTHY OSBORN, = SIR WILLIAM   JOHN AUBREY, F.R.S.
the letter writer.   TEMPLE.   b. 1626, d. 1697.

...E, 1st Earl
..., Aubrey's
...699.

APPENDIX B

Aubrey's Library

This catalogue of the books given by Aubrey to the Ashmolean was compiled by the late Dr R. T. Gunther. Only footnotes have been added.

It is likely that John Aubrey would have desired that in any account of his printed books given to the Ashmolean Museum, early mention should be made of the 'Arithmetical warlike treatise' of 1590 (Ash. 1553), in which he wrote 'Jo. Aubrey R.S.S. This was one of my honoured Grandfather Mr. Isaac Lyte's bookes.' It is signed 'ex libris Isaaci Lyti', and at the end is a manuscript page of Dr. Pell's solution to Digges's questions. We have not noted any other family books except the much later J. Vaillant's 'Numismata', 1694 (D.9), inscribed 'Bibl. Ashmol. dedit v. ornatissimus Dom. Joannes Aubrey de Lan Trydhyd in Glamorgania, Bar^{tus}'.

Unfortunately, less than one half of his books bear the date at which he acquired them; but as he seems to have varied the character of his signature and description at different periods, a clue to the period is sometimes possible. For instance, the signature 'Jo. Aubrey R.S.S.' and the like must be more recent than his admission into the Royal Society in May 1663, and similarly the forms 'Sum Johis Aubrey de Easton-Piers 1656' (H.4), 'Jo. Aubrey de Easton Piers 1658' (G.6), and 'Jo: Aubrey de Easton-Pierse R.S.S. 1666' (G.19), in books which contain his book-plate, while others do not, show a distinct method in his procedure, as do also the references to the Middle Temple 'Sum Joannis Aubrij et Societat. Medij Templi 1654' (Ash. 1554) and the variants in C.27 and D.65.

The earliest date, 1647, occurs in F. Beaumont's Poems, 1640 (Ash. 1663), and in a small volume of poems by Corbet (E.15), 'Liber Johannis Aubrij Coll. Trin. Oxon. 1647', when Aubrey was 21 years of age, which he afterwards inscribed 'For the Musaeum'. An unusual collection of well-thumbed school-books might reasonably be referred to an earlier period, and so we may begin our compilation of his library-list with them—ranging them in the order of their publication dates.

1560.   Cicero. Epistolae ad Atticum (A.50).
           Earlier owner 'Edw. Fytton'.

1578.   Cicero. Epistolae familiares (A.49).
           Earlier owners 'Nicholas Stanninger', 'Hen: Anderson',
           'Barbeau'.

1583.   Hierocles. Comm. in Pythagoreorum carmina. (A.9). ⎫ 'Sum
                                                             ⎬ J.A.pd.
1585.   Marcilius. Aurea Pythagoreorum carmina.   ⎭ 1ˢ 9ᵈ.'

1604.   Homer. Ileas, &c. (A.20).

1619.   Scapula, J. Lexicon Graeco-Lat. novum (G.22).
           'Bibl. Ash. dedit v.c. J.A., R.S.S.'

1632.   Virgilius. Opera (A.35).

1636.   Palissy, B. Moyen de devenir riche (D.63).

1639.   Dugres, G. Dialogi Gallico-Anglico-Latini (C.14).

1649.   Lovelace, R. Lucasta (B.14).

1652.   The School's Probation (A.29).
           'Given to me by the Rt. Hon. the Lady Gerard of Bromley.'

1655-7.   Alvarus, E. Grammatica Latina (B.13).
           'Dr. J. Pell sayes positively that double translation is the
           best and shortest way of being mastre of a language qd N.B.'

1658.   Osborn, F. Advice to a son (1309).
           'Sum J.A. 1658. Oxon xiid.'

1665.   Comenius. Janua linguarum (Index) (B.2).

1668.   La logique ou l'Art de penser (A.28).

1669.   M(ilton), J. Accedence commenc't grammar (A.4).

1669.   Rich, J. The pen's dexterity compleated: or Mr. Riches
           short-hand (A.27).

1674.   French Grammar by the Academy (A.36).

1676.   Walker, W. Art of teaching (B.4).

1687.   Goad. Rode for the Latin scholar (B.16).
           'Ex dono autoris.'

Our enumeration has now wandered far past the requirements of a
boy *in statu pupillari*, but it explains incidentally how the books of his
boyhood have come to be preserved in a great scientific library, as it
was piously hoped the Ashmolean Museum might come to possess.
Aubrey retained a great interest in educational methods, and in 1692 was
in close correspondence with John Ray, the great naturalist, about his
Idea of the Education of Young Gentlemen, a manuscript idea that never got
into type (MS. Aubrey 13, f. 180). In the case of his death Aubrey

even desired Ray to leave it with Dr Hooke at Gresham College to be put 'into my Chest which is marked "Idea" wch is full of Books for this Designe'.

If we now attempt to make a survey of his dated volumes on stricter chronological lines, we find that as a rule he was not in the habit of dating books except in the case of presentation copies. These usually arrived when the books were still new, and their inscriptions record the extent of Aubrey's literary circle. The arrangement is now in order of the accession-dates as written in the volumes.

1647.	Beaumont F. Poems, 1640 (1663).
1647.	Corbet, R. Certain elegant poems, 1647 (E.15).
	'Liber Johannis Aubrij. Coll. Trin. Oxon. 1647. For the Musaeum.'
1650.	Bacon, F. De ventis, 1648 (A.42).
	'J. Aubrey 1650. Mus. Ash. dedit v.c. Jo. Aubrey Arm. R.S.S.'
1651.	Dürer, A. De urbibus, Paris, 1535 (F.8).
	'Liber Johannes Aubrij 1651.'
1651.	Bacon, F. Remaines, 1648 (Ash.1621).
	'Sum Jo. Aubrij 1651.'
1654.	Selden, J. Jani Anglorum facies altera, 1610 (1555).
	'Sum Joannis Aubrij et Societat. Medij Templi p^{rt} iii. 1654 Dec. 11.'
1655.	Virgil's Georgics. Englished by T. May, 1628 (1561).
1655.	Hobbes. T. Elementorum philosophia, 1655 (C.27).
	'J. Aubrey med. Templi 1655 for the Musaeum.'
1655.	(Ward. Seth). Vindiciae Academiarum, 1654 (Ash. 1621).
1656.	Davidson, W. Philosophia pyrotechnica, 1641 (1551).
	'Pt. 4^{s}6^{d}.' With a note on the author: 'This booke sc. his Cursus Chymiatricus was recommend to me by Mr Robert Boyle, as the best then extant: but he advised me not to read the Philosophia Pyrotechnica. Mr Tho. Hobbes Malmesburiensis told me that he knew him very well at Paris, and that he went through a Course of Chymistrie with him. His Laboratorie was at ye upper end of the King of France's Physick-Garden. About 1660 he left France, and went into Poland to gett acquaintance with the Brothers of the Rosie-cross: where he ended his daies.'
1656.	Laurus, J. Antiquae urbis (Romae) splendour, 1612 (H.4).
	'Sum Johis Aubrey de Easton Piers 1656.' [Book-plate.]

1658.   Osborn, F. Advice to a son, 1658 (1309).
        'Oxon xii d.'

1658.   Willis, T. De fermentatione, 1659 (D.65).
        'John Aubrey 1658 é Societ. Medij. Templi pt. 3ˢ6ᵈ.'

1658.   Harrington, J. Oceana, 1658 (G.6). See above.
        'Sum Jo: Aubrij. 1658'. [Book-plate.]

1662.   Digby, Sir K. Vegetation, 1661 (1590).
        'J.A. 1662 Oxon. Julij.'

1662.   The legend of Capt. Jones, 1659 (C.21).

1662.   Charlton, W.¹ Consilium hygiasticum, 1661 (E.39).
        'Sum J. Aubrey 10ᵇᵉʳ 1662 donum authoris.'

(1663.) Miscellanea variegata, 1663 (1559).
        'Donum autoris Mri John White de Chert in agro Wilton.
        J. A.'

1666.   Mersenne, P. Optique, 1651 (G.19).
        Nicéron, P. Perspective curieuse, 1652.
        'J. A. de Eston Piers R.S.S. 1666.' [Book-plate.]

1668.   Mercator, N. Logarithmo-technia, 1668 (1661).

1669.   The Children's petition, 1669 (A.3).

1670.   S., R. F. 16 revelations, 1670 (1598).
        'D. Guliel. Rozen Hosp. Linc. Arm. Jo. Aubrio 1670.

1673.   Marvel, A. The Rehearsall transpos'd. Pt.2, 1673 (1585).
        'Liber Xrisforus Iles.' 'Sum Johis Aubrij R.S.S.'

1677.   Bonnettus, T. Medicinal councils, 1677 (1632).
        'J. A. dedit Tho. Shirley M.D.'

1679/80. H(obbes), T. Behemoth, 1680 (1587).

1680.   La logigue ou l'Art de penser, 1668 (A.28)
        'J.A. R.S.S. 3ˢ.' See above.

1681.   Grevil, F. Life of Sir P. Sidney, 1652 (1565).
(Jan.)

1681/2. Wither, G. Fragmenta prophetica, 1669 (1584).

1682.   Milton, J. Pro populo Anglicano, 1652 (1589).
        '2s. Octob. 3. Oxon. 1682.'

1682.   Collins, J.ª Salt of fishing, 1682 (1629).
        'J.A. dedit author.'

1682.   Collins, J. Salt of fishing, 1682 (1635).
        'Sum J.A. ex dono author.'

---

¹ Dr Walter Charleton, physician to King Charles II.
  'a learned mathematician, fellow of the Royal Society'. (MS. Aubr.
6, f. 2.)

1682.   Petty, W. Growth of City of London, 1683, with 7 other
           tracts (1632).
           'J.A. donum (authoris).'

1682.   Philipps, F. Reforming registry, 1671 (1635).
           'J.A. R.S.S. donum authoris June 1682.'
           'This book did cost the author *li* 100 and he never gott a
           penny by it, he told me. Mr F. P. payd 11ˢ ye sheet for
           printing his booke a M copies.'

1684/5.   Burnet, T. Theory of the earth, 1684 (G.26).
           'Sum Johis Aubrij.'

1686.   Gadbury, J.¹ Festum festorum, 1686 (1556).
           'Dedit author.'

1686.   16 Tracts including Sir E. Forde's Experimented Proposals,
           1666 and Ephemeris ad ann. 1686 (1639).
           'Jo. Aubrey R.S.S. ex dono Edm. Halley.'

1686.   Philipps, F. Pourveyance for the King, 1663 (1660).
           'Sum Johis Aubrij R.S.S. ex dono Fabiani Philips May 4,
           1686.'
           'This booke did cost my honᵈ friend yᵉ author, sixscore
           pounds the printing: yᵉ K. never gave him anything but good
           words.'

1687-8.   Bidelli, J. Vita, 1682 (1563).
           'Liber Jo. Aubrey ex dono Iohn Farington J.C. Templi
           interioris amici autoris Datum 1687/8.'

1688.   Leycester's commonwealth, 1641 (1557).
           'Sum Jo. Aubrij Com. Leic. 6 Sept. 1688.'

1688.   L., G. Observations on the life of R. Polus, 1686 (1586).
           'Liber Jo. Aubrij R.S.S. ex dono Gulielmi Joyner (alias
           Lyde) A. M. Autoris, collegii St. Mariae Magdalenae
           Oxon: Soc: 1688.'

1690.   Newton, I. Principia, 1687 (F.21).
           'Sum Johis Aubrij ex dono Honoratissimi Thomae Comitis
           Pembrochiae et Montgom: April 22, 1690.'

1692.   Merlini liberator, 1692 (E.39).
           'E dono Johis Aubrey—Jo. Gadbury astronomus.'

1692-3.   49 tracts bound in three volumes (1064-6).
           'Musaeo Ashmoleano dedit v.c. Johannes Aubrey 1692/3.'

1693.   Beaumont, J. on Burnet's Theory of the earth, 1693 (E.2).
           'Sum Jo. Aubrey ex dono autoris.'

                    ¹ John Gadbury, the astrologer.

1693. Cardanus, H. Somniorum synesiorum libri IV, 1562 (D.56).
'Sum Joh. Aubrey ex dono rev. et mihi amicissimi Will.
Holder D.D., R.S.S. Aug. 1693.'

1694. (Book of remedies for sickness etc., n.d.) (1331).
'This book was given to me John Aubrey R.S.S. by my old
friend Absolom Leech of Kingston sup Thames in 1694.'

1696. Aubrey's Miscellanies (E.11).
'Liber Mus. Ash. ex dono clar. authoris superstitiosi.'

1696. Wase, Chr. Senarius, 1687 (E.4).
'Sum Jo. Aubrij R.S.S. 1696 Oct. 6. This booke was given
to me by Mr Chr. Wase C.C.C. Soc. son of Chr. the author
of this book, who was of my oldest acquaintance, and my
singular friend.'

Law Books

Donellus, H. Comm ad tit. Inst. de actionibus, 1630 (B.33).
  'Sum Jo Aubrij R.S.S.'

Malynes, G. Lex mercatoria, 1636 (H.3).
  'Jo. Aubrey M. Templi Soc. pret 5ˢ the 4 day of October 1671
Katherine Hancox her booke, cost 1ˢ4ᵈ'

Books specially presented to the Ashmolean Museum

The following are inscribed 'Mus. Ash. dedit clariss. v. Johannis
Aubrey Arm.' or with words to that effect.

Digby, E.[1] De duplici methodo, n.d. (1596).

Smyth, T. Syntagma de Druidum moribus, 1664 (1572).

Scapula, J. Lexicon Graeco-Lat. novum, 1619 (G.22).

Augustinus, L. Gemmae et sculpturae, 1685 (1659).

Barba, A. A. Art of medals, 1674 (D.25).
  'pd. ijˢ'

Vaillant, J. Numismata, 1694 (D.9).

Livy. Historiarum tomi II & III, 1678 (D.23–4).

Valuation of eccles. preferments, 1680 (C.22).

Brown, T. Certain miscellaneous tracts, 1684 (C.23).

[1] 'Sir Everard Digby was a most gallant gentleman and one of the
handsomest men of his time. He writ something in Latin *de Methodo*,
which I did light upon 23 years ago at a country man's howse in Herefordshire'—Aubrey to Wood: 6 July, 1672. (MS. Wood F.39, f. 178.)

Donors &c. of books

Donor

Bagshaw, M.: Life of V. Powell, 1671 (1571).
  'Margaret Bagshaw vidua Th.[1] B.'

Bagshaw, Ed.: Diss. anti-Socinianae, 1657 (B.16a). With six others
  dated 1679–98.
  'Jo. Aubrey dedit author.'

Beaumont, J.: Venette, N. Of pruning fruit trees, 1685 (C.31).
  'This book was given me by my worthy friend Mr John Beaumont,
  who translated it into English.'

Chapman, Laurence: Ptolomaeus, Geographie opus, n.d. (H.34).
  'Sould to Mr John Aubrey this book for 5.[s] This book perfect
  Laurence Chapman. With note addressed to Edw. Floyd.' (G)

Garden, J.: Wallace, J. Isles of Orkney, 1693 (C.63).
  'ex dono Rev. Jacobi Garden Theol. Prof. in Univ. Aberdoniae.'

Gibbon, J.: Day-Fatality, n.d. (1672).

Iles: Rehearsal transposed, 1672 (1591).
  'Liber Xhristoforus Iles.'

More, J.: Benese, R. Measuring land, n.d. (1638).
  'John More.'

Lloyd, M.: Regius, H. Philosophia naturalis, 1654 (F.22).
  'The gift of my worthy friend Mr Meredith Lloyd.'

Malpighi, M.: His 'De structura glandularum epist.', 1689 (1692).
  'Jo: Aubrey ex dono autoris.'

Pocock, Edw.: Philosophus autodidactus, 1671 (1634).
  'Sum Jo. Aubrey R.S.S. ex dono Honoratiss. Thomae Comitis
  Pembrokiae etc. Presented to his lordship by the translator Dr.
  Edw. Pocock.'

Ray, J.: Pliny, Historie of the world, 1601 (G.17).
  'For Mr. John Ray Botanist at his house at Black Notley near
  Brayntry in Essex. He was born in the house where he lives . . .
  from Bullock Esq: went to school at Brayntry.'

Sherburne, E.: Blondel, M. Pindar and Horace, 1696 (D.58).
  'Ex dono Edwardi Sherburne militis.'

Shirley, T.: Mayerne, T. Medicinal councels, 1677 (1632).
  'Jo. Aubrey Dedit Thos. Shirley M.D.'

---

[1] This is presumably a slip for E[dward] B[agshaw], a friend of
Aubrey's imprisoned at the same period as Vavasor Powell.

Donor

Whitney, J.: Munster, S. Rudimenta mathematica, 1551 (F.7).
    'Given him by Mr James Whitney B.D.[1] and parson of Dunted St.'

Miscellaneous works bearing Aubrey's autograph

Erasmus. Fam. colloquia, 1673 (690). '9^d'

Lemnius, L. De habitu et constit. corporis, 1596 (1373).

Jones, T. Heart and its soveraign, 1678 (1554). 'pt. 2:6.'

Memoirs of dutchess Mazerine, 1676 (1558).

Denham, J. Cato major of old age, 1669 (1560).

Edlyn, R. Observationes astrol., 1659 (1564).

Wase, C. Grati Falisci Cynegeticon, 1654 (1567). With MS. note on
    Capt. Hamden.

M., G. Yorkshire ale, 1685 (1573). 'pt. 10^d'

18 Pamphlets, 1597–1684, bound in one vol. (1621).

Epistolae fratris R. Baconis, 1618 (1600).

D., T. John Winscomb, 1672 (1631). Probably one of Aubrey's books.

Hobbes, T. Hist. ecclesiastica, 1688 (1637).

20 Pamphlets with 4 pp. of MS. notes at end (1672).

Plot, R. Natural History of Oxfordshire (1722). See B.Q.R., vol. vi, p. 165.

Invasion and conquest of Florida, 1686 (C.12).

Account of Dr Bentley's humanity, 1699 (C.11). With E. Lhwyd's
    notes at end.

9 Pamphlets, 1657–95, presumably Aubrey's (C.67).

Pliny. Naturalis historiae tomi tres, 1668–9 (C.19–21).
    With Aubrey's book-plate and MS. notes.

Lister, M. De fontibus medic. Angliae, 1684 (D.45).

The Eternal gospel vindicated, 1681 (D.46).

Gadbury's Almanack, 1696 (D.60). With 4 other pieces: the volume
    originally contained 7.

Palissy, B. Moyen de devenir riche, 1636 (D.63).

Charleton, W. Two discourses; 1, concerning the different wits of
    men; 2, the mysterie of vinters (D.64). 'pt .1^s'

Graunt, J.[2] Observations on the bills of mortality, 1662 (F.23).

---

[1] 'My old cosen, parson Whitney', who had been at Oxford with
Raleigh's son, Walter.

[2] 'He wrote *Observations on the bills of Mortality* very ingeniosely (but I
beleeve, and partly know, that he had his hint from his intimate and
familiar friend Sir William Petty) . . . He was my honoured and
worthy friend.' (MS. Aubr. 6, f. 97, and MS. Wood F. 39, f. 270.)

Sir F. Drake's W. Indian voyage, 1652. Sir F. D. revived, 1653,
World encompassed by Drake, 1652 (F.24).
Cosin, R. Ecclesiae Anglicanae politeia, 1684 (G.29).

And to these should be added the five volumes of Aubrey's History
of Surrey (E.33–37) which were placed next to Ashmole's Berkshire
(E.29–32) and were inscribed 'Ashmole's Study'.[1]

This terminates Dr Gunther's list of Aubrey's books at the Bodleian.
Among volumes that seem to have disappeared may be noted Holyoake's
Dictionary. 'I gave my Holyoke's dictionary to the Museum. Pray looke
on the blank leaves at the end of it, and you will find a thundering copy
of Verses that he [Henry Birkhead] gave me in praise of this king of
France. Now he is dead, it may be look't-upon.' (MS. Tan. 24, f. 159.
21 Nov. 1696.)

Aubrey's much annotated copy of Robert Plot's *Natural History of
Oxfordshire*, 1677, is now MS. Ash. 1722. It turns out that a proportion
of the library was deposited in another place, in fact at Worcester
College.

On November 27, 1675, Aubrey wrote to Wood: 'As you were
saying, if I could be Principall of Gloucester hall that were a fine way
of ending my dayes in peace and ingeniose innocency. I would undertake to make it an ingeniose Nest and would decoy thither several
honest and ingeniose persons of either University and some from
Beyond the Sea'. It was probably with this design in mind that Aubrey
presented a number of books to Gloucester Hall (now Worcester
College); though, perhaps not surprisingly, this patronage did not have
the required effect of Aubrey's appointment as Head of that House.
Worcester College kindly allowed the following list of these books to be
made; and I am grateful to the late Colonel C. H. Wilkinson, Dean and
Librarian, for showing them to me. More may, in due course, be traced,
because, although Aubrey did not always inscribe his name, he often
made notes, did sums, or merely left his own characteristic blots, on
margins or end-papers. This catalogue which appeared in the *Times
Literary Supplement* 13 and 20 January, 1950 supplements that made by
Dr Gunther. The Worcester College collection adds about forty volumes,
mostly dealing with mathematical subjects. One book belonged to Ben
Jonson; another was presented to Aubrey by Thomas Hobbes. They are
here arranged in order of publication dates.

1515.   Almagestu Ptolemei. 'Jo: Aubrey, R.S.S.' (E.V.1.)

1641.   Mydorgius, Claudius. Prodromi catoptricorum et dioptri-
          corum sive conicorum . . . libri quatuor priores. 'Jo: Aubrey.
          1659' Inscribed in Aubrey's hand '12s,' presumably the price.
          (I.7.7.)

1544.   Stifelius, Michael. Arithmetica Integra. Inscribed 'Thomas
          Allen.' Aubrey wrote: 'I have Stifelius' Arithmetique that
          was his [Thomas Allen's] which I find he had much perused,
          and no doubt Mastered.' (MS. Aubr. 6, f. 95v.) (QQ.S.14.)

1557.   [Record, Robert.] The Whetstone of Witte. 'Jo: Aubrey,
          R.S.S.' Aubrey wrote: 'The Whetstone of Witte, which is
          the second part of Arithmetick, containing to extraction of
          rootes, etc.' (MS. Aubr. 8, f. 71v.) See Records of Arith-
          meticke at Castle of Knowledge below. (E.2.4.)

1558.   Dee, John. Brevis et Perspicua Ratio Indicandi Genituras,
          etc. 'Ex Dono humanissimi mei Amici Tho. Fludd, Cantiam.
          Armig.' Aubrey wrote: 'My honoured and learned friend
          Thomas Fludd, esq., a Kentish gentleman (aged 75, 1680)
          was a neighbour and acquaintance to Sir Robert Filmore, in
          Kent, who was very intimately acquainted with Mr.
          Camden . . .' (MS. Aubr. 6, f. 119) (E.2.6.) Fludd had also
          known William Oughtred, the mathematician. (MS. Aubr.
          8, f. 8.)

1569.   Peel, James. The Pathewaye to Perfectnes in th'Accomptes
          of Debitour, and Creditour. 'Jo: Aubrey, R.S.S. Apr. 1682.
          pd. 5s. od.' Aubrey adds: 'Here is wanting the Errata, which
          vide at the last leafe of Mr. Sadler's [? 'Cowper' written
          above 'Sadler'] in Little Britaine.' Aubrey wrote of Peel:
          'He is drawne before his booke in his gowne and a cap
          (scilicet, like the cappes the undergraduates weare), short
          haire and long beard.' (MS. Aubr. 8. f. 72.) (GG.3.4.)

1570.   Dee, John. De Superficierum Divisionibus Liber Machometo
          Bagdedino. 'Sū Jo: Aubrij de Easton Piers.' Bought by Aubrey
          during his French tour, marked 'Parisys 1664.' (E.V.4.)

1573.   Leouitius, Cyprianus. De Coniunctionibus Magnis In-
          signioribus Superiorum Planetarum, etc. 'Jo: Aubrey, R.
          Societ. Soc. pd. 1s. 6d.' (Bound in with other works of which
          Conciliorum Synopsis, 1651, is inscribed, 'John Prideaux
          Episcopi Vigorniensis': The Divine Warrant of Infant
          Baptism, by John Church, 1652, inscribed: 'R. Bouchier':

also Jehovah Praeside, &c., by Franciscus Constantius Pielat, 1694; and Oxonium Poema, 1667.) (CC.8.29.) The latinized form of the name of the author of the first of these slightly suggests Cyprian Lucar, the mechanician; but the latter does not appear to have published anything at that date. John Prideaux, Bishop of Worcester (1578–1650), when deprived of his epis-copal estates had to sell his library to provide for his family.

1583.   Urbinatus, Federicus Commandinus. Heronis Alexandrini Spiritalium Liber. 'Jo: Aubrey. Empt. Parisys. Sept. 1664': Aubrey's bookplate. (E.V.2.)

1591.   Digges, Thomas. A Geometrical, Practical Treatize Named Pantometria. Inscribed on title-page: [above] 'Tanqũ Explor-ator' [below] 'Sũ Ben: Jonsonij liber ex dono Dud: Digges Authoris filii.' (II.11.2.) Some arithmetical calculations on the fly-leaf are in Aubrey's writing. 'Elements of Geometrie, 1571,' also by Thomas Digges, although without Aubrey's auto-graph, was probably his gift. Aubrey wrote: '*Pantometria*, containing longimetria, planimetria, stereometria—was writ by Leonard Digges, esq., but published by his sonne Thomas Digges esqr. and dedicated to Sir Nicholas Bacon, knight, Lord Keeper, lately reviewed and augmented by the author, printed at London, 1591.' (MS. Aubr. 8. f. 75.)

1596.   [Record, Robert] Castle of Knowledge. Inscribed: 'Johannes FFisher. pres, 2s 4d' 'Jo. Aubrey R.S.S. prs 1s 0d': marked in Aubrey's writing. 'For Gloucester Hall.' Aubrey wrote: 'The Castle of Knowledge, printed at London, 1596, quarto, and is dedicated etc.' (MS. Aubr. 8. f. 7.) See Records of Arithmeticke below. (II.t.3.)

1609.   Origanoglacensis, Davidis. Motuum Cœlestium Ephemerides. 'Sum Johis Aubrij R.S.S. 1670': also 'Jo Aubrey de Eston Pierse Wiltes 1670 R.S.S.' (E.II.2.)

1611.   Hopton, John. The Topographicall Glasse. Arithmetical calculations in Aubrey's hand on end-papers. (II.11.6.)

1612.   Pitiscus, Bartholomaeus. Trigonometriae. 'Sum Johannis Aubrij de Easton-Piers. This was old Mr. Oughtred's booke and the notes are of his owne handwriting.' Aubrey wrote: 'I myselfe have his [William Oughtred's] Pitiscus, embellished with his excellent marginall notes, which I esteeme a great rarity' (MS. Aubr. 6. f. 43.) (E.Z.1.)

1615.   Record, Robert. Records of Arithmeticke. 'Jo Awbrey Trin:

Coll: Oxon.' Aubrey wrote: 'Robert Record, M.D. . . was the first that wrote a good arithmetical treatise in English, which hath been printed a great many times' (M.S. Aubr. 8. f. 71v). See Whetstone of Witte and Castle of Knowledge above. (E.X.5.)

1618   The Surveiors Dialogue. 'Sum Johannis Aubrey R.S.S. 1670.' (E.Z.5.)

1624.   Michaelis. M. Epitome Astronomiae. 'Jo: Aubrey Coll: Trin: Oxon 1648' (E.X.9.)

1628.   Tables of Leasses and Interest. 'Jo: Aubrey R.S.' (E.X.7.)

1631.   Gunter, Edmond. The Description and Use of the Sector-Cross-Staffe. Aubrey wrote: 'Mr. Edmund Gunter . . . His booke of the quadrant, sector, and crossestaffe did open men's understandings and made young men in love with that study.' (MS. Aubr. 8. f. 78v.) Calculations in Aubrey's hand at end. (II.t.5.)

1635.   Gellibrand, Henry. An Institution Trigonometricall. Aubrey wrote: 'Henry Gellibrand . . . He was Astronomy Professor in Colegio Greshamensi, Lond. Scripsit Trigonometriam.' (MS. Aubr. 6. f. 49.) Traces of Aubrey's writing visible. (II.t.9.)

1635.   Gibson, Thomas. Syntaxis Mathematica. Price of book just visible in Aubrey's writing. (II.W.9.)

1638.   De Pisis, H. Opus Geomantiae Completum. 'John Awbrey R.S.S. May 31 1671 London 2s 6d.' On the end-paper, in Aubrey's hand: 'John ye Sonne of Mr Th: Tyndale and Orian (twinnes) were baptised at Kington St Michael ye (?) of Novemb. 1629. Alexandr. son of H. Sydenh (?) bur. ye 12th Jan 1630.' Thomas Tyndale was a Wiltshire neighbour of Aubrey's, regarded by him as a typical gentleman of the old school. The second surname is perhaps an abbreviation of 'Sydenham,' a local family. Another note, almost illegible, refers to 'Corn: Agrippa,' 'Mr. Saunders' and 'DesCartes.' (Q.Q.9.14.)

1640.   Blaev, Guilielmus. Institutio Astronomica. 'Jo: Aubrey, Coll: Trin: Oxon:' and 'Jo: Awbrey 1647.' (E.X.2.)

1643.   Cardanus, Hieronymus. De Propria Vita Liber. 'Jo: Aubrey R.S.S. 1674. pt. 1s 6d.' (E.2.7.)

1644.   Argolus, Andrea. Tabulae Primi Mobilis. 2 vols. 'Sum Johis Aubrij R.S.S. 1s 4d.' (E.V.6–7.)

1651.   Kauffman, Nicolaus. Cosmographia Sive Descriptio Coeli et
          Terrae In Circulos. 'Jo: Aubrey R.S.S. Ex dono Authoris'.
          On p. 1, Aubrey notes ' . . alternation of the plane of the
          Ecliptick, Mr R. Hooke.' and on p. 7, 'from here to the end
          neglect.' Aubrey wrote: 'Mr Nicholas Mercator . . . The
          first booke he printed was his Cosmographia, where he uses
          his German name.' (MS. Aubr. 8. f. 59.) (GG.n.1.)

1651.   Thaumaturgus Mathematicus. 'Liber Johannis Aubrey
          1652 pt 2s 3d.' (E.X.3.)

1656.   Norwood, Richard. Trigonometrie: or the Doctrine of
          Triangles. 'Sum Johis Aubry de Easton-Piers 1664.' Aubrey
          wrote of this book: 'My edition is the third, 1656; and there
          hath been one since.' (MS. Aubr. 8. f. 79v.) (E.Z.3.)

1659.   Argoli, Andrea. Ptolemaeus Parvus In Genethliacis Iunctus
          Arabibus, former owner, 'G. Parm'. 'Jo: Aubrey R.S.S.
          1680 4s od.' (HH.11.3.)

1660.   Hobbes, Thomas. Examinatio & Emendatio Mathematicae
          Hodiernae. 'For my noble friend Mr Aubrie From his servant
          Tho: Hobbes.' (E.V.3.)

1661.   Streete, Thomas. A New Theorie of the Coelestial Motions
          'J. A. [monogram] pd 5s 6d 1660 (sic)' (E.X.1.)

1665–6.   Philosophical Transactions Giving Some Accompt of the
          Undertakings, Studies and Labours of the Ingenious in
          Many Considerable Parts of the World. Vol. I. 'Sum
          Johannis Aubrij de Easton-Pierse R.S.S. 1667' (E.V.5.)
          'Liber Aulae Glocistrinsis Oxon Ex dono ex'my Vir Rei gs
          Naturalis Indagatoris maxime curiosa Joannis Aubrey de
          Easton Peirse in agro Wiltoniensi Armigeri R.S.S. dignitissm.
          IV Non Juny MDCLXXXXV (1695). Aubery.'

1668.   Brancker, Thomas. An Introduction to Algebra. 'This book I
          have carefully corrected by Dr Pell's: and it is to be valued as
          a jewell of price. Jo: Aubrey R.S. p: 5s': Aubrey's bookplate.
          Aubrey wrote: 'In the booke called Branker's Algebra that
          which is purely Dr Pell's beginnes at p.79 and so continues to
          Finis—this I had from his owne mouth.' (MS. Aubr. 6. f. 55.)
          (E.Z.2.)

1670.   Wallis, Johannis. Mechanica: Sive De Motu etc. Bound up
          with this is A Treatise of Quantities, 1678, by Tho: Strode,
          inscribed 'J. Awbrey': also Analysis Æquationum, 1690, by
          Joseph Raphson, R.S., inscribed 'Jo: Aubrey R.S.S.' (E.V.8.)

1673.   Kersey, John. Elements of that Mathematical Art commonly
called Algebra. Notes in Aubrey's hand: 'By this Theorem
Thomas Fludd of Kent Esq ordered the taxes of the Country:
and, for brevity sake, did it by a large line of numbers, the
circle of Proportion': also contains, 'Twelve problems touching Compound Interest and Annuities in a New Method very
briefe and yet plain and perspicuous, first presented in twelve
short lines to the right Honb. the Lord Delamer, and afterwards humbly offered with the annexed explications to the
famous Royal Society by Mr John Collins with the consent of
the Inventor. [Signed] Adam Martindale.' (E.11.1.) There is a
drawing by Aubrey of an armorial design for a bookplate:
full achievement with crest, helmet, and mantling, quartering:
Aubrey, Eynon, Morgan, Danvers, Blount of Mangotsfield,
and Lyte, with motto 'J'Aime mon honneur plus que ma
vie.' A letter has been attached, endorsed in Aubrey's hand:
'Mr Paschel's letter of my mother's last desire.' This letter,
dated June 11, 1686, is from Andrew Paschall, 'On my hart
it [friendship with Aubrey] can never faile, this is not onely
from my own inclinations, but also what was written in the
last letter I had from your dear dying mother, in whome I lost
one of the sincerest friends I had on earth. But she is in
peace. For her sake, for your own, and for God's sake, do all
in you lyes to have all differences made up if any there be
between you and your brother and to live with him in
perfect amity—pardon me, dear Sr! in this I performe the
Will of the deceased . . .'

1674.   Petty, Sir William. The Discourse made before the Royal
Society 26 November 1674 concerning the use of Duplicate
Preposition. 'Dedit Author John Aubrio R.S.S. 1674.'
(E.X.4.)

1676.   Lilly, William. Anima Astrologiae: or a Guide for Astrologers.
'Jo: Aubrey. For Gloucester hall. pr. 1s.' (E.X.6.) Aubrey
has made some astrological notes at the end, possibly referring
to himself, as one seems to speak of stuttering.

1681.   Moore, Sir Jonas. A System of Mathematics. (E.11.3.) 'Sum
Jo: Aubrij R.S.S. 1686 psd. 11l 5s 0d.' Aubrey wrote: 'Sir
Jonas Moore . . . came to the Middle Temple, London, where
he published his Arithmetique, and taught it in Stanhop-
street.' (MS. Aubr. 6. f. 96.)

1686.   Speidell, Euclid. An Arithmetical Extraction. 'Jo: Aubrey Aug 7 1686' : A note in Aubrey's hand refers to 'Mr. J. Ward, his much shorter Rule of Practise.' Aubrey wrote: 'Mr. Spiedell: he taught mathematiques in London and published a booke in quarto named Spiedel's Geometrical Extractions which made young men have a love to geometrie.' (MS. Aubr. 8. f. 85.) (E.X.8.)

1691.   Gadbury, John. Nauticum Astrologicum: or the Astrological Seaman. 'Sum Jo: Aubrij R.S.S. ex dono Authoris 1692.' Gadbury, like Lilly and Coley, mentioned below, was an astrologer friend of Aubrey's. (E.X.10.)

The following books are bound up with sheets of blank paper, most of which has been covered with Aubrey's mathematical calculations:

1620.   Commandini Mercatoris Astronomica. 'Jo Aubrey Trin: Coll: Oxon 1648.' On the last page is a note regarding 'Mr. [Laurence] Rooke', only partly legible. Bound up with this work is Nicholas Mercator's Hypothesis Astronomia Nova, 1664. 'Su Jo: Aubrij R.S.S. 1672 Donä Authoris.' Among the blank pages that follow is the note in Aubrey's hand: 'This Slip of Parchment for Timber measure, I found by chance in Digges's Tectonicon.' i.e. 'Leonard Digges's Tectonicon, briefly showing the exact measuring and speedy reckoning all manner of land, etc.' (MS. Aubr. 8. f. 72v.) On the last page a note refers to 'Mr. [Edmund] Wyld' and 'Mr. Oldcastle.' (MS.5.4.)

1660.   Art of Species. 'Mr. Nich: Mercator's Lessons some which are a good Commentary on Mr. Oughtred's Clavis Mathem. A.J. [monogram].' Bound up with this work is Nicholas Gunton's Arithmetica Decimalis. 'Sum Johannis Awbrij 1660.' Among various calculations the names of Sir Isaac Newton, John Collins, Thomas Fludd, and Dr. Davenant occur; and such problems as: 'to find a Number which may be measured by 19, and being divided by 28 shall leave one.' There is a memorandum: 'Mr. E. Wyld's way of Proving Division (after the cancelled way) by adding to Division below and the Remainder above which aequates the Dividend: of this he learned from old Mr. Spiedell [inform] H. Coley de hoc.' On one page is written 'Sum Jo: Aubrey R.S.S. 1674.' (MS.4.9.)

A *4to* MS. Mathematical and Algebraical Matter. 'Sum Jo: Aubrey R.S.S. from Jo: Pell D.D. Sept 30 1684.' Later title-page: Algebra Literalis Auctore Edvardo Davenant de Gillingham in Agro Dorset. (MS.5.5.) 'Sum Johannis Aubrij de Easton Pierse Wiltes, 1659. This Algebra I transcribed from ye MS of Mris Anne Ettrick the eldest daughter of Dr Davenant: who is a very good Logist.' Notes follow: 'This Question was invented and resolv'd first by my Lord Brereton; and given me to be proposed by Dr Pell': 'This solution was done by Mr Jonas Moore': 'Mr. Davenant A.M. Fellow of Oriell Coll in Oxford hath all his Father's Mathematical MSS, where this is fully explained: *qd vide* I brought Dr. J. Wallis to him to peruse them: and he liked the above—sayd Progression very well.' 'A man makes his Will, his wife being great with child, and orders that if his wife shall have a Son, that His part should be double his Mothers: if a Daughter, that then the Mother's share should be double Hers: The husband dies and his Relict brought both a Son and Daughter. The Question is what share each ought to have. John Collins F.R.S.'s Discourse to prove that equation can be solved by tables, 1670.' 'Dr. Pell was wont to say that, in the Solution of Questions, the Maine Matter was *the well-stating of them*; wch requires mother-witt, & Logick, as well as Algebra: for let the question be but well-stated, it will worke almost of itselfe: as for example, the most Difficult Probleme, being thus clearly stated; the working of it becomes very easie.' 'Sum Jo: Aubrij Aug 1683.'

The collection recalls the fact that Aubrey proposed at one period to write a history of the English Mathematicians, while the many pages of calculations in Aubrey's hand draw attention to his keen interest in mathematics, a side of him that is sometimes overlooked.

Notes

1. In 1974 a miniature, said to have descended through the Wyld family, attributed perhaps to Hoskyns the Younger, was catalogued as Aubrey at Christie's, but not so regarded by the National Portrait Gallery.
2. Readers are recommended Michael Hunter's *John Aubrey and the Realm of Learning* (1975).
3. Facsimile copies of *Monumenta Britannica*, edited by John Fowles, annotated by Rodney Legg, have now been published, Parts I and II, 1980, Parts III and IV, 1982.

BIBLIOGRAPHY

So far as Aubrey's own letters and papers are concerned, nearly all manuscript sources are to be found in the Bodleian. Liberties have occasionally been taken in altering Aubrey's punctuation, expanding abbreviations, and discarding capital letters, where, as sometimes happens, the meaning in quotation is otherwise obscured. In any case of possible alternative reading, added words or letters are enclosed in square brackets. John Britton's *Memoir* is the only full-length biography of Aubrey, but printed sources for the general picture of his life are, of course, extensive. The reader is referred to Godfrey Davies' *Bibliography of British History, Stuart Period*, 1928; and sources mentioned in notes, together with some other works—chiefly family histories—which have been useful, are listed below, with abbreviations. Dates are given in '*New Style*', e.g. March 1649/50' is written 'March 1650'.

MANUSCRIPT SOURCES

Add. MSS.	Additional Manuscripts, British Museum.
Ash. MSS.	Ashmole Manuscripts, Bodleian Library
Aubr. MSS.	Aubrey Manuscripts, Bodleian Library.
Ballard MSS.	Ballard Manuscripts, Bodleian Library.
B.M.	British Museum.
Bodl.	Bodleian Library, Oxford.
Egerton MSS.	Egerton Manuscripts, British Museum.
Eng. Hist. MSS.	English Historical Manuscripts, Bodleian Library.
Lansdowne MSS.	Lansdowne Manuscripts, British Museum.
Malone MSS.	Malone Manuscripts, Bodleian Library.
P.C.C.	Prerogative Court of Canterbury.
P.R.	Parish Register.
P.R.O.	Public Record Office.
Rawl. MSS.	Rawlinson Manuscripts, Bodleian Library.
Tanner MSS.	Tanner Manuscripts, Bodleian Library.
Wood MSS.	Anthony Wood's Manuscripts, Bodleian Library.

PRINTED SOURCES

Adamson's Education.	A Short History of Education, J. W. Adamson, 1919.
Allen's Lambeth.	History of Lambeth, Thomas Allen, 1827.

Ashmole's Diary.	Diary and Will of Elias Ashmole. Ed. R. T. Gunther, 1927.
Ath. Ox.	Anthony Wood's Athenae Oxonienses; and Fasti. Ed. P. Bliss, 1813-20.
Avebury Publ.	Publications regarding Avebury of the Morven Institute of Archaeological Research.
Bertie Fam.	Five Generations of a Loyal House, Lady G. Bertie, 1845.
B.L.	Aubrey's Brief Lives. Ed. Andrew Clark, 1898.
Bodl. Quart. Rec.	Bodleian Quarterly Record.
Bramston.	Sir John Bramston's Autobiography, 1845.
B.R.S.	British Record Society's publications.
Bryant's Pepys I.	Samuel Pepys: the Man in the Making, Arthur Bryant, 1933.
Burnet.	Bishop Burnet's History of My Own Time, 1818.
Cam. Hist. Eng. Lit.	Cambridge History of English Literature.
Cam. Soc.	Camden Society.
Cath. Rec. Soc.	Catholic Record Society's publications.
Clarendon.	Clarendon's History of the Rebellion. Ed. W. D. Macray, 1888.
Comp. Peer., Baronet.	The Complete Peerage, Baronetage.
C.S.P.D.	Calendar of State Papers, Domestic Series.
Danvers Fam.	Memorials of the Danvers Family, F. N. Macnamara, 1895.
Dee's Diary.	The Private Diary of Dr John Dee. Ed. J. O. Halliwell, 1842.
D.N.B.	Dictionary of National Biography.
Dorset Proc.	Proceedings of the Dorset Natural History and Antiquarian Field Club.
Dwnn.	Lewis Dwnn's Heraldic Visitations of Wales. Ed. Meyrick, 1846.
Eng. Ant.	The English Antiquaries of the 16th–18th centuries, H. B. Walters, 1934.
Evelyn.	Diary of John Evelyn. Ed. A. Dobson, 1908.
Fac. Off. Mar. Lic.	Faculty Office Marriage Licences B.R.S., G. E. Cokayne and E. A. Fry, 1905.
Folklore Soc.	Publications of the Folklore Society.
Gen. N.S.	The Genealogist, New Series.

Hamper's Dugdale.	Life, diary, etc., of Sir William Dugdale, W. Hamper, 1827.
Harl. Soc.	Harleian Society's publications.
Hartlib Papers.	Hartlib, Dury, and Comenius: gleanings from Hartlib's papers, G. H. Turnbull, 1947.
Hearne.	Thomas Hearne's Remarks and Collections. Ed. H. E. Salter, 1914–21.
Herald. Visit.	Heraldic Visitations.
Hist. Ant. Ox.	Anthony Wood's Historia et Antiquitates Universitatis Oxoniensis. Ed. in Eng. Andrew Clark, 1889–99
Hist. Parl.	History of Parliament, J. C. Wedgewood and A. D. Holt, 1936–38.
Hist. R. S.	History of the Royal Society, H. B. Wheatley, 1905
H.M.C.	Historical Manuscripts Commission.
Hooke's Contemp.	Robert Hooke on his Literary Contemporaries. Margaret Wattie, Review of English Studies, April 1937.
Hooke's Diary.	Diary of Robert Hooke. Ed. H. W. Robinson and W. Adams, 1935.
Jones's Brecknock.	History of Brecknock, Theophilus Jones. Ed. Lord Glenusk, 1909.
Kilvert.	Rev. Francis Kilvert's Diary. Ed. W. Plomer, 1939.
L. & I. of R.H.S. & Cam. Soc.	Lists and Indexes of Royal Historical Society and Camden Society, H. Hall, 1925.
Le Neve's Knights.	P. Le Neve's Pedigrees of Knights. Ed. G. W. Marshall, 1873.
Limb. Pat. Morg.	Limbus Patrum Morganiae et Glamorganiae, G. T. Clark, 1886.
Lond. Mar. Lic.	London Marriage Licences, 1521–1869. Ed. J. Foster, 1887.
Lond. Mar. Lic. Alleg. (Bp. Lon.)	London Marriage Licence Allegations (Bishop of London). Ed. R. M. Glencross, 1940.
Long Fam.	Historical account of the family of Long of Wilts, W. Chitty, 1889,
Luttrell.	A Brief Historical Relation of State Affairs, 1678–1714, Narcissus Luttrell, 1857.

Lyte Fam.	The Lytes of Lytescary, H. C. Maxwell Lyte, Somerset. Arch. Soc. Vol. 38, 1892.
Misc.	Aubrey's Miscellanies, 1784 edition.
Misc. Gen. Herald.	Miscellanea Genealogica et Heraldica.
Nat. Hist. Wilts.	Aubrey's Natural History of Wiltshire. Ed. John Britton, 1847.
Normans in Glam.	The Normans in Glamorgan, Gower, and Kidweli, Lewis D. Nicholl, 1936.
Ox. Hist. Soc.	Oxford Historical Society's publications.
Pepys.	Samuel Pepys's Diary. Ed. H. B. Wheatley, 1893–6.
Ray Soc.	Publications of the Ray Society.
Seymour Fam.	The Seymour Family, A. A. Locke, 1911.
Shaw's Knights.	The Knights of England, W. A. Shaw, 1906.
Somerset Arch. Soc.	Somerset Archaeological and Natural History Society's publications.
Stawell Fam.	A Quantock family: history of the Stawells, G. D. Stawell, 1910.
Surrey.	Aubrey's Perambulation of the County of Surrey. 1718–19.
Toland's Druids.	John Toland's History of the Druids. Ed. R. Huddleston, 1814.
Tufton Fam.	Memorials of the Tufton Family, Earls of Thanet, R. Pocock, 1800.
Vaughan.	Henry Vaughan: a Life and Interpretation, F. E. Hutchinson, 1947.
Wilts. Arch. Mag.	Wiltshire Archaeological and Natural History Society's Magazine.
Wilts. Col.	Aubrey's Wiltshire Collections ('Description of the North Division of Wiltshire'). Ed. Canon J. E. Jackson, 1862.
Wilts. N. & Q.	Wiltshire Notes & Queries, 1892–1916.
Wilts. Wool Indust.	The Wiltshire Wool Industry in the 16th and 17th Centuries, G. D. Ramsay, 1943.
Wood's L. & T.	Life and Times of Anthony Wood. Ed. Andrew Clark, 1891–1900.
	The Times Literary Supplement dated 5 July, 1947, contains a note by Katharine A. Esdaile regarding points in MS. Aubr. 4 (Surrey) and Aubrey's acquaintance with Bushnell and Cibber.

BIBLIOGRAPHICAL NOTES

Since Andrew Clark always notes manuscript sources, references taken from his edition of the *Brief Lives* are indicated as ' *B.L.*', followed by the name of the subject of the biography in which the information is to be found; or, alternatively, by volume and page. p.=page: f.=folio: l.=line: n.=note.

INTRODUCTION

PAGE
9   l. 1, H.M.C. Portland VII, 36.
14   l. 25, *Quarrels of Authors*, III, 55, 76.
16   l. 10, *B.L.* 1, 42; l. 14, B.M. MS. Stowe 182, f. 33b.

CHAPTER ONE: I

19   l. 1 *et seq.*, *B.L.* Hobbes; l. 6, *North Wilts.* (Leigh Delamere); l. 19 *B.L.* 1, 35.
20   l. 12, MS. Aubr. 7, f. 3.

II

20   n., *Wilts. Visit.*, North Wilts. (South Wraxall).
21   l. 5, Dwnn, *Limb. Pat. Morg.*; l. 7 *et seq.*, *B.L.* William Aubrey; l. 12, MS. Aubr. 2, f. 34v, MS. Aubr. 8, f. 78v; n., MS. Aubr. 2, f. 34v, Coll. Somerset 1, 2, Old Foed. VII, 371.
22   l. 16 & n., MS. Aubr. 2, f. 34v; l. 24, *B.L.* Dee.
23   n., MS. Aubr., 6, f. 21.
24   l. 1 *et seq.*, Jones's *Brecknock* IV, 8 *et passim*.

III

25   l. 10 *et seq.*, Dee's Diary, *B.L.* Whitson & William Aubrey; n., MS. Rawl. D, 727, f. 96; l. 24, inform. Rev E. C. Benson of Burghill.
26   l. 18, MS. Aubr. 23, f. 81v, *Wilts. Visit.* (Metcalfe, 1897); l. 21, *Wilts. Arch. Mag.* IV, *Som. Arch. Soc.* XXXVIII (II), 1–100, Lyte Fam.; l. 25, *Nat. Hist. Wilts.* II, ii; n., Aubr. 2, f. 32v.
27   l. 5, MS. Aubr. 7, f. 3; n., *Nat. Hist. Wilts.* II, iv, *B.L.* Henry Lyte.

IV

27   l. 10 *et seq.*, *Wilts. Arch. Mag.* IV, North Wilts. (Appendix LXI), *Nat. Hist. Wilts.* IX, *Wilts. N. & Q.* VI.
28   l. 1, MS. Aubr. 4, f. 59v, *North Wilts.* (Malmesbury), *Nat. Hist. Wilts.* IX; l. 11 *et seq.*, MS. Aubr. 17; l. 19, *Nat. Hist. Wilts.* II, 6.
29   l. 1, Britton, 26; n. I, Britton's *Autobiography*; n. 2, Kilvert.

V

30   l. 1, MS. Rawl. J, f. 6, f. 30, *North Wilts.* (Malmesbury).
31   l. 1, *Gentilism*, 71, MS. Aubr. 14, f. 50v; l. 11, *North Wilts.* (Kington); l. 28, MS. Aubr. 7, ff. 3–5; l. 33, MS. Aubr. 16, f. 52; l. 37, *B.L.* 1st Earl of Pembroke.

32   l. 21, MS. Aubr. 3, f. 65v; l. 22, *Wilts, N. & Q.* 1, 50, 106; n., *Wilts. Arch. Mag.* XVIII, 81.

33   l. 1, *Nat. Hist. Wilts.* IX; l. 12, *B.L.* Waller; l. 13, MS. Aubr. 8, f. 6v; l. 19, MS. Aubr. 15, f. 200a; l. 22, MS. Aubr. 7, f. 4v; l. 34, MS. Aubr. 1, f. 162, *Nat. Hist. Wilts.*, 74

34   l. 7, MS. Aubr. 1, f. 125; l. 14, *B.L.* Sir Philip Sydney, *Nat. Hist. Wilts.* III.

VI

34   l. 30, MS. Aubr. 3, f. 30; l. 32, B.M. MS. Lansdowne 231, f. 113.

35   l. 3 *et seq.*, *B.L.* Raleigh, *passim*; l. 5, *B.L.* Camden; l. 31 *B.L.* Bushell.

36   l. 8, *North Wilts.* (Intro.); l. 18, *Gentilism*, 124, MS. Aubr. 6, f. 11; l. 21, MS. Aubr. 6, f. 11v; l. 26, B.M. MS. Lansdowne 231, f. 128v, 129, Chaucer, *The Franklin's Tale* (left uncorrected to retain Aubrey's own impression of the passage).

37   l. 3, MS. Aubr. 2, f. 18v, *Nat. Hist. Wilts.* XVI; l. 17, *Wilts. Wool Indust.*; l. 32, *Gentilism*, 22; l. 34, *ibid.*, 24.

VII

37   l. 25, *Gentilism*, 171, MS. Aubr. 21, f. 95; l. 33, B.M. MS. Lansdowne 231, f. 109v.

38   l. 1, *ibid.*, f. 111; l. 4 & n., MS. Aubr. 15, f. 208v; l. 7, B.M. MS. Lansdowne 231, f. 179v; l. 16, MS. Aubr. 1, f. 21 *et seq.*, *Nat. Hist. Wilts.* (Intro.)

VIII

39   l. 9 *et seq.*, MS. Aubr. 7, f. 3; l. 19, *Nat. Hist. Wilts.* XVI.

40   l. 4, MS. Aubr. 10, f. 83; l. 13, *B.L.* Sutton, *Ath Ox.* 111, 634 (William James), Hutchins's *Dorset* 1, 220 *et passim*, *B.L.* Lancelot Andrewes; l. 24, MS. Aubr. 10, f. 8v; l. 34, MS. Aubr. 10, f. 89.

41   l. 11, *B.L.* Stephens; l. 19, *B.L.* Raleigh; l. 27, *MS.* Aubr. 10, f. 166; n., MS. Aubr. 1, f. 19, *Nat. Hist. Wilts.* (Intro.)

42   l. 8, MS. Aubr. 7, f. 3; n. 1, *B.L.* Woodenote, *D.N.B.*, *Cam. Hist. Eng. Lit.* VII, 10; n. 2, *B.L.* 1, 51, n. 13.

43   l. 1, *B.L.* Burghley; l. 10, MS. Aubr. 10; l. 21, *Clarendon* VI, 23; n., *B.L.* Morton.

CHAPTER TWO: I

44   l. 3, MS. Rawl. J, f. 6, f. 30; l. 8 *et seq.*, *B.L.* Kettle, MS. Ballard 14, f. 127.

46   l. 10, B.M. MS. Lansdowne 231, f. 235v.

II

46   l. 21, MS. Aubr. 7, f. 3v, *B.L.* Sanderson & Webb.

47   l. 1 *et seq.*, Wood's *L. & T.*, Mar.–Aug., 1642, *passim*; l. 10, *Misc.* (Apparitions), B.M. MS. Lansdowne 231, f. 114v; l. 27, *B.L.* Coryat; l. 29, *B.L.* Kettle; l. 36, *ibid.*

48   l. 18, MS. Aubr. 7, f. 3v; l. 27, MS. Aubr. 14, f. 21, *Wilts. Arch. Mag.* XXVI, 220

III

48 l. 23, *Misc.* (Local Fatality); l. 30, *Misc.* (Omens); n., *North Wilts.* (Antiquaria).
49 l. 11, *B.L.* Kettle.; l. 22, Wood's *L. & T.*, 1642, *passim.*
50 l. 1, *Clarendon* VI, 99; l. 8, MS. Aubr. 14, f. 266; l. 15, *Misc.* (Omens); l. 21, *B.L.* Cartwright, *Gentilism*, 69; l. 24, MS. Aubr. 7, f. 3v.
51 l. 11, Wood's *L. & T.*, May, 1644; l. 14, *B.L.* Poyntz, *B.L.* Radford; l. 23, MS. Aubr. 8, f. 3; l. 32, *B.L.* Kettle.
52 l. 16, Wood's *L. & T.*, April, 1643; l. 17, *B.L.* Hales; n., *Cam. Hist. Eng. Lit.* V. 111, 119, & VI. 297.

IV

53 l. 1 *et seq.*, MS. Aubr. 7, f. 3v, *B.L.* Birkenhead; l. 23, MS. Aubr. 1, f. 152, *Nat. Hist. Wilts.* XIV; l. 29, *Nat. Hist Wilts.* I; l. 33, *B.L.* Taylor.
54 l. 22, *B.L.* Howe & Taylor.
55 l. 3, *B.L.* Harvey; l. 16, MS. Aubr. 10; l. 22, Wood's *L. & T.*, Oct., 1673; l. 25, *B.L.* Jonson; l. 30, *B.L.* Potters.

V

56 l. 28, MS. Aubr. 12, f. 35, 36.
57 l. 1, *Wilts. Arch. Mag.* XXVI, 347, XV, 4; l. 9, *B.L.* E. Broughton & MS. Aubr. 3, f. 153; l. 21, *B.L.* Jonson; l. 27, MS. Aubr. 7, f. 3v.
58 l. 11, MS. Aubr. 10, f. 69; l. 28, MS. Wood F. 49, f. 42, *B.L.* Rolle.
59 l. 12, *B.L.* Coke; l. 16, *B.L.* Denham; n., MS. Wood F. 49, f. 42.

VI

59 l. 19, MS. Aubr. 7, f. 3v.
60 l. 4, MS. Aubr. 14, f. 23 *et seq.* (*North Wilts.* Selkley); n., MS. Aubr. 14, f. 37.
61 l. 12, *Comp. Peer*; l. 27, *D.N.B.*, *Wilts. Arch. Mag.*; n. 2, *Oliver Cromwell and the insurrection of 1655*, F. D. Palgrave.
62 n. 1, *Wilts. Arch. Mag.* XXVI, n. 2, *North Wilts.* 190, *Wilts. Arch. Mag.* XXIII, 331.
63 l. 5, Wood's *L. & T.*, March 1692, *Wilts. N. & Q.* VI, 25, *Wilts. Arch. Mag.* XXIV, 96.
64 l. 6, *Avebury Publ.*; l. 22, MS. Aubr. 14, f. 35, *North Wilts.* (Selkley).

VII

64 l. 32, MS. Aubr. 12, ff. 41–50, *B.L.* Chillingworth.
65 l. 1, MS. Aubr. 2, f. 19v; l. 5, MS. Aubr. 2, f. 2v; l. 8, MS. Aubr. 8, f. 20; l. 11, *B.L.* Digby; l. 14, *B.L.* Harcourt; l. 19, MS. Aubr. 12; l. 27, Wood's *L. & T.*, Oct. 1649; l. 30, *Misc.*, MS. Aubr. 2, f. 306.
66 l. 31, MS. Aubr. 1, f. 52.

CHAPTER THREE: I

67 l. 8, MS. Aubr. 23, f. 82; l. 13, MS. Rawl. J, f. 6; l. 24, *P.C.C.*
68 l. 6, *P.R. Harl. Soc.*; l. 13, *Harl. Soc.* 24, *Lond. Mar. Lic.*; l. 22, *Harl. Soc.* XCII; l. 26, *B.L.* Andrewes; l. 30, *B.L.* Hyde.; n., *Nat. Hist. Wilts.* 1.

69 l. 1, *Essex Visit.* (Harl. Soc.); l. 18, P. R. *Harl. Soc.* 32; l. 23, *Lond. Mar. Lic.*; n., *Lond. Mar. Lic. Alleg.*, *Harl. Soc.* 5, & 10, Shaw's *Knights*, B.L. Jonson and Suckling, *Comp. Baronet.*

II

70 l. 1, *Misc.* (Omens), *D.N.B.*; l. 15, MS. Wood F. 39, f. 247.

71 l. 5, MS. Aubr. 12, ff. 141–45; l. 14, MS. Aubr. 13, f. 162; l. 17, B.L. Harvey; l. 24, MS. Aubr. 12, f. 157; l. 32, B.L. Harvey; l. 34, MS. Aubr. 13, f. 29.

72 l. 3, *Misc.* (Knockings); l. 8, *North Wilts.* (Kington); l. 13, *P.C.C.*; l. 22, MS. Aubr. 3, f. 65v; *North Wilts.* (Damerham); n., B.L. Brome, *D.N.B.*, *Broad Chalke* P. R. ed. Moore, MS. Aubr. 8, f. 38v.

III

73 l. 5, Seth Ward's *Notitia* III, f. 10 *et passim* (*Bp's Reg.*, Salisbury); l. 7, *Nat. Hist. Wilts.* II, 8, MS. Aubr. 2, f. 112 *et seq.*; l. 24, *Nat. Hist. Wilts.* II, 8; n., B.L. Sydney.

74 l. 5, MS. Aubr. 7, f. 3v; l. 10, MS. Aubr. 6, f. 62v; l. 13, MS. Aubr. 2, f. 33; l. 20, B.L. Denham; n. 1, *Surrey* 11, 306; n. 2, MS. Aubr. 8, f. 94v.

75 l. 7, MS. Aubr. 1, f. 135v; l. 13, MS. Aubr. 12, f. 312; l. 20, MS. Aubr. 7, f. 3v.

76 l. 1 *et seq.*, B.L. Falkland, Chillingworth & Davenant; l. 10, MS. Aubr. 21, f. 75.

77 l. 3, *Nat. Hist. Wilts.* I; l. 9, MS. Aubr. 21, f. 112; l. 15, MS. Aubr. 6, f. 66v; l. 19, MS. Aubr. 4, 202; l. 25, B.L. Hales.

78 l. 9, MS. Rawl. J, f. 6, f. 30.

IV

78 l. 11 *et seq.*, *Wilts. Arch. Mag.* XXXII, 73, MS. Aubr. 14, f. 23v, *North Wilts.* (Selkley); l. 22, MS. Aubr. 14, f. 24

79 l. 20, MS. Aubr. 14, f. 31.

V

80 l. 9, MS. Rawl. J, f. 6, f. 30; l. 16, MS. Aubr. 4, f. 82v; l. 20, *Wilts. Arch. Mag.* XLIX.

81 l. 3, B.L. Richard Corbet; l. 8, MS. Aubr. 1, f. 156v; l. 11, B.L. Coke; l. 13 *et seq.*, B.L. Romsey.

82 l. 1, B.L. Lee; l. 4, MS. Aubr. 3, f. 63v; l. 8 *et seq.*, B.L. Overall; l. 19, B.L. Harvey; l. 23, MS. Rawl. J, f. 6, f. 30.

83 l. 2, MS. Aubr. 12, f. 25; l. 5, MS. Rawl. J, f. 6, f. 30; l. 11, *P.C.C.*; l. 23, Hutchins's *Dorset*; l. 34, MS. Aubr. f. 66.

84 l. 1 *et seq.*, *Wilts. Arch. Mag.* XLVII, 379, *Nat. Hist. Wilts.* IV; l. 4, *Genealogist*, April 1897; l. 22, B.L. Harvey; l. 32, *e.g.* in MS. Aubr. 10.

VI

85 l. 3, MS. Aubr. 1, f. 163; l. 10, *Nat. Hist. Wilts.* I, MS. Aubr. 1, f. 163; l. 15, MS. Aubr. 1, f. 126; l. 20, MS. Aubr. 2, f. 81; l. 26, *Nat. Hist. Wilts.* IV; l. 29, MS. Aubr. 1, f. 60; l. 31, MS. Aubr. 1, f. 60.

86 l. 1, MS. Aubr. 1, f. 42; l. 3, *Nat. Hist. Wilts.* VI; l. 13, *Eton Register*, *Alum. Cant.*, B.L. Waller; l. 22, B.L. Morehouse, *Gentilism*, 81; l. 32, B.L. Coke.

87 l. 4, B.L. Robartes; l. 10, B.L. Sloper & Oughtred.

VII

87 l. 19, *Misc.* (Omens); l. 25 *et seq.,* *North Wilts.* (Intro.), MS. Aubr. 3,
    f. 10.
88 l. 7, *North Wilts., passim, Wilts. Arch. Mag.* XXVI, 389, *Wilts. Visit;*
    l. 15, *North Wilts., passim, Wilts. Arch. Mag.* XIV *et passim, Wilts.
    Visit;* n., Danvers Fam.
89 l. 8, *North Wilts., passim;* l. 14, *ibid., passim, Wilts. N. & Q.* III,
    505, 539, *Wilts. Arch. Mag.* VI, 135, *Ath. Ox.;* l. 19, *Wilts. Arch.
    Mag.* VI, 135.

VIII

90 l. 23, *B.L.* Lyte; l. 24, MS. Rawl. J, f. 6, f. 30v; l. 29, *B.L.* Hobbes;
    l. 33, MS. Aubr. 13, f. 230v.
91 l. 18, MS. Aubr. 2, f. 83; l. 29, *B.L.* Monk; n., *Comp. Peer.*
92 l. 1, MS. Wood F. 39, f. 141; l. 5 *et seq., B.L.* Monk; n., *D.N.B.*

IX

92 l. 25 *et. seq.;* n. 2, *B.L.* Harrington.
93 *ibid.*
94 l. 6, Pepys, Jan. 1660.
95 l. 16, Wood's *L. & T.,* Sept. 1658; l. 21, *et seq., B.L.* Monk.
96 *B.L.* Monk.

CHAPTER FOUR: I

97 l. 8, MS. Aubr. 8, f. 28v; l. 14, Wood's *L. & T.,* May 1660; l. 19,
    North Wilts. (Malmesbury); l. 24 *et seq., B.L.* Harrington.
98 l. 22, *Clarendon* VI, 267; l. 26, MS. Aubr. 13, f. 205; l. 26, Pepys, June
    1664, Wood's *L. & T.,* March 1659; l. 35, *Alum. Ox.*

II

99 l. 3 *et seq., B.L.* Hobbes; n., *B.L.* Falkland.
100 l. 6, *B.L.* Descartes; l. 10, MS. Aubr. 1, f. 21; l. 12 *et seq., B.L.* Hollar;
    l. 27 MS. Aubr. 9, f. 39v.
101 ll. 1–7, *B.L.* Halley and Drayton, *Times Lit. Sup.,* 5 June, 1947 (K.
    Esdaile); l. 9, MS. Aubr. 1, f. 85v.

III

101 l. 16, MS. Rawl. J, f. 6, f. 30v; l. 31, *Misc.* (Omens); l. 33, MS. Aubr. 14,
    f. 73v.
102 l. 4, Britton, 37; l. 12, MS. Aubr. 9, f. 54v, *B.L.* Hobbes; l. 15, MS.
    Aubr. 12, f. 175; l. 18, *ibid.,* f. 190; l. 26, MS. Aubr. 13, f. 231; n.,
    Bryan's Dict. of Painters.
103 l. 18, *Bryan's Dict. of Painters, D.N.B.;* l. 23, *Bryan's Dict. of Painters;*
    l. 29, MS. Aubr. 13, f. 235.
104 l. 1, *B.L.* Cavendish.

IV

104 l. 24, MS. Aubr. 6, f. 13; l. 26, MS. Aubr. 8, slip at f. 6; *B.L.* Wilkins.
105 l. 17, Evelyn, July 1669; l. 25, MS. Aubr. 21, f. 29 *et seq.;* l. 30, *Thomson's
    Hist. R.S.*

PAGE

106 l. 1, MS. Aubr. 4, f. 75; l. 5, MS. Aubr. 15, f. 237v; l. 10, *Comp. Peer.*;
l. 15, MS. Aubr. 6, f. 14v; l. 31, *North Wilts.* (Selkley), MS. Aubr. 14,
f. 2v *et seq.*; l. 35, *D.N.B.*

107 l. 1 *et seq.*, MS. Aubr. 14, f. 24 *et seq.*, *Ath. Ox.* IV, 751; n., MS. Aubr. 11,
f. 13v; l. 21, MS. Aubr. 14, f. 24v; l. 28, *Nat. Hist. Wilts.* XIII; n.,
MS. Aubr. 11, f. 13v.

108 l. 6, *Surrey* IV, 71; l. 11, MS. Aubr. 14, f. 25; l. 18, *ibid.*; l. 29, MS.
Aubr. 14, f. 31v; n., MS. Aubr. 15, f. 20.

109 l. 1, Pepys, June 1668.

V

109 l. 6, MS. Aubr. 7, f. 4; l. 7, MS. Aubr. 23, f. 82; l. 9, *B.L.* Willis, *Ath.
Ox.*, MS. Aubr. 13, ff. 254, 255; l. 16, *B.L.* Broughton; l. 22, MS.
Aubr. 12, f. 85.

110 l. 12, MS. Aubr. 1, f. 38; l. 31, MS. Aubr. 12, f. 194.

111 l. 5, *B.L.* Hobbes; l. 19, MS. Rawl. J, f. 6, f. 30v, MS. Aubr. 9, f. 43;
l. 22, MS. Aubr. 12, f. 164; l. 37, MS. Rawl. J, f. 6, f. 30v.

112 l. 3, *Gentilism*, 67; l. 7, MS. Aubr. 21; l. 10, MS. Aubr. 1, f. 20v; l. 23,
MS. Aubr. 12, f. 102; l. 34, *Nat. Hist. Wilts.* II.

113 l. 1, MS. Aubr. 1, f. 23v; l. 4, MS. Aubr. 1, f. 21v; l. 10, MS. Aubr.
8, f. 2.

VI

113 l. 11 *et seq.*, *B.L.* Hobbes; l. 32, *B.L.* Rochester.

VII

114 l. 25, MS. Aubr. 8, f. 63; n., Pepys, May 1665.
115 l. 2, Britton, 79

VIII

115 l. 31, MS. Rawl. J, f. 6, f. 30v; l. 34, *Surrey* (Intro.).

116 l. 2, *Mar. Lic.* (*Salisbury*), *Gen. N.S.* 4, 38; l. 14 *et seq.*, *North Wilts.*,
passim; *Gen. N.S.* XXXV (A. Schomberg's article), *Wilts. Wool.
Indust.*; l. 34, *Nat. Hist. Wilts.* II, 9.

117 l. 5, *North Wilts.* (Melksham); l. 26, MS. Aubr. 1, f. 34 *et seq.*; l. 31,
MS. Aubr. 3, f. 157, *Nat. Hist. Wilts.* II, 11.

118 l. 18 *et seq.*, *Gen. N.S.* XXXV (Schomberg), *passim*, *Wilts. Visit.*
Harl. Soc. Wilts. Arch. Mag. IV, 97, *Wilts. N. & Q.* VIII, 529; l. 32,
MS. Aubr. 3, f. 168, *North Wilts* (Seend); n., MS. Aubr. 26, 15.

119 l. 4, *Wilts. N. & Q.* II, 478–9; l. 16, *Nat. Hist. Wilts.* 14, MS. Aubr. 1,
f. 159; l. 27, MS. Aubr. 24, f. 96; l. 31, *Gen. N.S.* XXXIII, 46.

120 l. 2, *Gen. N.S.* XXXIII 46, XXIV–XXXVIII, *passim*; l. 6 *et seq.*, MS.
Rawl. J, f. 6, f. 30v; l. 27, *P.R.O.* C. 9, 477/1; n., *Gen. N.S.* XXXIII,
46.

121 l. 18, *P.R.O.* C/5/563/19; l. 32, *North Wilts.* (Gore pedigree); n., MS.
Aubr. 1, f. 144.

122 l. 4, *B.L.* Randolph.

123 l. 16, C. 33/234; l. 20, *P.R.O.* C. 9/402/15; l. 26, *Gen. N.S.* XXIV–
XXXVIII, *passim*; l. 34, *P.C.C.*

124 l. 3, MS. Wood F. 39, f. 122, *Wilts. N. & Q.* VI, 135, VIII, 529; l. 15,
MS. Wood F. 39, f. 122.

125 l. 27, MS. Wood F. 39, f. 199.
126 l. 3, *Wilts. Arch. Mag.* IV, 89; n., *Wilts. Arch. Mag.* L, 103. *Wilts.
N. & Q.* VIII, 529, *North Wilts* (Stanton St Quintin), MS. Aubr. 26,
f. 2v, MS. Wood F. 39, f. 386.

CHAPTER FIVE: I

127 l. 9, *e.g.* MS. Aubr. 7, f. 4v (*Amici*); l. 14 *et seq.*, Wood's *L. & T.,*
passim.
128 l. 11, Wood's *L. & T.*, 1653; l. 35, Hearne 15, Oct. 1705.
129 l. 29, Wood's *L. & T.*; n., *Ath. Ox.* IV.
130 l. 32, *e.g. B.L.* Gwyn.
131 l. 33, Wood's *L. & T.*, Aug. 1667.
132 l. 1, Wood's *L. & T.*, Jan. 1667–8; l. 6, MS. Wood F. 39, f. 118;
l. 8, MS. Ballard 14, f. 81; l. 18, MS. Ballard 14, f. 84; l. 22, MS.
Ballard 14, f. 80; l. 30 MS. Ballard 14, f. 80v; n., MS. Wood F. 39,
f. 188, MS. Tanner 456a, f. 31.
133 l. 2, MS. Wood F. 39, f. 122.

II

133 l. 25, Wood's *L. & T.*, Nov. 1660; n., *Som. Arch. Soc.* XXXVIII, 50.
134 l. 23, MS. Aubr. 12, f. 157.

III

134 l. 33, MS. Rawl. J, f. 6, f. 30v.
135 l. 1 *et seq.*, *B.L.* Davenant; l. 9, *B.L.* Fletcher; l. 13, *B.L.* Hobbes;
l. 16, MS. Aubr. 10, f. 2; l. 21, MS. Aubr. 17; l. 28, MS. Wood F. 39,
f. 123.
136 l. 2, MS. Ballard 14, f. 88; l. 5, MS. Aubr. 4, f. 142v; l. 9, MS. Aubr.
13, f. 256; n., *Comp. Peer.*
137 l. 2, MS. Tanner 456a, f. 9.

IV

137 l. 15, *Wilts. Arch. Mag.* IV, 72, 107; l. 21, MS. Aubr. 23, f. 101, MS.
Aubr. 7, f. 4; n., MS. Wood F. 39, f. 411.
138 l. 12 *et seq.*, MS. Aubr. 7, f. 4; l. 28, MS. Aubr. f. 4v.
139 l. 14, MS. Aubr. 12, f. 66, MS. Aubr. 23, f. 54.
140 l. 1, MS. Wood F. 39, f. 131; l. 11, MS. Aubr. 23, f. 104; l. 23, MS.
Wood F. 39, f. 141.
141 l. 33, *D.N.B.*; n., MS. Wood F. 39, f. 138.
142 l. 11, *Wilts. Arch. Mag.* IV, 107; l. 15, MS. Aubr. 8, f. 7v, *D.N.B.*;
l. 19, MS. Aubr. 21; n., MS. Aubr. 12, f. 140.
143 l. 3, MS. Aubr. 13, f. 163; l. 23, MS. Wood F. 39, f. 144; l. 27, *ibid.*,
f. 147.
144 l. 4, MS. Wood F. 39, f. 149; l. 12, MS. Aubr. 13, ff. 2, 3, 18, etc.

V

144 l. 14, MS. Wood F. 39, f. 192; l. 21, MS. Aubr. 13, f. 209.
145 l. 10, MS. Ballard 14, f. 92; l. 16, *B.L.* Massinger; l. 24, MS. Aubr. 9,
f. 51; l. 29, MS. Wood F. 39, f. 181; n. 1, *ibid.*, f. 252.
146 l. 14, MS. Aubr. 13, f. 211.

PAGE

VI

147 l. 2, MS. Wood F. 39, f. 196v; l. 16, *ibid.*, f. 257; n. 1, *B.L.* Selden; n. 2, Wood's *L. & T.*, Feb. 1674.

148 l. 18, MS. Aubr. 12; l. 22, MS. Wood F. 39, f. 199; l. 34, MS. Aubr. 23, f. 51.

149 l. 1, MS. Wood F. 39, f. 202; l. 14, MS. Aubr. 1, f. 3; l. 22, *B.L.* Ogilby; n., MS. Aubr. 4, f. 221.

150 l. 2, MS. Aubr. 2, f. 163; l. 6, *Surrey* (Intro.); l. 14, MS. Aubr. 4; l. 19, MS. Rawl. J, f. 6, f. 31; l. 24, MS. Wood F. 39, f. 214; n., MS. Rawl. J, f. 6, f. 31, *Harl. Soc.* VIII, *ibid.*, *Visit. Cumbs.*

151 l. 3 *et seq.*, *B.L.* Moray; l. 19, MS. Wood F. 39, f. 221; l. 23, *ibid.*, f. 231.

152 l. 4, S. Piggott's Stukely, 1950; l. 25, *B.L.* Radford, MS. Ballard 14, f. 96.

VII

153 l. 5 *et seq.*, Hooke's *Contemp.*, Hooke's *Diary, passim*; l. 11, MS. Aubr. 23, f. 97v; l. 15, MS. Wood F. 39, f. 261; l. 29, *B.L.* Graunt, MS. Wood F. 39, f. 261.

154 l. 3, MS. Ballard 14, f. 98; l. 31, *B.L.* Hobbes.

155 l. 3, MS. Ballard 14, f. 99; l. 20, *B.L.* Twisse; l. 25, MS. Wood F. 39, f. 268; l. 27, *ibid.*, f. 270; n., *ibid.*, f. 133.

156 l. 3, *Hist. Ant. Ox.* 11, 297; l. 9, MS. Ballard 14, f. 105; l. 19, *B.L.* Hobbes; l. 25, MS. Ballard 14, f. 111; l. 35, *ibid.*, f. 84.

157 l. 10, *B.L.* Potter; l. 21, MS. Aubr. 12, f. 211; n. 2, *B.L.* Tonge, *D.N.B.*

VIII

158 l. 32, MS. Ballard 14, f. 107; l. 34, *D.N.B.*

159 l. 3, *B.L.* Triplett; l. 15, MS. Ballard 14, f. 110; l. 23, MS. Wood F. 39, f. 282; n. 1, *B.L.* Gill.

160 l. 1, MS. Wood F. 39, f. 288; l. 15, *ibid*, f. 291; l. 21, MS. Aubr. 13, f. 266.

161 l. 6, MS. Aubr. 12, f. 105; l. 14, MS. Ballard 14, f. 115; l. 20, MS. Aubr. 13, f. 107; l. 27, *ibid.*, f. 109; l. 30, MS. Wood F. 39, f. 265; l. 37, *ibid.*, f. 296.

IX

162 l. 3, MS. Aubr. 12 f. 213; n., *Comp. Pees*

163 l. 13, MS. Aubr. 13, f. 217.

164 l. 3, MS. Aubr. 13, f. 218.

165 l. 4, MS. Aubr. 13, f. 228; l. 15, *ibid.*, f. 224.

X

165 l. 24, MS. Wood F. 39, f. 299; l. 25, MS. Tanner 456a, f. 19; l. 32, MS. Aubr. 4, f. 28; n., see Wood's *L. & T.* II, 398.

166 l. 13, *Nat. Hist. Wilts.* (Intro.); l. 19, MS. Aubr. 13, f. 137, MS. Aubr. 4, f. 163; l. 35, *Ath. Ox.* IV, 778.

167 l. 6, MS. Wood F. 39, f. 302; l. 14, MS. Aubr. 23, f. 117; l. 23, MS. Ballard 14, f. 119.

168 l. 8, MS. Aubr. 9, f. 27v; l. 22, *D.N.B.*

169 l. 3, MS. Aubr. 26; l. 9, *B.L.* Davenant; l. 16, MS. Aubr. 6, f. 43; l. 18, *Dorset Soc. Proc.* XXXVII, 34; n., *North Wilts.*, 29, Hartlib Papers, 441.

170 l. 1, *B.L.* Venetia Digby, MS. Aubr. 6, f. 101v; l. 10, Hooke's *Diary.*

171 l. 1 *et seq.*, Ashmole's *Diary*, Allen's *Lambeth*; l. 18, MS. Aubr. 23, slip
     at f. 23v.
172 l. 2, MS. Aubr. 13, f. 115; l. 9, MS. Wood F. 39, f. 314.

II

172 l. 18 *et seq.*, Hearne, July 1724, MS. Wood F. 51 (*Life of Sheldon*), *Ath.*
     Ox.; l. 22, MS. Wood F. 39, f. 162; l. 30, Wood's *L. & T.* July, 1671.
173 l. 15, Wood's *L. & T.*, July 1679; l. 21, MS. Wood F. 39, f. 347; Aug.
     1680; l. 23, MS. Wood F. 39, f. 347; l. 32, *B.L.* Overall & Monk.
174 l. 4 *et seq.*, Wood's *L. & T.*, *passim*; l. 13, MS. Wood F. 44, f. 96 *et seq.*;
     l. 23, Hooke's *Diary*; l. 26, MS. Wood F. 44, f. 111; n. 1, Bryant's
     Pepys I, 187; n. 2, Wood's *L. & T.*, Nov. 1678.

III

175 l. 1, MS. Aubr. 13, f. 227; l. 11 *et seq.*, *Tufton Fam.*; l. 30, MS. Aubr. 13,
     f. 120; l. 34, MS. Wood F. 39, f. 324.
176 l. 9, MS. Wood F. 39, f. 328; n. 2, *see* MS. Aubr. 21, *North Wilts.*, 247.
177 l. 4, MS. Aubr. 9, f. 14; l. 29, MS. Aubr. 7, f. 3, *B.L.* Hobbes *et passim*.
178 l. 2, *B.L.* Ent, Hooke's *Diary*, Sept. 1679, *Misc.* (Knockings); l. 6 *et*
     seq., *B.L.* Hobbes; l. 19, MS. Aubr. 9; l. 27, *B.L.* Blackbourne,
     D.N.B.; l. 31, MS. Aubr. 9, f. 28v.
179 l. 15, MS. Aubr. 9, f. 28; l. 16, MS. Ballard 14, f. 131; l. 28, MS. Wood
     F. 39, f. 351v; n., MS. Aubr. 6, f. 49v, *D.N.B.*
180 l. 2, MS. Ballard 14, f. 131.
180 l. 5, MS. Wood F. 39, f. 338; l. 9, MS. Ballard 14, f. 131.
181 l. 6, *B.L.* Petty; l. 9, *B.L.* Jenkins; l. 19, *MS.* Ballard 14, f. 131; l. 26,
     MS. Wood F. 39, f. 340; n., MS. Aubr. 6, f. 2.
182 l. 28, MS. Aubr. 6, f. 12.
184 l. 15, Hearne.

V

184 l. 23 *et seq.*, *B.L.* Hobbes.
185 l. 20, MS. Wood F. 39, f. 347; l. 23, *B.L.* Butler; n. 2, *P.R.O.* C/5/563/
     19; n. 3, *Comp. Peer.*, *Wilts. Arch. Mag.*, XXV, 86.
186 l. 3, *B.L.* Jonson; l. 8, *Wilts. Arch. Mag.* XLIX, 554; l. 29, MS. Aubr.
     8, slip at f. 6; l. 31, *Gentilism*, 206; n. 1, Bodl. MS. Autogr. c. 8, f. 2;
     n. 2, *Wilts. Arch. Mag.* XLVII, 396.

VI

187 l. 5, MS. Aubr. 12; l. 10 *et seq.*, *Comp. Peer.*; l. 23, MS. Ballard 14,
     f. 129v; l. 31, MS. Wood F. 44, f. 131.
188 l. 1, MS. Wood F. 39, f. 354v; l. 21, *ibid.*, f. 397; l. 27, MS. Wood F.
     39, f. 360; l. 31, MS. Aubr. 6, ff. 14, 15.
189 l. 2, *B.L.* Wallis & Holder; l. 3, MS. Wood F. 39, f. 360; l. 18, *B.L.*
     Bagshawe & Camden, *D.N.B.* Busby; l. 25, MS. Aubr. 13, f. 190;
     n., MS. Aubr. 26, f. 14, MS. Aubr. 12, f. 8.

VII

190 l. 1, MS. Ballard 14, f. 134; l. 18, *ibid.*, f. 135; l. 23, MS. Wood F. 39,
     f. 362; n. 1, MS. Wood F. 39, f. 357; MS. Aubr. 6, f. 109; n. 2, MS.
     Aubr. 8, f. 4v.

191   l. 17, MS. Wood F. 39, f. 362; l. 30, *ibid.*, f. 369; n., *B.L.* Hales.

192   l. 9, MS. Ballard 14, f. 187; l. 19, MS. Aubr. 13, f. 98, l. 23, MS. Aubr.
26, 9; n., *B.L.* Jonson, *North Wilts.*, 94, MS. Aubr. 8, f. 16v,
MS. Aubr. 10.

193   l. 9, MS. Aubr. 26, 14; l. 21, MS. Aubr. 13, ff. 1–89, *B.L.* Erasmus;
l. 30., *ibid.*, 2, 3, 18; l. 34, *B.L.* Moore.

194   l. 4, MS. Aubr. 13, f. 347; l. 10, MS. Aubr. 10; l. 14, MS. Aubr. 1,
f. 115, North's *Lives*.

VIII

194   l. 22, *Wilts. Arch. Mag.* XIV; l. 28, Wood's *L. & T.*, July, 1684.

195   l. 8 *et seq.*, Wood's *L. & T.*, Dec. 1683 *et passim*; l. 26, MS. Wood F.
32, Hamper's *Dugdale*; l. 31, MS. Aubr. 13, f. 65v; n., MS. Wood F.
144, f. 133.

196   l. 5, Hamper's *Dugdale*, 442 *et passim*; l. 13, MS. Wood F. 41, *passim*;
l. 17, Hamper's *Dugdale*.

IX

196   l. 24, *Misc.* (Omens); l. 33, MS. Aubr. 12, f. 273.

197   l. 9, to Lhwyd, 29 March, 1694, MS. Ash. 1814; l. 16, MS. Wood F.
39, f. 374.

X

197   l. 28, MS. Wood F. 39, f. 377; n. 1, MS. Aubr. 6, note on f. 80v;
n. 2, *D.N.B.*

198   l. 10, *B.L.* Deborah Aubrey; l. 12, MS. Ballard 14, f. 139; n. 1, MS.
Aubr. 23, f. 8v, MS. Wood F. 39, f. 404; n. 2, Hamper's *Dugdale*,
D.N.B.

199   l. 9, *Nat. Hist. Wilts.* X, Wood's *L. & T.*, *passim*, *D.N.B.*; l. 10, MS.
Ballard 14, f. 134; l. 16, *B.L.* Philips, *D.N.B.*

200   l. 1, MS. Aubr. 26, f. 6; n., *ibid.*, f. 98.

XI

200   l. 18, Britton, 60, MS. Aubr. 2.

201   l. 9, MS. Aubr. 1, f. 3; l. 12, *Nat. Hist. Wilts.* II, X; l. 17, MS. Aubr. 2,
f. 80v; l. 21, MS. Ballard 14, f. 141; l. 29, MS. Wood F. 39, f. 384;
l. 31, MS. Aubr. 14, f. 71; l. 36, *Nat. Hist. Wilts.* IX.

202   l. 3, MS. Wood F. 39, f. 392; l. 23, *B.L.* Petty.

XII

202   l. 28, Ashmole's *Diary*; l. 30, Wood's *L. & T.*, March 1683 *et passim*.

203   l. 2, MS. Tanner 456a, f. 34; n., Wood's *L. & T.*, Hearne, *passim*,
D.N.B.

204   l. 31, Luttrell.

205   l. 1, MS. Aubr. 12, f. 2; n., Evelyn.

206   l. 31, MS. Aubr. 12.

207   l. 16, MS. Aubr. 12, f. 178; l. 21, *ibid.*, f. 176; l. 31, MS. Aubr. 3, f. 72;
n. 1, *Comp. Peer.*; n. 2, MS. Aubr. 6, f. 25, *Wilts. Arch. Mag. passim.*

208   l. 11, MS. Aubr. 12, f. 182.

XIII

208 l. 19, MS. Wood F. 39, f. 386; n., MS. Aubr. 26, f. 2v, *D.N.B.*

209 l. 1 *et seq.*, *B.L.* Ward; l. 26, MS. Wood F. 39, f. 389; n. 2, *D.N.B.*; n. 3, *B.L.* Rushworth, *D.N.B.*

210 l. 4, MS. Wood F. 40, f. 372; l. 12, MS. Wood F. 39, f. 395.

211 l. 4, MS. Aubr. 6, f. 30; l. 14, MS. Wood F. 39, f. 412; l. 19, MS. Aubr. 12, f. 4; l. 28, MS. Aubr. 8, f. 69.

212 l. 5, MS. Aubr. 8, f. 70; l. 14, *ibid.*, f. 69; l. 18, MS. Wood F. 39, f. 402.

213 l. 12, MS. Ballard 14, f. 142; l. 18, MS. Wood F. 39, f. 405.

214 l. 19, MS. Wood F. 39, f. 411.

215 l. 1, MS. Wood F. 39, f. 414; n., *see* Werden, *D.N.B.*

XIV

215 l. 22, MS. Ballard 14, f. 354v; l. 25, MS. Aubr. 5, f. 2.

216 l. 5, MS. Wood F. 39, f. 426; l. 12, *ibid.*, f. 427; 29, *ibid.*, f. 433; MS. Tanner 456a, f. 40.

217 l. 5, MS. Aubr. 13, f. 174; l. 10, *D.N.B.*, Ray Soc.; l. 20, *Surrey*, V, 408, MS. Aubr. 13; l. 25, MS. Aubr. 1, f. 13; n. 1, *D.N.B.*, Grainger's *Biog. Hist. Eng.*, *Wilts. N. & Q.* IV, 4; n. 2, MS. Aubr. 13, f. 140.

218 l. 6, Britton, 79–82; l. 10, *North Wilts.* (Alington); l. 22, MS. Wood F. 39, f. 435.

XV

219 l. 1, MS. Wood F. 39, f. 438; l. 10, MS. Ballard 14, f. 146; l. 17, *Ray Soc.*; l. 22, MS. Aubr. 12, f. 123 *et seq.*; l. 30, *ibid*, f. 55, *Eton Reg.*; l. 33, MS. Wood F. 39, f. 437.

CHAPTER SEVEN: I

221 l. 9, Wood's *L. & T.*, Jan. 1691; l. 12, *ibid.*, Aug. 1692; l. 21, MS. Wood F. 51, f. 4.

222 l. 1 *et seq.*, *Ath. Ox.*; l. 25, MS. Ballard 14, f. 153, MS. Wood F. 51; n., Hooke's *Diary*, *B.L.* Harrington.

223 l. 4 *et seq.*, Wood's *L. & T.*, *passim*; l. 14, *B.L.* Jenkins; l. 19, *Ath. Ox.*; l. 23, *ibid.*; l. 30, MS. Aubr. 7, f. 2; n., MS. Wood F. 39, f. 160v, *ibid.*, f. 128.

224 l. 14, MS. Aubr. 6, ff. 8–10; l. 23, MS. Tanner 456a, f. 41; n., *B.L.* Marvell.

II

225 l. 13, MS. Wood F. 39, f. 360; l. 23, MS. Aubr. 12; l. 27, MS. Wood F. 51, f. 5.

226 l. 23, MS. Aubr. 25, f. 103v; n. 1, *D.N.B.*, Tuke; n. 2, *D.N.B.*, *North Wilts.*, *Wilts. Arch. Mag.* XIII, 59.

227 l. 4, MS. Aubr. 13, f. 199; l. 16, *ibid.*, f. 196; l. 18, MS. Tanner 25, f. 59.

III

228 l. 17, MS. Aubr. 6, f. 12; l. 26, *B.L.* I, 13; n., c.; l. 29, *ibid.* 8.

IV

228 l. 33, MS. Tanner 25, f. 66.

229 l. 4, MS. Tanner 25; l. 8, MS. Wood F. 51, f. 6; n. 1, MS. Tanner 25, f. 14; n. 2, *D.N.B.*

230 l. 19, MS. Aubr. 13.

PAGE   **V**

230   l. 23, MS. Aubr. 23, f. 103v; l. 24, MS. Aubr. 10, f. 2.
231   l. 12, MS. Wood F. 39, f. 440; l. 20, *ibid.* 442; l. 31, *Misc.*
232   l. 5, MS. Wood F. 39, f. 277; l. 26, MS. Ballard 14, f. 135.
233   n. 2, MS. Wood F. 39, f. 350, *B.L.* Bushell.
234   l. 8, MS. Ash. 1814, f. 116; l. 21, MS. Wood F. 39, f. 448; n. 1, Wood's
      L. & T., passim, Bucks., Vic. Co. Hist.; n. 2, *D.N.B.*
235   l. 1, MS. Tanner 456a, f. 48.
236   n. 1, MS. Ballard 14, f. 108, MS. Wood F. 39, f. 307, 350.
237   l. 25, Hearne, Aug. 1719; n., MS. Wood F. 39, f. 169, Hutchinson's
      Vaughan, 206.
238   l. 1, MS. Aubr. 13, f. 240; l. 21, MS. Aubr. 12, f. 164; l. 28, MS. Wood
      F. 39, f. 450; n., *Comp. Peer.*
239   l. 1, MS. Aubr. 1, f. 44.

VII

239   l. 7, MS. Ash. 1829, f. 25; l. 16, MS. Wood F. 39, f. 45v; l. 19, MS.
      Wood F. 51, f. 9; n., *D.N.B.,* Toland's *Druids,* 157.
240   l. 17, MS. Ash. 1829, ff. 28, 78; l. 20, MS. Wood F. 51, f. 11; n. 1,
      D.N.B.; n. 2, MS. Wood F. 51, f. 11.
241   l. 8, MS. Ash. 1829, f. 31; l. 16, Wood's *L. & T.* Oct. 1695; l. 20, *ibid.*
      MS. Tanner 456b, f. 45v; l. 17, Wood's *L. & T.* June 1669 *et passim.*
242   l. 5, Appendix IV, *Ath. Ox.* ed. 1813 (Huddersfield); l. 22, Bodl. MS.
      Eng. Misc. d. 10; l. 29, MS. Tanner 24, f. 108.

VIII

243   l. 29, MS. Tanner 24, f. 198.
244   l. 11, MS. Tanner 25, f. 30; l. 19, Hearne, June 1720; n. *D.N.B.*
245   l. 1, MS. Tanner 22, f. 126; l. 8, Bodl. MS. Eng. Hist. c. 11, f. 9 *et
      seq.*; l. 16, MS. Tanner 21, f. 174.

X

245   l. 31, MS. Aubr. 3, f. 71.
246   l. 5, MS. Tanner 456a, f. 27; l. 10, MS. Aubr. 5, 122; l. 35, MS. Aubr.
      15, f. 21.

CHAPTER EIGHT: I

248   l. 3, MS. Aubr. 7, f. 4v.

II

249   l. 20, Wood's *Hist. Ant. Ox.* II, 581, *B.L., passim*; l. 25 *et seq., Dorset
      Proc.,* XXXVII, 26 (Fletcher), Hutchins's *Dorset, passim,* Burke's
      L. G. (Ettrick); l. 27, MS. Aubr. 6, f. 57; l. 35, R. Soc. MS. (Wilts.)
      f. 363.
250   l. 15, *Misc.,* 121; l. 21, *B.L.* Davenant.

III

250   l. 27, *Wilts. Arch. Mag.* XXIX, 296; l. 30, *D.N.B.*
251   l. 4, *B.L.* Potter.

PAGE   IV

251   l. 32 *et seq.*, *D.N.B.*, *Comp. Baronet.*, Burke's *L. G.*, *Alum. Ox.*, *B.L.*,
      passim.

                                       V

253   l. 1, *B.L.* Wyld *et passim*, *Alum. Ox.*, *Visit of Worcs.*, *Essex*, *Beds.*, *Vic.
      Co. Hist. Beds.* VI, 80 & *Worcs.* III, 234, North's *Lives* II, 180, *Nat.
      Hist. Wilts.*, *passim*.
254   l. 10, MS. Aubr. 1, f. 115; l. 31, *Misc.* (Local-fatality); l. 37, MS. Wood
      F. 39, f. 387.
255   l. 1, *B.L.* Smythe, MS. Aubr. 23, f. 31; l. 7, B.M. MS. Lansdowne
      231, f. 201v; l. 16, *Nat. Hist. Wilts.* V; l. 20, *ibid.*; l. 32, *ibid.*, IX; l. 25,
      Surrey (Lambeth); l. 36, MS. Aubr. 6, f. 14, *Hist. Parl.*
256   l. 1, *B.L.* Petty; l. 3, MS. Aubr. 6, f. 96; l. 8, *ibid.* 63v; l. 13, *B.L.*
      Blount; l. 21, *B.L.* Raleigh; n. 1, *Hist. Parl.* Hamper's *Dugdale*;
      n. 2, MS. Aubr. 6, f. 102.
257   l. 6, MS. Lansdowne, 231, ff. 200v, 201.
258   l. 8, *Gentilism*, 239; l. 11, *B.L.* Colet; l. 19 *et seq.*, Hooke's *Diary*; l. 28,
      Osborne Letters, MS. Aubr. 8, f. 9, Brown's *Bunyan*.

                                       VI

258   l. 31 *et seq.*, *B.L.* Hooke, Waller's *Hooke*, *D.N.B.*, Hooke's *Diary*,
      Hooke's *Contemp.*
259   l. 31, Waller's *Hooke*.
260   l. 9, *B.L.* Hooke; l. 11, Hooke's *Diary*, *passim*.

                                       VII

260   l. 24, *B.L.* Hobbes *et passim*; l. 25, Wood's *L. & T.*, *B.L.*, *passim*;
      l. 27, *B.L.* Petty, *D.N.B.*, *Sir W. Petty* (Fitzmaurice, 1895).
261   l. 16 *et seq.*, *Wilts. Arch. Mag.* XLIV, 305 (Lansdowne).
262   l. 15, MS. Aubr. 6, f. 14v.

                                       V

262   l. 18, *B.L.* Long, *D.N.B.*, *Clarendon*, *passim*, *Wilts. N. & Q.* V, 380,
      Wilts. Arch. Mag. XXIV, 308 *et passim*, *Long Fam.*, *Misc. Gen.
      Herald.* N.S. III; l. 20, *B.L.* Venetia Digby; l. 26, MS. Aubr. 3,
      f. 187.
263   l. 11, *Clarendon* IV, 12, *Wilts. Arch. Mag.* XII, 301.

                                       IX

263   l. 25, *North Wilts.*, *passim*, *D.N.B.*, *Comp. Peer.*; n., MS. Aubr. 7, f. 4v.
264   l. 11 *et seq.*, *Stawell Fam.*, *passim*.

                                       X

264   l. 26, *D.N.B.*, *Stawell Fam.*; l. 28, MS. Aubr. 13, f. 191; l. 32, *Clarendon*,
      VII, 98.
265   l. 15, *Comp. Peer.*, Wood's *L. & T.* 11, 48.

                                       XI

265   l. 21, *B.L.* Ward, *D.N.B.*, *Wilts. Arch. Mag.* XLIX; l. 23, MS. Aubr. 6,
      f. 86.
266   l. 22, MS. Aubr. 9, f. 54; l. 24, *ibid.*, f. 7v; l. 26, *Ath. Ox.*; l. 35, MS.
      Wood F. 39, f. 149.

PAGE   XII
267 l. 22, *B.L.* Holder, *D.N.B.*
268 l. 16, MS. Aubr. 6, f. 87v; l. 19, B.M. MS. Sloane, 1388, f. 149.

XIII

268 l. 23, MS. Aubr. 7, f. 3v.
269 l. 3, *North Wilts.*, 91, *Misc.* (Omens).
270 MS. Aubr. 6, f. 11v.

APPENDIX A: I

271 l. 11, MS. Aubr. 5, f. 123v.
272 l. 18, B.M. MSS. Lansdowne 231.

II

272 l. 20, MSS. Aubr. 1 & 2, *Bod. Cat.*
273 l. 6, MS. Aubr. 1, f. 62; l. 10, *Nat. Hist. Wilts.* (Intro.); l. 13, *ibid.* 1; l. 16,
     MS. Aubr. 2, f. 177v; l. 26, MS. Aubr. 1, f. 144; l. 28, *Nat. Hist.
     Wilts.* (Intro.); l. 30, MS. Aubr. 1, f. 45v.; l. 33, MS. Aubr. 2, f. 43v.

III

274 l. 1, MS. Aubr. 3, *Bodl. Cat.*; l. 4, *North Wilts.* (Selkley); l. 19, *Wilts.
     Arch. Mag.* VII, 76, *N. & Q.*, 6th ser., XI; n., MS. Aubr. 3, f. 215.
275 l. 13, *North Wilts.* (Tisbury & Seend); l. 33, MS. 3, f. 10v *et seq.*
276 n. 2, *North Wilts.* (Calne).

IV

278 l. 30, MS. Aubr. 4, *Bodl. Cat.*
279 l. 2, MS. Aubr. 4, 82v; l. 30, *ibid.*, f. 35; l. 33, *ibid.*, f. 37; l. 35, *ibid.*,
     f. 133.
280 l. 1, MS. Aubr. 4, f. 155; l. 3, *ibid.*, f. 68; l. 7, f. 65; l. 10, *ibid*, f. 170;
     l. 22, *ibid.*, 93v.

V

281 l. 6, MS. Aubr. 5, *Bodl. Cat.*; l. 27, *Scandals & Credulities of J.A.*,
     Collier, 1931: *Brief Lives and Other Selected Writings*, Powell, 1949:
     Brief Lives, Dick, 1949.

VI

281 l. 17, MSS. Aubr. 6, 7, 8, & 9, *Bodl. Cat.*, *B.L.* (Intro.); n., MS. Malone
     33, f. 1.

VII

282 l. 30, MS. Aubr. 10., *Bodl. Cat.*
283 l. 14 *et seq.*, Adamson's *Education, Hartlib Papers.*
284 l. 14, *Hartlib Papers*, 59; l. 22, MS. Aubr. 3, f. 30.
285 n., *B.L.* Pell, *D.N.B.*
286 l. 12, MS. Aubr. 10, f. 137; l. 24, *ibid.*, f. 139; l. 33, *ibid.*, f. 152v; l. 35,
     ibid., f. 11v.
287 l. 7, MS. Aubr. 10, f. 133; l. 17, *ibid.*, f. 146.

VIII

287 l. 21, MSS. Aubr. 14, 15, & 16, *Bodl. Cat.*; l. 31, MS. Aubr. 15, f. 6.
288 l. 2, MS. Aubr. 15, f. 152v.

PAGE

IX

288   l. 15, MS. Aubr. 17.

X

288   l. 22, MS. Aubr. 21, *Bodl. Cat.*, *B.L.* Appendix II.
289   l. 14, MS. Aubr. 21, f. 8; l. 31, *ibid.*, ff. 19, 2.
290   l. 1, MS. Aubr. 21, f. 19; l. 12, *ibid.*, f. 11; l. 25, *ibid.*, f. 10 *et passim.*

XI

291   n., H.M.C. Portland, VII, 36, *Misc.* (Magic).
292   l. 1, *Apparitions*; l. 19, *Miranda.*

XII

292   l. 30, B.M. MS. Lansdowne 231, f. 101; l. 32, *ibid.*, f. 133.
293   l. 16, *ibid.*, f. 113; l. 24, *ibid.*, f. 116.
294   l. 6, *ibid.*, f. 167; l. 25, *ibid.*, f. 198v; l. 29, *ibid.*, f. 209; l. 36, *ibid.*, f. 199.

APPENDIX B

295 *et seq.*, *Bodl. Quart. Rec.* VI, 69, 1931 (Gunther).